A HANDBOOK OF

MUSIC

AND

MUSIC LITERATURE

IN

SETS AND SERIES

A HANDBOOK OF

MUSIC

AND

MUSIC LITERATURE

IN

SETS AND SERIES

Sydney Robinson Charles

THE FREE PRESS · NEW YORK

Collier-Macmillan Limited · London

CONTENTS

INTRODUCTION

INTRODUCTION

This book was started with the idea of lessening some of the problems attendant on music research at an academic level. A great many of these problems arise in using that sizable percentage of the most basic material for research which is contained in the large, and presently rapidly growing repertory of sets and series. The nature of the difficulties encountered can readily be seen by noting the tiny proportion of the 340 sets listed in this book which contain any sort of index. Of those which do, the number which contain really complete and workable indices is far smaller. Two further factors add difficulties: first, citations of this body of literature, even those in some of the most recent and authoritative reference works, do not always clarify the location of a given item within a set, and may even fail to mention that a set is involved at all. Second, library card catalogs may or may not include cards for the individual contents of a set, depending on such factors as the library's policy, the age of the set, or its completeness. When one adds the further consideration that a very large number of sets either are organized on totally random lines, or are "super-organized" with considerable, and sometimes inconsistent, complexity, it is plain that the music investigator requires long experience and an excellent memory to locate material in sets with even a modicum of efficiency.

No single work, of course, can rectify the situation entirely. The present book is meant to supplement, not to duplicate, excellent existing works in the field. It makes no effort to cover all music sets and series, for the admirable comprehensive coverage of Anna Harriet Heyer in her index to monuments and complete works, the valuable listing of current music monograph series by Fred Blum, and various lists of periodicals in MGG, Grove's and elsewhere, make this quite unnecessary. Instead, those sets from each of these four categories which the compiler feels are most central and useful in present-day music research have been selected for listing in detail. The primary object has been to clarify the contents and organization of each set from the point of view of its would-be user, by means of alphabetical indices, explanatory paragraphs and the like, wherever they seem to be needed. Nearly every set has its own individual characteristics, so no attempt has been made to establish a single arbitrary formula for presentation.

Selection of material The basic criterion for selection of material has been its value for general musical research purposes. However, in the interests of compactness, the following classes have been excluded: (1) Sets in which volumes are not numbered (for these are generally catalogued as separates and present no problem in use). (2) Works which are essentially a single unit divided into volumes because of length (such as Rokseth's *Polyphonies du XIIIme Siècle*), which again present no problem in use. (3) Sets which have been superseded by later and more authoritative editions.

Organization   There are four principal divisions in this book, followed by a single index. The four divisions: (A) monuments, (B) complete works, (C) monographs and (D) periodicals, have been considered useful, even though there are many items which stubbornly refuse to fit any of them precisely, such as the monument sets which include complete works, and the periodicals which turn into monograph series. The general policy has been to place a set according to its predominant contents *except* when it is divided into self-contained series which would belong to different categories, in which case it is so divided.

This book is meant to be used by a user who wishes to know what a given set contains as well as by the user who starts from the index. For this reason, many cross references, dates, and explanatory notes have been placed in the body of the book. The index, however, also includes these, and should be checked for complete coverage, or for an item which might appear to be missing.

Monuments   This section contains principally sets of music by several composers. However any set or series which contains some volumes of music, including facsimiles, has been placed here in preference to the other sections. The number of performance editions has been kept to a minimum of the most ubiquitous. Many old standbys in monuments lists are missing here, because the compiler feels that most of the older sets are best used only by the expert who knows what to expect of them and can evaluate their possibilities for accuracy.

Complete works   In this section are listed complete works of a single composer in more than one volume. *Selected works* and segments of works such as *Complete keyboard works* have been included only if they are (a) fairly extensive, (b) not duplicated in a more complete set, and (c) represent an important category of the composer's work. Some long defunct sets which produced only a few volumes have not been included. Complete works which are in non-consecutive volumes of monuments sets receive only cross references in this section. For each composer for whom a works set is included, the following are listed if pertinent: thematic catalog, year-book, recent bibliography, facsimile series, other series, index.

Monographs   This section lists series which either wholly or chiefly issue

Introduction

volumes on a single subject by a single author. Facsimile series of theory and other music literature works are included. Some series, however, which fairly consistently issue volumes in which a single specific subject is treated by several authors are also included here. In this section and the next only series wholly or partly in English, German, French, Italian or Spanish, and only series whose basic subject matter is music have been included.

Periodicals   In this section the emphasis is on periodicals with general musical coverage and a scholarly approach, and only a limited number of those devoted to specialized topics has been included. The term "periodical" has been interpreted quite broadly, to include any series, of whatever publishing regularity, which generally consists of collected articles on different subjects by different authors.

No attempt has been made to list all of the contents, but particularly extensive articles which could well have formed separate studies had they been so published are cited, as is also the case with the yearbooks listed in section B.

Index   The index includes all composers and editors named in the body of the book. Titles of sets and the names of societies, organizations and other institutions editing them are also included. Subject entries for music are used only for large collections and for individual volumes which cannot be assigned any proper-name entry but have been supplied for music literature. Some effort has been made to keep cross-references to a minimum by simply repeating short entries under different legitimate spellings and the like. Abbreviations are included in the index rather than in a separate table. The index also includes a few brief explanatory notes such as the Latin names of cities where these differ significantly from modern form.

I have personally examined the greater part of the volumes listed here, relying on secondary sources as little as possible, in the hope of attaining a high degree of accuracy. It is, however, all too likely that in a book so full of details some errors will have escaped attention; I can only hope that they will be few and minor and offer my sincere apologies to the user. I will welcome corrections and suggestions from any user about how the book's usefulness can be improved in future editions.

I am most happy to take this opportunity to thank those without whose friendly interest and kind helpfulness this work could not have been written. First and foremost, Dr. Vincent Duckles and his wonderful staff at the music library of the University of California at Berkeley, particularly Mrs. Harriet Nicewonger, Mr. C.R. Nicewonger and Mrs. Addie Smith must be named. My deepest thanks are also due to all those who so patiently listened to my many queries about the difficulties of using various sets and who responded with excellent suggestions, especially Dr. Joseph Kerman,

Introduction

Dr. Theodore Karp, and Professor Richard Swift. I was also fortunate to have the cheerful and efficient assistance of Mrs. Carol Kozielski on many tedious details. I am most grateful to the Research Committee of the University of California at Davis for their generous grant of research funds; and last, but far from least, must offer a belated word of appreciation to those endlessly kind members of the acquisitions and cataloguing departments of the library of the University of California at Davis whose lot it has been to cope with music sets, music series, and a persistent music faculty member over the years.

S. R. C.

SECTION A

SETS AND SERIES CONTAINING MUSIC OF SEVERAL COMPOSERS, AND SETS AND SERIES CONTAINING BOTH MUSIC AND MUSIC LITERATURE

1

American Institute of Musicology, Rome. General director, Armen Cara-petyan. 1947–

This Institute publishes the following six series, which are listed in detail elsewhere in this book, as indicated:

Corpus mensurabilis musicae, **A 28**
A Corpus of early keyboard music, **A 29**
Corpus scriptorum de musica, **C 21**
Miscellanea, **A 2**
Music disciplina, **D 34**

2

American Institute of Musicology, Rome. Miscellanea. 1951–

Ser. 1   CLAUDE LE JEUNE (1528–1601), *Airs,* ed. D. P. Walker.

         v. 1   *Premier livre,* part 1

         v. 2   *Premier livre,* part 2

         v. 3–4 (in 1). *Second livre*

Ser. 2   JOSEPH SMITHS VAN WAESBERGHE, *A textbook of melody*

Ser. 3   JEAN-PHILIPPE RAMEAU (1683–1764), *Complete theoretical writings,* ed. Erwin R. Jacobi

v. 1   *Traité de l'harmonie...* [facsimile of Rameau's copy with his authograph annotations]

v. 2   *Nouveau système...* [facsimile]

v. 3   *Géneration harmonique...; Démonstration du principe de l'harmonie...; Observations sur notre instinct pour la musique...*

This series is still in progress, being planned as follows: v. 1–4 major works, v. 5 minor works, v. 6 articles, letters &.

3

Anthology of Music. A collection of complete musical examples illustrating the history of music. General editor Karl Gustave Fellerer. Cologne, Arno Verlag; Philadelphia, Theodore Presser; 1960–

This series with English text is identical with the series *Das Musikwerke* which has a German text.

v. 1   WALTER GEORGI, *400 years of European keyboard music*

v. 2   FRIEDRICH GENNRICH, *Troubadours, Trouvères, Minnesang, und Meistergesang*

v. 3   HANS ENGEL, *The sixteenth-century part song in Italy, France, England, and Spain*

v. 4   WALTER WIORA, *European folk song*

v. 5   ANNA AMALIE ABERT, *The opera,* part 1

v. 6   K. STEPHENSON, *The classical age*

v. 7   ERICH SCHENK, *The Trio sonata*

v. 8   WILLY KAHL, *The character piece*

v. 9   HEINRICH HUSMANN, *Medieval polyphony*

v. 10   HELMUTH OSTHOFF, *The German part song*

v. 11   KURT VON FISCHER, *The variation*

v. 12   ERNEST T. FERAND, *Improvisation*

v. 13   EGON WELLESZ, *The Music of the Byzantine church*

v. 14   HANS J. MOSER, *The German solo song and the ballad*

From vol. 33 on, all vols. on series number above

4

Antiqua Chorbuch, ed. Helmuth Mönkemeyer. Mainz, B. Schott's Söhne, 1951

This set is divided into two parts each of which contains five volumes numbered 1–5. Part I contains sacred music: part II secular music. The

arrangement within each part is roughly chronological. There is a table
of contents in each volume; a composer index to the entire set follows:

HÄNDEL, GEORG FRIEDRICH (1685–1759)   II,5
HAGIUS, KONRAD (*ca.* 1550–after 1615)   II,3
HAIDEN, HANS CHRISTOPH (*fl.* 1601–1614)   II,4
HAMMERSCHMIDT, ANDREAS (1612–1675)   I,5
HANDL (GALLUS) JACOB (1550–1591)   I,3–4
HARNISCH, OTTO SIEGFRIED (*fl.* 1586–1621)   I,4; II,3
HASSLER, HANS LEO (1564–1612)   I,4; II,4
HAUSSMAN, VALENTIN (d. 1612)   II,4
HEINTZ, WOLF (1490–1532)   II,1
HELLINCK, LUPUS (*ca.* 1495–1541)   I,1
HOFHAIMER, PAUL (1459–1537)   II,1
HOLLANDER, CHRISTIAN JANSZON (*fl.* from 1549, d. before 1570) I,2
HOYOUL, BAUDOIN (1548–1594)   I,2

ISAAC, HEINRICH (*ca.* 1450–1517)   I,1; II,1

JACOBI, MICHAEL (1618–1663)   II,5

KERLE, JOHANNES DE (1532–1591)   I,2
KUGELMANN, JOHANN (d. 1542)   I,1

LANGE, HIERONYMUS GREGOR (1540–1587)   II,3
LANGENAU, JOHANN LEONHARD VON (b. *ca.* 1500)   II,1
LAPICIDA, ERASMUS (1445/50–1547)   II,1
LASSO, ORLANDO DI (1532?–1594)   I,3–4; II,3
LE MAISTRE, MATTHEUS (*ca.* 1505–1577)   I,2; II,2
LECHNER, LEONHARD (1553–1611)   I,3; II,3
LEMLIN, LORENZ (*ca.* 1485–1540)   II,1
Lochamer Liederbuch   II,1

MAHU, STEPHAN (*ca.* 1485–1541)   I,1; II,1

OSIANDER, LUCAS (1534–1604)   I,3
OTHMAYR, KASPAR (1515–1553)   II,2

PAMINGER, LEONHARD (1495–1567)   I,1
PEURL, PAUL, (*fl.* 1602–1625)   II,5
PRAETORIUS, MICHAEL (1572–1621)   I,4; II,4

RASELIUS, ANDREAS (1563–1602)   I,4
RAUCH, ANDREAS (1592–1656)   I,4; II,4
REGNART, JACOB (1540–1589)   II,3
RESINARIUS, BALTHASAR (*ca.* 1480–after 1543)   I,1
REYTTER, OSWALD (*fl. ca.* 1520)   II,1
ROSTHIUS, JOHANN KASPAR NIKOLAUS (*fl.* 1583–1613)   II,4

SARTORIUS, PAUL (1569–1609)	II,4
SCANDELLO, ANTONIO (1517–1580)	I,2
SCHÄRER, M., (*fl.* late 16th c.)	I,4; II,3
Schedelsche Liederbuch	II,1
SCHEIN, JOHANN HERMANN (1586–1630)	I,5; II,5
SCHMELTZL, WOLFGANG (1500/5–1561)	II,2
SCHÖNFELDER, GEORG (*fl.* early 16th c.)	II,1
SCHÜTZ, HEINRICH (1585–1672)	I,5; II,5
SCHULTZ, JOHANN (d. 1653)	II,5
SENFL, LUDWIG (*ca.* 1490–1542/3)	I,1; II,2
STADEN, JOHANN (1581–1634)	I,5; II,5
STOBAEUS, JOHANN (1580–1646)	I,5
STOLZER, THOMAS (*ca.* 1470–1526)	I,1; II,1
UTENDAL, ALEXANDER (d. 1581)	II,2
VENTO, IVO DE (*ca.* 1540–1575)	I,3; II,3
VULPIUS, MELCHIOR (*ca.* 1560–1615)	I,3; II,4
WALTER, JOHANN (1496–1570)	I,2; II,1
WIDMANN, ERASMUS (1572–1634)	II,4
WOLFF, MARTIN (*fl.* early 16th c.)	I,1
ZANGIUS, NICHOLAUS, (d. 1619)	I,4

5

Antiquae Musicae Italicae Bibliotheca. Pubblicazioni dell'Associazione "Antiquae Musicae Italicae Studiosi" (Università degli Studi, Bologna; Antiqua Musica Italica, Milano; Centri Studi sull'Ars Nova Italiana del Trecento, Certaldo, Firenze). Bologna, Arnaldo Forni Editore.

This title includes the following series:

Antiqua musica italicae:
  Monumenta Bononiensia, **A 6**
  Monumenta Lombarda, **A 7**
  Monumenta Veneta, **A 8**
  Monumenta Veronensia, **A 9**
  Scriptores, **C 4**
  Subsidia didascalica, **C 5**
  Subsidia historica, **C 6**
  Subsidia theorica, **C 7**
Corpus mensurabilis more antiquo musicae, **A 27**
Momumenta lyrical medii aevi italica, **A 62**

6

Antiquae Musicae Italicae: Monumenta Bononiensia [Bologna]

See **A 5**. This series, like **A 7–9**, is divided into two parts: the *Monumenta* proper, and a series called *Excerpta* devoted to shorter works. Both *Monumenta* and *Excerpta* may or may not be further subdivided. Only works actually published so far, or currently in preparation, are listed. The latter are placed in parentheses.

MONUMENTA

v. 2   JOHANNIS SPATARII [GIOVANNI SPATARO, (*ca.* 1548–1541)], *Opera omnia,* ed. Giuseppe Vecchi.
  1 *Bartholomei Ramis Pareie honesta defensio in Nicolai Burtii Parmensis opusculum.* Bologna, 1491 [fascimile edition].
  2 *Utile e breve regule di canto (Cod. Londin., British Museum Add. 4920).* [facsimile].

v. 4   ANDRAE ROTAE [ANDREA ROTA, (*ca.* 1553–1597)], *Opera omnia.* See **B 77**.

v. 5   HIERONYMI JACOBII [GIROLAMO GIACOBBI (1567–1629)], *Opera omnia.* See **B 42**.

v. 11   ALEXANDRI PICCININI, *Opera I: Intavolatura di liuto e di chitarrone, libro primo,* ed. M. Caffagni.
  1 *Riproduzione fotografica dell'opera.*
  2 *Testi per liuto.*
  (3 *Testi per chitarrone).*

v. 12   ADRIANI BANCHIERI (1568–1634), *Opera omnia.* See **B 6.**

(v. ?   GIACOMO ANTONIO PERTI (1661–1756), *La pasione di Cristo (1685),* ed. V. Gibelli).

(v. ?   G. A. PERTI, *I responsori della settimana santa,* ed. G. Vecchi).

EXCERPTA

A.   *Monumenta sacra polichoralis*

  (1   ADRIANI BANCHIERI, *Missa "Paratum cor meum" a 8 voci, dai "Concerti ecclesiastici"* (1595), ed. E. Capaccioli).

  (2   A. BANCHIERI, *Ecce sacerdos magnus, motectum cum 8 vocibus (1595),* ed. G. Vecchi).

(3   J. JACOBII [G. GIACOBBI], *Dilecta nostra candida, motectum cum 8 vocibus,* ed. G. Vecchi).

(4   J. JACOBII [G. GIACOBBI], *Laudate Dominum, a 9 voci (due cori) dai "Salmi concertati a due e più cori" (1609),* ed. V. Gibelli).

B. *Madrigalia cantiones*

1   A. BANCHIERI, *La battaglia, a 8 voci (1596),* ed. G. Vecchi.

2   A. BANCHIERI, *Due intermedii . . . da "La pazzia senile" (1598),* ed. G. Vecchi.

(3   GASPARO COSTA, *Canzonette a tre voci, libro I (1581),* ed. F. Giannelli).

C *Instrumentalia*

1   A. BANCHIERI, *La carissima, canzone a 8 strumenti (due cori),* ed. G. Vecchi.

2   A. BANCHIERI, *Canzoni alla francese a 4 voci per sonare* (1595–6), ed. G. Vecchi.

3   AURELIO BONELLI, *La Cleopatra, canzone a 8 strumenti (due cori),* ed. P. Beraldo.

7
Antiquae Musicae Italicae: Monumenta Lombarda. 1964–
See A 5–6

MONUMENTA

A *Madrigalia cantiones*

1   LUDOVICI GROSSI DE VIADANA (1564–1645), *Canzonette a tre voci (1594),* ed. G. Vecchi.

2   LUCA MARENZIO (*ca.* 1560–1599), *Il primo libro delle villanelle (1584),* ed. M. Baroni.

3   GIOVANNI CAVACCIO, *Canzonette a tre voci (1592),* ed. F. Angius.

B *Polifonia sacra*

JOHANNIS CAVACII [G. CAVACCIO], *Magnificat omnitonum. Liber primus (1581),* ed. F. Haberl.

C   *Instrumentalia*

  I   GIOVANNI ANTONIO TERZI (*fl.* 1593–1599), *Opere: Intavolature di liuto, libro primo,* ed. M. Caffagni.
      I   *Riproduzione della stampa originale.*
      (II–III *Studio critico e trascrizione.* . .)

  2   G. A. TERZI, *Opere: Il secondo libro de intavolatura di liuto,* ed. M. Caffagni.
      I   *Riproduzione della stampa originale.*
      (II   *Studio critico e transcrizione* . . .).

  3   VINCENZO PELLEGRINI (*fl.* 1599–1631), *Canzoni de intavolatura d'organo, libro primo (1599),* ed. P. Beraldo.

EXCERPTA

V. I   IULII CAESARIS GABUTII [GUILIO CESARE GABUSSI (GABUCCI), (*ca.* 1555–1611)], *Defecit gaudium, motectum octonis vocibus decantandum,* ed. G. Vecchi.

V. 2   CONSTANTII PORTAE [CONSTANZO PORTA (*ca.* 1530–1601)], *Motecta quaedam cum quattuor vocibus,* ed. B. Ippolito.

V. 3   LUCAE MARENTII [LUCA MARENZIO], *Cantines sacrae (1580),* ed M. Baroni.

8

Antiquae Musicae Italicae: Monumenta Veneta. 1964–

See A 5–6

MONUMENTA

A   *Sacra*

V. I   ANTONII ROMANI (*fl.* 1414–1423), *Opera,* ed. F. A. Gallo.

EXCERPTA

V. I   IOANNIS A CRUCE CLODIENSIS [GIOVANNI CROCE (*ca.* 1557–1609)], *Missa prima sexti toni (1596),* ed. G. Cattin.

V. 2   G. CROCE, *Canzonette a tre voci, libro primo (1601),* ed. G. Vecchi.

9

Antiquae Musicae Italicae: Monumenta Veronensia. 1963–

See A 5–6

MONUMENTA

v. 1   VINCENT II RUFI (*ca.* 1510–1587), *Opera omnia.*
             See **B 78**

v. 2   IOANNIS MATTHAEI ASULAE [GIOVANNI MATTEO ASOLA (*fl.
             from* 1578, *d.* 1609)], *Opera omnia.*
             See **B 4**

EXCERPTA

A   *Sacra*

        1   MARCI ANTONII INGIGNERII [INGEGNERI (*ca.* 1545–1592)],
             Missa Gustate et videte (ex libr. I missarum, 1573), ed. G.
             Vecchi.

10

Antiquitates Musicae in Polonia. Institute of musicology of Warsaw University. Edited by Hieronim Feicht. Warsaw, Warsaw University Press. 1965–

v. 1   *The Pelplin Tablature* [organ tablature: Pelplin, Diocesan
             Seminary Library, Mss 304–308a, *ca.* 1620–40]. *A thematic
             catalog,* ed. Adam Sutkowski and Alina Osostowicz-Sutkow-
             ska.

v. 2–7   [Facsimile of the Pelplin tablature in 6 parts].

v. 8–14   Not yet published

v. 15   *The organ tablature of Warsaw musical society,* ed. Jerzy Golos.
             [Transcription]

11

Archives des Maîtres de l'Orgue des XVIᵉ, XVIIᵉ, et XVIIIᵉ Sièles, publiées par ALEXANDRE GUILMANT et ANDRÉ PIRRO. Paris, A. DURAND, 1898–1910.

The v. of this set with more than one composer are divided into self-contained sections, with separate title pages and notes. A currently available reprint

edition issues each composer in a separate booklet, without using the
original v. numbers. Composers included in the reprint are marked with
asterisks.

v. 1   *JEAN TITELOUZE (1563–1633), *Oeuvres complètes d'orgue.*

v. 2   ANDRÉ RAISON (*fl.* 1687–1714), *Livre d'orgue (1688).*

v. 3   FRANÇOIS ROBERDAY (*ca.* 1620–*ca.* 1690), *Fugues et caprices.*
            LOUIS MARCHAND (1669–1732), *Pièces choisies.*
            *LOUIS NICHOLAS CLÉRAMBAULT (1676–1713), *Livre d'orgue.*
            *PIERRE DU MAGE (*fl.* 1703–1713), *Livre d'orgue.*
            *LOUIS CLAUDE D'AQUIN (1694–1772), *Livre de noëls.*

v.   *NICHOLAS GIGAULT (*ca.* 1625–*ca.* 1707), *Livre de musique.*

v. 5   *NICHOLAS DE GRIGNY (1671–1703), *Livre d'orgue.*
            *FRANÇOIS COUPERIN, SIEUR DE CROUILLY (*ca.* 1632–*ca.* 1701),
            Pièces d'orgue.
            *LOUIS MARCHAND, *Pièces d'orgue.*

v. 6   JACQUES BOYVIN (*ca.* 1653–1706), *Oeuvres complètes d'orgue.*

v. 7   *JEAN FRANCOIS DANDRIEU (1682–1738), *Premier livre de
            pièces d'orgue (1739).*
            *JEAN ADAM GUILLAUME GUILAIN (*fl.* early 18th c.), *Pièces
            d'orgue pour le magnificat.*

v. 8   *SEBASTIAN ANTON SCHERER (1631–1712), *Oeuvres d'orgue.*

v. 9   *NICHOLAS LEBÉQUE (*ca.* 1630–1702), *Oeuvres.*

v. 10   Liber fratrum cruciferorum Leodiensium (Ms from Liège,

            early 17th c.).
            PETER PHILIPS (*ca.* 1561–1628), *Trios.*
            PETER CORNET (*fl.* 1593–1633), *Pièces.*

12

Archivium musices metropolitanum Mediolanense [Milan]. Collana musicale
diretta da LUCIANO MIGLIAVACCA . . . ANGELO CICERI, EUGENIO CONSONNI.
Veneranda fabbrica del Duomo di Milano. 1958–

v. 1   FRANCHINO GAFURIO (1451–1522), *Messe,* ed. AMERIGO
            BORTONE.

Contains Masses: *a tre, Montana, Carneval, Sexti toni irregularis.*

v. 2   F. GAFURIO, *Messe,* ed. A. BORTONE.
Contains Masses: *Omnipotens genitor, Primi toni brevis, Trombetta, Touts biens pleine, a quattro.*

v. 3   F. GAFURIO, *Messe,* ed. A. BORTONE.
Contains Masses: *Quarti toni (Sanctae Catharinae V. et M.), Brevis et expedita, Brevis eiusdem toni, O clara luce, Brevis octavi toni, a quattro.*

v. 4   F. GAFURIO, *Magnificat. Sono undici Magnificat in varie modalità ecclesiastiche musicali . . . ,* ed. FABIO FANO.

v. 5   F. GAFURIO, *Motetti,* ed. LUCIANO MIGLIAVACCA.

v. 6   Anonimi, *Messe,* ed. F. Fano.
Contains Masses and Mass sections from Milan, Cathedral Library *Libroni II* (Ms 2268) and *III* (Ms 2267), contemporary with Gafurio.

v. 7   Anonimi, *Magnificat,* ed. F. FANO.
Contains works from Milan Cathedral Library *Libroni I* (Ms 2269) and *III* (Ms 2267).

v. 8–9   Anonimi, *Motetti,* ed. L. MEGLIAVACCA.
From the sources of v. 6–7.

v. 10   HEINRICH ISAAC (*ca.* 1450–1517), *Messe,* ed. F. FANO.
Contains Masses: *La bassadanza (o La spagna), Quant j'ai, Chargé de deul, Wohlauf gesell von Hinnen.*

v. 11   GASPAR VAN WEERBECKE (*ca.* 1445–after 1514), *Messe e motetti,* ed. GIAMPIERO TINTORI.
Contains *Missa Ave regina caelorum, motets.*

v. 12   JOHANNES MARTINI (late 15th c.), *Magnificat e messe,* ed. BENVENUTO DISERTORI.
Masses: *Corda pavon, Ma bouche rit, Io ne tengo quanto te.* Includes parody models.

13

Attaingnant, Pierre (d. 1552/3), Treize livres de motets parus chez Pierre Attaingnant en 1534 et 1535, ed. ALBERT SMIJERS. Paris, Oiseau-Lyre, 1934–64.

v. 9–14 ed. ARTHUR TILLMAN MERRITT. There are complete INDICES in v. 13.

v. 1   *Liber primus quinque et viginti musicales quatuor vocum motetos complectitur . . . Aprili 1534.*

v. 2   *Liber secundus: quatuor et viginti musicales quatuor vocum motetos habet . . . Maii 1534.*

v. 3   *Liber tertius: viginti musicales quinque /sex/ vel octo vocum motetos habet . . . Junio 1534.*

v. 4   *Liber quartus. XXIX. musicales quatuor vel quinque parium vocum modulos habet . . . Junio 1534.*

v. 5   *Liber quintus. XII. trium priorum tonorum magnificat continet. . . Augusti 1534.*

v. 6   *Liber sextus. XIII. quinque ultimorum tonorum magnificat continet . . . Septemb. 1534.*

v. 7   *Liber septimus. XXIIIJ trium/quatuor/quinque/sex vocum modulos domenici adventus/nativitasque eius/ac sanctorum eo tempore occurrentium habet . . .*

v. 8   *Liber octavus. XX. musicales motetos quatuor/quinque vel sex vocum modulus habet. Meuse decemb. M. d. XXXIIII.*

v. 9   *Lib. nonas. XVIII. Daviticos musicales psalmos habet. Mense Januarii. M. d. XXXIIII* [1535].

v. 10   *Lib. decimus: Passiones dominice in ramis palmarum veneris sancte: necnon lectiones feriarum quinte/sexte/ac sabbati hebdomade sancte: multaque alia quadragesime congruentia continet. Mense Februario 1534* [1535].

v. 11   *Lib. undecimus. XXVI. musicales habet modulos quatuor et quinque vocibus editos . . . Mense Martio m. d. XXXIIII* [1535].

v. 12   *Lib. duodecimus. XVII. musicales ad virginem christiparam solutationes habet . . . Mense Martio m.d. XXXV. post pascha.*
        Contains 8 settings of *Regina coeli,* 7 of *Salve regina,* 2 of *Ave regina coelorum.*

v. 13   *Lib. decimus tertius. XVIII. musicales habet modulos quatuor quinque vel sex vocibus editos. Opus sone totius armonie flos nuncupandum . . . Mense Mayo. m.d. XXXV.*

v. 14   *Liber decimua quartus. XIX musicas cantiones continet P. de*

Manchicourt [*ca.* 1510–1564] *insignis Ecclesie Turonensis prefecto authore.* M.d. XXXIX.

14

c‹M2
.B28

Barcelona. Biblioteca de Catalunya, publicacions del department de música, Institut d'estudio Catalans. 1921–

v. 1   JOAN BRUDIEU (*fl. from* 1538, *d.* 1591), *Els marigals i la missa de defunto* . . . , ed. FELIPE PEDRELL, Higini Anglès.

v. 2   *Catàleg dels manuscrits musicals de la collecció Pedrell,* ed. H. Anglès.

v. 3   JOANNIS PUJOL (1573?–1626), *Opera omnia,* ed. H. Anglés. v. 1 of PUJOL's works, containing *Missa pro defunctis;* music for the feast of St. George. v. 2 = v. 7 below.

v. 4   *Musici organici* JOHANNIS CABANILLES (1644–1712), *Opera omnia,* ed. H. Anglés. v. 1 of CABANILLES works, containing 25 *Tiento.* v. 2 = v. 8 below; v. 3 = v. 13; v. 4 = v. 17.

v. 5   CASIANO ROJO Y GERMÁN PRADO, *El canto Mozárabe. Estudio historico-critico de su antigüedad y estado actual.*

c‹M.484.935 v. 6   H. ANGLÉS, *El códex musical de Las Huelgas*
w 3 vols.   In 3 separately bound parts: 1. *Introducció,* 2. *Facsimil,* 3. *Transcripció musical.*

v. 7   J. PUJOL, v. 2 (see series v. 3 above), containing 4 Masses; music for the feast of St. George.

v. 8   J. CABANILLES, v. 2 (see series v. 4 above), containing *Tientos, Pasacalles, Batallas, Folias* &.

v. 9   ANTONI SOLER (1729–1783), *Sis quintets per a instruments d'arc i orgue o clave obligat,* ed. ROBERTO GERHARD, H. ANGLÉS.

v. 10   H. ANGLÉS, *La música a Catalunya fins al segle XIII.*

v. 11   JUAN HIDALGO (*fl.* 1633–1690), *Celos aun del aire matan. Opera del siglo XVII,* ed. JOSÉ SUBIRÁ.

v. 12   VINCENÇ RIPOLLÉS, *El villancico i la cantata del segle XVIII a València.*

v. 13   J. CABANILLES, v. 3 (see series v. 4 above), containing 25 *Tientos.*

v. 14 DOMINGO TERRADELLAS (1713–1751), *La Merope. Opera en tres actos,* ed. R. GERHARD.

v. 15 *La música de las Cantigas de Santa María del Rey Alfonso el Sabio,* ed. H. ANGLÉS.
This v. contains the transcription; v. 18 below contains the *Estudio crítico* in two separately bound parts; v. 19 contains the facsimile.

v. 16 MATEO FLECHA (1530–1604) *Las ensaladas* (Praga, 1581), ed. H. ANGLÉS.

v. 17 J. CABANILLES, v. 4 (see series v. 4 above), containing 16 *Tientos.*

v. 18–19 See v. 15.

v. 20 - 23 *Antología de organistas españoles del siglo XVII, Tomo 1: Transcripcion y estudio,* ed. H. ANGLÉS.
Contains works by SEBASTIÁN AGUILERA DE HEREDIA (1585–1618), FRANCISCO CORREA DE ARAUXO (*ca.* 1576–*after* 1636), GABRIEL MENALT (*d.* 1687), PABLO BRUNA, and J. CABANILLES.

v. 24

Biblioteca de Raritá Musicali, see **A 20** (Chilesotti).

15

Bibliotheca musica Bononiensis: Musica pratica.

See **C 14** This series is principally composed of facsimiles of the original prints or manuscripts.

v. 1 EMILIO DEL CAVALIERE (*ca.* 1550–1602), *Rappresentatione di Anima et di Corpo,* Roma, 1600. Facsimile.

v. 2 JACOPO PERI (1561–1633), *Le musiche sopra l'Euridice,* Firenze, 1600. Facsimile.

v. 3 GUILIO CACCINI (*ca.* 1546–1618), *L'Euridice composta in musica in stile rappresentativo,* Firenze, 1600. Facsimile.

v. 4 MARCO DA GAGLIANO (*ca.* 1575–1642), *La Dafne,* Firenze, 1607. Facsimile.

v. 5 GIROLAMO GIACOBBI (1567–1629), *Dramatodia overo Canti rappresentativi . . . sopra l'Aurora ingannata,* Venetia, 1608. Facsimile.

v. 6   CLAUDIO MONTEVERDI (1567–1643), *L'Orfeo, Favola in musica,* Venezia, 1609. Facsimile.

v. 7   M. DA GAGLIANO, *La Flora,* Firenze, 1628. Facsimile.

v. 8   BIAGIO MARINI (1597–1665), *Le lacrime d'Erminia in stile recitativo,* Parma, 1623. Facsimile.

v. 9   DOMENICO MAZZOCCHI (1592–1665), *La catena d'Adone,* Venezia, 1626. Facsimile.

v. 10   D. MAZZOCCHI, *Dialoghi e sonetti,* Roma, 1638. Facsimile.

v. 11   STEFANO LANDI (*ca.* 1596–*ca.* 1655), *S. Alessio,* Roma, 1634. Facsimile.

v. 12   MICHELANGELO ROSSI (*ca.* 1600–1660), *Erminia sul Giordano,* Roma, 1637. Facsimile.

v. 13   ANTONIO MARIA ABBATINI (*ca.* 1598–1680), *Il pianto di Rodomonte,* Orvieto, 1633. Facsimile.

v. 14   FRANCESCO MARIA VERACINI (1690–*ca.* 1750), *Adriano (Favorite songs),* London, n.d. Facsimile.

v. 15   FERDINANDO GIUSEPPE BERTONI (1725–1813), *Orfeo,* Venezia, 1776. Facsimile.

v. 16   NICOLO PICCINNI (1728–1800), *Didon, tragédie lyrique en trois actes,* Paris, n.d. Facsimile.

v. 17   ANTONIO SACCHINI (1730–1786), *Oedipe à Colone, opéra en trois actes,* Paris, n.d. Facsimile.

v. 18   ANTONIO SALIERI (1750–1825), *Les Danaides, tragédie lyrique en cinq actes,* Paris, n.d. Facsimile.

v. 19   ATTILIO ARIOSTI (1666–1740), *Il Coriolano,* London, 1723. Facsimile.

v. 20   GIOVANNI BONONCINI (1670–1755), *Astartus,* London, 1720. Facsimile.

v. 21   OSCAR CHILESOTTI, *Saggio sulla melodia popolare del Cinquecento.* Milano, 1888. Reprint.

v. 22–30. Reprint of CHILESOTTI's *Biblioteca di Rarità Musicali,* listed separately in **A 20**.

v. 31   O. CHILESOTTI, *Lautenspieler des 16. Jahrhunderts.* Leipzig, 1891. Reprint.

v. 32   O. CHILESOTTI, *Da un codice Lauten-Buch del Cinquecento.* Lipsia, 1892. Reprint.

v. 33   FABRIZIO CAROSO (*fl.* late 16th c.), *Nobiltà di dame,* Venezia, 1600. Facsimile.

v. 34   R. A. FEUILLET, *Recueil de dances,* Paris, 1704. Facsimile.

v. 35   CESARE NEGRI, "Il Trombone" (*fl.* 1602–4), *Le gratie d'amore,* Milano, 1602. Facsimile.

v. 36   GIOVANNI PICCHI (*fl.* early 17th c.), *Intavolatura di balli d'arpicordo,* Venetia, 1621. Facsimile.

v. 37   *Libro primo delle laudi spirituali.* RACCOLTA DI FRA SERAFINO RAZZI, Venezia, 1563. Facsimile.

v. 38   S. VEROVIO, *Lodi della musica,* Roma, 1595 (Canzonette a 3 voci con l'intavolatura del cembalo e del liuto). Facsimile.

v. 39   GIOVANNI BASSANO (*fl.* 1585–1615), *Madrigali e canzonette per canto e liuto,* Venezia, 1602. Facsimile.

v. 40   ADRIANO BANCHIERI (1568–1634), *Terzo libro dei nuovi pensieri ecclesiastici,* Bologna, 1613. Facsimile.

v. 41   JOHANN HIERONYMUS KAPSBERGER (*fl.* 1604–1640), *Libro primo d'intavolatura di Lauto,* Roma, 1611. Facsimile.

v. 42   *Musica di diversi autori. La bataglia francese delli Uccelli.* Venezia, A. GARDANO, 1577. Facsimile.

v. 43   A. VALENTE, *Versi spirituali,* Napoli, 1580. Facsimile.

v. 44   CONSTANZO ANTEGNATI (1549–1624), *L'Antegnata, intavolatura di ricercari d'organo,* Venezia, 1608. Facsimile.

v. 45–49   Not yet published.

v. 50   *Intabolatura nova di varie sorte de balli da sonare . . . libro primo.* Venezia, A. GARDANE, 1551. Facsimile.

v. 51   *Intavolatura d'organo facilissima accomodata in versetti sopra gli otto tuoni ecclesiastici,* Venezia, 1598. Facsimile.

v. 52   BERNHARD SCHMID, the younger (*b.* ca. 1548), *Tabulatur Buch von allerhand ausserlesenen, schönen, lieblichen Praeludijs, Toccaten, Motteten, Canzonetten, Madrigalen und Fugen von 4. 5. und 6. Stimmen . . .* Strassburg, 1607. Facsimile.

v. 53   JOHANN WOLTZ (*fl.* 1577–1617), *Nova musices organicae tabulatura . . .,* Basel, 1617. Facsimile.

v. 54   GUILIO CESARE ARESTI (1625–1701), *Partitura di modulationi precettive.* Facsimile.

v. 55   G. C. ARESTI (ed.), *Sonate da organi di vari autori.* Facsimile.

v. 56   JOHANN ULRICH HAFFNER (publisher), *Raccolta musicale. . di sonate per il cembalo solo,* Norimberga, n. d. Facsimile.
         In 3 parts.

v. 57   P. G. SANDONI (*fl.* early 18th c.?), *Cantate da camera e sonate per cembalo.* Facsimile.

v. 58   *30 componimenti per organo in istile legato di autori bolognesi del secolo XVIII,* raccolti da ALESSANDRO BUSI, Trieste-Bologna.

v. 59–80 Not yet published?

v. 81   C. MONTEVERDI, *L'incoronazione di Poppea.* Facsimile of Ms (Venice, Bibl. Marciana It. IV).

v. 82   ALESSANDRO STRADELLA (*ca.* 1645–1682), *Susana* (oratorio). Facsimile of Ms in Biblioteca Estense, Modena.

v. 83   GIACOMO ANTONIO PERTI (1661–1756), *Oratorio della passione.* Facsimile of Ms in Archivio di S. Petronio, Bologna.

v. 84   G. A. PERTI, *Il Mosè, oratorio per soli (5) e strumenti.* Facsimile of autograph score in Archivio di S. Petronio, Bologna.

v. 85   G. A. PERTI, *Tre cantate morali e storiche per voce e archi.* Facsimile of autograph score in Archivio di S. Petronio, Bologna.

v. 86   G. A. PERTI, *La notte illuminata, cantata morale per basso e archi.* Facsimile of Ms in Archivio di S. Petronio, Bologna.

v. 87   GIUSEPPE TORELLI (*ca.* 1650–1708), *Sinfonie e concerti per archi e due trombe.* Facsimile of autograph score in Archivio di S. Petronio, Bologna.

v. 88   GIUSEPPE TORELLI, *Sinfonie per archi e tromba.* Facsimile of autograph score in Archivio di S. Petronio, Bologna.

v. 89   G. TORELLI, *Sinfonia a due cori con trombe e oboe.* Facsimile of autograph score in Archivio di S. Petronio, Bologna.

Brokklyn, Institute of mediaeval music: publications, see A 50: The Institute...

16

Cantantibus organis: Sammlung von Orgelstücken alter Meister, ed. Eberhard Kraus. Regensburg, Friedrich Pustet, 1958–

A composer index follows the listing of volume titles.

v. 1   *Die Orgel im Kirchenjahr: Advent/Weihnachten.*

v. 2   *Orgelmusik an Europäischen Kathedralen: Venedig/Augsburg/ München.*

v. 3   *Orgelmusik im Baierischen Raum.*

v. 4   *Die Orgel im Choralamt IX. Messe: Cum jubilo*

v. 5   *Orgelmusik in Benediktinerklöstern: Kremsmünster, Prüfening, Rott am Inn.*

v. 6   *Orgelmusik in Europäischen Kathedralen II: St. Peter in Rom.*

v. 7   *Orgelmusik in Benediktinerklöstern: Augsburg, Garstin, St. Lambrecht, Mariazell.*

v. 8   *Die Orgel im Kirchenjahr II: Ostern.*

v. 9   *Orgelmusik in Benediktinerklöstern III: Irsee, Mailand, Neresheim.*

v. 10   *Orgelmusik der Franziskaner.*

v. 11   *Orgelmusik in Europäischen Kathedralen III: Bergamo, Passau.*

v. 12   *Die Orgel im Kirchenjahr III: Zwischen Weihnachten, Ostern.*

v. 13   *Orgelmusik an den Höfen der Habsburger Wien zur Zeit Kaiser Leopolds I.*

AICHINGER, GREGOR (1564–1628)   7
AMMERBACH, ELIAS NIKOLAUS (ca. 1530–1597)   11

ANDREAS, CAROLUS (late 16th–early 17th c.)   9
Anonymous; Bavarian (18th c.)   1,3
Anonymous; English (16th c.)   12
APEL, NIKOLAS (*fl.* 1504)   8,12
AQUIN, LOUIS CLAUDE d' (1694–1772)   1
ARCADELT, JACOB (*ca.* 1514–1557)   6
ARRESTI, GIULIO CESARE (1625–1701)   12
ASOLA, GIOVANNI MATTEO (*d.* 1609)   9
ATTAINGNANT, PIERRE (publisher) (*d.* 1552/3)   12

BAKFARK, VALENTIN (1507–1576)   6,12
BELLI, GUILIO (*ca.* 1560–1613)   10
BLITHEMAN, WILLIAM· (*d.* 1591)   12
BOYLEAU, SIMON (16th c.)   12
BRIGNOLI, GIACOMO (*fl. ca.* 1600)   11
Buxheimer Orgelbuch   4,8,12

CANTONE, SERAFINO (late 16th-early 17th c.)   9
CARLETON, NICHOLAS (16th c.)   12
CAVACCIO, GIOVANNI (*ca.* 1556–1626)   11
CAVAZZONI, GIROLAMO (*ca.* 1500–1560)   4
CLÉMENT, JACOB (C. non. Papa) (ca. 1510–1555?)   12

DAÇA, ESTEVAN (*fl.* 1576)   8,12
DANDRIEU, JEAN FRANÇOIS (1684–1740)   1,8
DAQUIN, LOUIS CLAUDE (1694–1772)   1
DEPRES, JOSQUIN (*ca.* 1450–1521)   4,6,8
DIRUTA, GIROLAMO (*f.* 1574–1612)   12
DUNSTABLE, JOHN (*d.* 1453)   12

EBERLIN, JOHANN ERNST (1702–1762)   3
EBNER, WOLFGANG (1612–1665)   13
ERBACH, CHRISTIAN (1570–1635)   2,4,9,12
ERTEL, SEBASTIAN (*d.* 1618)   7
ETT, JOHANN CASPAR (1788–1847)   3

FASOLO, FRA GIOVANNI BATTISTA (17th c.)   1,4,8,10
FERRABOSCO, DOMENICO MARIA (16th c.)   6
FINCK, HEINRICH (1444–1527)   8
FRESCOBALDI, GIROLAMO (1583–1643)   6
FROBERGER, JOHANN JACOB (1616–1667)   13
FUX, JOHANN JOSEPH (1660–1741)   13

GABRIELI, ANDREA (*ca.* 1510–1586)	2
GABRIELI, GIOVANNI (1557–1612)	2
GIOVANELLI, RUGGIERO (*ca.* 1560–1625)	6
Glogauer Liederbuch	8
GRÄTZ, JOSEPH (1760–1826)	3
GRINGY, NICOLAS DE (1641–1703)	1
GUAMMI, GIOSEFFO (1540–1611)	2
HASENKNOPF, SEBASTIAN (*ca.* 1545–1597)	12
HASSLER, HANS LEO (1564–1612)	2,12
HOFHAIMER, PAUL (1459–1537)	11
HUGL, FRANZ ANTON (18th c.)	3,11
KERLL, JOHANN KASPAR (1629–1693)	2,13
KÖNIGSPERGER, FR. MARIANUS (1708–1769)	1,5
KOLB, KARLMANN (1703–1765)	3
LASSO, ORLANDO DI (1532?–1594)	1,2,6,9
LE BÈGUE, NICOLAS (1630–1702)	1,12
MARENZIO, LUCA (*ca.* 1560–1599)	6
MASSAINO, TIBURTIO (*ca.* 1550–*ca.* 1609)	12
MAYR, SIMON (1763–1845)	11
MERULO, CLAUDIO (1533–1604)	2
METSCH, PLACIDUS	5
MORALES, CRISTÓBAL DE (*ca.* 1500–1553)	6
MUFFAT, GOTTLIEB (1690–1770)	1,3,8
MURSCHHAUSER, FRANZ XAVER ANTON (1663–1738)	2,3
Orgelbuch von St. Ulrich und Afra, Neresheim	8,9,12
ORTO, MARBRIANO DE (15th c.)	6
PAIX, JACOB (1550–1644)	1,2,6
PALERO, FRANCISCO FERNANDEZ (16th c.)	6
PALESTRINA, GIOVANNI PIERLUIGI DE (1525–1594)	1,6
PASTERWITZ, GEORG (1730–1803)	5
POGLIETTI, ALESSANDRO (*fl. from* 1661, *d.* 1683)	13
PONZIO, PIETRO (1532–1595)	11
PRESTON, THOMAS (16th c.)	8,12
REDFORD, JOHN (1485–1545)	1,12
REUTTER, GEORG (1656–1738)	13
RICHTER, FERDINAND TOBIAS (*ca.* 1649–1711)	13

SCANDELLO, ANTONIO (1517–1580)   11
SCARLATTI, DOMENICO (1685–1757)   6
SCHMID, BERNHART, the elder (1520–1592)   1,6,9
SCHMID, BERNHARD, the younger (*b. ca.* 1548)   6,7,12
SENFL, LUDWIG (*ca.* 1490–1542/3)   12
SICHER, FRIDOLIN (1490–1546?)   9,12

TALLIS, THOMAS (1505–1585)   1
TECHELMANN, FRANZ MATTHIAS (*ca.* 1649–1714)   13
TITELOUZE, JEAN (1563–1633)   1,8,12

VASARTO (16th c. Spanish)   8
VICTORIA, TOMÀS LUIS DE (1549–1611)   6
VINCI, PIETRO (1540-*ca.* 1584)   11
VOGLER, ABBÉ GEORG JOSEPH (1749–1814)   3

WOLTZ, JOHANN (*fl.* 1577–1617)   7

ZIANI, PIETRO ANDREA (*ca.* 1620–1684)   11

17

Cantio sacra. Geistliche Solokantaten, ed. Rudolf Ewerhart. Köln, Edmund Bieler. 1958–
"In der Reihe 'Cantio sacra' erscheinen bisher ungedruckte der schwer zugängliche Solomotetten und Solokantaten mit lateinischem Text aus dem reichen Schatz geistlicher Musik der Generalbass-Epoche." The 68 v. issued to date are arranged below alphabetically by composer.

ANERIO, GIOVANNI FRANCESCO (*ca.* 1567-*ca.* 1621)
  √ *Drei geistliche Konzerte*   14 √

Anonymous, Spanish, 18th c.
  Drei Motetten   21

———, ———, *ca.* 1700
  Intonuit de coelo   35

BERNABEI, ERCOLE (*ca.* 1620–1687)
  Heu me miseram et infelicem   44
  In hymnis et canticis   52

Barcelona, Bibl. Cen. Mss 546, 553, 555
  Anonymous 18th c. motets   21

———, ———, Ms 539
  Intonuit de coelo   35

BASSANI, GIOVANNI BATTISTA (*ca.* 1657–1712)
  ⌐ *Nascere, nascere, dive puellule*   2 √

18

Capolavori polifonici del secolo XVI, ed. BONAVENTURA SOMMA. Roma, Edizioni de Santis, 1940–1953.

v. 1   ADRIANO BANCHIERI (1568–1634), *Festino della sera del giovedì grasso avanti cena, a 5 voci miste (1608),* ed. B. Somma.

v. 2   ORAZIO VECCHI (1550–1608), *Le veglie di Siena, ovvero i vari umori della musica moderna, a 3, 4, 5, 6 voci (1604),* ed. B. Somma.

v. 3   GIOVANNI CROCE (*ca.* 1567–1609), *Triaca musicale a 4, 5, 6, 7 voci miste (1596),* ed. R. Schinelli.

v. 4   ALESSANDRO STRIGGIO (*ca.* 1535–1587?), *Il cicalamento delle donne al bucato. Commedia armonica in 5 parti a 4 e 7 voci (1567),* ed. B. Somma.

v. 5 *M1585 .V43 A5*   O. VECCHI, *Amfiparnasso. Commedia armonica a 5 voci miste (1597),* ed. B. Somma.

v. 6   A. BANCHIERI, *La pazzia senile. Ragionamenti vaghi et dilettevoli a 3 e 6 voci miste (1607),* ed. B. Somma.

v. 7 *M1584 .T67F5 1967*   GASPARO TORELLI (*fl.* 1593–1600), *I fidi amanti. Favola pastorale del Signor Ascanio Ordei Milanese con vari et piacevoli intermedii a 4 voci miste (1600),* ed. B. Somma.

v. 8   O. VECCHI, *Convito musicale, a 3, 4, 5, 6, 7, e 8 voci (1597)*,
             ed. G. Martin.
             (1600), ed. B. Somma.

Catalunya, Institut d'estudio Catalans see **A 14.**

M2.C26 v. 9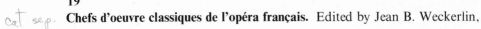

19

Cat sep.
See Heyer

Chefs d'oeuvre classiques de l'opéra français. Edited by Jean B. Weckerlin,

Vincent d'Indy and others.] Leipzig, Breitkopf & Härtel. [copyright 1880].
These operas are all in vocal score. The set was originally without volume
numbers: those given below are evidently to apply to a reprint edition
currently announced by Broude Bros., N. Y..

v. 1   BALTAZARINI [BALTHASAR DE BEAUJOYEAULX], *(fl. from ca.
             1555, d. ca. 1587), Ballet comique de la Reine* (1582).

v. 2   ROBERT CAMBERT *(ca. 1628–1677), Les peines et les plasirs
             d'amour* (1671).

v. 3   CAMBERT, *Pomone* (1671).

v. 4   ANDRÉ CAMPRA (1660–1744), *L'Europe galant* (1697).

v. 5   CAMPRA, *Les festes Vénetiennes* (1699).

v. 6   CAMPRA, *Tancrède* (1702).

v. 7   CATEL, CHARLES SIMON (1773–1830), *Les Bayadères* (1810).

v. 8   PASCAL COLASSE (1649–1709), *Les saisons* (1695).

v. 9   P. COLASSE, *Thétis et Pelée* (1689).

v. 10   ANDRE-CARDINAL DESTOUCHES (1673–1749), *Issé* (1697).

v. 11   DESTOUCHES, *Omphale* (1701).

v. 12   ANDRE ERNEST MODESTE GRETRY (1741–1813), *La caravan
             de Caire* (1783).

v. 13   GRÉTRY, *Céphale et Procris* (1775).

v. 14   MICHEL-RICHARD DE LALANDE (1657–1726) and A. DESTOU-
             CHES, *Les éléments* (1721).

v. 15   JEAN FRANÇOIS LESUEUR (1760–1837), *Ossian, ou les Bardes*
             (1804).

v. 16   JEAN BAPTISTE LULLY (1632–1687), *Alceste* (1674).

v. 17   LULLY, *Armide* (1686).

v. 18   LULLY, *Atys* (1676).

v. 19   LULLY, *Bellérophon* (1679).

v. 20   LULLY, *Cadmus et Hermione* (1673).

v. 21   LULLY, *Isis* (1677).

v. 22   LULLY, *Persée* (1682).

v. 23   LULLY, *Phaéton* (1683).

v. 24   LULLY, *Proserpine* (1680).

v. 25   LULLY, *Psyché* (1678).

v. 26   LULLY, *Thesée* (1675).

v. 27   FRANÇOIS ANDRÉ DANICAN PHILIDOR (1726–1795), *Ernelinde* (1767).

v. 28   NICCOLA PICCINNI (1728–1800), *Didon* (1783).

v. 29   PICCINNI, *Roland* (1778).

v. 30   JEAN-PHILIPPE RAMEAU (1683–1764), *Castor et Pollux* (1737).

v. 31   RAMEAU, *Dardanus* (1739).

v. 32   RAMEAU, *Les fêtes d'Hébé* (1739).

v. 33   RAMEAU, *Hippolyte et Aricie* (1733).

v. 34   RAMEAU, *Les Indes galantes* (1735).

v. 35   RAMEAU, *Platée, ou Junon jalouse* (1745).

v. 36   RAMEAU, *Zoroastre* (1749).

v. 37   ANTONIO MARIA GASPERE SACCHINI (1734–1786), *Chimène, ou le Cid* (1773, 1783).

v. 38   SACCHINI, *Renaud [Rinaldo]* (1780, 1783).

v. 39   ANTONIO SALIERI (1750–1825), *Les Danaïdes* (1784).

v. 40   SALIERI, *Tarare [Axur, Re d'Ormus]* (1787).

20

Chilesotti, Oscar, Biblioteca di Rarjtà Musicali. Milano, Ricordi, 1884–1915
This set has been reprinted as volumes 22–30 of *Bibliotheca musica Bono-niensis: Musica pratica* (**A 15**).

v. 1   *Danze del secolo XVI. . .*
            Contents: Excerpts from FABRIZIO CAROSO (*fl.* 1581–1600),

Nobiltà di dame; and CESARE NEGRI "Il Trombone" (*fl.* 1602–4), *Le gratie d'amore.*

v. 2   *Balli d'arpicordo di Giovanni Picchi, organista della Casa Grande in Venetia (1621).*

v. 3   *Affetti amorosi. Canzonette ad una voce sola, raccolte da Giovanni Stefano (1621).*

v. 4   *Arianna. Inteccio scenico-musicale di Benedetto Marcello* [1686–1739] *Nob. Veneto (1727).*

v. 5   *Arie, Canzonette e Balli a tre, a quattro e a cinque voci con liuto di Horatio Vecchi* [1550–1608] *(1590).*

v. 6   *Partite sopra La Romanesca, La Monica, Ruggiero e La Follia di Girolamo Frescobaldi* [1583–1643] *dalle Toccate e Partite d'intavolatura di Cimbalo. Libro primo (Roma 1614).*

v. 7   *Airs de Court (secolo XVI) dal Thesaurs Harmonicus* [1603] *di J. B. Besard* [*b. ca.* 1567].

v. 8   *Musica del passato (da intavolature antiche).*

v. 9   *Madrigali, Villanelle ed Arie di danza del Cinquecento (dalle opere di J. B. Besard).*

21
Le Choeur des muses: Les Luthistes. Paris, Editions du Centre national de la recherche scientifique, 1959–

v. 1   *La luth et sa musique: colloque internationale,* ed. Jean Jacquot.

v. 2   THOMAS MACE (*ca.* 1613–1709?), *Musick's Monument (1676).* [Part I: Facsimile].

v. 3   GUILLAUME MORLAYE (*fl. mid*-16th c.). *Psaumes de Pierre Certon réduits pour chant et luth (1554),* ed. Richard de Morcourt.

v. 4   ADRIAN LE ROY (*d.* 1589?), *Oeuvres: Premier livre de tabulature de luth (1551),* ed. André Souris, R. de Morcourt.

v. 5   A. LE ROY, *Oeuvres: Fantaisies et danses (Instruction de 1568),* ed. P. Jansen.

v. 6   A. LE ROY, *Oeuvres: Psaumes (Tiers Livre 1552–Instruction 1574),* ed. R. de Morcourt.

22

Das Chorwerk, herausgegeben von Friedrich Blume. Berlin, Kallmeyer, 1929–

The first 52 volumes issued 1929–1939 have been reprinted since the war by Mösler Verlag, Wolfenbüttel, who are also continuing to publish the series, now edited by Blume and Kurt Gudewill.

v.   1   JOSQUIN DESPREZ (*ca.* 1450–1521), *Missa Pange lingua*, ed. F. Blume.

v.   2   JACOBUS VAET (*d.* 1567),   *Sechs Motetten*, ed. Hermann Mayer.

v.   3   JOSQUIN DESPRES und andere Meister. *Weltliche Lieder*, ed. F. Blume.

   Includes works by LOYSET COMPÉRE (*ca.* 1450–1518), MATTHAEUS PIPELARE (late 15th c.), and PIERRE DE LA RUE (*d.* 1518).

v.   4   JOHANNES OCKEGHEM (*ca.* 1420–1495), *Missa mi-mi*, ed. Heinrich Besseler.

v.   5   ADRIAN WILLAERT (*ca.* 1485–1562) und andere Meister, *Italienische Madrigale*, ed. Walter Wiora.

   Includes works by JACOB ARCADELT (*ca.* 1514–*after* 1557); PHILIPPE VERDELOT (*d. ca.* 1540), and CYPRIANO DE RORE (1516–1565).

v.   6   THOMAS STOLTZER (*ca.* 1470–1526), *Der 37. Psalm "Erzürne dich nicht"*, ed. Otto Gombosi.

v.   7   HEINRICH ISAAC (*ca.* 1450–1517), *Missa carminum*, ed. Reinhold Heyden.

v.   8   ADRIAN WILLAERT und andere Meister, *Volkstümliche italienische Lieder*, ed. Erich Hertzmann.

v.   9   HEINRICH FINCK (1445–1527), *Acht Hymnen*, ed. Rudolf Gerber.

v.   10   GIOVANNI GABRIELI (1457–1612), *Drei Motetten*, ed. H. Besseler.

v.   11   PIERRE DE LA RUE (*d.* 1518), *Requiem und eine Motette*, ed. F. Blume.

v.   12   JOHANN HERMANN SCHEIN (1586–1630), *Sechs deutsche Motette*, ed. Adam Adrio.

v. 13   ORLANDO DI LASSO (1532?–1594), *Madrigale und chansons*, ed. H. Besseler.

v. 14   DI LASSO [*et al.*], *Sieben chromatische Motetten des Barock*, ed. F. Blume.
         Includes works by HANS LEO HASSLER (1564–1612), J. H. SCHEIN, JAN PIETERSZOON SWEELINCK (1562–1621), HIERONYMUS PRAETORIUS (1560–1629).

v. 15   JOHANNES LUPI (16th c.), *Zehn weltliche Lieder*, ed. Hans Albrecht.

v. 16   JOHANN THEILE (1646–1724), CHRISTOPH BERNHARD (1627–1692), *Zwei Kurzmessen*, ed. R. Gerber.

v. 17   HENRY PURCELL (1658/9–1695), *Fünf geistliche Chöre*, ed. F. Blume.

v. 18   DESPRES, *Vier Motetten*, ed. F. Blume.

v. 19   GUILLAUME DUFAY (*ca.* 1400–1474), *Zwölf geistliche und weltliche Werke*, ed. H. Besseler.

v. 20   DESPREZ, *Missa Da pacem*, ed. F. Blume.

v. 21   H. FINCK, *Missa In summis*, ed. Musik-Institut der Universität Tübingen, Karl Hasse.

v. 22   GILLES BINCHOIS (*ca.* 1400–1460), *Sechzehn weltliche Lieder*, ed. Willibald Gurlitt.

v. 23   DESPREZ, *Drei Evangelien-Motetten*, ed. F. Blume.

v. 24   MELCHIOR FRANCK (*ca.* 1573–1639), *Fünf Hohelied-Motetten*, ed. Anna Amalie Abert.

v. 25   ANTONIO CALDARA (1670–1736), *Ein Madrigal und achtzehn Kanons*, ed. Karl Geiringer.

v. 26   THOMAS SELLE (1599–1663), *Johannes-Passion*, ed. R. Gerber.

v. 27   CHRISTOPH DEMANTIUS (1567–1643), *Deutsche Johannes-Passion*, ed. F. Blume.

v. 28   GALLUS DRESSLER (1533–*ca.* 1585), *Fünf Motetten*, ed. Manfred Ruetz.

v. 29   *Fünfzehn deutsche Lieder aus Peter Schöffers Liederbuch (1513)*, ed. Musik-Institut der Universität Tübingen, Karl Hasse.

v. 30   DESPREZ [*et al.*], *Acht Lied- und Choralmotetten*, ed. Helmuth Osthoff.
Includes works by MATTHAEUS LE MAISTRE (*d.* 1577), JACOB REGNART (1540–1599), IVO DE VENTO (*ca.* 1540–1575), ALEXANDER UTENDAL (*d.* 1581), CHRISTIAN HOLLANDER (*fl. from* 1549, *d. before* 1570).

v. 31   JOHANNES AULEN (*fl. late* 15th c.), *Dreistimmige Messe*, ed. Herbert Birtner.

v. 32   Deutsche Meister des 15. Jahrhunderts, *Zwölf Hymnen*, ed. R. Gerber.
Includes works by ADAM VON FULDA (*ca.* 1445–1505), HEINRICH FINCK and others.

v. 33   DESPRES, *Drei Psalmen*, ed. F. Blume.

v. 34   LASSO, *Busstränen des heiligen Petrus, Teil I*, ed. Hans Joachim Therstappen.
Part 2 = v. 37; Part 3 = v. 41.

v. 35   *Neun Madrigale nordischer Gabrieli-Schüler*, ed. R. Gerber.
Works by JOHANN GRABBE (1585–1685), MOGENS PEDERSØN (*ca.* 1585–1620), and HANS NIELSEN (1580–1626).

v. 36   SCHEIN, DEMANTIUS, *Der 116. Psalm*, ed. R. Gerber.

v. 37   DI LASSO, *Busstränen . . . 2* [See v. 34].

v. 38   M. FRANCK, *Musikalische Bergkreyen*, ed. Bruno Grusnick.

v. 39   DEMANTIUS, *Deutsche Motetten*, ed. A. A. Abert.

v. 40   ALESSANDRO GRANDI (*ca.* 1570–1630), *Drei konzertierende Motetti*, ed. Blume.

v. 41   DI LASSO, *Busstränen . . . 3* [See v. 34].

v. 42   DESPREZ, *Missa De beata virgine*, ed. Blume.

v. 43   *Karnavalslieder der Renaissance*, ed. Kurt Westphal.

v. 44   JOHANNES HÄHNEL (*b. ca.* 1490), *Ostermesse über das Lied "Christ ist erstanden"*, ed. Blume, Willi Schulze.

v. 45   *Deutsche Lieder aus fremden Quellen*, ed. Heinz Funck.

v. 46   JOHANNES MARTINI (late 15th c.), *Drei geistliche Gesänge*, ed. R. Gerber.

v. 47   BALTHASAR HARZER (Resinarius, *ca.* 1480–*after* 1543), *Johannes-Passion,* ed. Blume, Schulze.

v. 48   DI LASSO, *Prophetiae Sibyllarum,* ed. H. J. Therstappen.

v. 49   DUFAY, *Sämtliche Hymnen,* ed. R. Gerber.

v. 50   JOHANNES GEORG KÜHNHAUSEN, *Matthäus-Passion,* ed. A. Adrio.

v. 51   LAMBERT DE SAYVE (late 16th c.), MICHAEL PRAETORIUS (1572–1621), *Teutsche Liedlein,* ed. Blume.

v. 52   AUGUSTIN PFLEGER, *Passionsmusik über die sieben Worte Jesu Christi am Kreuz,* ed. Fritz Stein.

v. 53   M. FRANCK, *Drei Quodlibet,* ed. Kurt Gudewill.

v. 54   DEPREZ, ARCADELT, DE RORE, WILLAERT, *Fünf Vergil-Motetten,* ed. H. Osthoff.

v. 55   LOYSET COMPÈRE (*ca.* 1450–1518), *Missa Alles regrets,* ed. Ludwig Finscher.

v. 56   *Missa anonyma II aus Breslau Codex Mf 2016,* ed. Fritz Feldmann.

v. 57   DESPREZ, *Drei Motetten,* ed. H. Osthoff.

v. 58   ARCADELT und andere Meister, *Sechs italienische Madrigale,* ed. Bernhard Meier.

v. 59   WILLAERT, *Ausgewählte Motetten,* ed. W. Gerstenberg.

v. 60   *Spanisches Hymnen um 1500,* ed. R. Gerber.
        Works by PEDRO ESCOBAR (*fl.* 1507–1514), ALONZO DALUA, FRANCISCO DE PEÑALOSA (*ca.* 1470–1528), and others.

v. 61   *Zwölf französische Lieder aus Jacques Moderns "La Parangon des Chansons"* [1538], ed. H. Albrecht.

v. 62   LUDWIG SENFL (*ca.* 1490–1542/3), *Zwei Marien-motetten,* ed. W. Gerstenberg.

v. 63   *Zehn weltliche Lieder aus Georg Forster "Frische teutsche Liedlein" (III–V),* ed. K. Gudewill.

v. 64   DESPREZ, *Zwei Psalmen,* ed. H. Osthoff.

v. 65   ANTONIO SCANDELLO (1517–1580), *Missa super epitaphium Mauritii,* ed. Lothar Hoffmann–Erbrecht.

✓ v. 66   AMBROSIUS BEBER, *Markuspassion,* ed. Simone Wallon.

✓v. 67   GIOVANNI GABRIELI (1557–1612), *Drei Motetten,* ed. Christiane Engelbrecht.

✓ v. 68   ANTOINE BRUMEL (*ca.* 1475–*ca.* 1520), *Requiem,* ed. Albert Seay.

✓v. 69   GEORG HEMMERLEY und andere deutsche Meister, *Vier Motetten,* ed. Wilfried Brennecke.

✓v. 70   JEÁN MOUTON (*ca.* 1470–1522), *Missa Alleluya,* ed. Paul Kast.

✓v. 71   DAVID KÖLER, *Drei deutsche Psalmen,* ed. L. Hoffmann–Erbrecht.

✓v. 72   JACOBUS CLEMENS NON PAPA (*ca.* 1510–1555?), *Drei Motetten,* ed. B. Meier.

✓v. 73   CLEMENT JANEQUIN (*ca.* 1485–*ca.* 1560), *Zehn Chansons,* ed. Albert Seay.

✓ v. 74   T. STOLTZER, *Ostermesse,* ed. L. Hoffmann–Erbrecht.

✓v. 75   ANTON GOSSWIN (*ca.* 1540–1594), *Newe teutsche Lieder mit dreyen Stimmen (1581),* ed. Karl Gustav Fellerer.

✓
   v. 76   MOUTON, *Fünf Motetten,* ed. Paul Kast.

✓ v. 77   GIOSEFFO ZARLINO (1517–1590), *Drei Motetten und ein geistliches Madrigal,* ed. Norman Flury.

✓v. 78   FRIEDRICH FUNCKE, *Mattäus-Passion,* ed. Joachim Birke.

✓v. 79   [*same,* bound with v. 78].

✓v. 80   *Madrigale von Mantuaner Komponisten,* ed. Denis Arnold.

✓v. 81   ISAAC, *Introiten I,* ed. Martin Just.

✓ v. 82   PIERRE CERTON (*ca.* 1510–1572), *Zehn Chansons,* ed. Albert Seay.

✓ v. 83   ANTONIUS DIVITIS (*ca.* 1475–*after* 1515), *Missa Quem dicunt homines,* ed. Lewis Lockwood (cf. v. 94).

✓v. 84   JOHN SHEPPARD (*ca.* 1520–*ca.* 1563), *Responsorien,* ed. Frank Llewelyn Harrison.

✓
   v. 85   JOHANNES HÄHNEL (GALLICULUS), und anonymi Meister, *Drei Weihnachtsmagnificat,* ed. Winfried Kirsch.

v. 86   L. DE SAYVE, *Vier Motetten*, ed. Georg Rebscher.

v. 87   MATHIAS GREITER (*ca.* 1500–1550), *Sämtliche weltliche Lieder*, ed. Hans-Christian Mueller.

v. 88   GIOVAN NASCO (*d.* 1561), *Fünf Madrigale auf Texte von Francisco Petrarca*, ed. B. Meier.

v. 89   JOHANN LUDWIG KREBS (1713–1780), JOHANN PHILIPP KIRNBERGER (1721–1783), GOTTFRIED AUG. HOMILIUS (1714–1785), *Vier Motetten der Bach-Schule*, ed. Georg Feder.

v. 90   THOMAS SELLE (1599–1663), *Zwei Kurzmessen*, ed. Joachim Birke.

v. 91   P. DE LA RUE, *Vier Motetten*, ed. Nigel Davison.

v. 92   *Fünfzehn flämische Lieder der Renaissance*, ed. René Lenaerts.

v. 93   CONSTANZO PORTA (*ca.* 1530–1601), *Missa La sol fa re mi*, ed. Oscar Mischiati.

v. 94   JEAN RICHAFORT (*ca.* 1480–1548), JEAN PIONNIER (*fl. from* 1539, *d.* 1573), NICHOLAS GOMBERT (*ca.* 1490–*after* 1556), *Drei Motetten über den Text "Quem dicunt homines"*, ed. Lewis Lockwood (cf. v. 83).

v. 95   DOMENICO MAZZOCCHI (1592–1665), *Acht Madrigale*, ed. Raymond Meylan.

v. 96   ANDREA GABRIELI (*ca.* 1510–1586), *Drei Motetten*, ed. Denis Arnold.

v. 97   ROBERT FAYRFAX (*ca.* 1464–1521), *Missa Tecum principium*, ed. Denis Stevens.

v. 98   HEINRICH HARTMANN (*fl.* 1613–1617), *Motetten*, ed. Adam Adrio.

v. 99   THOMAS MORLEY (1557–1603) und andere Meister, *Englische Madrigale*, ed. F. Ll. Harrison.

v. 100   ISAAC, *Vier Marienmotetten*, ed. Martin Just.

v. 101   ADAM RENER (*ca.* 1485–*ca.* 1520), *Missa carminum*, ed. Jürgen Kindermann.

v. 102   *Drei Te Deum-Kompositionen des 16. Jahrhunderts*, ed. Winfried Kirsch.
          Contains 2 anonymous, 1 by THOMAS CREQUILLON (*d.* 1557).

√v. 103   CLAUDE GOUDIMEL (*ca.* 1510–1572), *Vier Festmotetten*, ed. Rudolf Häussler.

v. 104   GEORG PHILIPP TELEMANN (1681–1767), *Vier Motetten*, ed. Wesley K. Morgan.

√v. 105   SEBASTIAN AQUILERA DE HEREDIA (1585–1618), *Drei Magnificat*, ed. Barton Hudson.

√v. 106   *Fünf Madrigale venezianischer Komponisten um Adrian Willaert*, ed. Helga Meier.
Works by LORENZO BENVENUTI, PERISSONE CAMBIO (*before* 1520–*after* 1551), GIROLAMO PARABOSCO (1520–1557) and BALDISSERA DONATO (*ca.* 1530–1603).

√v. 107   Not yet published.

v. 108   ORAZIO VECCHI (1550–1605), *Missa in resurrectione Domini*, ed. Raimund Rüegge.

√. 109
√. 110
√. 111
√. 113

23

I Classici Italiani della Musica, published under the auspices of the Council of Music of UNESCO, general editor Alfredo Bonaccorsi. Roma, del Turco, 1958–

This set and the following should not be confused with each other, nor with *I Classici della Musica Italiana* (general editor Gabriele d'Annunzio, Milan, 1919ff), which is not listed in this book.

v. 1   LUIGI BOCCHERINI (1743–1805), *4 Quintets, op. 30; 6 quintets, op. 33,* ed. Pina Carmirelli.

v. 2   ANTONIO VIVALDI (*ca.* 1676–1741), *Concerto in do magg.; Concerto in fa magg. (dai concerto di Dresda),* ed. Piero Giorgi.

v. 3   GAETANO BRUNETTI (1753–1808), *Sinfonia no. 33 (Il Maniatico); Sinfonia in g no. 22,* ed. Newell Jenkins.

v. 4   L. BOCCHERINI, *Sinfonia a più instrumenti obbligati, op. 37; Grande-sinfonia a grande orchestra, op. 21 no. 3,* ed. P. Carmirelli.

xx M2
.C633   **24**

I Classici Musicali Italiani. Milano, 1941–2.

See **A 23.**

v. 1   MARCO ANTONIO CAVAZZONI (*ca.* 1490–*after* 1569), GIACOMO FOGLIANO (1468–1548), GUILIO SEGNI (*ca.* 1498–1561), ed anonimi, *Ricercari e Ricercati,* ed. Giacomo Benvenuti.

v. 2   BENEDETTO MARCELLO (1686–1739), *Cantate per contralto e per soprano,* ed. G. Benvenuti.

v. 3   FELICE DE' GIARDINI (1716–1796), *Sonate per cembalo con violino o flauto traverso, op. 3,* ed. Enrico Polo.

v. 4   LUIGI BOCCHERINI (1743–1805), *Sonate per cembalo con violino obbligato. op. 5,* ed. E. Polo.

v. 5   ANDREA GABRIELI (*ca.* 1510–1586), *Musiche de chiesa da cinque a sedici voci (1587),* ed. Giovanni d'Alessi.

v. 6   GIARDINI, *Quartetti, op. 23 n. 3 e 4,* ed. Alberto Poltronieri.

v. 7   NICOLA PICCINNI (1728–1800), *La buona figliola,* ed. G. Benvenuti.

v. 8   MARCELLO, *Gioaz* [oratorio], ed. G. Benvenuti.

v. 9   CLAUDIO MONTEVERDI (1567–1643), *L'Orfeo,* ed. G. Benvenuti.

v. 10   SIGISMUNDO d'INDIA (*fl.* 1606–1627), *Madrigali a cinque voci, Lobro I,* ed. Federico Mompellio.

v. 11   PADRE GIAMBATTISTA MARTINI (1706–1784), *Concerti per cembalo e orchestra,* ed. Guido Agosti.

v. 12   GIOVANNI BATTISTA GRAZIOLI (*ca.* 1750–*ca.* 1820), *Dodici sonate per cembalo,* ed. Ruggero Gerlin.

v. 13   ALESSANDRO SCARLATTI (1659–1725), *Primo e secondo libro di Toccate,* ed. R. Gerlin.

v. 14   PIETRO LOCATELLI (1693–1764), *Sei sonate da camera per violino e basso, op. 6,* ed. G. Benvenuti, E. Polo.

v. 15   CARLO GRAZIANI (*d.* 1787), *Sei sonate per violoncello e basso continuo, op. 3,* ed. G. Benvenuti, Gilberto Crepax.

25

M2
C6433

Collana di Musiche Veneziane inedite o rare. Fondazione Giorgio Cimi,
Centro di cultura e civilità. Scuola di San Giorgio per lo studio della musica
e teatro. Istituto di lettere musica e teatro. Venice, 1951–

v. 1 *I diporti della villa in ogni stagione* [Venice, Angelo Gardano,
1601], ed. Siro Cisilino.
GIOVANNI MARIA NANINO (1545–1605), *Proemio;* GIO-
VANNI CROCE (1560–1609), *La primavera;* LELIO BERTANI
(1523–1600), *L'estate;* IPPOLITO BACCUSI (1530–1609),
L'autunno; FILIPPO DE MONTE (1521–1603), *Il verno.*

v. 2 GIOVANNI MATTEO ASOLA (1524–1609), *Missa Regina coeli,*
ed. S. Cisilino.

v. 3 JOSEFFO ZARLINO (1517–1590), *Nove Madrigali.*

v. 4 ADRIANO WILLAERT (1480–1562) *et al. Nove madrigali,* ed.
Gian Francesco Malipiero.
Contains works by WILLAERT, VINCENZO RUFFO (*ca.* 1510–
1587), MARCANTONIO INGEGNERI (*ca.* 1545–1592), and
CLAUDIO MONTEVERDI (1567–1643).

v. 5 GIOVANNI BATTISTA BASSANI (1657–1716), *Cantate a voce
sola,* ed. G. F. Malipiero.

v. 6 BALDASSARE GALUPPI DETTO IL BURANELLO (1706–1785),
Passatempo al cembalo, ed. Franco Piva.

v. 7 ANTONFRANCESCO DONI (1513–1574), *Dialogo della musica*
[1544], *Dialogo della musica,* ed. G. F. Malipiero, Virginio
Fagotto.

26

M2
.C6436

Collegium musicum, gen. ed. Leo Schrade. Yale University, 1955–

v. 1 ALESSANDRO SCARLATTI (1660–1725), *Passio D. N. Jesu
Christi secundum Johannem,* ed. Edwin Hanley.

v. 2 *Thirty chansons for three and four voices from Attaingnant's
collections,* ed. Albert Seay.

v. 3 MICHAEL HAYDN (1737–1806), *Te Deum in C (1770),* ed.
Reinhard G. Pauly.

v. 4   *The Wickhambrook lute manuscript,* ed. Daphne, E. R. Stephens.

v. 5   *Missae Caput, by Guillaume Dufay* [*ca.* 1400–1474], *Johannes Ockeghem* [*ca.* 1420–1495], *Jacob Obrecht* [*ca.* 1453–1505], ed. Alejandro Enrique Planchart.

v. 6   *Thirty-five conductus for two and three voices,* ed. Janet Knapp.

27

Corpus mensurabilis more antiquo musicae. 1952, 1967–

A sub-series of *Antiqua Musicae Italicae* (**A 4**).

v. 1   PETRI TRITONII (*late* 15th–*early* 16th c.), *Melopoiae sive harmoniae tetracenticae (1507),* ed. Giuseppe Vecchi.

v. 2   NICOLAI FABRI, *Melodiae Prudentiae et in Virgilium (1533),* ed. G. Vecchi.

v. 3   PAULI HOFEIMERI [PAUL HOFHAIMER, 1459–1537], *Harmoniae poeticae (1539),* ed. C. Massei. (In preparation).

28

✱✱ **Corpus Mensurabilis Musicae.** Rome, American Institute of Musicology, 1947–

M3.D9   Ser. 1   GUILLAUME DUFAY, *Opera omnia.* See **B 31**.

M3.C9   Ser. 2   GUILLAUME DE MACHAUT (*ca.* 1300–*ca.* 1377), *Mass,* ed. Guillaume de Van.

M3.W55   Ser. 3   ADRIANO WILLAERT, *Opera omnia.* See **B 95**.

M3.C6   Ser. 4   JACOBUS CLEMENS NON PAPA, *Opera omnia.* See **B 24**.

M3.B78   Ser. 5   ANTONIE BRUMEL, *Opera omnia.* See **B 16**.

M3.G7   Ser. 6   NICHOLAS GOMBERT, *Opera omnia.* See **B 45**.

M3.B37   Ser. 7   JACOBUS BARBIREAU, *Opera omnia.* See **B 7**.

           Ser. 8   *Music of fourteenth-century Italy,* ed. Nino Pirrotta.

xxM3
.P5   ✓ v. 1   *Collected works of Giovanni Bartolomeo, Gherardello da Firenze.*

✓ v. 2   *Collected work of Maestro Pierro, compositions from Vatican Ms Rossi 215, and madrigals and cacce from other Ms sources.*

✓ v. 3   *Collected works of Lorenzo da Firenze, Donato da Firenze, Rosso da Collegrano and anonymous works.*

N. 4   *Collected works of Jacobo da Bologna and Vincenzo da Rimini.*

✓v. 5   *Andreas de Florentia, Guilielmus de Francia, Bonaiutus Corsini, Andrea Stefani, Ser Foe, Jacopo Piaelaio, Gian Toscano, anonymous.*

R43L5 Ser. 9   JOHANNES REGIS, *Opera omnia.* See **B 73.**

G2 Ser. 10   FRANCHINUS GAFURIUS, *[Opera].* See **B 39.**

Ser. 11   *Early fifteenth-century music,* ed. Gilbert Reaney.

M2 R237

✓v. 1   BAUDE CORDIER (*b. ca.* 1380), J. CESARIS, J. TAPIS-SIER (*fl. ca.* 1400–1418): *Collected works.*

✓v. 2   *67 compositions by 23 composers, some from the Avignon papal court, some from the papal court after the schism.*
   Works of FRANCHOIS LEBERTOUL (*fl.* 1409–10), GUILLAUME LE GRANT (*fl.* 1419–21), JOHANNIS LE GRANT, BOSQUET (*fl.* 1394), CARDOT (RICHARD DE BELLENGUES, 1380–1470), MALBECQUE (*d.* 1465), Oxford, Bodl. Lib. Ms Can. misc 213, and others.

✓v. 3   *Collected works of Richard Loqueville [d. 1418], Etienne Grossin [fl. 1410–21], R. Libert [fl. ca. 1424] and Benoit [fl. 1420–40].*
   v. 4

G16 Ser. 12   GIOVANNI GABRIELI, *Opera omnia.* See **B 38.**

148 4578 1957 Ser. 13   *Missa Tornacensis (The Tournai Mass),* ed. Charles Van den Borren.

R65 Ser. 14   CIPRIANO DI RORE, *Opera omnia.* See **B 76.**

C7 Ser. 15   LOYSET COMPÈRE, *Opera omnia.* See **B 25.**

C3 Ser. 16   ROBERT CARVER, *Collected works.* See **B 21.**

F25 Ser. 17   ROBERT FAYRFAX, *Collected works.* See **B 33.**

M3.T55F7   Ser. 18   JOHANNES TINCTORIS, *Opera omnia.* See **B 89**.

M3. F95   Ser. 19   WALTER FRYE (*d.* 1475?), *Collected works,* ed. Sylvia Kenney. (Complete in 1 v.).

M2. S53T7   Ser. 20   PIERRE ATTAINGNANT (publisher, *d.* 1552/3). *Transcriptions of chansons for keyboard (1531),* ed. Albert Seay.
3 books in 1 v., including vocal versions.

Ser. 21   *Cypriot-French Repertory (15th c.): Polyphony in Ms J. II. 9 of the National Library in Turin,* ed. Richard J. Hoppin.

X< M2
.T95   v. 1   *Mass material.*

v. 2   *Motets.*

v. 3   *Ballades.*

v. 4   *Virelais and rondeaux.*

M3. A 35   Ser. 22   ALEXANDER AGRICOLA, *Opera omnia.* See **B 2**.

M3. G4   Ser. 23   JOHANNES GHISELIN-VERBONNET, *Opera omnia.* See **B 41**.

M3. W45   Ser. 24   GIACHES WERT, *Opera omnia.* See **B 94**.

Ser. 25   CONSTANZO FESTA, *Opera omnia.* See **B 34**.

Ser. 26   NICOLA VICENTINO (*ca.* 1511–1572), *Collected works,* ed. Henry H. Kaufmann. (Complete in 1 v.).

Ser. 27   NICHOLAS LUDFORD, *Collected works.* See **B 57**.

Ser. 28   PHILIPPE VERDELOT, *Opera omnia.* See **B 90**

Ser. 29   *Fourteenth-century Mass music in France,* ed. Hanna Stäblein-Harder.
X< M2
.576   Includes works from the Apt Ms; Ivrea, Bibl. Cap. Ms; Barcelona, Bibl. cent. Ms M. 971 (*olim* M. 946); Paris, Sorbonne, Institut de musicologie, Ms. Critical text in *Musicological studies and documents* (**C 54**), v. 7.

Ser. 30   JEHAN LESCUREL (*d.* 1303), *Collected works,* ed. Nigel E. Wilkins. (Complete in 1 v.).

Ser. 31   JACOBUS ARCADELT, *Opera omnia.* See **B 3**.

Ser. 32   *Music of the Florentine Renaissance,* ed. Frank d'Accone.

v. 1   BERNARDO PISANO (*early* 16th c.), *Collected works.*

v. 2   *Collected works of Alessandro Coppini [ca.* 1465–1527]*,
Bartolomeo degli Organi* [1474–1539]*, Giovanni Seragli
[fl.* 1502–1527]*, and 3 anonymous works.*

Ser. 33   JOHN HOTHBY (*d.* 1487), *Collected musical works,* ed. A. Seay.
(Complete in 1 v.).

Ser. 34   MATTEUS PIPELARE, *Opera omnia.* See **B 69**.

Ser. 35   JOHANNES BRASSART, *Opera omnia.* See **B 14**.

Ser. 36   *A 14th century repertory from the codex Reina* [Paris, Bibl. nat.,
nouv. acq. fr. 6771], ed. Nigel E. Wilkins.

Ser. 37   *A 15th century repertory from the codex Reina,* ed. N. E. Wilkins.

Ser. 38   *Canons in the Trent codices,* ed. Richard Logan.

Ser. 39   *The motets of the manuscripts Chantilly, Musée Conté 564
(olim 1047) and Modena, Biblioteca Estense a. M. 5.24 (olim
lat. 568),* ed. Ursula Günther.

Ser. 40   *The Pepys manuscript 1236,* ed. Sydney Charles.

Ser. 41   JOHANNES PULLOIS (*fl. from* 1447. *d.* 1478), *Opera omnia,* ed.
Peter Gülke. (Complete in 1 v.).

Ser. 42   *The unica in chansonnier cordiforme (Paris, Bibl. nat., Roth-
schild 2973),* ed. Edward L. Kotlick.

Ser. 43   JEAN MOUTON, *Opera omnia.* See **B 63**.

Ser. 44   ADAM DE LA HALE (*ca.* 1240–*ca.* 1286), *Lyric works,* ed. Nigel
E. Wilkins.

Ser. 45   PASSEREAU (*fl.* 1510?–1547?), *Opera omnia,* ed. Georges Dotten. (Complete in 1 v.).

29

A Corpus of Early Keyboard Music. Rome, American Institute of Musicology, 1963–

Ser. 1   *Keyboard music of the fourteenth and fifteenth centuries,* ed.
Willi Apel.

Ser. 2   MARCO FACOLI, *Intavolatura di balli (1588),* ed. W. Apel.

√ Ser. 3   GIOVANNI SALVATORE (*d.* 1688), *Collected keyboard works,* ed. Barton Hudson.

√ Ser. 4   HIERONYMUS PRAETORIUS (1560–1629), *Magnificats,* ed. Clare G. Rayner.

√ Ser. 5   BERNARDO PASQUINI (1637–1710), *Collected works for keyboard,* ed. M. B. Haynes.

   v. 1   [Miscellaneous works].

   v. 2   *Suites, arias.*

   v. 3   *Variations.*

   v. 4   *Variations.*

   v. 5   *Toccatas.*

   v. 6   *Toccatas.*

   v. 7   *Figured bass pieces.*

√ Ser. 6   JAN OF LUBLIN (*fl.* 1537–1548), *Tablature of keyboard music,* ed. John R. White.

   v. 1   *Organ perambula, masses, mass ordinary sections.*

   v. 2   *Introits, sequences, hymns, antiphons.*

   v. 3   *Motet intabulations.*

   v. 4   *French, German, Italian compositions.*

   v. 5   *Dances, Polish songs &*

   v. 6   *Tones of the psalms, magnificat &*

Ser. 7   BERNARDO STORACE, *Selva di varie compositioni d'intavolatura per cimbalo ed organo . . . In Venetia 1644,* ed. B. Hudson.

Ser. 8   *Keyboard dances from the earlier sixteenth century,* ed. Daniel Heartz.

Ser. 9   COSTANZO ANTEGNATI (1549–1624), *L'Antegnata, intavolatura de ricercari de organo,* ed. W. Apel.

Ser. 10   *Organ music from Polish manuscripts,* ed. George Golos and Adam Sutkowski.

v. 1   *Organ chorales by Peter Hasse [ca. 1617–1672] and Ewaldt.*

v. 2   *Organ chorales by Heinrich Scheidemann [ca. 1596–1663] and Franz Tunder [ca. 1614–1667].*

v. 3   *Fantasias from Ms 300. R. Vv123, Archivium Wojewódzkie Gdánsk.*

v. 4   DIOMEDES CATO (*ca.* 1576–*after* 1615), MARTIN WARTECKI (*fl.* 1564–5), PIOTR ZELECHOWSKI (17th c.), and Anonymous, [*Works*].

Ser. 11   GREGORIO STROZZI (*fl.* 1634–1687), *Capricci da sonare, cembali et organi (1687),* ed. B. Hudson.

Ser. 12   ERCOLE PASQUINI (*ca.* 1560–*before* 1620), *Collected keyboard works,* ed. W. R. Schindle.

Ser. 13–14   Not yet published.

Ser. 15   MICHELANGELO ROSSI (*ca.* 1600–1660), *Collected Keyboard works,* ed. J. R. White.

Ser. 16   [JOHANN] ADAM REINCKEN (1628–1722), *Collected keyboard works,* ed. W. Apel.

Ser. 17   Not yet published.

Ser. 18   CHRISTOPHER GIBBONS (1615–1676), *Keyboard compositions,* ed. Clare Rayner.

Ser. 19–23   Not yet published.

Ser. 24   *Neapolitan keyboard compositions (ca.* 1600) [London, B. M. Add. Ms 30491], ed. Roland Jackson.

Ser. 25–6   Not yet published.

Ser. 27   SAMUEL MARESCHAL (1554–*after* 1640), *Selected works,* ed. Jean-Marc Bonhot.

Ser. 28–9   Not yet published.

Ser. 30   GIROLAMO FRESCOBALDI (1583–1643), *Keyboard compositions preserved in manuscripts,* ed. W. R. Schindle.
 v. 1 *Toccatas.*
 v. 2 *Capricci, canzoni and other contrapuntal compositions.*
 v. 3 *Hinni, partiti, corrente.*

Ser. 31   Not yet published.

Ser. 32   *Seventeenth-century keyboard music in the Chigi manuscripts
of the Vatican Library,* ed. Harry B. Lincoln.
  v. 1   *Liturgical and imitative forms.*
  v. 2   *Toccatas, dances and miscellaneous forms.*
  v. 3   *Variation forms.*

30
Dania sonans. Kilder til musikens historie i Danmark.

V. 1 of this set was issued in 1933. In 1966 the set began to publish again
with v. 2–3.

v. 1   *Vaerker af Mogens Pedersøn* [*ca.* 1585–1623?], ed. Knud
Jeppesen.
    Contents: *Pratum spirituale* (1620), *Madrigali a cinque voce,
libro primo (1608).* The latter is also in v. 3 below.

v. 2   *Madrigaler fra Christian IV's tid,* ed. Jens Peter Jacobsen.
    Contents: HANS NIELSEN (Giovanni Fonteiio, *ca.* 1585–
after 1626), *Il primo libro di madrigali a cinque voci, 1606;*
TRUID AAGESEN (THEODORICO SISTINO), *Cantiones trium
vocum, 1608;* HANS BRACHROGGE (GIOVANNI BRACHROGGI),
Madrigaletti, 1609.

v. 3   *Madrigaler fra Christian IV's tid* [part 2].
    Contents: MOGENS PEDERSØN (MAGNO PETREO DANO),
*Madrigali a cinque voci libro primo (1608); . . . libro
secundo (1611);* MELCHIOR BORCHGREVINCK (d. 1632) og
NICOLO GISTON, *4 madrigaler fra Giardino novo I–II,
1605–6.*

31
Denkmäler der Tonkunst in Bayern *(Denkmäler Deutscher Tonkunst,
Zweite Folge: Bayern).* Veröffentlicht durch die Gesellschaft zur Her-
ausgabe von Denkmälern in Bayern unter Leitung Adolf Sandberger.
Braunschweig, H. Litolff's Verlag, 1900–1938.

Common abbreviation: DTB. Numbered by both *Jahrgang* and volume.

This set and its parent set, DDT (**A 33**), were superseded in 1936 by *Das Erbe Deutscher Musik* (**A 43**), the last two volumes of DTB having appeared also as part of the latter set. Plans for a reprint and/or revised edition have been announced by the Gesellschaft für Bayerische Musikgeschichte for many years, but by 1968 only volumes 9 and 20 have appeared.

v. 1   (Jg. 1). EVARISTO FELICE DALL'ABACO (1675–1742), *Ausgewählte Werke, 1. Teil*, ed. A. Sandberger.
Contents: 12 solo sonatas, 4 trio sonatas, 4 concerti da chiesa. Part 2 = v. 16.

v. 2   (Jg. II, 1). JOHANN PACHELBEL (1633–1706), *Klavierwerke*, ed. Max Seiffert.
Includes works by WILHELM HIERONYMUS PACHELBEL (1686–1764). See also v. 6.

v. 3   (Jg. II, 2). JOHANN KASPAR KERLL (1627–1693), *Ausgewählte Werke, 1. Teil*, ed. A. Sandberger.
Includes 22 keyboard, 9 *Geistliche Concerte*, 1 chamber sonata. Part 2 never published.

v. 4   (Jg. III, 1) *Symphonien der pfaelzbayerischen Schule (Mannheimer Symphoniker), 1. Teil*, ed. Hugo Riemann.
Contains works by JOHANN STAMITZ (1717–1757), FRANZ XAVER RICHTER (1709–1789) and ANTON FILZ (*ca.* 1725–1760). Also contains: *Verzeichnis der Druckausgaben von Sinfonien der Mannheimer Komponisten . . . Thematischer Katalog der Mannheimer Sinfonien mit Angabe der Fundorte erhaltener Exemplare in Druck und Handschrift*. Composers included in this catalog are: J. STAMITZ, F. X. RICHTER, A. FILZ, IGNAZ HOLZBAUER (1711–1763), JOSEPH TOESCHI 1724–1788), CHRISTIAN CANNABICH (1731–1798), CARL STAMITZ (1746–1801), ANTON STAMITZ (1753–1820), IGNAZ FRÄNZL (1736–1803), and GEORG ZARTH (CZARTH; TZARTH, 1708–1774). Additions were made in Part 2 (v. 13). Cf. v. 27–8 for chamber music of these composers.

v. 5   (Jg. III, 2). LUDWIG SENFL (*ca.* 1490–1542/3), *Werke*, 1. Teil, ed. Theodor Kroyer, Adolf Thürlings.
See **B 86** for full list of SENFL's *Works*.

v. 6   (Jg. IV, 1). J. PACHELBEL, *Orgelkompositionen*, ed. Max Seiffert.
Includes works by W. H. PACHELBEL.

v. 7   (Jg. IV, 2). CHRISTIAN ERBACH (1573–1635), *Ausgewählte Werke für Orgel und Klavier;* HANS LEO HASSLER (1564–1612), *Werke, 1. Teil: Werke für Orgel und Klavier,* ed. Ernest von Werra.
      Includes works by JACOB HASSLER (*b.* 1585). Other HASSLER *Works* in this set: v. 8–9, 20.
      See **B 51** for fuller listing.

v. 8–9   (Jg. V, 1–2, bound together). HASSLER, *Werke, 2. Teil: Bemerkungen zur Biographie Hans Hasslers und seiner Brüder sowie zur Musikgeschichte der Städte Nürnberg und Augsburg im 16. und zu Anfang des 17. Jahrhunderts,* [by A. Sandberger], and HASSLER's *Canzonette und Neue Teutsche Gesang von 1596,* ed. Rudolf Schwartz.

v. 10   (Jg. VI, 1). *Nürnberger Meister der zweiten Hälfte des 17. Jahrhunderts: Geistliche Konzerte und Kirchenkantate,* ed. M. Seiffert.
      Works by PAUL HAINLEIN (1626–1686), HEINRICH SCHWEMMER (1621–1696), GEORG KASPAR WECKER (1632–1695), J. PACHELBEL, JOHANN PHILIPP KRIEGER (1649–1725), JOHANN KRIEGER (1651–1735).

v. 11   (Jg. VI, 2). AGOSTINO STEFFANI (1654–1728), *Ausgewählte Werke, 1. Teil,* ed. H. Riemann.
      Contains chamber duets, scherzi, cantatas, and thematic catalog of duets, scherzi.
      Part 2 = v. 21; part 3 = v. 23.

v. 12   (Jg. VII, 1). JOHANN STADEN (1581–1634), *Ausgewählte Werke, 1. Teil,* ed. Eugen Schmitz.
      Contains Latin and German motets. Part 2 = v. 14.

v. 13   (Jg. VII, 2). *Sinfonien der pfaelzbayerischen Schule, 2. Teil* [First half], ed. H. Riemann.
      Works of J. STAMITZ, F. X. RICHTER, A. FILZ, I. HOLZBAUER, J. (G.) TOESCHI. Additions to thematic catalogs of v. 4, plus new listings for FRANZ BECK (1730–1809); ERNEST EICHNER (1740–1777); THOMAS ALEXANDER ERSKINE, EARL OF KELLY (1732–1781); and FRANZ DANZI (1763–1826). Part 1 = v. 4; part 2, 2nd half = v. 15.

v. 14   (Jg. VIII, 1). STADEN, *Ausgewählte Werke, 2. Teil,* ed. E. Schmitz.
Contains sacred solo and ensemble music, secular songs, instrumental music. Part 1 = v. 12.

v. 15   (Jg. VIII, 2). *Sinfonien der pfaelzbayerischen Schule, 2. Teil, 2. Hälfte,* ed. Riemann.
Works by C. CANNABICH, CARL STAMITZ, FRANK BECK, ERNST EICHNER.

v. 16   (Jg. IX, 1). DALL'ABACO, *Ausgewählte Werke, 2. Teil,* ed. A. Sandberger.
Contains ensemble sonatas. Part 1 = v. 1 above.

v. 17   (Jg. IX, 2). LEOPOLD MOZART (1719–1787), *Ausgewählte Werke,* ed. Max Seiffert.
Includes thematic catalog.

v. 18   (Jg. X, 1). GREGOR AICHINGER (1564–1628), *Ausgewählte Werke,* ed. T. Kroyer.

v. 19   (Jg. X, 2). ADAM GUMPELZHAIMER (1559–1625), *Ausgewählte Werke,* ed. Otto Mayr.
Includes list of his works.

v. 20   (Jg. XI, 1). H. L. HASSLER, *Werke, 3. Teil. Madrigale* [1596], ed. R. Schwartz.
Parts 1–3 = v. 7–9.

v. 21   (Jg. XI, 2). A. STEFFANI, *Ausgewählte Werke, 2. Teil,* ed. H. Riemann.
Contains *Alarico* (opera, 1687). Part 1 = v. 11; Part 3 = v. 23.

v. 22   (Jg. XII, 1). ANTON ROSETTI (1750–1792), *Ausgewählte Sinfonien,* ed. Oskar Kaul [Part 1 of *Ausgewählte Werke*].
Contains 5 symphonies, thematic catalog. Part 2 = v. 33.

v. 23   (Jg. XII, 2). A. STEFFANI, *Ausgewählte Werke,* [*3. Teil*]: *Agostino Steffani als Opernkomponist,* ed. H. Riemann.
Contains excerpts from 13 operas.

v. 24   (Jg. XIII). JOHANN ERASMUS KINDERMANN (1616–1665), *Ausgewählte Werke, 1. Teil,* ed. Felix Schreiber.
Part 2 = v. 32.

v. 25   (Jg. XVI, 1). TOMMASO TRAETTA (1727–1779), *Ausgewählte Werke* [*1. Teil*], ed. Hugo Goldschmidt. Contains excerpts from *Il Farnace* and *Tantarudi*. Part 2 = v. 29.

v. 26   (Jg. XIV, 2). CHRISTOPH WILLIBALD GLUCK (1714–1787), *Le Nozze d'Ercole d'Ebe (1747)*, ed. Hermann Abert.

v. 27   (Jg. XV). *Mannheimer Kammermusik des 18. Jahrhunderts, 1. Teil: Quartette und Quintette ohne Klavier*, ed. H. Riemann. Works of A. HOLZBAUER, J. (G.) TOESCHI, E. EICHNER, ABT GEORG JOSEPH VOGLER (1744–1814), JOHANN BAPTIST WENDLING (1720–1797), CHRISTIAN CANNABICH, K. (C.) STAMITZ, A. STAMITZ.

v. 28   (Jg. XVI). *Mannheimer Kammermusik des 18. Jahrhunderts, 2. Teil*, ed. H. Riemann. Works of J. STAMITZ, TOESCHI, FILZ, EICHNER, WILHELM CRAMER (1745–1799), K. STAMITZ, JOHANN FRIEDRICH EDELMANN (1749–1794), FRANZ XAVER STERKEL (1750–1817). Also: *Verzeichnis der Druckausgaben und Thematischer Katalog der Mannheimer Kammermusik des XVIII. Jahrhunderts: Duos, Trios, Quartette, Quintette usw. mit und ohne Klavier*, with listings for: JOSEPH BAUER (*d.* 1797), FRANZ BECK (1730–1809), MARTIN FRIEDRICH CANNABICH (VATER; 1723–1758), CHRISTIAN CANNABICH, WILHELM CRAMER, JOHANN FRIEDRICH HUGO (FREIHERR VON DALBERG; 1752–1812), FRANZ DANZA, MARGARETHE DANZI (geb. MARCHAND 1767–1799), ANTON DIMALER (1756–1815), JOHANN FRIEDRICH EDELMANN, ERNST EICHNER, KARL MICHAEL ESSER (1736–ca. 1795), ANTON FILZ, A. E. FORSTMEYER (in Karlsruhe), IGNAZ FRÄNZL, FERDINAND FRÄNZL (1770–1833), GEORG FRIEDRICH FUCHS (1752–1821), JOSEPH GITTER, PETER ROMANUS HOFFSTATTER (*d.* 1785), IGNAZ HOLZBAUER, ALEXANDER ERSKINE (LORD PETTENWEEN, EARL OF KELLY), HUGO FRIEDRICH VON KERPEN (*fl. ca.* 1790), JOHANN KÜCHLER, LUDWIG AUGUST LEBRUN (1746–1790), FRANZISKA LEBRUN (geb. DANZI, 1756–1791), ANTON JOSEPH LIBER, GEORG METZGER (1746–1793), FRANZ METZGER (1785–1808), FRANZ XAVER RICHTER, ANTON RIEGEL (*fl.* 1807), PETER RITTER (1763–1846), VALENTIN RÖSER, JOHANN STAMITZ, ABT FRANZ XAVER STERKEL (1750–

1817), LUDWIG TANTZ (*d.* 1790), FRANZ TAUSCH (1762–1817), JOSEPH (GIUSEPPE) TOESCHI, GIOVANNI BATTISTA TOESCHI (*d.* 1800), GEORG TZARTH (CZARTH, ZARTH), ABT GEORG JOSEPH VOGLER, JOHANN BAPTIST WENDLING (*ca.* 1740–1800), PETER WINTER (1754–1825), JOHANN ZACH (1699–1773?).

v. 29   (Jg. XVII), *Traetta, Ausgewählte Werke, 2. Teil,* ed. H. Goldschmidt.
Contains selected scenes from *La Sofonisba.* Part 1 = v. 25.

v. 30   (Jg. XVIII). JOHANN KRIEGER (1651–1735), FRANZ XAVER ANTON MURSCHHAUSER (1663–1738), JOHANN PHILIPP KRIEGER (1649–1725), *Gesammelte Werke für Orgel und Klavier,* ed. Max Seiffert.

v. 31   (Jg. XIX–XX). PIETRO TORRI (*ca.* 1665–1737), *Ausgewählte Werke,* 1. Teil, ed. Hermann Junker.
Contains *Le Merope* (opera, 1719) and other opera excerpts. Part 2 never published.

v. 32   (Jg. XXI–XXIV). KINDERMANN, *Ausgewählte Werke, 2. Teil,* ed. F. Schrieber, Bertha Antonia Wallner. Part 1–v. 24.

v. 33   (Jg. XXV). ROSETTI, *Ausgewählte Werke, 2. Teil: Orchester- und Kammermusik,* ed. O. Kaul.
Part 1 = v. 22.

v. 34   (Jg. XXVI). JACOBUS DE KERLE (1532?–1591), *Ausgewählte Werke, 1. Teil: Preces speciales für das Konzil zu Trient, 1562,* ed. Otto Ursprung.

v. 35   (Jg. XXVII–XXVIII). JOHANN CHRISTOPH PEZ (1684–1716), *Ausgewählte Werke,* ed. B. A. Wallner.
Contains instrumental music, excerpts from *Trajano* (opera, 1696–9), sacred vocal music.

v. 36   (Jg. XXIX–XXX). ANDREAS RASELIUS (*ca.* 1563–1602), *Cantiones sacrae,* ed. Ludwig Roselius.

v. 37–8 see *A* **43***:* Ldsdm. Bay. v. 1–2.

31A
Denkmäler der Tonkunst in Bayern: Neue Folge. Veröffentlicht von der Gesellschaft für Bayerische Musikgeschichte, Wiesbaden, Breitkopf & Härtel, 1967–

Sonderband.

v.   1   C. RUSSELL CROSBY JR. *Die Flötnerschen Spielkarten und andere Curiosa der Musiküberlieferung des 16. Jahrhundert aus Franken.*

32

Denkmäler der Tonkunst in Österreich. General editor Guido Adler. Vienna, Artaria, 1894–

Common abbreviations: DTO, DTOe. The first 83 volumes have both *Jahrgang* and volume numbers. They have been reprinted since the war by Universal Edition, Vienna, who are also the publishers of the later volumes. The present general editor is Erich Schenk. Volume 84 (1942) also appeared as part of the series *Das Erbe Deutscher Musik* (**A 43**).

v.   1   (Jg. I, 1). JOHANN JOSEPH FUX (1660–1741), *Messen,* ed. Johannes Habert, Gustav Glossner.

v.   2   (Jg. I, 2). GEORG MUFFAT (*ca.* 1643–1704), *Florilegium primum für Streichinstrumente,* ed. Heinrich Rietsch.
         See v. 4.

v.   3   (Jg. II, 1). J. J. FUX, *Motetten,* ed. J. E. Habert.

v.   4   (Jg. II, 2). GEORG MUFFAT, *Florilegium secundum . . .,* ed. H. Reitsch.
         See v. 2.

v.   5   (Jg. III, 1). JOHANN STADLMAYR (*ca.* 1560–1648), *Hymnen,* ed. J. E. Habert.

v.   6   (Jg. III, 2). MARC'ANTONIO CESTI (1623–1664), *Il pomo d'oro (Prolog und 1. Akt),* ed. Guido Adler.
         See v. 9.

v.   7   (Jg. III, 3). GOTTLIEB MUFFAT (1690–1770), *Componimenti musicali per il cembalo: sechs Suiten und eine Ciaccona für Klavier,* ed. G. Adler.

v. 8   (Jg. IV, 1). JOHANN JAKOB FROBERGER (1616–1667), *Orgel-
           und Klavierwerke, I*, ed. G. Adler.
           II = v. 13; III = v. 21.

v. 9   (Jg. IV, 2). CESTI, *Il pomo d'oro (2.–5. Akt)*, ed. G. Adler.
           See v. 6.

v. 10   (Jg. V, 1). HEINRICH ISAAC (*ca.* 1450–1517), *Choralis Constan-
           tinus I*, ed. Emil Bezecny, Walter Rabl.
           See v. 32.

v. 11   (Jg. V, 2). HEINRICH JOHANN FRANZ BIBER (1644–1704), *Acht
           Violinsonaten*, ed. G. Adler.

v. 12   (Jg. VI, 1). JACOBUS GALLUS (Jakob Handl, 1550–1591),
           *Opus musicum: Motettenwerk für das ganze Kirchenjahr, I
           Teil: Vom 1. Adventsonntag bis zum Sonntag Septuagesima*,
           ed. E. Bezecny, Josef Mantuani.
           II = v. 24; III = v. 30; IV = v. 40; V = v. 48; VI = v. 51–2.

v. 13   (Jg. VI, 2). JOHANN J. FROBERGER, *Klavierwerke II: Suiten
           für Klavier*, ed. G. Adler.

v. 14–15   (Jg. VII; bound together). *Trienter Codices I: Geistliche und
           weltliche Kompositionen des XV. Jahrhunderts*, ed. G. Adler,
           Oswald Koller.
           Contains indices, thematic catalogs. II = v. 22; III = v. 38;
           IV = v. 53; V = v. 61; VI = v. 76.

v. 16   (Jg. VIII, 1). ANDREAS HAMMERSCHMIDT (1611/12–1675),
           Dialogi, ed. A. W. Schmidt.

v. 17   (Jg. VIII, 2). JOHANN PACHELBEL (1653–1706), *94 Komposi-
           tionen: Fugen über das Magnificat für Orgel oder Klavier*, ed.
           Hugo Botstiber, Max Seiffert.

v. 18   (Jg. IX, 1). OSWALD VON WOLKENSTEIN (1377–1445), *Geist-
           liche und weltliche Lieder*, ed. Josef Schatz, Oswald Koller.

v. 19   (Jg. IX, 2). J. J. FUX, *Mehrfach besetzte Instrumentalwerke:
           zwei Kirchensonaten und zwei Ouvertüren (Suiten)*, ed. G.
           Adler.

v. 20   (Jg. X, 1). ORAZIO BENEVOLI (1605–1672), *Festmesse und
           Hymnus zur Erweihung des Doms in Salzburg, 1628*, ed. G.
           Adler.

v. 21   (Jg. X, 2). J. J. FROBERGER, *Orgel- und Klavierwerke III*, ed. G. Adler. See v. 8.

v. 22   (Jg. XI, 1). *Trienter Codices II*, ed. G. Adler, O. Koller. Contents: 3 Masses on *O rosa bella;* secular works. See v. 14–15.

v. 23   (Jg. XI, 2). GEORG MUFFAT, *Concerti grossi I: 1701*, ed. Erwin Luatz. II = v. 89.

v. 24   (Jg. XII, 1). J. GALLUS, *Opus musicum II: Vom Sonntag Septuagesima bis zur Karwoche*, ed. E. Bezecny, J. Mantuani. See v. 12.

v. 25   (Jg. XVII, 2). H. J. F. BIBER, *Sechzehn Violinsonaten*, ed. G. Adler.

v. 26   (Jg. XIII, 1). ANTONIO CALDARA (*ca.* 1670–1736), *Kirchenwerke*, ed. Eusebius Mandyczewski.

v. 27   (Jg. XIII, 2). *Wiener Klavier- und Orgelwerke in der zweiten Hälfte des 17. Jahrhunderts*, ed. Hugo Botstiber. Works by ALESSANDRO POGLIETTI (*fl. from* 1661, d. 1683), FERDINAND TOBIAS RICHTER (1649–1711), GEORG REUTTER (the elder, 1656?–1738).

v. 28   (Jg. XIV, 1). H. ISAAC, *Weltliche Werke*, ed. Johannes Wolf [See *Nachtrag*, v. 32].

v. 29   (Jg. XIV, 2). MICHAEL HAYDN (1737–1806), *Instrumentalwerke*, ed. Lothar Herbert Pergea. Includes thematic index of instrumental works.

v. 30   (Jg. XV, 1). J. GALLUS, *Opus musicum III: von der Karwoch bis zum Dreifaltigkeitsfest*, ed. E. Bezecny, J. Mantuani.

v. 31   (Jg. XV, 2). *Wiener Instrumentalmusik vor und um 1750, I*, ed. Karl Horwitz, Karl Riedel. Works by GEORG REUTTER (the younger, 1708–1772), GEORG CHRISTOPH WAGENSEIL (1715–1777), GEORG MATTHIAS MONN (1717–1750), MATTHAEUS SCHLÖGER (1722–1766), JOSEF STARZER (1727–1787). Part II = v. 39.

v. 32   (Jg. XVI, 1). H. Isaac, *Choralis Constantinus II; Nachtrag zu dem Weltliche Werke,* ed. Anton von Webern, J. Wolf. *Weltliche Werke* = v. 28.

v. 33   (Jg. XVI, 2). Johann Georg Albrechtsberger (1736–1809), *Instrumentalwerke,* ed. Oskar Kapp.

v. 34–5   (Jg. XVII; bound together), J. J. Fux, *Costanza e Fortezza,* ed. Egon Wellesz.

v. 36   (Jg. XVIII, 1). Ignaz Umlauf (1746–1796), *Die Bergknappen,* ed. Robert Haas.

v. 37   *Oesterreichische Lautenmusik im 16. Jahrhundert,* ed. Adolf Koczirz.

Works by Hans Judenkönig (*ca.* 1445–1526), Hans Newsidler (*ca.* 1509–1563), Simon Gintzler (*fl.* 1547), Valentin [Greff] Bakfark (1507–1576), *Lautenbuch der Stephan Craus aus Ebenfurt* (Vienna Hofbibl. Ms 18688), Vienna Hofbibl Ms 18827, *Lautenbuch des Herrn Jörg Fugger* (Vienna Hofbibl. Ms 18790), *Lautenbuch des Octavianus Secundus Fugger* (Vienna Hofbibl. Ms 18821), Vienna Hofbibl. Ms 19259.

v. 38   (Jg. XIX, 1). *Trienter Codices III,* ed. O. Koller, Franz Schegar, Margarethe Loew.

Contents: Masses by Guillaume Dufay (*ca.* 1400–1474), Johannes Ockeghem (*ca.* 1420–1495), and anonymous masses. See v. 14–15.

v. 39   (Jg. XIX, 2). *Wiener Instrumentalmusik vor und um 1750, II,* ed. Wilhelm Fischer.

Works by G. M. Monn, Johann Christoph Monn. Part I = v. 31.

v. 40   (Jg. XX, 1). J. Gallus, *Opus musicum, IV. Teil: vom Dreifaltigkeitsfest bis zum Advent,* ed. E. Bezecny, J. Mantuani. See v. 12.

v. 41   (Jg. XX, 2). *Gesänge von Frauenlob, Reinmar von Zweter und Alexander, nebst einem anonymen Bruchstück nach der Handschrift 2701 der Wiener Hofbibliothek,* ed. Heinrich Rietsch.

v. 42–44   (Jg. XXI; bound together). Florian Leopold Gassmann (1729–1774), *La Contessina (Die junge Gräfin),* ed. Robert Haas.

v. 44a   (Jg. XXI, 4). CHRISTOPH WILLIBALD GLUCK (1714–1787), *Orfeo ed Euridice. Originalpartitur der Wiener Fassung von 1762*, ed. Hermann Abert.

v. 45   (Jg. XXII). M. HAYDN, *Drei Messen,* ed. Anton Maria Klafsky.

v. 46   (Jg. XXIII, 1). ANTONIO DRAGHI (1635–1700), *Kirchenwerke: zwei Messen, eine Sequenz, zwei Hymnen*, ed. G. Adler.

v. 47   (Jg. XXIII, 2). J. J. FUX, *Concentus musico-instrumentalis: enthaltend sieben Partiten, vier Ouvertüren, zwei Sinfonien, eine Serenade*, ed. Heinrich Rietsch.

v. 48   (Jg. XXIV). J. GALLUS, Opus musicum V: *Gesänge für die Feste der Heiligen*, ed. E. Bezecny, J. Mantuani.
See v. 12.

v. 49   (Jg. XXV, 1). *Messen für Soli, Chor und Orchester in dem letzen Viertel des 17. Jahrhunderts*, ed. G. Adler.
Works by FRANZ HEINRICH BIBER (1644–1704), HEINRICH SCHMELTZER (1630–1680), JOHANN CASPAR KERLL (1627–1693).

v. 50   (Jg. XXV, 2). *Oesterreichische Lautenmusik zwischen 1650–1720*, ed. A. Koczirz.
Works by JOHANN GOTTHARD PEYER, FERDINAND IGNAZ HINTERLEITHNER (*fl.* 1699), JOHANN GEORG WEICHENBERGER, GRAF LOGI, WENZEL LUDWIG [FREIHERR VON] RADOLT (1687–1716), JOHANN THEODOR HEROLD, JACQUES DE SAINT LUC (1616–*after* 1684).

v. 51–2   (Jg. XXVI; bound together). J. GALLUS, *Opus musicum VI (Schluss): Gesänge für die Feste der Heiligen*, ed. E. Bezecny, J. Mantuani.

v. 53   (Jg. XXVII, 1). *Trienter Codices IV*, ed. Rudolf Ficker, Alfred Orel.
Works by REGINALDUS LIEBERT (*fl. ca.* 1424), G. DUFAY, JOHN DUNSTABLE (*d.* 1453), LEONEL [POWER] (d. 1437), MERQUES, TOURONT (*fl.* 1450–1480), BATTRE, and GILLES BINCHOIS (*ca.* 1400–1460). See v. 14–15.

v. 54   (Jg. XXVII, 2). *Das Wiener Lied von 1778 bis zu Mozarts Tod*, ed. Margarete Ansion, Irene Schlaffensburg.
Works by JOSEPH ANTON STEFFAN (1736–1797), CARL

FRIBERTH (1736–1813), LEOPOLD HOFMANN (1738–1793), JOHANN HOLZER (*fl.* 1779), WILHELM POHL (*fl. ca.* 1780), MARTIN RUPRECHT (1750–1800), LEOPOLD KOZELUCH (1748–1818), J. J. GRÜNWALD (*fl. ca.* 1780), MARIA THERESE PARADIS (1759–1824), JOHANN CHRISTOPH HACKEL (1758–1814), FRANZ ANTON HOFFMEISTER (1754–1812).

v. 55   (Jg. XXVIII, 1). JOHANN ERNST EBERLIN (1702–1762), *Oratorium: Die blutschwitzende Jesus; Stücke aus anderen Oratorien,* ed. Robert Haas.

v. 56   (Jg. XXVIII, 2). *Wiener Tanzmusik in der 2. Hälfte des 17. Jahrhunderts,* ed. Paul Nettl.
Works by J. H. SCHMELTZER, JOHANN JOSEPH HOFFER, ALEXANDER POGLIETTI.

v. 57   (Jg. XXIX, 1). CLAUDIO MONTEVERDI (1567–1643), *Il ritorno d'Ulisse in patria,* ed. R. Haas.

v. 58   (Jg. XXIX, 2). GOTTLIEB MUFFAT, *12 Toccaten und 72 Versett für Orgel und Klavier,* ed. G. Adler.

v. 59   (Jg. XXX, 1). *Drei Requiem für Soli, Chor und Orchester aus dem 17. Jahrhundert,* ed. G. Adler.
Works by CHRISTOPH STRAUS (1575–1630), F. H. BIBER, J. C. KERLL.

v. 60   (Jg. XXX, 2). C. W. GLUCK, *Werke, II. Band* [*sic*]*: Don Juan* [ballet], ed. R. Haas.

v. 61   (Jg. XXXI). Trienter Codices V, ed. R. Ficker.
Masses and Mass sections by: *Anglicanus,* BARTOLOMAEUS DE BRUOLLIS, BATTRE, BEDINGHAM, BENET, BINCHOIS, BODOIL, BOURGOIS, JOHANNES CICONIA, DUFAY, DUNSTABLE, FOREST, GEORGIUS A BRUGIS, GROSSIN, HUGO DE LANTINS, LEONELLUS [POWER], RICHARD MARKHAM, SORBI, ZACHARIAS DE TERAMO, and anonymous works. See v. 14–15.

v. 62   (Jg. XXXII, 1). M. HAYDN, *Kirchenwerke,* ed. Anton Maria Klafsky.
Includes thematic catalog of church music.

v. 63   (Jg. XXXII, 2). JOHANN STRAUSS (the younger, 1825–1899), *Walzer,* ed. Hans Gál.

v. 64   (Jg. XXXIII, 1). *Deutsche Komödienarien, 1754–1758*, ed. R. Haas.
Commentary: *Studien zur Musikwissenschaft* (**D 57**), XII, 3.

v. 65   (Jg. XXXIII, 2). JOSEPH LANNER (1801–1843), *Ländler und Walzer*, ed. Alfred Orel.

v. 66   (Jg. XXXIV). JOHANN SCHENK (1753–1836), *Der Dorfbarbier*, ed. R. Haas.

v. 67   (Jg. XXXV, 1). EMANUEL ALOYS FÖRSTER (1748–1823), *Zwei Quartette, Drei Quintette*, ed. Karl Weigl.
Includes thematic catalog of chamber music.

v. 68   (Jg. XXXV, 2). JOHANN STRAUSS (the elder, 1804–1849), *Walzer*, ed. H. Gál.

v. 69   (Jg. XXXVI, 1). STEFFANO BERNARDI (*d.* 1635), *Kirchenwerke*, ed. Karl August Rosenthal.

v. 70   (Jg. XXXVI, 2). PAUL PEUERL (*fl.* 1602–1625), ISAAC POSCH (*fl.* 1621), *Instrumental- und Vokalwerke*, ed. Karl Geiringer.
Contents: PEUERL, *Neue Paduanen* (1611), *Weltspiegel* (1613), *Ganz neue Paduanen* (1625). Posch: *Musikalische Tafelfreud* (1621).

v. 71   (Jg. XXXVII, 1). NEIDHART VON REUENTHAL (*ca.* 1180–*ca.* 1240), *Lieder*, ed. Wolfgang Schmieder, Edmund Wiessner.
Includes Ms facsimiles. See *Studien zur Musikwissenschaft* (**D 57**), XVII.

v. 72   (Jg. XXXVII, 2). *Das deutsche Gesellschaftlied in Oesterreich von 1480 bis 1550,* ed. Leopold Nowak, A. Koczirz, Anton Pfalz.
Works by ARNOLDUS VON BRUCK (*ca.* 1470–*ca.* 1554), HEINRICH FINCK (1445–1527), WOLFGANG GREFINGER (*b. ca.* 1485), PAUL HOFHAYMER (1459–1537), ERASMUS LAPICIDA, STEPHAN MAHU, GREGOR PESCHIN, JOHANN SIES, THOMAS STOLZER (*ca.* 1470–1526), H. ISAAC.

v. 73   (Jg. XXXVIII, 1). BLASIUS AMON (*ca.* 1560–1590), *Kirchenwerke I*, ed. P. Caecilianus Huigens.

v. 74   (Jg. XXXVIII, 2). JOSEF STRAUSS (1827–1870), *Walzer*, ed. Hugo Botstiber.

v. 75   (Jg. XXXIX). A. CALDARA, *Kammermusik für Gesang*, ed. E. Mandyczewski.

v. 76   (Jg. XL). *Trienter Codices VI,* ed. R. von Ficker.
Sacred and secular works by ALANUS DE ANGLIA, BATTRE, BRASART, CRISTOFORUS DE MONTE, DUFAY, DUNSTABLE, FRANCHOS, FOREST, LUDBICUS DE ARIMINO, MERQUES, VERBEN, DE VITRY; Anon. works. See v. 14–15.

v. 77   (Jg. XLI). *Italienische Musiker und das Kaiserhaus 1567–1625: Dedikationsstücke und Werke von Musikern im Dienste des Kaiserhauses,* ed. Alfred Einstein.
Madrigals by FILIPPO DI MONTE (1521–1603), FRANCESCO PORTINARO (*b. ca.* 1517), ANDREA GABRIELI (*ca.* 1510–1586), ANNIBALE PADOANO (1527–1575), MATTEO FLECHA (1530–1604), CARLO LUYTHON (1556–1620), LAMBERTO DE SAYVE (1549–1614), GIACOMO REGNART (1540–1589), FRANCESCO ROVIGO (1531–1597), ALESSANDRO OROLOGIO, CAMILLO ZANOTTI (*fl.* 1586–1591), GIOVANNI PRUILI (*d.* 1629).

v. 78   (Jg. XLII, 1). JACOB GALLUS, *Messen,* ed. Paul Amadeus Pisk.

v. 79   (Jg. XLII, 2). *Wiener Lied von 1792 bis 1815,* ed. Hermann Maschek, Hedwig Kraus.
Songs by ANTON TEYBER (1754–1822), ANTON EBERL (1765–1807), EMILIAN GOTTFRIED VON JACQUIN (1767–1792), MORITZ VON DIETRICHSTEIN (1775–1864), JOHANN FUSS (1777–1819), SIGMUND NEUKOMM (1778–1858), NIKLAS VON KRUFFT (1779–1818), CONRADIN KREUTZER (1780–1849).

v. 80   (Jg. XLIII, 1). *Salzburger Kirchenkomponisten,* ed. K. A. Rosenthal, Constantin Schneider.
Works by CARL H. BIBER (1681–1749), M. S. BIECHTELER (*d.* 1744), J. ERNST EBERLIN (1702–1762), A. C. ADLGASSER (1729–1777).

v. 81   (Jg. XLIII, 2). KARL DITTERS VON DITTERSDORF (1739–1799), *Drei Sinfonien, eine Serenata,* ed. Victor Leithlen.

v. 82   (Jg. XLIV). C. W. GLUCK, *L'innocenza giustificata . . . (Festa teatrale, 1755),* ed. A. Einstein.

v. 83   (Jg. XLV). FLORIAN LEOPOLD GASSMANN (1729–1774), *Kirchenwerke,* ed. Franz Kosch.

v. 84   *Wiener Lautenmusik im 18. Jahrhundert,* ed. Karl Schnürl.
Works by JOHANN ANTON LOSY (Graf von Losintal, *ca.* 1645–1721), JOHANN GEORG WEICHENBERGER (1676–1749),

ANDREAS BOHR VON BOHRENFELS (*ca.* 1663–1728), FERDI-
NAND FRIEDRICH FICHTEL (1687–1722), FRANCESCO CONTI
(1681–1732), J. J. FUX, JOHANN FRIEDRICH DAUBE (1733–
1797), KARL KOHAUT (1726–1782).

v. 85   J. J. FUX, *Werke für Tasteninstrumente,* ed. Erich Schenk.

v. 86   *Tiroler Instrumentalmusik im 18. Jahrhundert,* ed. Walter Senn.
Works by GEORG PAUL FALK, JOHANN ELIAS DE SYLVA,
FRANZ SEBASTIAN HAINDL (1727–1812). NONNOSUS MADL-
SEDER (1730–1797), STEFAN PALUSELLI (1748–1805).

v. 87   NICHOLAUS ZANGIUS (*fl.* 1594–1612), *Geistliche und weltliche
Gesänge,* ed. Hans Sachs, Anton Pfalz.

v. 88   GEORG REUTTER (the younger, 1708–1772), *Kirchenwerke,*
ed. P. Norbert Hofer.

v. 89   GEORG MUFFAT, *Armonico tributo (1682), Exquisitiores har-
moniae instrumentalis grave-jucundae selectus primus (1701),
Concerti grossi II,* ed. E. Schenk.
Concerti grossi 1 = v. 23.

v. 90   *Niederländische und Italienische Musiker der Grazer Hofkapelle
Karls II, 1564–1590,* ed. Hellmut Federhofer, Robert John.
Works by JOHANNES DE CLEVE (*ca.* 1529–1582), LAMBERT
DE SAYVE (1549–1614), JACOB VON BROUCK (*ca.* 1545–*ca.*
1590), ANNIBALE PADOVANO (1527–1575), SIMONE GATTO
(*ca.* 1545–1594/5), FRANCESCO ROVIGO (1530/31–1597),
GIOVANNI BATTISTA GALENO (1550/55–*after* 1626), PIETRO
ANTONIO BIANCO (*ca.* 1540–1611), MATTHIA FERRABOSCO
1550–1616).

v. 91   A. CALDARA, *Dafne (1719),* ed. Constantin Schneider.

v. 92   J. J. F. BIBER, *Harmonia artificiosa-ariosa,* ed. Paul Nettl,
Friedrich Reidinger.

v. 93   JOHANN HEINRICH SCHMELZER (*ca.* 1628–1680), *Sonate unarum
fidium (1664). Violinsonaten handschriftlicher Überlieferung,*
ed. E. Schenk.

v. 94–5   J. GALLUS, *Fünf Messen zu acht und sieben Stimmen,* ed. P. A.
Pisk.

v. 96   H. J. F. BIBER, *Mensa sonora seu musica instrumentalis, sonatii
aliquot liberus sonantibus ad mensam (1680),* ed. E. Schenk.

v. 97   H. J. F. BIBER, *Fidicinium sacro-profanum . . . (1683)*, ed. E. Schenk.

v. 98   JAKOB VAET (*ca.* 1529–1567), *Sämtliche Werke I*, ed. Milton Steinhardt.
Contents: Motets, 3–5 v. (D–Ecce). II = 100; III = 103–4; IV = 108–9; V = 113–14; VI = 116.

v. 99   ARNOLD VON BRUCK (*ca.* 1500–1554), *Sämtliche lateinische Motetten*, ed. Othmar Wesseley.

v. 100   J. VAET, *Sämtliche Werke II*, ed. M. Steinhardt.
Contents: Motets, 5 v. (E–V). See v. 98.

v. 101–2   *Geistliche Solomotetten des 18. Jahrhunderts*, ed. Camillo Schoenbaum.
Works by MARC'ANTONIO ZIANI (1653–1715), A. CALDARA, FRANCESCO CONTI (1682–1732), J. J. FUX.

v. 103–4   J. VAET, *Sämtliche Werke III*, ed. M. Steinhardt.
Contents: Motets, 6–8 v. See v. 98.

v. 105   J. H. SCHMELZER, *Duodena selectarum sonatarum (1659)* [Trio sonatas], *Werke handschriftlicher Überlieferung*, ed. E. Schenk.

v. 106–7   H. J. F. BIBER, *Sonatae tam aris quam aulis servientes (1676)* [ensemble sonatas], ed. E. Schenk.

v. 108–9   J. VAET, *Sämtliche Werke IV*, ed. M. Steinhardt.
Contents: Masses, 4–6 v. See v. 98.

v. 110   TIBURTIO MASSAINO (*ca.* 1550–*ca.* 1609), *Liber primus cantionum ecclesiasticarum (1592); Drei Instrumentalcanzonen (1608)*, ed. Raffaello Monterosso.

v. 111–12 J. H. SCHMELZER, *Sacro-profanus concentus musicus fidium aliorumque instrumentorum (1662)*, ed. E. Schenk.

v. 113–14 J. VAET, *Sämtliche Werke V*, ed. M. Steinhardt.
Contents: Masses, 6–8 v. See v. 98.

v. 115   *Suiten für Tasteninstrumente von und um Franz Mathias Techelmann* [*ca.* 1649–1714], ed. Herwig Knaus.
Contents: 2 suites by TECHELMANN, 13 anonymous from Göttweig Ms "Kerll 2".

v. 116   J. VAET, Sämtliche Werke VI, ed. M. Steinhardt.
           Contents: settings of *Salve Regina, Magnicat*. See v. 98.

v. 117   J. GALLUS, *Drei Messen zu sechs Stimmen*, ed. P. A. Pisk.

33

Denkmäler Deutscher Tonkunst. Herausgegeben von der Musikgeschichtlichen Kommission. [General editor Max Seiffert]. Leipzig, Breitkopf & Härtel, 1892–1931.

Common abbreviation: DDT. The double volumes are paged continuously. This set, like its second series, DTB (**A 31**), is superseded by *Das Erbe Deutscher Musik* (**A 43**). During the 1950's the original publishers reprinted DDT with added pages of additions and corrections, all by Hans Joachim Moser except where otherwise stated below.

v. 1   SAMUEL SCHEIDT (1587–1634), *Tabulatura nova*, ed. Max Seiffert.

v. 2   HANS LEO HASSLER (1564–1612), *Cantiones sacrae für 4–12 Stimmen*, ed. Hermann Gehrmann, with additions by C. Russell Crosby, Jr.

v. 3   FRANZ TUNDER (1614–1667), *Gesangwerk*, ed. Max Seiffert.

v. 4   JOHANN KUHNAU (1660–1711), *Klavierwerke*, ed. Karl Päsler.

v. 5   JOHANN RUDOLF AHLE (1625–1673), *Ausgewählte Gesangswerke*, ed. Johannes Wolf.

v. 6   MATTHIAS WECKMANN (1621–1674), CHRISTOPH BERNHARD (1627–1692), *Solokantaten und Chorwerke mit Instrumentalbegleitung*, ed. M. Seiffert.

v. 7   H. L. HASSLER, *Messen*, ed. Joseph Auer; additions by C. R. Crosby, Jr.

v. 8–9   IGNAZ HOLZBAUER (1711–1783), *Günther von Schwarzburg* [opera], ed. Hermann Kretschmar.

v. 10   *Orchestermusik des XVII Jahrhunderts*, ed. Ernst von Werra.
           Contents: JOHANN KASPAR FERDINAND FISCHER (*ca.* 1665–1746), *Journal de printemps;* D. A. SCHMICORER (*fl.* 1649), *Zodiacus*.

v. 11   DIETRICH BUXTEHUDE (1637–1707), *Instrumentalwerke,* ed.
             Carl Stiehl.
             Contains ensemble sonatas, op. 1–2.

v. 12–13   HEINRICH ALBERT (1604–1651), *Arien,* ed. Eduard Bernoulli,
             H. Kretschmar

v. 14   D. BUXTEHUDE, *Abendmusiken und Kirchenkantaten,* ed. M.
             Seiffert.

v. 15   CARL HEINRICH GRAUN (1701–1759), *Montezuma,* ed. Albert
             Mayer-Reinach.

v. 16   MELCHIOR FRANCK (*ca.* 1573–1639), VALENTIN HAUSSMANN
             (*d. ca.* 1612), *Ausgewählte Instrumentalmusik,* ed. Franz
             Boelsche.

v. 17   JOHANN SEBASTIANI (1622–1683), JOHANN THEILE (1646–
             1724), *Passionsmusik,* ed. Friedrich Zelle.

v. 18   JOHANN ROSENMÜLLER (*ca.* 1620–1684), *Sonate da camera,*
             ed. Karl Nef.

v. 19   ADAM KRIEGER (1634–1666), *Arien,* ed. Alfred Heuss.

v. 20   JOHANN ADOLPH HASSE (1699–1783), *La conversione di
             S. Agostino,* ed. Arnold Schering.

v. 21–2   FRIEDRICH WILHELM ZACHOW (1663–1712), *Gesammelte
             Werke,* ed. M. Seiffert.

v. 23   HIERONYMUS PRAETORIUS (1560–1629), *Ausgewählte Werke,*
             ed. Hugo Leichtentritt.

v. 24–5   H. L. HASSLER, *Sacri concentus, für 4–12 Stimmen,* ed. J. Auer;
             additions by C. R. Crosby Jr.

v. 26–7   JOHANN GOTTFRIED WALTHER (1684–1748), *Gesammelte Werke
             für Orgel,* ed. M. Seiffert.

v. 28   GEORG PHILIPP TELEMANN (1681–1767), *Der Tag des Ge-
             richts* [oratorio], *Ino* [cantata], ed. Max Schneider.

v. 29–30   *Instrumentalkonzerte deutscher Meister,* ed. Arnold Schering.
             Works of JOHANN GEORG PISENDEL (1687–1755), J. A.
             HASSE, KARL PHILIPP EMANUEL BACH (1714–1788),

CHRISTOPH GRAUPNER (1683–1760), GOTTFRIED HEINRICH STÖLZEL (1690–1749).

v. 31   PHILIPPUS DULICHIUS (1562–1631), *Prima pars Centuriae octonum et septenum vocum. Stetini (1607),* ed. Rudolph Schwartz.
Secunda pars = v. 41.

v. 32–3   NICOLA JOMMELLI (1714–1774), *Fetonte,* ed. Hermann Abert.

v. 34   *Newe deudsche geistliche Gesange für die gemeinen Schulen (Georg Rhau, 1544),* ed. J. Wolf.
Works by MARTIN AGRICOLA (1486–1556), ARNOLD VON BRUCK (*ca.* 1500–1554), SIXTUS DIETRICH (*ca.* 1492–1538), BENEDICTUS DUCIS (*ca.* 1480–1544), LUPUS HELLINGK (*ca.* 1495–1541), STEPHAN MAHU, BALTASAR RESINARIUS (*ca.* 1480–*after* 1543), LUDWIG SENFL (*ca.* 1492–1542/3), THOMAS STÖLZER (*ca.* 1470–1526), and others.

v. 35–6   SPERONTES (i.e. JOHANN SIGISMUND SCHOLZE, 1705–1750), *Die singenden Muse an der Pleisse* [1736], ed. Edward Buhle.

v. 37–8   REINHOLD KEISER (1674–1739), *Der hochmütige, gestürzte und wieder erhabene Croesus, 1730 (1710); erlesene Sätze aus L'Inganno fedele, 1714,* ed. M. Schneider.

v. 39   JOHANN SCHOBERT (*ca.* 1720–1767), *Ausgewählte Werke,* ed. Hugo Riemann.
Includes thematic catalog.

v. 40   ANDREAS HAMMERSCHMIDT (1611/12–1675), *Ausgewählte Werke,* ed. H. Riemann.

v. 41   P. DULICHIUS, *Secunda pars Centuriae octonum et septenum vocum. Stettini, 1608,* ed. R. Schwartz.
Prima pars = v. 31.

v. 42   JOHANN ERNST BACH (1722–1777), *Sammlung auserlesener Fabeln.* VALENTIN HERBING (*d.* 1766), *Musikalische Versuche,* ed. H. Kretschmar.

v. 43–4   *Ausgewählte Ballette Stuttgarter Meister aus der 2. Hälfte des 18. Jahrhunderts,* ed. H. Abert.
Contents: FLORIAN JOHANN DELLER (1729–1773), *Orfeo;* JOHANN JOSEPH RUDOLPH (1730–1812), *Rinaldo, La mort d'Hercule, Medea.*

v. 45   HEINRICH ELMENHORSTS (1662–1704) *geistliche Lieder,* ed. Josef Kromolicki, Wilhelm Krabbe.
Works by GEORG BÖHM (1662–1733), JOHANN WOLFGANG FRANCK (*ca.* 1641–*after* 1695), PETER LAURENTIUS WOCKENFUSS (*fl.* 1708–1714).

v. 46–7   PHILIPP HEINRICH ERLEBACH (1657–1714), *Harmonische Freude musikalischer Freunde,* ed. Otto Kinkeldey.

v. 48   J. E. BACH, *Passionsoratorium,* ed. J. Kromolicki.

v. 49–50   *Thüringische Motetten der ersten Hälfte des 18. Jahrhunderts,* ed. M. Seiffert.
Contains motets from Königsberg, Universitätsbibl. Gottholdsche Sammlung Ms 13661 by JOHANN MICHAEL BACH (1648–1694), NIKOLAUS NIEDT, JOHANN TOPFF and others.

v. 51–2   CHRISTOPH GRAUPNER (1683–1760), *Ausgewählte Kantaten,* ed. Friedrich Noack.
For commentary see *Beihefte,* v. 1 (listed below).

v. 53–4   JOHANN PHILIPP KRIEGER (1649–1725), *21 Ausgewählte Kirchenkompositionen,* ed. M. Seiffert.

v. 55   CARLO PALLAVICINO (1630–1688), *La Gerusalemme liberata (Das befreyte Jerusalem). Dramma per musica,* ed. H. Abert.

v. 56   JOHANN CHRISTOPH FRIEDRICH BACH (1732–1795), *Die Kindheit Jesu (1773), Die Auferweckung Lazarus (1775),* ed. Georg Schünemann.

v. 57   GEORG PHILIPP TELEMANN, *24 Oden.* JOHANN VALENTIN GÖRNER (1702–*after* 1752), *Sammlung neuer Oden und Lieder,* ed. W. Krabbe.

v. 58–9   SEBASTIAN KNÜPFER (1633–1676), JOHANN SCHELLE (1648–1701), JOHANN KUHNAU (1660–1722), *Ausgewählte Kirchenkantaten,* ed. A. Schering.

v. 60   ANTONIO LOTTI (*ca.* 1667–1740), *Messen,* ed. Hermann Müller.

v. 61–2   G. P. TELEMANN, *Tafelmusik (Hamburg, 1733),* ed. M. Seiffert.
For commentary see *Beihefte,* v. 2 (listed below).

v. 63   JOHANN PEZEL (*fl. from* 1672, *d.* 1694), *Turmmusik und Suiten,* ed. A. Schering.

v. 64   GEORG BENDA (1722–1795), *Der Jahrmarkt* [opera], ed. Theodor W. Werner.

v. 65   THOMAS STOLZER (*ca.* 1470–1526), *Sämtliche lateinische Hymnen und Psalmen,* ed. Hans Albrecht, Otto Gombosi.

BEIHEFTE ZU DEN DENKMÄLERN DEUTSCHER TONKUST
v. 1   FRIEDRICH NOACK, *Christoph Graupner als Kirchenkomponist: Ausführungen zu Band LI/LII der Denkmäler deutscher Tonkunst . . .*

v. 2   MAX SEIFFERT, *Georg Philipp Telemann (1681–1767) Musique de Table: Ausführungen zu Band LXI und LXII der Denkmäler deutscher Tonkunst . . .*

Denkmäler deutscher Tonkunst, zweite Folge: Bayern see **A 31**

34
Denkmäler Rheinischer Musik, herausgegeben von der Arbeitsgemeinschaft für Rheinische Musikgeschichte, *ca.* 1950–

v. 1   *Sinfonien um Beethoven,* ed. Ludwig Schiedermair.
         Contents: FERDINAND ERNST GABRIEL, GRAF VON WALD-STEIN (1762–1823), *Sinfonie in D;* CHRISTIAN GOTTLOB NEEFE (1748–1798), *Partita in Es.*

v. 2   *Das Kölnische Volks- und Karnevalslied: Ein Beitrag zur Kulturgeschichte der Stadt Köln von 1823 bis 1923 im Lichte des Humors,* ed. Paul Mies.

v. 3   CUNRADUS HAGIUS RINTELIUS (i.e. Konrad Hagius, *ca.*1550–after 1615), *Die Psalmen Davids nach Kaspar Ulenberg (Köln 1582) für vier Stimmen. Düsseldorf 1589, Oberursd 1606,* ed. Johannes Overath.

v. 4   *Liederbuch der Anna von Köln (um 1500),* ed. Walter Salmen, Johannes Koepp.

v. 5   CARL LEIBL (1784–1870), *Festkantate zur Feier der Grundsteinlegung für den Fortbau des Kölner Doms, 1842,* ed. P. Mies.

35

Documenta liturgiae polychoralis Sanctae Ecclesiae Romanae. [Edited by Lorenzo Feininger]. Roma, Societas Universalis S. Ceciliae, 1957–

M2
D58

A 35 **Documenta liturgiae polychoralis Sanctae Ecclesiae Romanae : 13**

v. 13   GIORGI, *Et manducantibus illis.*

v. 14   CANICCIARI, *Confirma hoc Deus.*

v. 15   CANICCIARI, *Vidi turbam magnam.*

v. 16   BENEVOLI, *Collocet eum.*

v. 17   BENEVOLI, *Et ecce terremotus.*

v. 18   GIACOMO CARISSIMI (1605–1674), *Christus factus est.*

v. 19   GIORGI, *Improperium exspectavit.*

36

Documenta maiora liturgiae polychoralis Sanctae Ecclesiae Romanae. [Edited by Lorenzo Feininger]. Tridenti, Societas Universalis S. Ceciliae, 1958–

v. 1   GIUSEPPE OTTAVIO PITONI (1657–1745), *Missa Cum clamarem.*

v. 2   PITONI, *Missa Sancta Maria.*

v. 3   PITONI, *Missa Sancta Dei genetrix.*

v. 4   PITONI, *Missa Sancta virgo virginum.*

v. 5   PITONI, *Missa pro defunctis V.*

v. 6   GIOVANNI GIORGI (*fl.* 1723), *Missa a 4 voci plena.*

v. 7   GIORGI, *Missa a 4 voci plena.*

v. 8   GIORGI, *Missa a 4 voci concertata.*

v. 9   GIORGI, *Missa a 4 voci concertata.*

v. 10   GIUSEPPE DE ROSSI (*d. ca.* 1719), *Graduale di S. Cecilia (1715).*

v. 11

37

Documenta majora polyphoniae liturgicae Sanctae Ecclesiae Romanae. [Edited by Lorenzo Feininger]. Tridenti, Societas Universalis S. Ceciliae, 1964–

v. 1   Anonymus, *Missa L'homme armé* (from Bologna, Bibl. mus. G. B. Martini Ms Q 16, ff. 86–96).

38

Documenta musicologica: Reihe II. [Facsimiles of musical manuscripts].
Kassel, Bärenreiter, 1951–

For *Reihe I* see **C 23.**

v.   1   *Das Buxheimer Orgelbuch: Handschrift mus. 3729 der Bayerischen Staatsbibliothek, München,* ed. Bertha Antonia Wallner.

v.   2   *Codex Escorial. Chansonnier. Biblioteca del Monasterio, Signatur MS. V. III. 24,* ed. Wolfgang Rehm.

39

Documenta polyphoniae liturgicae Sanctae Ecclesiae Romanae. [Edited by Lorenzo Feininger]. Roma, Societas Universalis S. Ceciliae, 1947–

Serie 1   *Ordinarium missae.*

a. [4 voices].

v.   1   GUILLAUME DUFAY (*ca.* 1400–1474), *Fragmentum missae.*

v.   2   LEONEL POWER (*d.* 1437), *Missa Alma redemptoris mater.*

v.   3   DUFAY, *Et in terra, ad modum tubae.*

v.   4   DUFAY, *Missa de SS. Trinitate.*

v.   5   GILLES BINCHOIS (*ca.* 1400–1460), *Missa de angelis.*

v.   6   STANDLEY (*fl. ca.* 1450), *Missa Ad fugam reservatam.*

v.   7   DUFAY, *2 Kyrie, et Gloria in dominicis diebus.*

v.   8   JOHN DUNSTABLE (*d.* 1453), *Gloria, Credo.*

v.   9   LEONEL (?), *Missa Fuit homo missus.*

v.   10   DUFAY, *Et in terra De quaremiaux.*

v.   11   FRANCHOYS DE GEMBLACO (*fl. ca.* 1425–1430), *Gloria, Credo.*

b. [6 voices]

v.   1   PIERRE DE LA RUE (*d.* 1518), *Missa Ave sanctissima.*

Serie IV   *Motectae.*

v.   I   STANDLEY (?), *Quae ista.*

40

Early English Church Music. Published by the British Academy with the support of the Pilgrim Trust. General editor Frank Ll. Harrison. London, Stainer & Bell, 1963–

v.   I   *Early Tudor Masses I,* ed. John D. Bergsagel.
Masses by RICHARD ALWOOD, THOMAS ASHWELL (*fl.* 1486–1518).

v.   2   WILLIAM MUNDY (*ca.* 1529–*ca.* 1591), *Latin antiphons and psalms,* ed. F. Ll. Harrison.

v.   3   ORLANDO GIBBONS (1583–1625), *Verse anthems,* ed. David Wulstan.

v.   4   *Early Tudor Magnificats,* ed. Paul Doe.
Works by ROBERT FAYRFAX (*ca.* 1484–1521), WILLIAM CORNYSH (*ca.* 1465–1523), EDMUND TURGES, HENRY PRENTYCE, NICHOLAS LUDFORD (*ca.* 1480–*ca.* 1542).

v.   5   THOMAS TOMKINS (1572–1656), *Musica Deo sacra I,* ed. Bernard Rose.

v.   6   *Early Tudor organ music I: Music for the Office,* ed. John Caldwell.
Works by JOHN REDFORD (*d.* 1547), and others.

v.   7   ROBERT RAMSEY (*fl.* 1616–1644), *English sacred music,* ed. E. Thompson.

v.   8   T. TOMKINS, *Musica Deo sacra II,* ed. B. Rose

v.   9   *Fifteenth-century liturgical music I: Antiphons and music for Holy Week and Easter,* ed. Andrew Hughes
Includes music from MSS Cambridge, Pembroke College 314 (*olim* Incun. C 47); London, B. M. Egerton 3307; Oxford, Bodl. Lib. Arch. Seldon B 26 and Add. C 87

41

M452 **The English Madrigalists,** edited by Edmund H. Fellowes. London, Stainer &
.A   Bell, 1913–1924; revised edition 1958–

18   The following volumes of the revised edition have reappeared to date: v. 6,
413   9, 12 (WILBYE, WEELKES) by Thurston Dart; and v. 14 (BYRD) by Philipp
      Brett. The first edition has been reprinted by Stainer & Bell.

ALISON, RICHARD, (*fl.* 1592–1606).
An hour's recreation in music (1608)   V. 33

BATESON, THOMAS (*ca.* 1570–1630)
First set of madrigals (1604)   21
Second set of madrigals (1618)   22

BENNET, JOHN (*fl.* 1599–1614)
Madrigals to 4 voices (1599)   23

BYRD, WILLIAM (1542/3–1623)
Psalms, songs and sonnets (1611)   16
Psalms, sonnets and songs for 5 voices (1588)   14
Songs of sundry natures (1589)   15

CARLTON, RICHARD (*ca.* 1558–*ca.* 1638)
Madrigals to 5 voices (1601)   27

CAVENDISH, MICHAEL (*ca.* 1565–1628)
Madrigals (1598)   36

EAST, MICHAEL (*ca.* 1580–1648)
First set of madrigals (1604)   29
Second set of madrigals (1606)   30
Third book of madrigals (1610)   31a
Fourth book of madrigals (1618)   31b

EDWARDS, RICHARD (*ca.* 1523–1566)
"In going to my naked bed"   36

FARMER, JOHN (*fl.* 1591–1601)
Madrigals to 4 voices (1599)   8

FARNABY, GILES (*ca.* 1560–*ca.* 1600)
Canzonets to 4 voices (1598)   20

GIBBONS, ORLANDO (1583–1625)
Madrigals and motets of 5 parts (1612)   5

Madrigals of 6 parts (1600)   V. 12

WILBYE, JOHN (1574–1638)
  First set of madrigals (1598)   6
  Second set of madrigals (1609)   7

YOULL, HENRY (*fl.* 1608)
  Canzonets to 3 voices (1608)   28

42
The English School of Lutenist Song Writers, edited by Edmond H. Fellowes. London, Winthrop Rogers, Stainer & Bell, 1920–1932; 1959–

This set is divided into two series: Series 1 contains lute and piano versions; Series 2 contains lute versions only. In 1932 the original set concluded with 16 volumes in each series. In 1959 it was revived under the editorship of Thurston Dart. The original 32 volumes were <u>reprinted</u> and by 1968 the following additions and revisions had appeared: new volumes in Series 1: 17–19 (COPERARIO, MAYNARD, Ms sources) and Series 2: 17–18 (JOHNSON, GREAVES, MASON, EARNDEN); revisions of Series 1: 1–3, 8–9 (DOWLAND, FORD, ROSSETER) by Dart and of Series 2: 16 (FERRABOSCO) by I. ~~Fink~~. Spink In the following alphabetical composer index, Series 1: 19 (miscellaneous songs from various manuscript sources) is not included.

ATTEY, JOHN (*fl. from* 1622, *d. ca.* 1640)
  First book of ayres (1622)   II,9

BARTLET, JOHN (*fl. ca.* 1606–1610)
  A book of ayres (1606)   II,3

CAMPION, THOMAS (1567–1620)
  Songs from Rosseter's Book of airs (1601), part 1   I,4

  . . . . part 2   I,13

  First book of ayres (1613)   II,1
  Second book of ayres (1613)   II,2
  Third book of ayres (1617)   II,10
  Fourth book of ayres (1617)   II,11

CAVENDISH, MICHAEL (*ca.* 1565–1628)
  Songs from Book of ayres (1598)   II,7

COPERARIO, GIOVANNI (*ca.* 1570–1627)
  Funerale teares . . . (1606)   I,17

CORKINE, WILLIAM (*fl.* 1610–12)
  First book of ayres (1610)   II,12
  Second book of ayres (1612)   II,14

DANIEL, JOHN (*ca.* 1565–1630)
  Songs for lute, viol and voice (1606)   II,8

DOWLAND, JOHN (1562–1626)
  First book of airs (1597)   I,1–2
  Second book of airs (1600)   I,5–6
  Third book of airs (1603)   I,10–11
  Fourth book of airs (1612), part 1

  . . . part 2   I,14

EARSDEN, JOHN (*fl.* 1618)
  Ayres (1618)   II,18

FERRABOSCO, ALFONSO (the younger, *ca.* 1575–1628)
  Ayres (1609)   II,16

FORD, THOMAS (*ca.* 1580–1648)
  Music of sundrie kindes (1607)   I,3

GREAVES, THOMAS (*fl.* 1604)
  Songs (1604)   II,18

JOHNSON, ROBERT (*ca.* 1583–1633)
  Ayres, songs and dialogues   II,17

JONES, ROBERT (*fl. ca.* 1597–1617)
  First book of ayres (1600)   II,4
  Second book of ayres (1601)   II,5
  Ultimum vale, third book of ayres (1608)   II,6
  Fourth book of ayres (1609)   II,14
  Fifth book of ayres (1610)   II,15

MASON, GEORGE (*fl.* 1618)
  Ayres (1618)   II,18

MAYNARD, JOHN (*fl.* 1611–12 ?)
  The twelve wonders of the world (1611/12 ?)   I,18

MORLEY, THOMAS (1557–1603)
  First book of airs (1600)   I,16

                         Misc. Mss.   I,19

PILKINGTON, FRANCIS (*fl. from* 1595, *d.* 1638)
  First book of airs (1605), part 1   I,7

  . . . part 2   I,15

ROSSETER, PHILIPP (*ca.* 1575–1623)
  Book of airs (1601)   I,8–9

43

Das Erbe Deutscher Musik. Herausgegeben von der Musikgeschichtlichen Kommission. Leipzig, Breitkopf & Härtel, 1935–1942, other publishers (see below), 1954–
Common abbreviation: EDM.

This is one of the most confusing series, bibliographically speaking. It began in 1935 as a continuation of *Denkmäler der Tonkunst in Bayern* [**A31**], and was initially divided into two series: 1) *Reichsdenkmale* (items of general interest), and 2) *Landschaftsdenkmale* (items of chiefly local interest), plus a small *Sonderreihe* category. Interrupted by the war, it resumed publication in 1954, reprinting the earlier volumes and adding new ones.
The set as issued since the war uses the old *Reichsdenkmale* volume numbers for the set as a whole, but now divides them among ten somewhat overlapping divisions *(Abteilungen).* Each *Abteilung* has its own numbering system in addition to the overall set volume numbers, and each is published by a different publishing house. In addition to the ten *Abteilungen,* there is a *Sonderband* (special volume) category, volumes of which are numbered both by that category and as volumes of EDM as a whole. Then there is a *Sonderreihe* (special series) category, volumes of which follow a single numbering system separate from the rest of the set. The post-war *Sonderreihe* includes the pre-war *Landschaftsdenkmale* series (which will not continue under its former title), as well as the *Sonderreihe* of the pre-war set, but with different volume numbers.
The first table below shows the numbering of volumes in the *Abteilungen* and the *Sonderband* category. It is followed by a list of the contents of each volume, arranged by EDM volume number, then a list of the new and old *Sonderreihe* volumes, then a list of the old *Landschaftsdenkmale* (arranged alphabetically by country). Pre-war volumes which have not been reprinted are placed in parentheses.

Abteilung 1. *Orchestermusik* (Wiesbaden, Breitkopf & Härtel)

v. 1 = v. 11   v. 4 = v. 41
v. 2 = v. 18   v. 5 = v. 51
v. 3 = v. 30

Abteilung 2. *Motette und Messe* (Lippstadt, Kistner & Siegel)

v. 1 = v. 5   v. 4 = v. 25
v. 2 = v. 13   v. 5 = v. 42
v. 3 = v. 24   v. 6 = v. 47

Abteilung 3. *Mehrstimmiges Lied* (Wolfenbüttel, Karl Heinrich Mösler Verlag)

v. 1 = v. 10   v. 3 = v. 20
v. 2 = v. 15   v. 4 = v. 29

Abteilung 4. *Oper und Sologesang* (Mainz, B. Schott's Söhne)

v. 1 = v. 6   v. 4 = v. 28
v. 2 = v. 19   v. 5 = v. 43
v. 3 = v. 27

Abteilung 5. *Kammermusik* (Kassel, Nagels Verlag)

v. 1 = v. 3   v. 5 = v. 31
v. 2 = v. 14   v. 6 = v. 44
v. 3 = v. 17   v. 7 = v. 49
v. 4 = v. 24

Abteilung 6. *Orgel, Klavier und Laute* (Frankfurt a.M., Henry Litolffs Verlag)

v. 1 = v. 9   v. 3 = v. 36
v. 2 = v. 12   v. 4 = v. 40

Abteilung 7. *Mittelalter* (Kassel, Bärenreiter Verlag)

v. 1 = v. 4   v. 6 = v. 34
v. 2 = v. 7   v. 7 = v. 37
v. 3 = v. 8   v. 8 = v. 38
v. 4 = v. 9   v. 9 = v. 39
v. 5 = v. 33

Abteilung 8. *Ausgewählte Werke einzelner Meister* (Frankfurt a.M., C. F. Peters)

v. 1 = v. 16   v. 2 = v. 22

v. 3 = v. 23   v. 5 = v. 48
v. 4 = v. 26   v. 6 = v. 57

Abteilung 9. *Oratorium und Kantate* (Kassel, Bärenreiter Verlag)
  v. 1 = v. 35
  v. 2 = v. 45   v. 4 = v. 50
  v. 3 = v. 46   v. 5 = v. 64

Abteilung 10. *Frühromantik* (München, G. Henle Verlag)
  v. 1 = v. 58

Sonderband. (Wiesbaden, Breitkopf & Härtel)
  1 = v. 1   2 = v. 2

a. v. 1   *Altbachisches Archiv aus Johann Sebastian Bachs Sammlung von Werken seiner Vorfahren. I. Teil: Motetten und Chorlieder*, ed. Max Schneider. *(Sonderband 1)*
             Works by JOHANN BACH (1604–1673), JOHANN MICHAEL BACH (1648–1694), JOHANN CHRISTOPH BACH (1642–1703).

    v. 2   *Altbachisches Archiv . . . II. Teil: Kantaten*, ed. M. Schneider. *(Sonderband 2)*.
             Works by HEINRICH BACH (1615–1692), GEORG CHRISTOPH BACH (1642–1697), JOHANN MICHAEL BACH, JOHANN CHRISTOPH BACH.

    v. 3   JOHANN CHRISTIAN BACH (1735–1782), *Sechs Quintette, op. 11*, ed. Rudolf Steglich. *(Kammermusik 1)*

    v. 4   *Das Glogauer Liederbuch, I. Teil: Deutsche Lieder und Spielstücke*, ed. Heribert Ringmann. *(Mittelalter 1)*
             Includes thematic catalog. Part 2 = v. 8.

    v. 5   LUDWIG SENFL (*ca.* 1490–1542/3), *Messen*, ed. Edwin Löhrer, Otto Ursprung. *(Motette und Messe 1)*
             Also is LUDWIG SENFL's *Sämtliche Werke*, v. 1. See v. 10, 13 and 15 below, and **B 86**.

    v. 6   GEORG PHILIPP TELEMANN (1681–1767), *Pimpinone, oder Die ungleiche Heirat*, ed. Theodor W. Werner. *(Oper und Sologesang 1)*

   (v. 7)   *Trompeterfanfaren, Sonaten und Feldstücke des 16.–17. Jahrhunderts*, ed. Georg Schünemann. (*Mittelalter 2* [sic])

✓ v. 8 *Das Glogauer Liederbuch, II. Teil: Ausgewählte lateinische Sätze,* ed. Heribert Ringmann *(Mittelalter 3)*
Part I = v. 4.

v. 9 *Orgelchöräle um Johann Sebastian Bach,* ed. Gotthold Frotscher. *(Orgel, Klavier und Laute 1).*
Works by ANDREAS ARMSDORFF (1670–1699), JOHANN HEINRICH BUTTSTEDT (1666–1727), JOHANN LUDWIG KREBS (1713–1788), JOHANN KRIEGER (1652–1735), ANDREAS NICOLAUS VETTER (1666–1734) and others.

✓ v. 10 LUDWIG SENFL, *Deutsche Lieder, I. Teil: Lieder aus handschriftlichen Quellen bis etwa 1533,* ed. Arnold Geering, Wilhelm Altwegg *(Mehrstimmige Lied 1; SENFL Werke 2).*
See v. 5.

✓ v. 11 *Gruppenkonzerte der Bachzeit,* ed. Karl Michael Komma. *(Orchestermusik 1)*
Concerti grossi by TELEMANN, JOHANN DAVID HEINICHEN (1683–1729), JOHANN FRIEDRICH FASCH (1688–1758).

✓ v. 12 *Lautenmusik des 17.–18. Jahrhunderts,* ed. Hans Neemann. *(Orgel, Klavier und Laute 2)*
Works by ESAIAS REUSNER (1636–1697) and SILVIUS LEOPOLD WEISS (1686–1750).

✓ v. 13 L. SENFL, *Motetten, I. Teil: Gelegenheitsmotetten und Psalmvertonungen,* ed. Walter Gerstenberg *(Motette und Messe 2; SENFL Werke 3).*
See v. 5.

✓ v. 14 *Deutsche Bläsermusik vom Barock bis zur Klassik,* ed. Helmut Schultz. *(Kammermusik 2).*
Works by ANDREAS BERGER, MATTHIAS SPIEGLER, JOHANN HEINRICH SCHMELZER (1630–1680), DANIEL SPEER (1636–1707), JOHANN GEORG CHRISTIAN STÖRL (1675–1719), P. PROWO *(fl. ca.* 1725), STRANENSKY, JOHANN DAVID SCHWEGLER (1759–1817), FRANZ DANZI (1763–1826).

v. 15 L. SENFL, *Deutsche Lieder, II. Teil: Lieder aus Hans Otts Liederbuch von 1534,* ed. Arnold Geering, W. Altwegg. *(Mehrstimmiges Lied 2; SENFL Werke 4).*
See v. 5.

v. 16   CASPAR OTHMAYR (1515–1553), *Ausgewählte Werke, I. Teil: Symbola,* ed. Hans Albrecht *(Ausgewählte Werke einzelner Meister 1).*
Part 2 = v. 26.

v. 17   JOHANN JAKOB WALTHER (1650–1717), *Scherzi da violono solo con il basso continuo, 1676,* ed. Gustav Beckmann *(Kammermusik 3).*

v. 18   CARL PHILIPP EMANUEL BACH (1714–1788), *Vier Orchestersinfonien mit zwölf obligaten Stimmen,* ed. R. Steglich. *(Orchestermusik 2)*

v. 19   VALENTIN RATHGEBER (1682–1750), *Ohrenvergnügendes und gemüthergötzendes Tafelconfect (Augsburg 1733/37/46),* ed. Hans Joachim Moser *(Oper und Sologesang 2).*

v. 20   GEORG FORSTER, *Frische teutsche Liedlein, I. Teil: Ein Ausszug guter alter und neuer teutscher Liedlein (1539),* ed. Kurt Gudewill, Wilhelm Heiske. *(Mehrstimmiges Lied 3)*
Part 2 not yet published.

v. 21   GEORG RHAU (publisher, 1488–1548), *Sacrorum hymnorum liber primus, I. Teil: Proprium de tempore,* ed. Rudolf Gerber. *(Motette und Messe 3)*
Contains list of contents for entire Rhau volume, transcriptions of nos. 1–74. Part 2 = v. 25.

v. 22   THOMAS STOLTZER (*ca.* 1470–1526), *Ausgewählte Werke, I. Teil,* ed. H. Albrecht. *(Ausgewählte Werke einzelner Meister 2)*
Contains masses, motets. Part 2 not yet published.

v. 23   SIXT DIETRICH (*ca.* 1492–1548), *Ausgewählte Werke, I. Teil: Hymnen (1545), 1. Abteilung,* ed. Hermann Zenck. *(Ausgewählte Werke einzelner Meister 3)*
Part I:2 not yet published.

v. 24   IGNAZ HOLZBAUER (1711–1783), *Instrumental Kammermusik,* ed. Ursula Lehmann. *(Kammermusik 4)*

v. 25   G. RHAU, *Sacrorum hymnorum liber primus, II. Teil: Proprium et commune sanctorum,* ed. R. Gerber. *(Motette und Messe 4)*
Part I = v. 21.

v. 26   CASPAR OTHMAYR, *Ausgewählte Werke, II. Teil: Cantilenae (1546), Epitaphium Luthers (1546), Bicinia (1547?), Tricinia (1549), Einzelne Werke aus verstreuten Quellen*, ed. H. Albrecht. *(Ausgewählte Werke einzelner Meister 4).*
Part I = v. 16.

v. 27   JOHANN ADOLF HASSE (1699–1783), *Arminio, I. Teil: 1. und 2. Akt*, ed. R. Gerber. *(Oper und Sologesang 3).*

v. 28   J. A. HASSE, *Arminio, II. Teil: 3. Akt und Kritischer Bericht*, ed. R. Gerber. *(Oper und Sologesang 4).*

v. 29   JOHANN JEEP (1582–1644), *Studentengärtlein, 1614*, ed. Rudolf Gerber. JOHANN STEFFENS (d. 1616), *Neue teutsche weltliche Madrigalia und Balletten, 1619*, ed. Gustav Fock. *(Mehrstimmige Lied 4).*

v. 30   JOHANN CHRISTIAN BACH, *Fünf Sinfonien*, ed. Fritz Stein *(Orchestermusik 3).*
Contains *op.* VI, 6; XXI, 1; XVIII, 5–6; Overture to *Temistocle.*

v. 31   GREGOR JOSEPH WERNER (1695–1766), *Musikalischer Instrumental-Kalender für zwei Violinen und Basso continuo*, ed. Fritz Stein. *(Kammermusik 5).*

v. 32   *Der Mensuralkodex Nikolas Apel, I. Teil*, ed. R. Gerber. *(Mittelalter 4).*
Contains nos. 1–84.

v. 33   ———, *II. Teil. (Mittelalter 5).*
Contains nos. 85–150.

(v. 34)   ———, *III. Teil. (Mittelalter 6).*
This v. was destroyed while in press and has never appeared.

v. 35   JOHANN GOTTLIEB GOLDBERG (1727–1756), GOTTFRIED KIRCHHOFF (1685–1746), *Kirchenkantaten*, ed. Alfred Dürr. *(Oratorium und Kantate 1).*

v. 36   *Lüneburger Orgeltabulatur KN 208[1]*, ed. Margarete Reimann. *(Orgel, Klavier und Laute 3).*

v. 37   *Das Buxheimer Orgelbuch, I. Teil*, ed. Bertha A. Wallner. *(Mittelalter 7).*
Contains nos. 1–105.

v. 38   ———, *II. Teil. (Mittelalter 8)*.
         Contains nos. 106–229.

v. 39   ———, *III. Teil. (Mittelalter 9)*.
         Contains nos. 230–256 and *Kritischer Bericht* for all 3 parts.

v. 40   *Die Lüneburger Orgeltabulatur Kn 208²*, ed. M. Reimann
         (Orgel, Klavier und Laute 4)
         N.B. This v. was announced in the prospectus as an edition
         of the Schedel Liederbuch by Besseler, an edition which
         has not yet appeared elsewhere in the set.

v. 41   *Klarinetten-Konzerte des 18. Jahrhunderts*, ed. Heinz Becker.
         (Orchestermusik 4).
         Contains 4 concertos by JOHANN MELCHIOR MOLTER (*ca.*
         1695–1765) and 2 by FRANZ XAVER POKORNY (1729–*after*
         1770).

v. 42   ADRIAN PETIT COCLICO (*ca.* 1500–1563), *Musica reservata*,
         1552, ed. Martin Ruhnke. *(Motette und Messe 5)*.

v. 43   ANDREAS HAMMERSCHMIDT (1611–1675), *Weltliche Oden*, ed.
         Hans J. Moser *(Oper und Sologesang 5)*.

v. 44   JOHANN SCHENK (1656–*before* 1715), *La Nymphe de Rheno*,
         für zwei Sologamben, ed. Karl-Heinz Pauls *(Kammermusik 6)*.

v. 47   LUDWIG DASER (*ca.* 1525–1589), *Motetten*, ed. Anton
         Schneiders *(Motette und Messe 6)*.

v. 48   CHRISTIAN GEIST (*ca.* 1640–1711), *Ausgewählte Kirchen-
         konzerte*, ed. Bo Lundgren *(Ausgewählte Werke einzelner
         Meister 5)*.

v. 49   ANDREAS HAMMERSCHMIDT (1611–1675), *Erster Fleiss (1636/
         1639)*. *Instrumentalwerke zu 5 und 3 Stimmen*, ed. Helmut
         Mönkemeyer. *(Kammermusik 7)*.
         This was v. 3 of the old *Sonderreihe*.

v. 50   AUGUSTIN PFLEGER (*ca.* 1635–*ca.* 1690), *Geistliche Konzerte
         no. 1–11*, ed. Fritz Stein. *(Oratorium und Kantate 4)*.
         Nos. 12–23 = v. 64.

v. 51   *Flötenkonzerte der Mannheimer Schule*, ed. Walter Lebermann.
         Orchestermusik 5).
         Contains works by ANTON FILTZ (*ca.* 1730–1760), FRANZ

XAVIER RICHTER (1709–1789), JOHANN STAMITZ (1717–1757), KARL STAMITZ (1746–1801), ANTON STAMITZ (1721–1768), KARL JOSEPH TOESCHI (*ca.* 1723–1758).

v. 57   HEINRICH FINCK (1445–1527), *Ausgewählte Werke, I. Teil: Messen und Motetten zum Proprium Missae,* ed. Lothar Hoffmann-Erbrecht. *(Aussgewählte Werke einzelner Meister 6).*
         Part 2 not yet published.

v. 58   JOHANN FRIEDRICH REICHARDT (1752–1814), *Goethes Lieder, Oden, Balladen und Romanzen mit Musik,* ed. Walter Salmen. *(Frühromantik 1).*

v. 64   A. PFLEGER, *Geistliche Konzerte nr. 12–23,* ed. Fritz Stein. *(Oratorium und Kantate 5).*
         Nos. 1–11 = v. 50.
         66

b. *Sonderreihe.*
The pre-war *Sonderreihe* was composed of 4 v., of which v. 1–2 were the same as below, v. 3 was the same as v. 49 above, and v. 4 was the same as v. 3 below. The following is the new *Sonderreihe* listing.

v. 1   CHRISTOPH DEMANTIUS (1567–1643), *Neue teutsche weltliche Lieder, 1595; Convivialum concentuum farrago, 1609,* ed. Kurt Stangl.

v. 2   JOHANN KUGELMANN (*fl. from* 1518, *d.* 1542), *Concentus novi, 1540,* ed. Hans Engel.

v. 3   ERASMUS WIDMANN (1572–1634), *Ausgewählte Werke,* ed. Georg Reichert.

v. 4   JOHANN SCHOBERT (*ca.* 1720–1767), *Sechs Sinfonien für Cembalo mit Begleitung von Violine und Hörner ad libitum, op. 9–10,* ed. Gustav Becking.

c. *Landschaftsdenkmale.*
   1. *Alpen-und Donau Reichsgaue*
   v. 1   Same as DTO [A 32], v. 84.

   2. *Bayern*
   These 2 v. were also published as v. 37–8 of DTB [A 31].

   v. 1   RUPERT IGNAZ MAYR, *Ausgewählte Kirchenkompositionen,* ed. Karl G. Fellerer.

v. 2   JOHANN WOLFGANG FRANCK (*ca.* 1641–*after* 1696?), *Die drey Töchter Cecrops,* ed. G. F. Schmidt.

3. *Kurhessen*

v. 1   MORITZ, LANDGRAF VON HESSEN-KASSEL (1572–1632), *Ausgewählte Werke,* ed. Herbert Birtner.

4. *Mecklenburg und Pommern*

v. 1   *Hochzeitsarien und Kantaten Stettiner Meister nach 1700,* ed. Hans Engel.

   Contains works by FRIEDRICH GOTTLIEB KLINGENBERG and MICHAEL ROHDE.

v. 2   DANIEL FRIDERICI (1584–1638), *Ausgewählter geistlicher Gesang,* ed. Erich Schenk.

5. *Mitteldeutschland.*

v. 1   FRIEDRICH WILHELM RUST (1729–1796), *Werke für Klavier und Streichinstrumente,* ed. Max Schneider.

6. *Niedersachsen*

v. 1   JOHANNES SCHULTZ (1582–1653), *Musikalischer Lüstgarte, 1622,* ed. Hermann Zenck.

v. 2   ANDREAS CRAPPIUS (1542–1623), *Werke,* ed. H. Zenck.

7. *Ostpreussen und Danzig.*

v. 1   *Preussische Festlieder zu Dichtungen Simon Dachs,* ed. Hans Engel.

   Contains works of HEINRICH ALBERT (1604–1651), CHRISTOPH KALDENBACH (1613–1698), GEORG KOLB, KONRAD MATTHAEI, JOHANN SEBASTIANI (1622–1683), JOHANN STOBÄUS (1580–1646), JOHANN WEICHMANN (1620–1652).

8. *Rhein-Main-Gebiet*

v. 1   JOHANN ANDREAS HERBST (1588–1666), *Drei mehrchörige Festkonzerte für die freie Reichstadt Frankfurt a.M.,* ed. J. M. Müller-Blattau.

9. *Schleswig-Holstein und Hansestädte*

v. 1   NICHOLAS BRUHNS (*ca.* 1665–1697), *Gesammelte Werke, I. Teil: Kirchenkantaten nr. 1–7,* ed. Fritz Stein.

v. 2   ———*2. Teil: Kirchenkantaten nr. 8–12.*

v. 3   JOHANN SIGISMUND KUSSER (1660–1727), *Arien, Duette und Chöre aus Erindo, oder Die unsträfliche Liebe,* ed. Helmuth Osthoff.

v. 4   MATTHIAS WECKMANN (1613–1679), *Gesammelte Werke,* ed. Gerhard Ilgner.

10. *Sudentenland, Böhmen und Mähren*
v. 1   Same as *Sonderreihe,* v. 1.

44

Florilège du concert vocal de la renaissance, edited by Henry Expert. Paris, Cité des Livres, 1928–
This series was reprinted unchanged by Broude Bros., New York, ca. 1967.

v. 1   CLÉMENT JANEQUIN (*ca.* 1485–*ca.* 1560), *Chantons, sonnons, trompetes . . .*

v. 2   ORLANDO DI LASSO (1532?–1594), *O temps divers.*

v. 3   JANEQUIN, *Les cris de Paris (1529).*

v. 4   GUILLAUME COSTELEY (1530–1606), *Arreste un peu.*

v. 5   PIERRE BONNET, *Airs et villanelles.*

v. 6   CLAUDE LEUJEUNE (1528–1600), *Las! ou vas-tu sans moy.*

v. 7   JACQUES MAUDUIT (1557–1627), *Psaumes mesurés à l'antique.*

v. 8   CLAUDIN DE SERMISY (*ca.* 1490–1562), PELLETIER, GUILLAUME LE HEURTEUR, and ANTOINE GARDANE (*fl.* 1538–1569), *Duos.*

45

Fort Hays Studies, new series: Music series. Fort Hays, Kansas State College, 1965–

v. 1   *Alessandro Rauerij's collection of Canzoni per sonare (Venice, 1608), v. 1: Historical and analytical study,* by Leland Earl Bartholomew.

v. 2   ————, v. 2: Edition.

Gesellschaft für Musikforschung: Publikationen see **A 88: Publikationen älterer praktischer und theoretischer Musikwerke.**

46

Harvard publications in music. Cambridge, Mass., Harvard University Press, 1968–

[Ser.   1]   *The complete works of Anthony Holborne (d.* 1602)*, ed.* Masakata Kanazawa.
v.   1   *Music for lute and bandora.*

[Ser.   2]   *The symphonies of G. B. Sammartini* (1695–1775)*, ed.* Bathia Churgin.
v.   1   *The early symphonies.*

The Lute music of Francesco Canova da Milano.

47

Hirsh, Paul. Veröffentlichungen der Musik-Bibliothek Paul Hirsch, unter Mitwirkung von Paul Hirsch, herausgegeben von Johannes Wolf. Berlin, H. Breslauer, 1922–1947.

Ser.   1

v.   1   FRANCESCO CAZA (*fl. late* 15th c.), *Tractato vulgare de canto figurato (Mailand 1492)*, ed. Wolf.

v.   2   GIOVANNI LUCA CONFORTO (*b. ca.* 1560), *Breue et facile maniera d'essercitarsi a far passaggi* (Roma, 1593, ?1603), ed. Wolf.

v.   3   *Neujahrsgrüsse empfindsamer Seelen. Eine Sammlung von Liedern mit Melodien und Bilderschmuck aus den Jahren 1770–1800,* ed. Max Schneider.

v.   4   GEORG PHILIPP TELEMANN (1681–1767), *Drei dutzend Klavierfantasien,* ed. Max Seiffert.

v.   5   HERCOLE BOTTRIGARI (1531–1612), *Il desiderio overo de' concerti di varii strumenti musicali, Venetia 1594,* ed. Kathi Meyer.

v.   6   KARL FRIEDRICH ZELTER (1758–1832), *Fünfzehn ausgewählte Lieder,* ed. Moritz Bauer.

v.   7   GIOVANNI SPATARO (*ca.* 1458–1541), *Dilucide et probatissime demonstratione . . . contra certo frivole et vane excusatione de Franchino Gafurio . . . 1521.*

v. 8   NICOLAUS LISTENIUS (*b. ca.* 1500), *Musica, ab authore denuo recognita . . . 1549,* ed. Georg Schünemann.

v. 9   CARL PHILIPP EMANUEL BACH (1714–1788), *Zwölf zwei- und dreistimmige kleine Stücke für die Flöte oder Violine und das Klavier (1770),* ed. Richard Hohenemser.

v. 10 CHRISTOPH SCHULTZE (1619–1683), *Lukas-Passion, Leipzig, 1633,* ed. Peter Epstein.

v. 11 MARTIN LUTHER (1483–1546), *Deutsche Messe und Ordnung Gottes Diensts,* ed. Wolf.

v. 12 WOLFANG AMADEUS MOZART (1756–1791), *The ten celebrated string quartets,* ed. Alfred Einstein.

Ser. 2   *Katalog der Musikbibliothek Paul Hirsch, Frankfurt am Main,* ed. Kathi Meyer, Paul Hirsch [The Hirsch collection is now in the British Museum, London].

v. 1   *Theoretische Drucke bis 1800.*

v. 2   *Opern-Partituren.*

v. 3   *Instrumental- und Vokalmusik bis etwa 1830.*

v. 4   *Erstausgaben, Chorwerke in Partitur, Gesamtausgaben, Nachschlagswerke, etc., Ergänzungen zu Bd. 1–3.*

48

Hortus Musicus. Kassel, Bärenreiter, 1936–

In this well-known performing edition, a few of the volumes have only parts and no score, as indicated below. In the following listing compositions belonging to the same group of works by a given composer are listed together. Alternate instruments are indicated by /, thus: flute/violin = flute *or* violin; flute, violin = flute *and* violin.

v. 1   JOHANN SEBASTIAN BACH (1685–1750), *Unschuld, Kleinod reiner Seelen.* Soprano, flute, oboe, violin, viola.

v. 2   ORLANDO DI LASSO (1532?–1594), *Bicinien.* 2 recorders/other instruments, of different range.

v.   3   JOHANN JOACHIM QUANTZ (1697–1773), *Sonate, D dur*. Flute/ oboe/violin, continuo.

v.   4   *Leichte Duette alte Meister des 16. Jahrhunderts*. 2 recorders/ other instruments, of equal range.

v.   5   *Leichte Duette alte Meister des 16. Jahrhunderts*. 2 recorders/ other instruments, of different range.

v.   6–13   GEORG PHILIPP TELEMANN (1681–1767), *Der getreue Musik-meister* [Selections].

v.   6   *Vier Sonaten*. Recorder, continuo.

v.   7   *Sonaten und Spielstücke*. Violin/flute/oboe, continuo.

v.   8   *Spielstücke*. Flute, continuo.

v.   9   *Spielstücke*. Keyboard/lute.

v.   10   *Triosonate, C-dur*. 2 recorders/violins/flutes, continuo.

v.   11   *Drei Duette:* no. 1, 2 recorders; no. 2, 2 violins; no. 3, violin, flute.

v.   12   *Lieder und Arien*. High voice, continuo; some also with violin.

v.   13   *Sonate*. Cello, continuo.
Also from *Getreue Musikmeister:*
v. 175 *Suite, g-moll*. Violin/oboe, continuo.
v. 189   *Sonate, G-dur*. Viola da gamba, continuo.

v.   14   *Englische Fantasien*. 3 viola da gamba/violin, viola, cello.

v.   15   GEORG FRIEDRICH HÄNDEL (1685–1759), *Triosonate, B-dur*. Oboe/violin, violin, continuo.

v.   16   GIOVANNI BATTISTA BASSANO (*ca.* 1657–1716), *Sieben Trios*. Violin, viola, viola da gamba.

v.   17   FISCHER, JOHANN (1646–1721), *Tafelmusik: Overtürensuite*. String quartet/string orchestra, with or without keyboard.

v.   18   DI LASSO, *Sechs Fantasien*. 2 violins/other instruments, of equal range.

v.   19   DI LASSO, *Sechs Fantasien*. 2 instruments of different range.

v.   20   G. P. TELEMANN, *Konzert, D-dur*. 4 violins alone.

v. 21   JOHANN VIERDANCK (*ca.* 1612–1646), *Capricci.* 2 and 3 violins/ other melodic instruments.

v. 22   TELEMANN, *Konzert, G-dur.* Viola, string orchestra, continuo.

v. 23   GIOVANNI GIACOMO GASTOLDI (*ca.* 1550–*after* 1581), *Spielstücke.* 2 instruments of equal range.

v. 24   GASTOLDI, *Spielstücke.* 2 instruments of different range.

v. 25   TELEMANN, *Triosonate, e-moll.* Recorder/flute/violin, oboe/ flute/violin, continuo.

v. 26   JOHANN FRIEDRICH FASCH (1688–1758), *Sonate, B-dur.* Recorder, oboe, violin, continuo.

v. 27   *Bicinien der Renaissance.* 2 instruments of equal range.

v. 28   *Bicinien der Renaissance.* 2 instruments of different range.

v. 29   HEINRICH ISAAC (*ca.* 1450–1517), *Sechs Instrumentalsätze.* String quartet.

v. 30   JOHANN JOSEPH FUX (1660–1791) *Triosonate (Kanon).* 2 viola da gamba/viola, continuo.

v. 31   GIOVANNI LEGRENZI (*ca.* 1625–1690), *Triosonate G-dur.* 2 violins, continuo.

v. 32   TELEMANN, *Konzert, a-moll.* Violin, string orchestra.

v. 33   Anonymous, *ca.* 1730, *Drei Sonaten.* Recorder, continuo.

v. 34   MAURIZIO CAZZATI (*ca.* 1620–1677), *Triosonate d-moll.* 2 violins, continuo.

v. 35   PIETRO LOCATELLI (1693–1764), *Drei Sonaten.* Flute, continuo.

v. 36   TELEMANN, *Triosonate, B-dur.* Keyboard, cello, lute.

v. 37   JOHANN CHRISTIAN BACH (1735–1782). *Drei Streichtrios.* 2 violins, cello. Parts only.

v. 38   TOMASO VITALI (*ca.* 1664–1692), *Sonate.* Violin, continuo.

v. 39–40   KARL FRIEDRICH ABEL (1725–1787), *Sechs Sonaten.* Viola da gamba/violin/flute, continuo. 3 in each v.

v. 41   JOSEPH HAYDN (1732–1809), *Zwölf deutsche Tänze.* 2 violins, cello.

v. 42   J. C. BACH, *Quintett, D-dur*. Flute, oboe, violin, cello, keyboard.

v. 43   JEAN-BAPTISTE LOEILLET (1680–1730), *Sonaten, Heft 1*. Re-
            corder/flute/violin/oboe, continuo.
            Contains *op. 1*, no. 1–3. *Heft 2* = v. 162: *Op. 3*, no. 9; *op. 4*,
            no. 9–10. *Heft 3* = v. 165: *Op. 3*, no. 12, *op. 4*, no. 11–12.

v. 44–5   FRANCESCO ANTONIO BONPORTI (1672–1749), *Inventionen,
            op. 10, "La Pace"*. Violin, continuo. 3 in each v. Part 3 =
            v. 77, with 4 more.

v. 46   KARL PHILIPP EMANUEL BACH (1714–1788), *Sonate, C-dur*.
            Violin, cello, keyboard.

v. 47   TELEMANN, *Die kleine Kammermusik: Sechs Partiten*. Violin,
            continuo.

v. 48   ALESSANDRO SCARLATTI (1659–1725), *Sinfonie IV, e-moll*.
            Chamber orchestra.
            Sinfonie I = v. 125; *Sinfonie II* = v. 146; *Sinfonie V* = v. 116;
            Sinfonie XII = v. 168.

v. 49   JOHANN WILHELM HERTEL (1727–1789), *Sonate, d-moll*.
            Keyboard.

v. 50   HENRY PURCELL (1659–1695), *Spielmusik zum "Sommernachts-
            traum" (The Fairy Queen)*. Strings, continuo.
            Contains Prelude, Hornpipe, Overture, Air, Rondeau,
            Prelude, Entry dance, Hornpipe, Dance for the fairies,
            Chaconne. V. 58 contains Air, Jig, Prelude, Dance for the
            followers of Night, Air, Dance for the green men, Monkey's
            dance, Air.

v. 51   J. J. FUX, *Partiten III und V in G-dur und F-dur*. 2 violins,
            continuo.

v. 52   TELEMANN, *Concerto, D-dur. Eine kleine Tanzsuite*. String
            quartet/string orchestra, continuo.

v. 53   GIUSEPPE TARTINI (1692–1770), *Sinfonie in A*. String quartet/
            string orchestra.

v. 54–6   JOHANN PACHELBEL (1653–1706), *Triosuiten*. 2 violins,
            continuo. 2 suites in each v.

v. 57   WILHELM FRIEDRICH ERNST BACH (1759–1845), *Trio, G-dur*.
            2 flutes, viola.

v. 58   See v. 50.

v. 59   J. FISCHER, *Vier Suiten*. Recorder/violin/flute/oboe, continuo.

v. 60   QUANTZ, *Triosonate, C-dur*. Recorder/flute/violin, flute/violin, continuo.

v. 61   JOHANN ERASMUS KINDERMANN (1616–1655), *Tanzstücke*. Keyboard.

v. 62   CHRISTLIEB SIGMUND BINDER (1724–1789), *Sonate, G-dur*. Violin, keyboard.

v. 63   JOHANN WALTHER (1496–1570), *Kanons in den Kirchentonen*. Recorder, violin.

v. 64   *Leichte Fantasien*. 3 viola da gamba.
          Contains works by G. B. BASSANI, THOMAS LUPO (17th c.), and THOMAS MORLEY (1557–1603).

v. 65   J. HAYDN, *Divertimenti, Heft, 1*. Baryton/violin/viola, viola, cello.
          Contains *Hob. XI:* 26, 35, 45. *Heft 2* = v. 94: *Hob. XI:* 30, 25, 44. *Heft 3* = v. 95: *Hob. XI:* 27, 37, 48.

v. 66–8   GIOVANNI ANTONIO BRESCIANELLO (*ca.* 1690–1757), *Concerti a tre*. 2 violins, cello. 2 in each v.

v. 69   GIUSEPPE TORELLI (*ca.* 1650–1708), *Sonate, G-dur*. Violin, continuo.

v. 70   GIOVANNI GABRIELI (1557–1612), *Sonate,* 3 violins, continuo

v. 71–2   K. P. E. BACH, *Sonaten*. Flute, continuo. 2 in each v.

v. 73   HANS LEO HASSLER (1564–1612), *Intraden aus dem "Lustgarten"*. 3 violins, 2 violas, cello.

v. 74   ERASMUS ROTENBUCHER (*fl. ca.* 1550), *Schöne und liebliche Zweigesänge*. 2 violins/recorders.

v. 75   JAN PIETERSZOON SWEELINCK (1562–1621), *Rimes françoises et italiennes à deux parties*. 2 violins or other melodic instruments.

v. 76   QUANTZ, *Konzert "Pour Potsdam"*. Flute, string orchestra, continuo.

v. 77   See v. 44.

v. 78   LEOPOLD MOZART (1719–1787), *Zwölf Duette.* 2 violins.

v. 79   KARL STAMITZ (1746–1801), *Concerto II, A-dur.* Cello, string
orchestra.
Concerto I = v. 104; *Concerto III* = v. 105.

v. 80   J. S. BACH, *Virga Jesse floruit (Einlagesatz aus dem Magnificat
Es-dur BWV 243a).* Soprano, bass, continuo.

v. 81   ESPRIT-PHILIPPE DE CHÉDEVILLE (*d.* 1782), *Sechs galante Duos.*
2 recorders/violins.

v. 82   CARLO RICCIOTTI (1686–1756) (attributed to G. B. PERGOLESI),
Concertino II. 4 violins, viola, continuo.
I = v. 158, *III* = v. 159, *IV* = v. 144, *V* = v. 154, *VI* = v. 155.

v. 83   GIOVANNI LEGRENZI, *Sonate.* 4 violins, continuo.

v. 84   LEGRENZI, *Sonate.* Violin, cello, continuo.

v. 85   JOSEPH BODIN DE BOISMORTIER (*ca.* 1691–1765), *Sonate.*
2 flutes alone.

v. 86   FRANZ XAVER RICHTER (1709–1789), *Sechs Kammersonaten,
Heft 1.* Flute/violin, cello, keyboard.
Heft 2 not yet published.

v. 87–8   GIOVANNI PLATTI (*ca.* 1700–1762), *Ricercati.* Violin, cello.
2 in each v.

v. 89   JOHANN THEODOR RÖMHILD (1684–1757), *Das neue Jahr ist
kommen. Solokantat.* Basso, oboe, 2 violins, continuo.

v. 90   JOHANN GOTTLIEB NAUMANN (1741–1801), *6 leichte Duette.*
2 violins.

v. 91   JOHANN GEORG PISENDEL (1687–1755), *Sonate.* Violin solo.

v. 92   KARL DITTERS VON DITTERSDORF (1739–1799), *Sechs Streichtrios.* 2 violins, cello. Parts only.

v. 93   WENZEL [JAN VACLAV] STICH [= GIOVANNI PUNTO] (1746–
1803), *Quartet, op. 2, no. 1.* Horn, violin, viola, cello.
Quartet op. 18, no. 1 = v. 171.

v. 94–5   See v. 65.

v. 96   SAMUEL SCHEIDT (1587–1654), *Canzon Bergamasca.* 3 violins,
viola, cello.

Canzon Intradam Aechiopicam = v. 140.

v. 97   TELEMANN, *Sonate.* 3 violins, continuo.

v. 98   J. HAYDN, *Streichquartette, E-dur* [Hob. III: E2].

v. 99   CHRISTIAN FRIEDRICH WITT (1660–1716), *Suite, F-dur.* 2 recorders/violins, c' recorder/violin, continuo.

v. 100   TOMASO VITALI, *Chaconne, g-moll.* Violin, continuo.

v. 101   JOHANN HELMICH ROMAN (1694–1758), *2 Sonaten.* Flute, continuo.

v. 102   ANTONIO VIVALDI (*ca.* 1676–1741), *Sonate, g-moll.* Violin, continuo.

v. 103   NICOLAUS ADAM STRUNGK (1640–1700), *Sonate.* 3 violins, 2 violas, cello, continuo.

v. 104   See v. 79

v. 105   See v. 79.

v. 106   See v. 79.

v. 107   TELEMANN, *Kleine Suite, D-dur.* 2 violins, 2 violas, continuo/3 violins, viola, continuo.

v. 108   TELEMANN, *Streichquartett A-dur.* Parts only.

v. 109   K. STAMITZ, *Quartett, D-dur, op. 8 no. 1.* Flute, violin, viola/horn, cello. Parts only.

v. 110   SALOMONE ROSSI (1587–1628), *Sonata detta la Moderna.* 2 violins, continuo.

v. 111   JOSEPH WÖLFL (1773–1812), *Sonate, op. 31.* Cello, piano.

v. 112   HÄNDEL, *Sonate.* Viola da gamba/viola, keyboard.

v. 113   WOLFGANG AMADEUS MOZART (1756–1791), *Duo, B-dur, K.424.* Violin, viola. Parts only.

v. 114   MOZART, *Duo, G-dur, K. 423.* Violin, viola. Parts only.

v. 115   MOZART, *12 Duette für 2 Bassethörner, K. 487.* Arranged for violin, viola.

v. 116   See v. 48.

v. 117   PHILIPP HEINRICH ERLEBACH (1657–1714), *Sonate I, D-dur.* Violin, viola da gamba, continuo.

v. 118   ERLEBACH, *Sonate III, A-dur.* Violin, viola da gamba, continuo.

v. 119   J. C. BACH, *Quartett, D-dur, op. 22 no. 2.* 2 flutes, viola, cello.

v. 120   CHRISTOPH GRAUPNER (1683–1766), *Sonata, G-dur.* String quartet or string orchestra.

v. 121   GRAUPNER, *2 Sonaten.* Violin, keyboard.

v. 122   FRIEDRICH KARL, GRAF ZU ERBACH (1680–1731), *6 Duos.* 2 cellos.

v. 123   *Leichte Spielmusik.* Viola da gamba, continuo.

v. 124   TELEMANN, *Konzert, e-moll.* Recorder, flute, string orchestra, continuo.

v. 125   See v. 48.

v. 126   JAN DISMAS ZELENKA (1679–1745), *Sonate I, F-dur.* 2 oboes/ violins, Bassoon/cello, continuo.
         II = v. 188, III = v. 177, IV = v. 147, V = v. 157, VI = v. 132.

v. 127–8   WILLEM DE FESCH (1687–1757), *Sechs Sonaten.* Violin/flute/ oboe, continuo.

v. 129   BIAGIO MARINI (1597–1665), *Sonate, d-moll.* Violin, string bass, continuo.

v. 130   TELEMANN, *Konzert, F-dur.* Recorder, string orchestra, continuo.

v. 131   TELEMANN, *Konzert, G-dur.* Flute, 2 violins, continuo.

v. 132   See v. 126.

v. 133   J. B. LOEILLET (doubtful attribution), *Quintett, h-moll.* 2 flutes, 2 recorders, continuo.

v. 134   *In nomine. Altenglische Kammermusik zu 4 und 5 Stimmen.*

v. 135   VIVALDI, *Il pastor fido: 6 Sonaten.* Flute/recorder/oboe/violin, continuo.

v. 136   T. MORLEY, *9 Fantasien.* 2 viola da gamba.

v. 137–8   *Carmina germanica et gallica. Ausgewählte Instrumental-stücke des 16. Jahrhundert.* Various string combinations.

v. 139   ANNE DANICAN-PHILIDOR (1681–1731), *Sonate, d-moll.* Re-corder/flute/oboe, continuo.

v. 140   See v. 76.

v. 141   PURCELL, *Die Nacht. 3 Arien.* High voice, string quartet.

v. 142   BENEDETTO MARCELLO (1686–1739), *Sonaten, op. 2, Heft 2.* Recorder/flute/violin, continuo.
          Heft 1 = v. 151, *Heft 3 =* v. 152.

v. 143   B. MARINI, *Sonate.* 2 violins, continuo.

v. 144   See v. 82.

v. 145   JOHANN ZACK (1699–1773), *2 Sinfonien.* 2 violins, continuo.

v. 146   See v. 48.

v. 147   See v. 126.

v. 148   CHRISTOPH DEMANTIUS (1567–1643), *Deutsche Tänze.* String quartet/string orchestra.

v. 149   JOHN JENKINS (1592–1678), *7 Fantasien.* 3 viola da gamba.

v. 150   HEINRICH ALBERT (1604–1651), *Duette.* Any 2 instruments, continuo.

v. 151–2   See v. 142.

v. 153   JEAN-JACQUES NAUDOT (*early* 18th c.), *Konzert, G-dur.* Re-corder/flute/oboe, 2 violins, continuo.

v. 154–5   See v. 82.

v. 156   CHRISTIAN ERBACH (1573–1635), *Canzona "la Paglia".* 3 violins, 2 cellos.

v. 157   See v. 126.

v. 158–9   See v. 82.

v. 160   BOISMORTIER, *Sonate, e-moll, op. 37 nr. 2.* Flute/oboe/violin, viola da gamba/bassoon/cello, continuo.

v. 161   JOHANN CHRISTOPH PEPUSCH (1667–1752), *Triosonate, d-moll.* Flute/recorder/violin, viola/viola da gamba, continuo.

v. 162   See v. 43.

v. 163   PURCELL, *Herr, zu dir will ich schreien*. Bass, strings, continuo.

v. 164   PURCELL, *Wie wonnig ist's auf blumigem Gefild*. Soprano, tenor, 2 recorders, continuo.

v. 165   See v. 43.

v. 166   JOHN LOEILLET (i.e. JEAN-BAPTISTE, 1680–1730), *Triosonate, op. II, 2*. Recorder/flute, oboe/violin, continuo.
           Op. 2, no. 6 = v. 176; *Op. 2, no. 4* = v. 181.

v. 167   MATTHEW LOCKE (*ca.* 1630–1677), *Duette*. 2 viola da gamba.

v. 168   See v. 48.

v. 169   FRANCESCO MARIA VERACINI (1690–*ca.* 1750), *Konzert, D-dur*.
           Violin, strings, continuo.

v. 170   IGNAZ VON BEECKE (1733–1803), *Streichquartette nr. 6*.

v. 171   See v. 93.

v. 172   LELIO COLISTA (1629–1680), *Triosonate, A-dur*. 2 violins, cello, continuo.

v. 173   FRANCESCO GEMINIANI (1687–1762), *Sonate, A-dur, op. I, 1*. Violin, continuo.

v. 174   GEMINIANI, *Sonate, D-dur, op. I, 4*. Violin, continuo.

v. 175   See v. 6–13.

v. 176   See v. 166.

v. 177   See v. 126.

v. 178   GEMINIANI, *Sonate, e-moll*. Oboe/flute/violin, continuo.

v. 179   TELEMANN, *Triosonate, B-dur*. Oboe/flute, violin, continuo.

v. 180   M. LOCKE, *6 Suiten*. 3 viola da gamba.

v. 181   See v. 166.

v. 182   J. J. NAUDOT, *Sonate, G-dur*. Recorder/flute, continuo.

v. 183–5   FRANCESCO BARSANTI (*ca.* 1690–*after* 1750), *Sonaten: C-dur, e-moll, B-dur*. Recorder/flute, continuo.

v. 186   BERTIN QUENTIN (*d.* 1767), *Sonate, d-moll, op. I, 1.* Recorder/ flute/violin, continuo.

v. 187   *Bicinien aus Glareans Dodekachordon.* 2 melodic instruments of equal range.

v. 188   See v. 126.

v. 189   See v. 6–13.

v. 190–91   MARTINI BITTI (*fl.* 1696–*ca.* 1715), *Sonaten.* Recorder/flute/ oboe/violin, continuo.

49

Instituta et Monumenta. Collezione de monumenti riprodutti in facsimile, di testi e studi interessantai la paleografia, la musica e la miniatura nell'antichita, nel medioevo e nel rinasciamento. Cremona, Athenaeum Cremonense, 1954–

Serie I. Monumenta

v. 1   *Le Frottole, nell'edizione principe de Ottaviano Petrucci,* ed. Gaetano Cesari, Raffaello Monterosso, Benvenuto Disertori. Contains Petrucci's Books I-III.

v. 2   *Sacre rappresentazioni nel manoscritto 201 della Bibliothèque municipale de Orleans.* Facsimile, eds. Giampiero Tintori, R. Monterosso.

v. 3   ANTONIO VIVALDI (*ca.* 1676–1741), *La fide ninfa,* ed. R. Monterosso.

4, 5, 6, 7 also issued

Serie II. Instituta

v. 1   ANNA MARIA MONTEROSSO VACCHELLI, *L'opera musicale di Antonfrancesco Doni* (1513–1574).

v. 2   RAFFAELLO MONTEROSSO, *Tecnica ed espressione artistica nella musica del secolo XII.*

v. 3

50

The Institute of Mediaeval Music, Brooklyn, N.Y.

This institute publishes the following four series listed in this book:

Publications of mediaeval musical manuscripts. **A 52.**
cat sep.   *Musical theorists in translation.* **C 51.**

Collected works. **A 51.**

Musicological studies. **C 53.**

51.

The Institute of Medieval Music. Collected Works. Brooklyn, 1960–

v.   1   FAUGUES (VINCENT? GUILLAUME?, *fl. late* 15th c.), *Collected works,* ed. George C. Schuetze.
Complete in 1 v. See also **A 52,** v. 7.

v.   2   ADAM RENER, *Collected Works.* See **B 74.**

v.   3   CLAUDE GOUDIMEL, *Collected works.* See **B 46.**

v.   4   ANTONIO DE CABEZÓN, *Collected works.* See **B 19.**

v.   6   Philippe Caron

52

The Institute of Medieval Music. Publications of Medieval Musical Manuscripts. Brooklyn, 1957–

v.   1   *Bibl. Nac. Madrid Ms 20486* [13th c.], ed. Luther Dittmer.

v.   2   *Wolfenbüttel Ms 1099 (1206)* [13th c.], ed. L. Dittmer.

v.   3   *A central source of Notre-Dame polyphony: Facsimile, reconstruction, catalogue raisonné, discussion and transcriptions,* by L. Dittmer.
(Munich, Bay. Staatsbibl, Ms gallo-rom. 42 [*olim* 4775] and related fragments).

v.   4   *Paris, B.N. Ms nouv. acq. fr. 13521 (La Clayette); Ms Lat. 11411. Facsimile, introduction, index, transcriptions,* by L. Dittmer.

v.   5   *Worcester, Chapter Library Ms Add. 68; London, Westminster Abbey Ms 33327; Madrid, B.N. Ms 192. Facsimile, introduction, index and transcriptions,* by L. Dittmer.

v.   6   *Oxford, Bodl. Lib. Ms lat. lit. d 20; London, British Museum Add. Ms 25031; Chicago, Univ. Lib. Ms 654 app. Facsimile, introduction, index, transcriptions,* by L. Dittmer.

v.   7   *Opera omnia Faugues: facsimile of the compositions of Faugues from the manuscripts Trent 88–Trent 91, Cappella Sistina 14,*

Cappella Sistina 51, Verona DCCLXI, Modena a.M.1.13 (olim Lat. 456), ed. George C. Schuetze.
See also **A 51,** v. 1.

v. 8   Facsimile reproduction of the manuscripts Sevilla 5–I–43 & Paris N. A. Fr. 4371 (part 1), ed. Dragan Plamenac.

v. 9   Carmina Burana. Facsimile reproduction of the manuscript [Munich] Clm 4660, 4660a, ed. Bernhard Bischoff.
Color facsimile.

v. 10–11   Firenze, Biblioteca Mediceo-Laurenziana, Pluteo 29, I, ed. L. Dittmer.
v. 10. fascicles I–VI (ff. 1–262). v. 11: fascicles VII–XI (ff. 263–476).

V. 12

53

Instituto Italiano per la Storia della Musica. Publicazioni. Roma, 1941–

[Series 1]   Antologie e raccolti.

v. 1   Villanelle alla napolitana a tre voci di musicisti Baresi del secolo XVI raccolte da Giovanni de Antiquis per le stampe del Gardano del 1574, ed. S. A. Luciani.

[Series 2]   Monumenti.

1   Madrigali di Carlo Gesualdo, principe di Venosa [1560–1613], ed. Francesco Vatielli.
Contains Books I, II.

2   Madrigali di Pomponio Nenna [ca. 1550–before 1618], ed. Eduardo Dagino.
Contains Books I, IV.

3   GIACOMO CARISSIMI. See **B 20.**

54

Istituzioni e monumenti dell'arte musicale Italiana. Milano, Ricordi, 1931–1939; new series 1956–
a. Old series.

v. 1   *Andrea e Giovanni Gabrieli e la musica strumentale in San Marco I,* ed. Giacomo Benvenuti.
Works by A. GABRIELI (*ca.* 1510–1586), G. GABRIELI (1557–1612), and ANNIBALE PADOVANO (1527–1575).

v. 2   ——— II. Preface by GAETANO CESARI.
Contains G. GABRIELI, *Sacrae symphoniae* (1597).

v. 3   *La cappelle musicali di Novarra dal secolo XVI a' primordi dell'ottocento,* ed. Vito Fideli.
Sacred works by GIACOMO (1665–1719) and GAUDENZIO BATTISTINI (1723–1800).

v. 4   *La camerata fiorentina: Vincenzo Galilei [ca.* 1520–1591], ed. Fabio Fano.
Includes discussion of G.'s theory works, chronological lists of works, transcriptions of lute compositions, and *Il secondo libro di madrigali . . .* (1587).

v. 5   *L'oratorio de Filippini e la scuola musicale di Napoli: la polifonia cinquecentesca ed i primordi del secolo XVII, Tomo I,* ed. Guido Pannain.
Contains sacred works by GIAN DOMENICO MONTELLA (*fl.* 1594–*d. ca.* 1602), GIOVANNI MARIA TRABACI (*d.* 1647), CARLO GESUALDO (1560–1613).

v. 6   *La musica in Cremona nella seconda metà del secolo XVI e i primordi dell'arte Monteverdiana,* ed. G. Cesari; preface by G. PANNAIN.
Contains madrigals by MARCO ANTONIO INGEGNERI (*ca.* 1545–1592); *Sacrae Cantiunculae,* canzonette by CLAUDIO MONTEVERDI (1567–1643).

b. New series (still in progress).

v. 1   *La capella musicale del duomo de Milano.*
1. FABIO FANO, *Le origini e il primo maestro di capella: Matteo da Perugia* (*fl.* 1402–1416).

v. 2   FAUSTO TORREFRANCA, *Giovanni Benedetto Platti* [1700–1763] *e la sonata moderna.*
Contains 18 keyboard sonatas.

v. 3   BENVENUTO DISERTORI, *Le frottole per canto e liuto intabulate da Franciscus Bossinensis* (*fl.* 1509–1511).

55

Italia sacra musica. *Musica corali italiane sconoscuite della prima metà del cinquecento,* ed. Knud Jeppesen. Copenhagen, Wilhelm Hansen, 1962–
Notes in Italian, English and German.

v. 1   Works by JACOPO FOGLIANO (1483–1548), LAURUS PATAVUS *fl. ca.* 1530), GIOVANNI SPATARO (*ca.* 1458–1541), GIULIANO BUONAUGURIS DA TIVOLI (*ca.* 1500–1587), GASPERO ALBERTI (*ca.* 1480–1545), *et al.*

v. 2   Works by RUFINO BARTOLUCCI DA ASSISI (*ca.* 1540), HIERONIMO MAFFONI (*ca.* 1540), SIMON DA FERRARA (*ca.* 1520), TIVOLI, *et al.*

v. 3   Works by GASPERO ALBERTI, BERNARDO PISANO (*ca.* 1520), PAOLO BIVI ((ARETINO, 1508–1584), PALESTRINA (1525–1594), *et al.*

56

Liber Organi. Herausgegeben von ERNST KALLER. Mainz, B. SCHOTT'S Söhne, 1931–1938, 1954–

v. 1–2   *Altfranzösische Orgelmeister (aus dem "Archives des maîtres de l'orgue" von Guilmant-Pirro ausgewählt und für den praktischen Gebrauch bezeichnet.*
v. 1: works by JEAN TITELOUZE (1563–1633), JEAN HENRI D'ANGLEBERT (1628–1691), NICOLAS GIGAULT (*ca.* 1625–*ca.* 1707), FRANÇOIS COUPERIN (SIEUR DE CROUILLY, *ca.* 1632–*ca.* 1701), NICOLAS LEBEGUE (*ca.* 1630–1702), LOUIS MARCHAND (1668–1732).
v. 2: works by TITELOUZE, FRANÇOIS ROBERDAY (*ca.* 1620–*ca.* 1690), JEAN ADAM GUILAIN (*fl. early* 18th c.), NICOLAS DE GRIGNY (1671–1703), LOUIS NICOLAS CLÉRAMBAULT (1676–1713), LOUIS CLAUDE D'AQUIN (1694–1772).

v. 3   *Altspanische Orgelmeister.*
Works by ANTONIO DE CABEZÓN (1519–1566), TOMÁS DE SANTA MARIA (*d.* 1570).

v. 4   *Altitalienische Orgelmeister.*
Works by GIROLAMO FRESCOBALDI (1583–1643), FRA GIOVANNI BATTISTA FASOLO (17th c.), ADRIAN BANCHIERI (1567?–1634), DOMENICO ZIPOLI (1645–*after* 1718).

v. 5 *Toccaten des XVII und XVIII Jahrhunderts.*
By Frescobaldi, Johann Jakob Froberger (1616–1667), Georg Muffat (*ca.* 1645–1704), Johann Pachelbel (1653–1706), Wilhelm Hieronymus Pachelbel (1686–1764).

v. 6–7 *Deutsche Meister des 16. und 17. Jahrhunderts.*
v. 6 Works by Christian Erbach (1573–1635), Samuel Scheidt (1587–1654), Dietrich Buxtehude (1637–1707), J. Pachelbel, Gottlieb Muffat (1690–1770).
v. 7 Johann Kaspar Ferdinand Fischer (*ca.* 1665–1738), *Ariadne musica.*

v. 8 *Orgelmeister der Gotik,* ed. Hans Klotz.
Works by Guillaume Dufay (*ca.* 1400–1474), Heinrich Isaac (*ca.* 1450–1517), Josquin de Pres (*ca.* 1450–1521), Paul Hofhaimer (1459–1537), Ludwig Senfl (*ca.* 1490–1542/3).

v. 9 *Süddeutsche Orgelmeister,* ed. Gregor Klaus.
Contains toccatas from Johannes Speth, *Ars magna consoni . . . Augsburg, Kroniger, 1693.*

v. 10 *Alte englische Orgelmeister,* ed. Gordon Philipps.
Works by John Redford (*ca.* 1485–1545), William Byrd (1542/3–1623), Richard Alwoode (*fl. mid*-16th c.), Thomas Tomkins (1572–1653), Orlando Gibbons (1583–1625), John Blow (1649–1708), Henry Purcell (1659–1695), Maurice Greene (1695–1755), William Boyce (1710–1779), Charles John Stanley (1713–1786), Samuel Wesley (1766–1837).

57
Madrigalisti Italiani. Roma, Edizioni A. de Santis.

v. 1 Luca Marenzio (*ca.* 1560–1599), *Madrigali a 4 e 5 voci, Fasc. I,* ed. L. Virgili.

v. 2 — — — Fasc. 2 (not yet published).

v. 3 Asprilio Pacelli (*ca.* 1570–1623), *Primo volume dei madrigali,* ed. M. Glinsky.

58

Maestri Bolognesi. Publicazioni della Biblioteca del Conservatorio Giovanni Battista Martini, Bologna. Ed. Guiseppe Vecchi.

v. 1   GIROLAMO GIACOBBO (*ca.* 1575–1630), *L'Aurora ingannata* (*1605*).

v. 2   FILIPPO AZZAIOLO (*fl.* 1557–1569), *Il secondo libro de vilotte del fiore alla padovana (1559)*.

v. 3   GHINOLFO DATTARI (1540–1617), *Le vilanelle (1563)*.

v. 4   ASCANIO TROMBETTI (*fl. late* 16th c.), *Il primo libro delle Napolitane (1573)*.

59

Maîtres anciens de la Musique Française. Collection publiée par l'Association des amis d'Henry Expert et de la musique française ancienne. Paris, Hugel. 1966–
Série des compositeurs et auteurs Parisiens.

↞ M2
.M17

v. 1   JEHAN PLANSON (*ca.* 1558–*after* 1612), *Airs mis en musique à quatre parties (1587)*, ed. Henry Expert, André Verchaly.

v. 2   PIERRE CERTON (*ca.* 1510–1572), *Chansons polyphoniques publiées par Pierre Attaingnant, livre I (1533–1539)*, ed. Verchaly, Expert

v. 3   CERTON, *Chansons polyphoniques . . . livre II (1540–1545)*, ed. Verchaly, Expert

v. 4   CERTON, *Chansons polyphoniques . . . Livre III (1546–1550)*, ed. Verchaly, Expert

60

Les Maîtres Musiciens de la Renaissance Française, edited by Henry Expert. Paris, Alphonse Leduc, 1894–1908.

v. 1   ORLANDO DE LASSO (1532?–1594), *Meslanges (1576)* [part 1].
     8042.148

v. 2   CLAUDE GOUDIMEL (*ca.* 1505–1572), *150 psaumes de David*
     8042.145   *(1580)* [part 1].
          Part 2 = v. 4; part 3 = v. 6.

v. 3   GUILLAUME COSTELEY (1531–1606), *Musique (1570)* [part 1].
Part 2 = v. 18; part 3 = v. 19.

v. 4   GOUDIMEL, *150 psaumes de David* [part 2].
See v. 2.

v. 5   *Trente et une chansons musicales (Attaingnant, 1529)*.

v. 6   GOUDIMEL, *150 psaumes de David* [part 3].
See v. 2.

v. 7   CLÉMENT JANEQUIN (*ca.* 1485–*ca.* 1560), *Chansons (Attaingnant, 1529)*.

v. 8   ANTOINE BRUMEL (*ca.* 1475–*ca.* 1520), *Missa de beata virgine;*
PIERRE DE LA RUE (*ca.* 1450–1518), *Missa Ave Maria (1516)*.

v. 9   JEAN MOUTON (*ca.* 1470–1522), *Missa Alma redemptoris;*
ANTOINE DE FEVIN (*ca.* 1473–1512), *Missa Mente tota (1516)*.

v. 10   JAQUES MAUDUIT (1557–1627), *Chansonettes mesurées de I. A. Baïf (1586)*.

v. 11   CLAUDE LEJEUNE (1528–1600/1), *Dodécacorde (1598)*, (part 1).

v. 12–14   LEJEUNE, *Le printemps (1603)*.

v. 15   FRANÇOIS REGNART (1540–*ca.* 1600), *Poésies de P. de Ronsard et autres poètes*.

v. 16   LEJEUNE, *Meslanges* (part 1).

v. 17   EUSTACHE DU CAURROY (1549–1609), *Mélanges*.

v. 18–19   COSTELY, *Musique (1570)*, (parts 2–3).
See v. 3.

v. 20–22   LEJEUNE, *Psaumes mesurez à l'antique*.

v. 23   CLAUDE GERVAISE (*fl.* 1550–1556), ESTIENNE DU TERTRE, and anonymous composers, *Danceries*.

61
Monumenta Liturgiae Polychoralis Sanctae Ecclesiae Romanae. Roma,
Societas universalis S. Ceciliae, [ed. L. Feininger], 1950–

Serie I A.   *Ordinarium missae cum quatuor choris.*

v. 1   ORAZIO BENEVOLI (1605–1672), *Missa Tu es Petrus.*

v. 2   BENEVOLI, *Missa Benevola.*

v. 3   BENEVOLI, *Missa Tira corda.*

v. 4   BENEVOLI, *Missa Si Deus pro nobis.*

v. 5   GIUSEPPE OTTAVIO PITONI (1637–1743), *Missa Albana.*

v. 6   P. PETTI, *Missa in honorem S. Ceciliae.*

v. 7   PITONI, *Missa S. Pietro.*

v. 8   BENEVOLI, *Missa pro gratiarum actione in angustia pestilentiae.*

Serie I B.   *Ordinarium missae cum tribus choris.*

v. 1   BENEVOLI, *Missa Angelus Domini.*

Serie I C.   *Ordinarium missae cum duobus choris.*

v. 1   BENEVOLI, *Missae pastoralis.*

v. 2   *Missae tres, octo vocum, quarum duo Joannis de Georgiis, tertio vero Vincentii Tozzi.*

Serie II A.   *Psalmodia cum sex choris.*

v. 1   BENEVOLI, *Dixit Dominus II. toni.*

Serie II B.   *Psalmodia cum quatuor choris.*

v. 1   BENEVOLI, *Dixit Dominus I. toni.*

v. 2   BENEVOLI, *Dixit Dominus VIII. toni.*

v. 3   BENEVOLI, *Laudate pueri VI. toni.*

v. 4   BENEVOLI, *Confitebor III. toni.*

v. 5   PITONI, *Psalmus Dixit I. toni.*

v. 6   PITONI, *Psalmus Dixit II. toni (1685).*

v. 7   PITONI, *Psalmus Dixit III. toni (1719).*

v. 8   PASCHALE PISARI, *Dixit dominus (1775).*

v. 9   BENEVOLI, *Magnificat III. toni.*

v. 10 STEFANO FABRO, *Magnificat VI. toni.*

v. 11   FABRO, *Magnificat VIII. toni.*

v. 12   FABRO, *Confitebor II. toni.*

Serie II C.   *Psalmodia cum tribus choris.*

v. 1   BENEVOLI, *Magnificat VI. toni.*

Serie II D.   *Psalmodia cum duobus choris.*

v. 1   BENEVOLI, *Magnificat VI. toni.*

Serie [III ?]   *Proprium de tempore.*

v. 1   GIORGI, *Liturgia Paschalis.*

Serie [IV ?]   *Proprium de Sanctis.*

v. 1-2 GIORGI, *Officium de beata virgine.*

62

Monumenta lyrica medii aevi Italica. [A subdivision of *Antiquae musicae Italicae Bibliotheca,* **A 5**]. Bologna, 1966–

Only volumes actually printed or currently in preparation are listed below, the latter placed in parentheses.

Series I. *Latina.*

v. 1   *Troparium sequentiarum nonantulanum (Cod. Casa-nat. 1741) . . . ,* ed. Joseph [Giuseppe] Vecchi.

Series III.   *Mensurabilia.*

(v. 1)   *I più antichi monumenti sacri italiani,* ed. G. Vecchi, F. A. Gallo.
    1. *Edizione fotografica.*
    2. *Parte storica.*

v. 2   *Il canzoniere musicale del Codice Vaticano Rossi 215 con uno studio sulla melica italiana del trecento,* ed. G. Vecchi.
    1. *Edizione fotografica.*
    (2.) *Parte storica.*

v. 3   *Il Codice 2216 della Biblioteca Universitaria di Bologna,* ed. F. A. Gallo.

1. *Edizione fotografica.*
(2.) *Parte storica.*

(v. 4)   *Il Codice Mancini dell'Archivio di Stato di Lucca e della Biblioteca Communale di Perugia,* ed. Kurt von Fischer.

v. 5   *I Codici Tridentini quattrocenteschi del Castello del Buonconsiglio nn. 87, 88, 89, 90, 91 e 92.*

   1. *Il Cod. 87 del Castello del Buonconsiglio di Trento,* ed. Lorenzo Feininger.

(v. 6)   *Il Codice Q 15 del Civico Museo Bibliografico di Bologna,* ed. Suzanne Clercx.

63

Monumenta monodica medii aevi. Herausgegeben im Auftrag des Instituts für Musikforschung Regensburg mit Unterstützung der Musikgeschichtlichen Kommission von Bruno Stäblein. Kassel, Bärenreiter, 1956–

Only v. 1 and 7 have been published so far; the rest are proposed.

v. 1   *Hymnen (I). Die mittelalterlichen Hymnenmelodien des Abendlandes,* ed. Bruno Stäblein.

v. 2   *Die Gradualgesänge der Handschrift Vat. lat. 5319 ("Altrömisches" Graduale),* ed. Margaretha Landwehr, B. Stäblein.

v. 3   *Introitus-Tropen I. Die südfranzösischen Quellen,* ed. Günther Weiss.

v. 4   *"Versarius Martialensis". Die ein- und mehrstimmigen Gesänge des sogenannten Repertoires von Saint-Martial,* ed. B. Stäblein.

v. 5   *Gesamtausgabe der Troubadour-Melodien,* ed. Adolf Lang.

v. 6   *Introitus-Tropen II. Die übrigen Quellen,* ed. G. Weiss.

v. 7   *Die Alleluia-Gesänge I. Von den Anfängen bis etwa 1100,* ed. Karl Heinz Schlager.

v. 8   *Die Alleluia-Gesänge II. Von etwa 1100 bis zum Ende des Mittelalters,* ed. K. H. Schlager.

v. 9   *Die Sequenzen der "klassichen" Epoche I (bis etwa 1050),* ed. B. Stäblein.

v. 10   *Die Sequenzen der "klassischen" Epoche II (bis etwa 1050)* [*sic*], ed. B. Stäblein.

64

Monumenta Musica Neerlandica. Vereniging vor Nederlandse muziek-geschiedenis, Amsterdam, 1959–

Includes commentary in English.

v. 1   PIETER HELLENDAAL (1721–1799), *6 Concerti grossi,* ed. Hans Brants Buys.

v. 2   *The clavier book of Anna Maria Van Eyl,* ed. Frits Noske. Compiled by Steenwick *(fl. from* 1663, *d.* 1679).

v. 3   *Dutch keyboard music of the 16th and 17th centuries,* ed. Alan Curtis.
Contents: The SUSANNE VON SOLDT Ms (British Museum Add. 29485, dated 1599); Leningrad, Library of the Academy of Sciences Ms QN 204.

v. 4   PIETRO LOCATELLI (1693–1764), *Opera quarta, prima parte: sei introduttioni teatrali,* ed. Arend Koole.

v. 5   CORNELIS THYMANSZOON PADBRUÉ (*ca.* 1592–1670), *Nederlandse Madrigalen,* ed. Frits Noske.

v. 6   *The Utrecht Prosarium. Liber sequentiarum ecclesiae capitulario Sanctae Mariae Ultraiectensis saeculi XIII. Codex Ultraiectensis universitatis bibliotheca 417,* ed. F. Noske.

v. 7   *Het geestelijk Lied van noord-nederland in de vijftiende eeuw: de nederlandse liedern van de handschriften Amsterdam (Wenen ONB 12876) en Utrecht (Berlijn MG 8^0 190),* ed. E. Bruning, M. Veldhuyzen, H. Wagenaar-Nolthenius.

65

Monumenta Musicae Belgicae. Uitgegeven door de Vereeniging voor muziekgeschiedenis te Antwerpen, 1932–.

Includes commentary in English.

v. 1   JEAN BAPTISTE LOEILLET (1680–1730), *Werken voor clavi-cembel,* ed. Jos. Watelet, Paul Bergmans.
Contents: *Lessons for the harpsichord or spinnet. Six suits of lessons for the harpsichord or spinnet.*

v. 2   A. VAN DEN KERCKHOVEN (*fl. mid*-17th c.), *Werken voor orgel,* ed. J. Watelet, I. de Jans.

v. 3   JOSEPH-HECTOR FIOCCO (1703–1741), *Werken voor clavi-cimbel,* ed. J. Watelet, Christiane Stellfield.

v. 4   CHARLES GUILLET (*d.* 1654), GIOVANNI MACQUE (*ca.* 1551–1614), CAROLUS LUYTHON (1556–1620), *Werken voor orgel of voor vier spieltiugen,* ed. J. Watelet, Anny Piscaer.

v. 5   JOSSE BOUTMY (1697–1774), *Werken voor klavicimbel,* ed. J. Watelet, Suzanne Clercx.

v. 6   DIEUDONNÉ RAICK (*ca.* 1700–*after* 1752), CHARLES-JOSEPH HELMONT (1715–1790), *Werken voor orgel en/of clavecimbel,* ed. J. Watelet, S. Clercx.

v. 7   GERHARDUS HAVINGHA (1696–1753), *Werken voor clave-cimbel,* ed. J. Watelet, Edgard Lemaire.

v. 8   PIERRE DE LA RUE (*ca.* 1450–1518), *Missa de beate virgine; Missa de virginibus (O quam pulchra est), Missa de Sancta Anna,* ed. René B. Lenaerts, Jozef Robijns.

v. 9   *Nederlandse polyfonie mit Spaanse bronnen,* ed. R. B. Lenaerts.
Contents: NOE BAULDEWIJN (*d.* 1530), *Missa En douleur et tristesse;* MATTHEUS GASCOGNE (*fl.* 1521–1554), *Missa Es hat ein Sin;* THEO VERELST, *Missa quatuor vocum.*

v. 10   EMANUEL ADRIAENSSEN (1550–1604), *Luitmuziek,* ed. Gode-lieve Spiessens.

66

Monumenta Musicae Byzantinae, ediderunt Carsten Hoeg, H. J. W. Tillyard, Egon Wellesz. Copenhague, Muunksgaard, 1935– .

a. *Serie Principale (Facsimilia)*

v. 1   STICHERARIUM. *Codex Vindebonensis theol. graec.,* ed. Høeg, Tillyard, Wellesz.

v. 2   *Hirmologium Athoum. Codex monasterii Hiberorum,* ed. Høeg.

v. 3   *Hirmologium Cryptense,* ed. L. Tardo.

v. 4   *Contacarium Ashburnhamense,* ed. Høeg.

v. 5:1   *Fragmenta Chiliandarica palaeoslavica,* ed. Roman Jakobson.

v. 5:2   *Sticherarium. Codex monasterii Chiliandarici.*

v. 6   *Contacarium palaeoslavicum Mosquense,* ed. Arne Bugge.

v. 7   *Specimina notationum antiquorum,* ed. Oliver Strunk.

v. 8   *Jerusalem Hirmologion Saba 83,* ed. J. Raasted.

b. *Serie subsidiae*

M2 .B99S9

v. 1:1   H. J. W. TILLYARD, *Handbook of the middle Byzantine musical notation.*

v. 1:2   C. HØEG, *La notation ekphonetique.*

v. 2   E. WELLESZ, *Eastern elements in Western chant: studies in the early history of ecclesiastical music.*

v. 3   P. VERDEIL, *La musique Byzantine chez les Bulgares et les Russes du IXe et XIVe siècle.*

v. 4   M. M. VELIMIROVIC, *Byzantine elements in early Slavic chant.*

c. *Serie transcripta*

M2 B99?7

v. 1   *Die Hymnen des Sticherarium für September,* ed. Wellesz.

v. 2   *The hymns of the Sticherarium for November,* ed. Tillyard.

v. 3   *The hymns of the Octoechus, Part 1,* ed. Tillyard Part 2 = v. 5.

v. 4   *Twenty canons from the Trinity Hirmologium,* ed. Tillyard.

v. 5   *The hymns of the Octoechus, Part 2,* ed. Tillyard Part 1 = v. 3.

v. 6   *The hymns of the Hirmologium, Part 1,* ed. Aglaia
Ayoutanti, Høeg.
See v. 8.

v. 7   *The hymns of the Pentecostarium,* ed. Tillyard.

v. 8   *The hymns of the Hirmologium Part 3:2. The third
plagal mode,* ed. A. Ayouanti, Tillyard.
See v. 6.

v. 9   *The Akathiostos hymn,* ed. Wellesz.

v. 10   *The hymns of the Sticherarium for January,* ed.
Tillyard.

d.   *Serie lectionaria,* ed. C. Høeg, G. Zuntz.

ᴬᶜ M2   v. 1   *Lectiones nativitatis et epiphaniae.*

.B99ᴸ3 v. 2   *Lectiones hebdomadarum primae et secundae Quadrigesimae.*

v. 3   *Lectiones hebdomadarum tertiae et quartiae Quadrigesimae.*

v. 4   *Lectiones hebdomadae quintae quadrigesimae et
hebdomadae in palmis.*

v. 5   *Lectiones sabbati sancti.*

67

Monumenta Musicae Svecicae. Published by the Swedish Society for music
research. Uppsala, 1958–   .

Commentary in English included.

Series I.

ᴬᴬ M2   v. 1   Johan Helmich Roman (1694–1758), I. *Assaggi
.M4833   à violino solo,* ed. Ingmar Bengtsson, Lars Frydén.
II = v. 4.

v. 2   Joseph Martin Kraus (1756–1792). *I. Sinfonie
c-moll (1783),* ed. Richard Engländer.

v. 3   *Musica svecicae saeculi XVII, I. St. John's Passion,*
ed. L. Reimers.

v.   4   J. H. ROMAN, *II. Sinfonie 1–3,* ed. I. Bengtsson.
I = v. 1.

Series II = FRANZ BERWALD *Complete works.* See **B 11.**

68
Monumenta Polyphoniae Italicae. A pontif. instituto musicae sacrae edita.
Roma, 1930–1936.

v.   1   *Missa Cantantibus organis, Caecilia,* ed. Raphael Casimiri.
             Mass sections by ANNIBALE STABILE (*ca.* 1540–*after* 1604),
             FRANCESCO SORIANO (1549–*after* 1621), GIOVANNI ANDREA
             DRAGONI (*ca.* 1540–1598), GIOVANNI PIERLUIGI DA PALES-
             TRINA (1525–1594) *et al.*

v.   2   CONSTANTIUS FESTA (*ca.* 1490–1545), *Sacrae cantiones 3, 4,*
             5, 6 vocibus, ed. Edvardus Dagino.

v.   3   C. FESTA, *Hymni per totum annum 3, 4, 5, 6 vocibus,* ed. Glen
             Haydon.

69
Monumenta Polyphoniae Liturgicae Sanctae Ecclesiae Romanae. Roma,
Societas universalis Sanctae Ceciliae, ed. Laurentius Feininger. 1947–   .

Serie I. *Ordinarium missae*

v.   1   *Missae super L'homme armé*
          1. GUILLAUME DUFAY (*ca.* 1400–1474)
          2. ANTONIUS BUSNOIS (*fl. from* 1467, *d.* 1492)
          3. FIRMINUS CARON (15th c.)
          4. G. FAUGUES (15th c.)
          5. JOHANNES REGIS (*ca.* 1430–1485)
          6. JOHANNES OCKEGHEM (*ca.* 1430–1485)
          7. MARBRIANO DE ORTO (*fl. from* 1484, *d.* 1529)
          8. PHILIPPUS BASIRON (15th c.)
          9. JOHANNES TINCTORIS (1446–1511)
          10. VAQUERAS, BERNARD (15th c.)

v.   2   *Missae de G. Dufay et anonymi*
          1. DUFAY, *Missa Caput:* Anonymous (Trent 89), *Missa*

Veterem hominem; Anonymous (Trent 88), *Missa Christus surrexit.*

2. DUFAY, *Missa Se la face ay pale;* Anonymous (Trent 88), *Missa sine nomine;* Anonymous (Rome, Cap. Sist. 14.10), *Missa Pax vobis ego (Gloria, Credo).*

3. DUFAY, *Missa Ave regina celorum;* Anonymous (Modena, Lat. 456), *Missa sine nomine.*

4. DUFAY, *Missa Ecce ancilla Domini;* Anonymous (Rome, Vat. Cap. Sist. 14), *Missa Puisque je vis.*

v. 3 *Anonymus Napoli Ms VI.E. Missa VI super L'homme armé* 1–5. [Masses 1–5].

v. 4

    1. GULIELMUS FAUGUES, *Missa Vinnus vina.*

Series II. *Proprium missae*

v. 1 Auctorum anonymorum, *Missarum propria XVI quorum XI Gulielmo Dufay auctori adscribenda sunt.*
    Contains anon. compositions from Trent 88.

70

Monumenti di Musica Italiana, editi a cura di Oscar Mischiati, Giuseppe Scarpat, Luigi Ferdinando Tagliavini. Brescia, Organo, 1961– .

Series I. *Organo e cembalo*

v. 1 TARQUINIO MERULA (*fl.* 1623–*after* 1652), *Composizioni per organo e cembalo,* ed. Alan Curtis.

v. 2 GIROLAMO FRESCOBALDI (1583–1643), *Nove toccate inedite,* ed. Sandro dalla Libera.

v. 3 GIOVANNI MARIA TRABACI (1575–1647), *Composizioni per organo e cembalo,* ed. Oscar Mischiati.

Series II. *Polyphonia*

v. 1 LODOVICO AGOSTINI, Ferrarese (1534–1590), *Canzoni alla Napolitana a cinque voci, Libro primo,* ed. Adriano Cavicchi e Riccardo Nielsen.

v. 2 LUZZASCHO LUZZASCHI, Ferrarese (1545–1607), *Madrigali per cantare e sonare a uno, due e tre soprani (1601),* ed. A. Cavicchi.

71

Monumenti Musicali Mantovani. Collana diretta da Claudio Gallico. Mantova, Instituto Carlo d'Arco per la Storia di Mantova, 1964- .

Series I.   *Musica vocale sacra*

    v.   1.   LODOVICO VIADANA (1564–1645), *Cento concerti ecclesiastici, opera duodecima (1602). Parte prima: Concerti a una voce con l'organo,* ed. C. Gallico.

72

Monumentos de la Musica Española, ed. Higini Anglés, 1941- .

    v.   1   *La musica en la corte de los reyes católicos, I. Polifonia religiosa,* ed. H. Anglés.
               Part II = v. 5, v. 10; Part III = v. 14.

    v.   2   *La musica en la corte de Carlos V. Con la transcription del Libro de cifra nueva para tecla, harpa e vihuela de Luys Venegas de Henestrosa (1557),* ed. H. Anglés.

    v.   3   LUYS DE NARVÁEZ (*fl.* 1538), *Los seys libros del delphin de musica de cifra para taner vihuela,* ed. Emilio Pujol.

    v.   4   JUAN VÁSQUEZ (*fl.* 1551–1561), *Recopilacion de sonetas y villancicos a quatro y a cinco (Seville, 1560),* ed. H. Anglés.

    v.   5   *La musica en la corte de los reyes católicos, II. Polifonia profana. Cancioniero musicale de Palacio, siglos XV–XVI, Vol. 1,* ed. H. Anglés.
               See v. 1.

    v.   6   FRANCISCO CORREA DE ARAUXO (1581?–1663?), *Libro de tientos y discursos de musica practica e theorica de organo intitulado Faculdad organica (Alcala, 1626), Vol. 1,* ed. Santiago Kastner.
               Vol. 2 = v. 12.

    v.   7   ALÓNSO DE MUDARRA (*fl.* 1546), *Tres libros de música en cifra para vihuela, 1546,* ed. E. Pujol.

    v.   8   *Cancionero musical de la casa de Medinaceli (siglo XVI), Vol. 1,* ed. Miguel Querol-Gavaldá.

    v.   9   –––, *Vol. 2.*

v. 10   *La música en la corte de los reyes católicos, II. Polifonia profana: Cancionero musical de Palacio, Vol.* **2**, ed. H. Anglés. See v. 1.

v. 11   CRISTÓBAL DE MORALES (*ca.* 1500–1553), *Opera omnia I: Missarum liber primus (Roma, 1544).*
Contains Masses: de Beata Virgine (4 v.); Aspice Domine (4 v.); Vulnerasti cor meum (4 v.); Ave maria stella (5 v.); Quaeramus com pastoribus (5 v.); L'homme armé (5 v.); Mille regretz (6 v.); Si bona suscepimus (6 v.).
The other v. of MORALES *Opera omnia* are:

v. 2 (= v. 13). *Motetes I-XXV.*
v. 3 (= v. 15). *Missarum liber secundus (Roma, 1544), I.*
Contains Masses: Benedicta es caelorum regina (4 v.); Ave Maria (4 v.); de Beata Virgine (5 v.); Pro defunctis (5 v.).
v. 4 (= v. 17). *XVI Magnificat (Venecia, 1545).*
v. 5 (= v. 20). *Motetes XXVI–L,*
v. 6 (= v. 21). *Missarum liber secundus . . . II.*
Contains Masses: Tu es vas electionis (4 v.); Gaude Barbara (4 v.); L'homme armé (4 v.); Quem dicunt homines (5 v.).
v. 7 (= v. 24). *Misas 17–21.*
Contains Masses: Caça (4 v.); Super fa re ut fa sol la (4 v.); Super ut re mi fa sol la (4 v.); Desilde al cavallero (4 v.); Tristezas me matan (5 v.).

v. 12   CORREA DE ARAUXO . . . part 2.
See v. 6.

v. 13   See v. 11.

v. 14   *La música en la corte de los reyes católicos, III. Polifonia profana. Cancionero musical de Palacio: estudio preleminar,* by JORGE RUBIO, JOSÉ ROMEU FIGUERAS.

v. 15   See v. 11.

v. 16   FRANCISCO GUERRERO (1527–1599), *Opera omnia,* ed. M. Querol-Gavaldá.
Contains *Canciones y villanescas espirituales (Venecia 1589), Primera parte a cinco voces.* v. 19 contains the *segunda parte.*

v. 17   See v. 11.

v. 18   *Romances y letras a tres voces* [Madrid, Bibl. Nac. Ms M. 1370–72], ed. M. Querol-Gavaldá.

v. 19   See v. 16.

v. 20, 21   See v. 11.

v. 22–3   ENRIQUES DE VALDERRABANO (*fl.* 1547), *Libro de musica de vihuela, intitulado Silva de serenas (Valladolid, 1547),* ed. E. Pujol.

v. 24   See v. 11.

v. 25   TOMÁS LUIS DE VICTORIA (1549–1611), *Opera omnia I: Missarum liber primus,* ed. H. Anglés.
    Contains Masses: Ave maris stella (4 v.); Simile est regum (4 v.); de Beata Maria (5 v.); Gaudeamus (6 v.).
The other v. of VICTORIA *Opera omnia* are:
    v. 26 *Motetes I–XXI.*
    v. 30 *Missarum liber secundus.*
    Contains Masses: Quam pulchra sunt (4 v.); O quam gloriosum (4 v.); Surge, propera (5 v.); Dum complerentur (6 v.).

v. 27–9   ANTONIO DE CABEZON (1510–1566), *Obras de musica para tecla, arpa, vihuela . . . recopiladas y puestas en cifra por Hernando de Cabezon su hijo (Madrid, 1578),* ed. H. Anglés.

73
Les Monuments de la Musique Française au temps de la Renaissance, ed. Henry Expert. Paris, Maurice Senart, 1924–1930.

v. 1   CLAUDE LEJEUNE (1528–1600/1), *Octonaires de la vanité et inconstance du monde (I–VIII).*
    Nos. IX–XII in v. 8.

v. 2   PIERRE CERTON (*ca.* 1510–1572), *Messes à quatre voix.*

v. 3   DIDIER LE BLANC (*fl.* 1570), *Airs de plusieurs musiciens reduits a quatre parties.*

v. 4   ANTHOINE DE BERTRAND (*ca.* 1545–1581), *Premier livre des amours de P. de Ronsard* (part 1).

v. 5   BERTRAND, *Premier livre . . .* (part 2).

v. 6   BERTRAND, *Second livre des amours de P. de Ronsard.*

v. 7   BERTRAND, *Troisième livre de chansons de P. de Ronsard.*

v. 8   LEJEUNE, *Octonaires de la vanité et inconstance du monde (IX–XII); Pseaumes des Meslanges de 1612; Dialogue à sept parties (1564).*
         Octonaires I–VIII in v. 1.

v. 9   CLAUDE GOUDIMEL (*ca.* 1505–1572), *Messes à quatre voix.*

v. 10   PASCHAL DE L'ESTOCART (1540–*after* 1584), *Premier livre des Octonaires de la vanité du monde.*

v. 11   L'ESTOCART, *Deuxième livre des Octonaires de la vanité du monde.*

v. 12   JEAN MOUTON (*ca.* 1570–1522), *Messe Quem discunt homines;* CLAUDE DE SERMISY (*ca.* 1490–1562), CRISPIN VAN STAPPEN (*ca.* 1470–1532/3), PHILIBERT JAMBE DE FER (*fl. from* 1549, *d.* 1572), EUSTACHE DU CAURROY (1549–1609), *Motets.*

v. 13   JEAN PLANSON (1558–1612), *Chansons à quatre voix mixtes.*

v. 14–15   GUILLAUME BONI (*fl.* 1579–1582), *Sonnets de Ronsard.*

74

Monuments of Music and Music Literature in Facsimile. New York, Broude Bros. *ca.* 1964– .

Series I. Music.

v. 1   HENRY PURCELL (1658/9–1695), *Orpheus Britannicus.* [First and second books] London, 1698, 1702.

v. 2   JOHN BLOW (1649–1708), *Amphion Anglicus.* London, 1700.

v. 3   JACQUES CHAMPION DE CHAMBONNIÈRES (*ca.* 1602–1672), *Les pièces de clavessin: Livre premier, Livre second.* Paris, 1670.

v. 4   JEAN HENRY D'ANGLEBERT (1628–1691), *Pièces de clavecin: Livre premier.* Paris, 1689.

v. 5   JOHANNES MATTHESON, *Pièces de clavecin en deux volumes.* London, 1714.

v. 6   GEORGE BICKHAM (*fl. from* 1736, *d.* 1758), *The musical entertainer,* and *Bickham's musical entertainer,* v. 1–2. Second corrected edition. London, 1740.

v. 7   JEAN-PHILIPPE RAMEAU (1683–1764), *Pièces de clavecin.* Paris, 1724.

v. 8   GOTTLIEB MUFFAT (1690–1770), *Componimenti musicali per il cembalo.* Vienna, 1739 (?).

v. 9   FRANÇOIS COUPERIN (1668–1733), *Pièces de clavecin. Premier, second, troisième et quatrième livres.* Paris, 1713, 1716 (?), 1722, 1730.

v. 10 OTTAVIANO PETRUCCI (1466–1539), *Harmonice musices odhecaton.* Venice, 1501.

v. 11 WILLIAM BYRD (1542/3–1623), JOHN BULL (*ca.* 1562–1628), ORLANDO GIBBONS (1583–1628), *Parthenia.* London, 1612–1613.

v. 12 [JOHN WATTS (*ca.* 1678–1763)], *The musical miscellany: being a collection of choice songs set to the violin and flute by the most eminent masters.* 6 v. London, 1729, 1730, 1731.

v. 13 JEAN-PHILIPPE RAMEAU, *Nouvelles suites de pièces de clavecin.* Paris, *ca.* 1728.

v. 14 JEAN-BAPTISTE CARTIER (1765–1841), *L'art du violon, ou collection choisie dans les sonates des écoles italienne, franc. & allemande.* Second edition. Paris, 1798.

v. 15 *New instructions for playing the harpsichord, pianoforte or spinnet wherein the Italian manner of fingering is explained by a variety of examples.* London, 1790 (?).

v. 16 *The preceptor for piano-forte, the organ or harpsichord. To which is added two celebrated lessons by James Hook.* London, *ca.* 1785.

v. 17 JAMES HOOK (1746–1827), *Guida di musica* (in two parts). London, *ca.* 1785, [1794].

v. 18 GOTTLIEB MUFFAT, *72 Versetl. sammt. 12 Toccaten besonders beim Kirchen-Dienst . . .* Vienna, 1726.

V. 19 GIOVANNI BATTISTA MARTINI (1706–1784), *Sonate (12) d'intavolatura per l'organo.* Amsterdam, 1741.

V. 20 BERNHARD SCHMID (d. J., b. 1589), *Tabulatur Buch von allerhand ausserlesenen, schönen, lieblichen Praeludijs, Toccaten, Motteten* . . . Strasbourg, 1607.

V. 21 *French court-aires, with their ditties Englished, of foure and five parts, together with that of the lute. Collected, translated, published by Ed. Filmer, Gent.* London, 1629.

V. 22 HENRY CAREY (*ca.* 1687–1743), *The musical century in 100 English ballads* . . . 2 v. London, 1737, 1740.

V. 23 *Clio and Euterpe, or British harmony. A collection of celebrated songs and cantatas by the most approved masters curiously engrav'd.* 4 v. London, *ca.* 1778.

V. 24 LOUIS-CLAUDE D'AQUIN (1694–1772), *Premier livre de pièces de clavecin.* Paris, 1735.

V. 25 JACQUES DUPHLY (1715–1789), *Pièces de clavecin, livres I–IV.* Paris, 1744–1768.

V. 26 HENRY PURCELL, *A choice collection of lessons for the harpsichord or spinnet.* London, 1696.

V. 27 THOMAS ROSEINGRAVE (1690–1766), *Eight suits of lessons for the harpsichord or spinet.* London, [1728].

V. 28 JACOPO PERI (1561–1633), *Le musiche sopra l'Euridice del. Sig. Ott. Rinuccini* . . . Florence, 1600.

V. 29 GIULIO CACCINI (*ca.* 1546–1618), *Le nuove musiche.* Florence, 1601.

V. 30 LUYS MILAN (*ca.* 1500–1561), *Libro de musica de vihuela de mano initualado El maestro.* Valencia, 1536.

V. 31 JOHANN PHILIPP KIRNBERGER (1721–1783), *Clavieruebungen mit der Bachischen Applicatur* . . . Berlin, 1762.

V. 32 ANTONIO DE CABEZON (1510–1566), *Obras de musica para tecla, arpa y vihuela* . . . Madrid, 1578.

v. 33   GABRIEL BATAILLE (*ca.* 1575–1650), *Airs de différents autheurs mis en tablature de luth.* 6 v. Paris, 1608–1615.

v. 34   ELIAS NICOLAUS AMMERBACH (*ca.* 1530–1597), *Orgel oder Instrument Tabulatur.* Leipzig, 1571.

v. 35   CLAUDE-BÉNIGNE BALBASTRE (1727–1799), *Pièces de clavecin, premier livre.* Paris, 1759.

v. 36   HENRY PLAYFORD (1657–*ca.* 1709), *The theater of music, or, a choice collection of the newest and best songs* . . . In four books. London, 1685–7.

v. 37   *Universal harmony, or the gentleman and lady's social companion, consisting of. . . English and Scots songs, cantatas &c.* London [1743].

Series II. Music literature. See **C 46.**

Series III. Manuscripts.

The following facsimiles are in preparation:

v. 1   *Chantilly, Musée Condé, Ms. 1047.* In color.

v. 2   *Paris, Bibliothèque de l'Arsenal, Ms. 5198* [Chansonnier de l'Arsenal].

v. 3   *Apt, Bibliothèque Capitulaire, Ms. 16 bis.* In color.

v. 4   *Paris, Bibliothèque nationale, Département de la Musique, Res. 823* (Ms. Milleran [lute]).

v. 5   *Paris, Bibliothèque nationale, Ms. fr. 15123* (Ms. Pixérécourt).

v. 6   BENJAMIN COSYN (*fl.* 1622–1646), *Virginal book: British museum Royal Lib. Ms. 23.1.4.*

75

Monuments of Renaissance Music. General editor, Edward E. Lowinsky. Chicago, University of Chicago Press, 1964– .

v. 1   *Musica nova accommodata per cantar et sonar sopra organi et altri strumenti composita per diversi excellentissimi musici. Venetia MDXL,* ed. E. E. Lowinsky, H. Colin Slim.

V. 2   OTTAVIANO PETRUCCI (1466–1539), *Canti B, numero cinquanta. Venice, 1502,* ed. Helen Hewitt, E. E. Lowinsky, Morton W. Briggs, Norman B. Spector.

V. 3   *The Medici codex of 1518. A choirbook of motets dedicated to Lorenzi de' Medici, Duke of Urbino. Historical introduction and commentary,* by E. E. Lowinsky.

V. 4   ———. *Transcription.*

V. 5   ———. *Facsimile.*

76

Musica Britannica. A national collection of music. Published by the Royal Musical Association. London, Stainer & Bell, 1951–   .

V. 1   *The Mulliner Book,* ed. Denis Stevens. 2nd rev. ed.

V. 2   MATTHEW LOCKE (*ca.* 1630–1677) and CHRISTOPHER GIBBONS (1615–1676), *Cupid and Death* [masque], ed. Edward J. Dent. 2nd rev. ed.

V. 3   THOMAS AUGUSTINE ARNE (1710–1778), *Comus* [masque], ed. Julian Herbage.

V. 4   *Medieval carols,* ed. John Stevens. 2nd rev. ed.

V. 5   THOMAS TOMKINS (1573–1653), *Keyboard music,* ed. Stephen D. Tuttle.

V. 6   JOHN DOWLAND (1562–1626), *Ayres for four voices,* ed. Edmund H. Fellowes, Thurston Dart, Nigel Fortune.

V. 7   JOHN BLOW (1649–1708), *Coronation anthems; anthems with strings,* ed. Anthony Lewis, Harold Watkins Shaw.

V. 8   JOHN DUNSTABLE, *Complete works,* ed. Manfred F. Bukofzer (Complete in 1 v.).

V. 9   *Jacobean consort music,* ed. Thurston Dart, William Coates. Works by GIOVANNI COPERARIO (*ca.* 1570–1629), ORLANDO GIBBONS (1583–1628), WILLIAM WHITE, JOHN WARD (*before 1613–before* 1641), JOHN BULL (*ca.* 1562–1628), THOMAS LUPO, THOMAS TOMKINS, ALFONSO FERRABOSCO II (*ca.* 1575–1628), MICHAEL EAST (*ca.* 1580–1648), ROBERT

JOHNSON, RICHARD DERING (*d.* 1630), THOMAS FORD (*ca.* 1580–1648), JOHN OKEOVER, WILLIAM BRADE, ANTHONY HOLBORNE, PETER PHILLIPS (*ca.* 1560–*after* 1633), THOMAS SIMPSON, TOBIAS HUME, and others.

v. 10–12   *The Eton Choirbook,* ed. Frank Ll. Harrison.
Works by JOHN BROWNE, WALTER LAMBE (*fl.* 1467–1499), RICHARD DAVY (*fl.* 1501–1516) and others.

v. 13   WILLIAM BOYCE (1710–1779), *Overtures,* ed. Gerald Finzi.

v. 14   JOHN BULL (*ca.* 1562–1628), *Keyboard music I,* ed. John Steele, Francis Cameron, Thurston Dart.
II = v. 19.

v. 15   *Music of Scotland 1500–1700,* ed. Kenneth Elliot, Helena Mennie Shire. 2nd rev. ed.

v. 16   STEPHEN STORACE (1763–1796), *No song, no supper,* ed. Roger Fiske.

v. 17   JOHN FIELD (1782–1837), *Piano concertos,* ed. Frank Merrick.
Contains nos. 1–3.

v. 18   *Music at the court of Henry VIII,* ed. John Stevens.
Transcription of British Museum Add. Ms. 31922.

v. 19   JOHN BULL, *Keyboard music II,* ed. T. Dart.

I = v. 14.

v. 20   ORLANDO GIBBONS (1583–1628), *Keyboard music,* ed. Gerald Hendrie.

v. 21   WILLIAM LAWES (1602–1645), *Select consort music,* ed. Murray Lefkowitz.

v. 22   *Consort songs,* ed. Philip Brett.
Works of the Elizabethan and early Jacobean period.

v. 23   THOMAS WEELKES (*ca.* 1576–1623), *Collected anthems,* ed. David Brown, Walter Collins, Peter Le Huray.

v. 24   GILES FARNABY (*ca.* 1566–1640) and RICHARD FARNABY (*b. ca.* 1594), *Keyboard music,* ed. Richard Marlow.

v. 25   RICHARD DERING (*d.* 1630), *Secular vocal music,* ed. Peter Platt.

(v. 26)   JOHN JENKINS (1592–1678), *Consort music of four parts* (In preparation, 1969).

v. 27   WILLIAM BYRD (1542/3–1623), *Keyboard music I,* ed. Alan Brown.

(v. 28)   ––––––, II (In preparation, 1969).

(v. 29)   PETER PHILIPS (*ca.* 1560–*after* 1633), *Select Italian madrigals* (In preparation, 1969).

77
Musica divina. Kirchenmusikalische Werke für Praxis und Forschung. Herausgegeben im Auftrag des Instituts für Musikforschung, Regensburg, von Bruno Stäblein. Regensburg, Friedrich Pustet, 1950– .

v. 1–4   FRANCESCO CAVALLI (1602–1676), *Vier Marianische Antiphonen (1686),* ed. B. Stäblein.

v. 1 *Ave regina;* v. 2 *Regina caeli;* v. 3 *Salve regina;* v. 4 *Alma redemptoris mater.*

v. 5   CONSTANZO PORTA (1530–1601), *Missa tertii toni (1578),* ed. Joseph Schmidt-Görg.

v. 6–8   *Gregorianische Choralvorspiele für die Orgel,* by CORBINIAN GINDELE.

v. 9   ORLANDO DI LASSO (1532?–1594), *Missa Beschaffens Glück "Il me suffit",* ed. P. Wilhelm Lueger.

v. 10   LUDOVICO GROSSI DA VIADANA (1564–1645), *Missa domenicalis (1609)* (Solo voice and organ), ed. August Scharnagl.

v. 11   GIOVANNI FRANCESCO ANERIO (*ca.* 1567–1630), *Missa della Battaglia,* ed. Karl Gustav Fellerer.

v. 12   JOHANN JOSEF FUX (1660–1741), *Missa sancti Johannis (1727),* ed. Jack H. Van der Meer.

v. 13   JOHANNES DE FOSSA (*fl. from* 1569, *d.* 1603), *Missa super Theutonicam cantionem "Ich segge a Dieu",* ed. A. Scharnagl.

v. 14   CORBINIAN GINDELE, *Kleine Orgelstücke.*

v. 15   TOMAS LUIS DE VICTORIA (1549–1611), *Missa pro defunctis cum responsorio Libera me Domine (1605)*, ed. Rudolf Walter.

v. 16   ALLARDO [JACOBUS ALARDY, *fl.* 1522–1550], *Missa (1580)*, ed. A. Scharnagl.

v. 17   GIACOMO CARISSIMI (1605–1674), *Missa a quattro*, ed. A. Scharnagl.

v. 18   PIERRE DE LA RUE (*ca.* 1450–1518), *Missa Assumpta est Maria*, ed. Ludwig Finscher.

v. 19   L. G. DA VIADANA, *Missa pro defunctis*, ed. A. Scharnagl.

78
Musica Hispana. Consejo superior de investigaciones científicas: Instituto Español de musicologia, Barcelona, 1952– .

Serie A. *Canción popular* [not listed here]

Serie B. *Polifonia*

v. 1   CRISTÓBAL DE MORALES (*ca.* 1500–1553), *Missa de beata virgine*, ed. H. Anglés.

v. 2   *Antologia polifonica española profana (siglos XV–XVII)*, ed. Miguel Querol Gavaldá.

Serie C. *Musica de camara*

v. 1   P. ANTONIO SOLER (1729–1783), *III concierto para dos instrumentos de tecla*, ed. Santiago Kastner.

Concerto I   = v. 3.
Concerto II = v. 4.
Concerto IV = v. 5.
Concerto V = v. 6.
Concerto VI = v. 8.

v. 2   FRANCISCO MANALT, *Sonatas ns. I y II para violin y piano*, ed. P. J. A. Donostia.
Sonatas II–IV = v. 7.
Sonatas V–VI = v. 9.

v. 3–6 See v. 1.

v. 7   See v. 2.

v. 8   See v. 1.

v. 9   See v. 2.

79

Musica Liturgica. Devoted to the publication of Renaissance sacred music. General editor Robert J. Snow. Cincinnati, World library of sacred music, 1958– .

v. 1/1   VINCENZO RUFFO (*ca.* 1510–1587), *Missa sine nomine, for five equal voices,* ed. R. J. Snow.

v. 1/2   CLAUDIN DE SERMISY (*ca.* 1490–1562), *Missa pro defunctis,* ed. Snow.

v. 1/3   CONSTANZO PORTA (*ca.* 1530–1601), *Musica in introitus missarum, nos. 1–4,* ed. Snow.
        Nos. 5–8 = v. 2/3.

v. 1/4   FRANCESCO CORTECCIA (*d.* 1571), *Hinnario secondo l'uso della chiesa Romana et Fiorentina, nos. 1–5,* ed. Glen Haydon.
        Nos. 6–10 = v. 2/2.

v. 1/5   PAOLO ISNARDI (*fl.* 1568–1590), *Missa Angelus Domini,* ed. Carol MacClintock.

v. 1/6   P. ARENTINO, *Passio Jesu Christi secundum Joannem,* ed. Kurt von Fischer.

v. 2/1   *Missa pro defunctis, from the Valladolid Codex,* ed. Sr. M. Sagues.

v. 2/2   CORTECCIA, *Hinnario . . . nos. 6–10.*
        See v. 1/4.

v. 2/3   PORTA, *Musica in introitus . . . nos. 5–8.*
        See v. 1/3.

80

Musiche vocali e strumentali sacre e profane, sec. XVII–XVIII–XIX, edited by Bonaventura Somma. Roma, Edizioni de Santis, 1941– .

V. 1   DOMENICO SCARLATTI (1685–1757), *Stabat mater per coro a 10 voci miste e organo*, ed. Riccardo Nielsen.

V. 2   ALESSANDRO SCARLATTI (1660–1725), *Toccata n. 11 per cembalo e organo*, ed. Ferruccio Vignanelli.

V. 3   D. SCARLATTI, *Quattro sonate*, trascritte per organo per F. Vignanelli.

V. 4   BERNARDO PASQUINI (1670–1710), *Introduzione e pastorale per organo*, ed. F. Vignanelli.

V. 5   B. PASQUINI, *Toccata con lo scherzo del cuccù per organo*, F. Vignanelli.

V. 6   CLAUDIO MONTEVERDI (1567–1643), *Salmo "Laetatus sum" per 6 voci, coro, organo e orchestra*, ed. Alfredo Casella.

V. 7   GIOVANNI BATTISTA PERGOLESI (1710–1736), *Stabat mater a 2 voci ugali, soli e cori, quintetto d'archi e organo*, ed. B. Somma. Piano-vocal score.

V. 8   Same, full score.

V. 9   MONTEVERDI, *Messa a quattro voci da cappella*, ed. B. Somma.

V. 10   ANTONIO VIVALDI (*ca.* 1676–1741), *Juditha triumphans: sacrum militare oratorium*, ed. Vito Frazzi, S. A. Luciani. Piano-vocal score.

V. 11–21   RICCARDO MANFREDINI (1688–1748), *Sinfonie op. 2, nri. 1–11.* Not yet published.

V. 22   R. MANFREDINI, *12ª sinfonia dell'op. 2.* . . . ed. R. Nielsen.

V. 23   GIUSEPPE TORELLI (1650–1708), *Concerto musicale op. 11 n. 1*, ed. Giuseppe Piccioli.

V. 24   TOMASO ALBINONI (1671–1750), *Concerto a cinque con violino concertante, op. 5 n. 1*, ed. G. Piccioli.

V. 25   PIETRO CASTRUCCI (1679–1752), *Sonata in sol minore op. 1*, ed. Aldo Priano.

V. 26   ATTILIO ARIOSTI (1666–1740), *Collection of lessons for the viol d'amore (1728)*, ed. A. Priano.

V. 27–8   ARIOSTI, *Sonata 1* [viola]; *Sonata 2* [violin] *(1728)*, ed. A Priano.

v. 29a–b   BENEDETTO MARCELLO (1686–1739), *Suonate a flauto solo con il suo basso continuo . . . opera secondo,* ed. Arrigo Tassinari, Riccardo Tora.
a: nos. 1–6; b: nos. 7–12.

✓ v. 30   GIOVANNI MARCO RUTINI (1723–1797), *Sei sonate per il cembalo, opera 3,* ed. Hedda Illy.

v. 31   RUTINI, *Concerto per il cembalo con violini e basso,* ed. H. Illy.

v. 32   RUTINI, *Sei sonate per il cembalo, opera 6,* ed. H. Illy.

v. 33   JOHANN CHRISTIAN BACH (1735–1782), *Sei concerti per cembalo o pianoforte con accompagnamento di due violini e violoncello, op. 7.*
Contains no. 5 only.

81

Musik Alter Meister. Beiträge zur Musik- und Kulturgeschichte Innerösterreichs, herausgegeben von Hellmut Federhofer. Graz, Akademische Druck- und Verlagsanstalt, 1954– .

✓ v. 1   JOHANNES DE CLEVE (1529–1582), *Missa Vous perdes temps,* ed. H. Federhofer.

✓ v. 2   JOHANNES BRASSICANUS (JOHANN KRAUT, ca. 1570/80–1634), *Sechs Choralbearbeitungen und das Quodlibet "Was wölln wir aber heben an",* ed. Othmar Wessely.

✓ v. 3   *Begräbnisgesänge Nürnberger Meister für Exulanten aus der Steiermark,* ed. H. Federhofer.
Works by DAVID SCHEDICH (1607–1687), PAUL HEINLEIN (1626–1686), HEINRICH SCHWEMMER (1621–1696), ERASMUS KINDERMANN (1616–1655).

✓ v. 4   JOHANNES HEROLD (*fl. from* 1594, *d.* 1604), *Historia des Leidens und Sterbens unser Herrn und Heilands (Mattäuspassion),* ed. Hans Joachim Moser.

✓ v. 5   VINCENTIUS JELICH (1596–*after* 1636), *Sechs Motetten aus Arion primus (1628),* ed. Albe Vidaković.

✓ v. 6   BENEDICTUS DUCIS (*ca.* 1480–1544), *Zwei Psalmmotetten,* ed. Hans Albrecht.

v. 7   PAUL HOMBERGER (1560?–1634), *Brautgesänge*, ed. Eva Badura-Skoda.

v. 8   JACOBUS VAET (*ca.* 1529–1567), *Zwei Hymnen*, ed. Milton
Steinhardt.

v. 9   *Zwei Orgelstücke aus einer Kärntner Orgeltabulatur des 16.
Jahrhunderts*, ed. Josef Klima.
Kärntner Landesarchiv in Klagenfurt, Ms 4/3. One work by
Ludwig Senfl (*ca.* 1490–1542/3).

v. 10   *Ausgewählte Werke aus der Ausseer Gitarretabulatur des 18.
Jahrhunderts*, ed. J. Klima.
Vienna Nationalbibliothek Ms. S.M. 9659.

v. 11   B. DUCIS, *Missa de beata virgine*, ed. H. Albrecht.

v. 12   J. DE CLEVE, *Missa Rex Babylonis venit ad locum*, ed. Milton
Steinhardt.
Includes motet model by J. Vaet.

v. 13   JOHANNES BRASSART (*fl.* 1422–1444), *Sechs Motetten*, ed.
Keith E. Mixter.

v. 14   MATTHAEUS LE MAISTRE (1505?–1577), *Missa Regnum mundi;
Motette Regnum mundi*, ed. Gernot Gruber.

v. 15   GEORG POSS (*fl. early* 17th c.), *Drei Motetten*, ed. August
Scharnagl.

v. 16   *Fünf Partiten aus einem Kärntner Lautenbuch*, ed. J. Klima.
Kärtner Landesarchiv Ms G. V. 5/37 (late 17th c.).

v. 17   *Ausgewählte Stücke aus einer Angelica- und Gitarrentabulatur
der 2. Hälfte des 17. Jahrhunderts*, ed. Hans Radke.

v. 18   J. DE CLEVE, *Missa De lustelijcke May*, ed. Albert Dunning.

v. 21–22   Dunning, comp, Staatsmotetten fuer Erherzog Karl II...

82

Musikalische Denkmäler. Akademie der Wissenschaften und der Literatur
in Mainz: Veröffentlichungen der Kommission für Musikwissenschaft.
Mainz, B. Schott's Söhne, 1955– .

v. 1   *Oberitalienische Figuralpassionen des 16. Jahrhunderts*, ed.
Arnold Schmitz.

Passions by JAN [NASCO (*fl. from* 1547, *d.* 1561)], CYPRIANO
DE RORE (1516–1565), JACHET VON MANTUA (*fl. from* 1527,
d. 1559), GIOVANNI MATTEO ASOLA (1524–1609).

v. 2   *Die Chansons von Gilles Binchois* [*ca.* 1400–1460], ed. Wolfgang
Rehm.

v. 3   *46 Choräle für Orgel von J. P. Sweelinck* [1562–1621] *und
seinen deutschen Schülern*, ed. Gisela Gerdes.
Works by SWEELINCK, JACOB PRAETORIUS (1586–1651),
HEINRICH SCHEIDEMANN (*ca.* 1596–1663), MELCHIOR
SCHILDT (*ca.* 1593–1667) and others.

v. 4   GIROLAMO FRESCOBALDI (1583–1643), *Arie musicale (Florenz,
1630)*, ed. Helga Spohr.

v. 5   GIORGIO MAINERIO [MAYNER] (*ca.* 1535–1582), *Il primo
libro di balli (Venedig 1573)*, ed. Manfred Schuler.

v. 6   *Mehrstimmige Lamentationen aus der ersten Hälfte des 16.
Jahrhunderts*, ed. Günther Massenkeil.
Works by BERNARDUS YEART (*b. ca.* 1440), MARBRIANO DE
ORTO (*d.* 1529), JOHANNES DE QUADRIS, BARTOLOMEO TROM-
BONCINO (*fl.* 1487–1513), ERASMUS LAPICIDA (*d. after* 1545),
JOHANNES GARDANO, THOMAS CREQUILLON (*d. ca.* 1557),
ANTONIO FEVIN (*ca.* 1473–*ca.* 1512), CLAUDIN DE SERMISY
(*ca.* 1490–1562), PIERRE DE LA RUE (*ca.* 1460–1518), and
anonymi from publications of Petrucci (1506) and Montanus
(1549).

83

Paléographie musicale. Recueil fondé par Dom A. Mocquereau. Les prin-
cipaux manuscrits de chant Grégorien, Ambrosien, Mozarabe, Galican,
publiés en facsimilés phototypiques par les Benedictins de Solesmes.
1889–1937, 1955– .

Although this series, as the sub-title suggests, consists largely of facsimiles,
most v. include extensive and wide-ranging commentary. The present
editor is Dom Joseph Gajard. A reprint of the first series has been recently
announced by Broude Bros.

[First series]

v. I   *Le codex 339 de la Bibliothèque de Saint-Gall (Xe siècle):
Antiphonale missarum Sancti Gregorii.*

v. 2–3   *Le Répons-Gradual "Justus ut palma" d'après plus de deux
cents antiphonaires manuscrits.*
v. 2: plates 1–107; v. 3: plates 108–211.

v. 4   *Le codex 121 de la Bibliothèque d'Einsiedeln (X^e — XIe siècle):
Antiphonale missarum Sancti Gregorii.*

v. 5–6   *L'antiphonaire Ambrosien* [London, British Museum Add.
Ms. 34209].
v. 5: facsimile; v. 6: transcription.

v. 7–8   *Le codex H. 159 de la Bibliothèque de l'Ecole de Médecin de
Montpellier (XIe siècle): Antiphonarium tonale missarum.*
v. 7: commentary; v. 8: facsimile, index.

v. 9   *Le codex 601 de la Bibliothèque capitulaire de Lucques (XIIe
siècle): Antiphonaire monastique.*

v. 10   *Le codex 239 de la Bibliothèque de Laon (IXe–Xe siècle):
Antiphonale missarum Sanctii Gregorii.*

v. 11   *Le codex 47 de la Bibliothèque de Chartres (Xe siècle): Antiphonale missarum Sancti Gregorii.*

v. 12   *Codex F. 160 de la Bibliothèque de la Cathédrale de Worcester
(XIIIe siècle): Antiphonaire monastique.*

v. 13   *Le codex 903 de la Bibliothèque Nationale de Paris (XIe siècle):
Graduel de Saint Yrieix.*

v. 14   *Le codex 10673 de la Bibliothèque Vaticane fonds Latin (XIe
siècle): Graduel Bénéventain.*

v. 15   *Le codex VI. 34 de la Bibliothèque de Bénévent (XIe–XIIe
siècle) avec prosaire et tropaire.*

v. 16   *Le manuscrit du Mont-Renaud (Xe siècle): Graduel et antiphonaire de Noyon.*

v. 17   *Fragments des manuscrits de Chartres.*

2me serie

v. 1   No. 390–391 de la Bibliothèque de Saint-Gall (Xe siècle):
          L'antiphonaire du B^e Hartker.

v. 2   Le codex 359 de la Bibliothèque de Saint-Gall (IXe siècle):
          Cantatorium.

84

Polifonia vocale sacra e profana sec. XVI, ed. Bonaventura Somma. Roma,
Edizioni de Santis, 1940– .

v. 1   JOANNE ANIMUCIA (d. 1571), Missa Ave maris stella (1564).

v. 2   GIOVANNI MARIA NANINO (1544–1607), Il primo libro delle
          canzonette a tre voci miste (1593).

v. 3   JOANNE PETRALOYSIO PRAENESTINO [G. P. DA PALESTRINA]
          (1525–1594), Missa Papae Marcelli (1567).

v. 4   PALESTRINA, Missa Aeterna Christi munera.

v. 5   Not yet issued.

v. 6   PALESTRINA, Missa brevis quatuor vocum (1580).

v. 7   PIERRE CERTON (ca. 1510–1572), Missa Sus le pont d'Avignon
          (1538).

85

Polyphonic music of the fourteenth century, ed. Leo Schrade. Monaco,
Éditions de l'Oiseau-lyre, 1956– .

The present general editor is Frank Ll. Harrison. Critical notes for volumes
1–4 are in separate mimeographed booklets.

v. 1   The Roman de Fauvel; The works of Philippe de Vitry [1291–
          1361]; French cycles of the ordinarium missae: Mass of Tournai,
          Mass of Toulouse, Mass of Barcelona.

v. 2, 3   GUILLAUME DE MACHAUT, Works. See **B 49.**

v. 4   FRANCESCO LANDINI (1325–1397), Works.

v. 6   Italian secular music [14th c] by Magister Piero, Giovanni da
          Firenze, Jacopo da Bologna, ed. W. Thomas Marrocco.

86

Portugaliae Musica. Lisboa, Fundaçao Caloriste Gulbenkian, 1959–
This set is in two series, although the volumes are numbered consecutively, regardless of series. In series A the v. are self-contained in one binding, while in Series B they include separate sets of complete performance parts. 'Letters following v. number below show the series.

v. 1 A   MANUEL RODRIGUEZ COELHO (*ca.* 1555–1635), *Florés de musica pera o instrumento de tecla & harpa, Vol. I: Livro de tentos,* ed. Macario Santiago Kastner.
Vol. II: *Composicioes sobre temas liturgicos* = v. 3 below.

v. 2 B   JOÃO DE SOUSA CARVALHO (1745–1798), *L'amore industrioso,* ed. Felipe de Sousa.

v. 3A   See v. 1.

v. 4 A   ESTÊVÃO LOPES MORAGO [= STEPHANUS LOPEZIUS] (17th c.), *Varias obras de música religiosa "a cappella",* ed. Manuel Joaquim.

v. 5–6 A   FREI MANUEL CARDOSO (1566–1650), *Liber primus missarum,* ed. José Augusto Alegria.

v. 7 A   JOÃO DA COSTA DE LISBOA (mid-17th c.), *Tençao,* ed. Cremilde Rosado Fernandes.

v. 8 B   JOÃO DOMINGOS BONTEMPO (1771–1842), *Sinfonia no. 1, op. 11,* ed. M. S. Kastner.

v. 9 B   MARCOS ANTONIO DA FONSECA PORTUGAL (1762–1830), *La Duca di Foix.*

v. 10 A   CARLOS SEIXAS (1704–1742), *Sonatas para instrumentos de tecla,* ed. M. S. Kastner.

Publicacions del department de música, Institut d'estudio Catalans, see **A 14, Barcelona** . . .

Publications of medieval musical manuscripts, see **A 50, The institute of mediaeval music** . . .

87

Publikationen älterer Musik. Veröffentlicht von der Abteilung zur Herausgabe älterer Musik bei der deutschen Musikgesellschaft. Für die Leitung: Theodor Kroyer. Leipzig, Breitkopf & Härtel, 1926–1940.

Jg. 1:1   GUILLAUME DE MACHAUT, *Musikalische Werke*, v. 1. See **B 49**.

Jg. 1:2   OCKEGHEM, *Sämtliche Werke*, v. 1. See **B 66**.

Jg. 2   LUYS MILAN (*ca.* 1500–1561), *Libro de musica de vihuela de mano intitulado El Maestro*, ed. Leo Schrade.

Jg. 3:1   GUILLAUME DE MACHAUT, v. 2. See Jg. 1:1.

Jg. 3:2   HERMANN ZENCK, *Sixtus Dietrich* [*ca.* 1492–1548]: *Ein Beitrag zur Musik und Musikanschauung im Zeitalter der Reformation*.

Jg. 4:1   LUCA MARENZIO (*ca.* 1560–1599), *Sämtliche Werke*, v. 1. *Madrigals, Books I–III*, ed. Albert Einstein. v. 2: *Madrigals, Books 4–6* = Jg. 6.

Jg. 4:2   GUILLAUME DE MACHAUT, v. 3. See Jg. 1:1.

Jg. 5   *Das Graduale der St. Thomaskirche zu Leipzig (14. Jahrhundert)*. *Erster Band*, ed. Peter Wagner.
Contents: *Von Advent bis Christi Himmelfahrt* 2. Bd.: *Von Christi Himmelfahrt bis Advent* = Jg. 7.

Jg. 6   See Jg. 4:1.

Jg. 7   See Jg. 5.

Jg. 8   OTTAVIANO PETRUCCI (1466–1539), *Frottole, Buch I und IV 1504–1505?)*, ed. Rudolf Schwartz.

Jg. 9   ADRIAN WILLAERT, Sämtliche Werke. See **B 95**.

Jg. 10   HELMUT SCHULTZ, *Das Madrigal als Formideal. Eine stilkundliche Untersuchung mit Belegen aus dem Schaffen des Andrea Gabrieli*.

Jg. 11   *Die drei- und vierstimmigen Notre-Dame-Organa*, ed. Heinrich Husmann.

88

Publikationen älterer praktischer und theoretischer Musikwerke, vorzugsweise des XV. und XVI. Jahrhunderts. Gesellschaft für Musikforschung unter Leitung Robert Eitner. Berlin, 1873–1905.

Sometimes called *Publikationen der Gesellschaft für Musikforschung* or

"Eitner *Publikationen*" to distinguish it from the preceding item. This series has both v. and *Jahrgang* numbers, both given below. It has recently appeared in an unchanged reprint edition.

v. 1–4   (Jg. 1–4:1). *Ein Hundert fünfzehn weltliche u. einige geistliche Lieder...gesammelt und im Jahre 1544 zu Nürnberg...herausgegeben von Johann Ott,* ed. Robert Eitner, Ludwig Erk, Otto Kade.

**M400.1   Contents: v. 1–2. Four voice songs by HEINRICH ISAAC (*ca.* 1450–1517), LIDWIG SENFL (*ca.* 1490–1542/3) *et al.*

v. 3. 4–6 voice songs by SENFL, VERDELOT (*d.* 1452), MAHU, *et al.*

**M.185.3   v. 4. *Einleitung, Biographieen, Melodieen und Gedichte zu Johann Ott's Liedersammlung von 1544.*

v. 5   (Jg. 4:2). *Musikalische Spicilegien über das liturgische Drama;*
**M.185.4   *Orgelbau und Orgelspiel; das ausserliturgische Lied und die Instrumentalmusik der Mittelalters,* by P. ANSELM SCHUBIGER.

v. 6   (Jg. 5). JOSQUIN DEPRES (*ca.* 1450–1521), *Eine Sammlung*
**M.400.2   *ausgewählter Kompositionen...,* ed. Raymund Schlecht, R. Eitner, Franz Commer.
          Contains *Missa L'homme armé super voces musicales,* motets, chansons.

v. 7   (Jg. 6). JOHANN WALTHER (1496–1570), *Wittembergisch*
**M.400.3   *geistlich Gesangbuch von 1524,* ed. O. Kade.

v. 8   *(Jg. 7). HEINRICH FINCK (1445–1527), HERMANN FINCK (1527–
**M.400.4   1558), *Eine Sammlung ausgewählter Kompositionen zu vier und fünf Stimmen,* ed. Eitner.

v. 9   *(Jg. 8). *Erhart Oeglin's Liederbuch zu 4 Stimmen (1512),*
*M.400.5   ed. Eitner, J. J. Maier.

v. 10   *(Jg. 9). `Die Oper von ihren ersten Anfängen bis zur Mitte des 18. Jahrhunderts. Erster Teil.`
          This is in five parts: part 2 = v. 12; part 3 = v. 14; part 4 = v. 17; part 5 = v. 18.
**M.400.6   Contents: Part 1. *Einleitung.* GUILIO CACCINI (1546–1618), *Euridice;* MARCO DA GAGLIANO (*ca.* 1595–1642), *Dafne;* CLAUDIO MONTEVERDI (1567–1643), *Orfeo.*

Part 2. FRANCESCO CAVALLI (1602–1676), *Il Giasone (1649),* Act 1; MARC'ANTONIO CESTI (1623–1669), *La Dori (1663),* Act I and excerpts from acts 2–3; *Le disgrazie d'Amore (1667),* excerpts; *La Semiramis (1667),* excerpts; *La magnamimitá d'Alessandro (1662),* excerpts.

– Part 3. JEAN-BAPTISTE LULLY (1632–1687), *Armide,* Acts 1–2; ALESSANDRO SCARLATTI (1659–1725), *La Rosaura,* Acts 1–2.

– Part 4. GEORG CASPAR SCHÜRMANN (*ca.* 1672–1751), *Lodovicus Pius oder Ludwig der Fromme (1726),* Act 2 complete; excerpts from acts 1, 3.

Part 5. REINHARD KEISER (1674–1739), *Der lächerliche Prinz Jodelet (1726).*

V. 11   (Jg. 10). SEBASTIAN VIRDUNG (*fl.* 1500–1510), *Musica getutscht,* Basel, 1511. Facsimile, indexed by Eitner.

V. 12   (Jg. 11). See v. 10.

V. 13   (Jg. 12). MICHAEL PRAETORIUS (1572–1621), *Syntagmatis musici. Tomus II de Organographia...1618,* ed. Eitner.

V. 14   (Jg. 13–14). See v. 10.

V. 15   *(Jg. 15). HANS LEO HASSLER (1564–1612), *Lustgarten. 50 Lieder . . . nebst einigen Instrumentalenwerken,* ed. Friedrich Zelle.

V. 16   (Jg. 16–18). HENRICUS GLAREANUS (1488–1563), *Dodeca-chordon (1547).* German transl. by Peter Bohn.

V. 17   (Jg. 19). See v. 10.

V. 18   (Jg. 20–22). See v. 10.

V. 19   *(Jg. 23). *Jacob Regnarts [d. 1600] deutsche dreistimmige Lieder nebst Leonhard Lechners [ca. 1550–1606] fünfstimmiger Bearbeitung.*

V. 20   (Jg. 24). MARTIN AGRICOLA (1486–1556), *Musica instrumentalis deudsch (Wittemberg 1528, 1545),* ed. Eitner.

V. 21   (Jg. 25). JOHANNES ECCARD (1553–1611), *Neue geistliche und weltliche Lieder...Königsberg, 1589,* ed. Eitner.

V. 22   * (Jg. 26). Joachim von Burck (*ca.* 1541–*ca.* 1610), *20 deutsche vierstimmige Lieder (1575); Die Passion nach dem Evangelisten Johannes...(1568); Die Passion nach dem 22. Psalmen Davids,* ed. August Halm, R. Eitner.

V. 23   * (Jg. 27). *60 Chansons zu vier Stimmen aus der 1. Hälfte des 16. Jahrhunderts von französischen und niederländischen Meistern,* ed. Eitner.

Contains works from chanson publications of Attaingnant, 1538–1549, by Jacob Arcadelt (*ca.* 1514–*after* 1567), Pierre Certon (*ca.* 1510–1572), Lupi [Hellinck] (*ca.* 1495–1541), Sandrin, Claude de Sermisy (*ca.* 1490–1562), *et al.*

V. 24   (Jg. 28). Gallus Dressler (1533–*ca.* 1585), *XVII Motetten zu vier und fünf Stimmen,* ed. A. Halm, R. Eitner.

V. 25   (Jg. 29). Gregor Langius (*d.* 1587), *Eine ausgewählte Sammlung Motetten,* ed. Reinhold Starke.

V. 26   (Jg. 30). Orazio Vecchi (1550–1605), *L'Amfiparnasso,* ed. R. Eitner.

V. 27   (Jg. 31). Jean-Marie Leclair l'aîné (1697–1764), *Zwölf Sonaten für Violine (oder Flöte) und Generalbass nebst einem Trio für Violine, Violoncell und Generalbass, 2. Buch der Sonaten, Paris circa 1732,* ed. R. Eitner.

V. 28   (Jg. 32). Martin Zeuner, *82 geistliche Kirchenlieder zu fünf Stimmen, Nürnberg, 1616,* ed. R. Eitner.

V. 29   (Jg. 33). Georg Forster, *Der zweite Teil der kurtzweiligen guten frischen teutschen Liedlein (1540),* ed. R. Eitner.

89

Le Pupitre. Collection de musique ancienne, dirigée par François Lesure. Paris, Heugel, 1967– .

V. 1   Jacques Duphly (1715–1739), *Pièces pour clavecin (1744–1768).* 4 livres représentant toute l'œuvre du compositeur en 1 volume. Ed. Françoise Petit.

V. 2   Claude Le Jeune (1528–1600/1), *Missa ad placitum (1607) pour 5 voix a cappella,* ed. Michel Sanvoisin.

V. 3   JEAN-JOSEPH DE MONDOVILLE (1711–1772), *Sonates en trio (1734)*, ed. Roger Blanchard.

V. 4   GIOVANNI LEGRENZI (*ca.* 1625–1690), *Sonate da chiesa, Op. 4, op. 8 (1656, 1663)*, ed. Albert Seay.

V. 5   *Chansons françaises pour orgue (16th c.)*, ed. Jean Bonfils.

V. 6   *Airs sérieux et à boire à 2 et 3 voix* (17th–18th c.), ed. Frédéric Robert.

V. 7   ANTONIO VIVALDI (*ca.* 1676–1741), *Motetti a canto solo con stromenti*, ed. R. Blanchard.

V. 8   FRANÇOIS COUPERIN (1668–1733), *Leçons de Ténèbres pour le Mercredy*, ed. Daniel Vidal.

V. 9   PIERRE ATTAINGNANT, *Danseries à 4 parties (deuxième livre, (1547)*, ed. Raymond Meylan.

V. 10   GIOVANNI GIACOMO GASTOLDI (*ca.* 1550–1622?), *Balletti a cinque voci (1591)*, ed. M. Sanvoisin.

V. 11   JOHANN ADOLPH HASSE (1699–1783), *Cantates*, soprano and orchestra, ed. Sven H. Hansell.

90
Recent Researches in the music of the baroque era. New Haven, A R editions.

V. 1   MARC-ANTOINE CHARPENTIER (1634?–1704), *Judicum Salomonis*, ed. H. Wiley Hitchcock.

V. 2   GEORG PHILIPP TELEMANN (1681–1767), *Forty-eight chorale preludes*, ed. Alan Thaler.

V. 3   JOHANN CASPAR KERLL (1627–1693), *Missa superba*, ed. Albert C. Giebler.

V. 4   JEAN-MARIE LECLAIR (1697–1764), *Sonatas for violin and basso continuo, Part I: Opus 5, sonatas I–V*, ed. Robert E. Preston.

V. 5   ———, *Part II: Opus 5 sonatas VI–XII*.

V. 6   *Ten eighteenth-century voluntaries*, ed. Gwilym Beechly.
          Works by JOHN BENNETT (*d.* 1784), WILLIAM WALOND (*ca.* 1725–1770) and WILLIAM HINE (1687–1730).

91

Recent Researches in the Music of the Renaissance. New Haven, A R editions.

v. 1   GIAMMATEO ASOLA (1524–1609), *Sixteen liturgical works,* ed. Donald M. Fouse.

v. 2   PHILIPPE ROGIER (1561–1596), *Eleven motets,* ed. Lavern J. Wagner.

v. 3   CHRISTOPHER TYE (*ca.* 1500–1572/3), *The instrumental music,* ed. Robert W. Weidner.

v. 4   THOMAS TOMKINS (1572–1653), *Thirteen anthems,* ed. Robert W. Cavanaugh.

v. 5   GIOVANNI MARIA NANINO (1545–1607), *Fourteen liturgical works,* ed. Richard J. Schuler.

v. 6   FRANCESCO CORTECCIA (1504–1571), *Eleven works to Latin texts,* ed. Ann McKinley.

92

Rhau, Georg (*ca.* 1488–1548), **Musikdrucke aus den Jahren 1538 bis 1545** in praktischer Neuausgabe. Herausgegeben von Hans Albrecht im Rahmen der Veröffentlichungen des Landesinstituts für Musikforschung, Kiel. Kassel, Bärenteiter, 1955– .

v. 1   BALTHASAR RESINARIUS (*ca.* 1480–*after* 1543), *Responsorium numero octoginta. Erster Band: De Christo, et regno eius, Doctrina, Vita, Passione, Resurrectione et Ascensione,* ed. Inge-Maria Schröder.

v. 2   ————, *Zweiter Band: De sanctis, et illorum in Christe fide et cruce.*

v. 3   *Symphoniae jucundae, atque adeo breves 4 vocum ab optimis quibusque musicis compositae, 1538,* ed. H. Albrecht.

v. 4   *Vesperarum precum officia* (Wittenberg, 1540), ed. Hans Joachim Moser.

v. 5–6   Not yet published.

v. 7   SIXTUS DIETRICH (*ca.* 1492–1548), *Novum ac insigne opus musicum 36 antiphonarum, 1541,* ed. Walter Buszin.

Rome, American Institute of Musicology, see 1 A, American . . .

93

Schweizerische Musikdenkmäler. Herausgegeben von der Schweizerischen Musikforschenden Gesellschaft. Kassel, Bärenreiter, 1955– .

v. 1   HENRICUS ALBICASTRO (*late* 17th c.), *Zwölf concerti a 4, op. 7,* ed. Max Zulauf.

v. 2   JOHANN MELCHIOR GLETLE (1626–1683), *Ausgewählte Kirchenmusik,* ed. Hans Peter Schanzlin, M. Zulauf, Adolf Layer.

v. 3   LOYS BOURGEOIS (*fl. from* 1545, *d. after* 1561), *Vingt-quatre Psaumes à 4 voix,* ed. Paul-André Gaillard.

v. 4   JOHANNES BENN (*before* 1600–*after* 1657), *Missae concertatae trium vocum, adiuncto choro secondo et una missa ab octo,* ed. M. Zulauf.

v. 5   *Das Liederbuch des Johannes Herr von Glarus: Ein Musikheft aus der Zeit des Humanismus (Codex 462 der Stiftsbibliothek St. Gallen),* ed. Arnold Geering, Hans Trümpy.

v. 6   *Tabulaturen des XVI. Jahrhunderts. Teil I: Die Tabulaturen aus dem Besitz der Basler Humanisten Bonifacius Amerbach,* ed. Hans Joachim Marx.

94

Smith College Music Archives, edited by Alfred Einstein. Northampton, Smith College, 1935– .

v. 1   FRANCESCO GEMINIANI (1687–1762), *Twelve sonatas for violin and piano,* ed. Ross Lee Finney.

v. 2   JOHANN JOSEF FUX (1660–1741), *Costanza e Fortezza, an opera in three acts,* ed. Gertrude Parker Smith.

v. 3   LUIGI BOCCHERINI (1743–1805), *Cello concerto (no. 3),* ed. Marion De Ronde.

v. 4   *Canzoni, sonetti, strambotti et frottole, libro tertio (Andrea Antico, 1517)*, ed. Alfred Einstein.

v. 5   *The chansons of Jacques Arcadelt* [*ca.* 1514–*after* 1567], ed. Everett B. Helm.

v. 6   *The madrigals of Cipriano de Rore for 3 and 4 voices*, ed. Gertrude Parker Smith.

v. 7   FRANCESCA CACCINI (1588–*after* 1626), *La Liberazione di Ruggiero dal Isola d'Alcina, a balletto*, ed. Doris Silbert.

v. 8   VINCENZO GALILEI (1520?–1591), *Contrapunti a due voci, 1584*, ed. Louise Rood.

v. 9   GIUSEPPE TARTINI (1692–1770), *Concerto in A minor; concerto in F major for solo violin and string orchestra*, ed. and provided with cadenzas by Gilbert Ross.

v. 10   JOSEPH HAYDN (1732–1809), *Symphony no. 87 in A major (Paris symphony no. 6, 1785)*, ed. A. Einstein.

v. 11   AGOSTINO STEFFANI (1624–1728), *Eight songs for solo voice, one or two woodwinds and continuo*, ed. Gertrude Parker Smith.

v. 12   TOMMASO ANTONIO VITALI (*ca.* 1665–1747), *Concerto di sonate, op. 4, for violin, violoncello and continuo*, ed. Doris Silbert, Gertrude P. Smith, Louise Rood.

v. 13   PAOLO QUAGLIATI (*ca.* 1555–1628), *La sfera armoniosa, Il carro di fedelta d'amore*, ed. Vernon Gotwals, Philip Keppler.

v. 14   GIOVANNI BATTISTA VITALI (*ca.* 1644–1692), *Artifici musicali opus XIII*, ed. Louise Rood, Gertrude P. Smith.

v. 15   *Folk songs for women's voices arranged by Johannes Brahms*, ed. Vernon Gotwals, Philip Keppler.

95
Societas universalis Sanctae Ceciliae: [Publications]

The following publications of this society are listed elsewhere in this book:
Documenta liturgiae polychoralis Sanctae Ecclesiae Romanae, **A 35**
Documenta maiora liturgiae polychoralis S. Ecc. Rom. **A 36**
Documenta majora polyphoniae liturgiae S. Ecc. Rom. **A 37**
Documenta polyphoniae liturgiae S. Ecc. Rom. **A 39**

Monumenta liturgiae polychoralis S. Ecc. Rom. **A 61**
Monumenta polyphoniae liturgiae S. Ecc. Rom. **A 68**
BENEVOLI, ORAZIO, *Opera omnia,* **B 9**

96
Société Française de Musicologie. Publications, Série I: Monuments de la musique ancienne. Paris, 1925– .

For series 2, 3 see **C 70**.

v. 1   *Deux livres d'orgue édités par Pierre Attaingnant (1531),* ed. Yvonne Rokseth.
           See also v. 5.

v. 2   *Oeuvres inédites de Beethoven,* ed. Georges de Saint-Foix.

v. 3–4   *Chansons au luth et airs de cour français du XVIe siècle,* ed. Adrienne Maire, Lionel de La Laurencie, Geneviève Thibault.

v. 5   *Treize motets et un prélude réduits en la tablature des orgues, transcription du 3e livre d'orgue édité par Attaingnant (1531),* ed. Y. Rokseth.
           Includes vocal versions of the intabulations. See also v. 1.

v. 6–7   *La rhétorique des dieux et autres pièces de luth de Denis Gaulthier . . .* ed. André Tessier, Jean Cordey.
           v. 6: facsimile; v. 7: transcription.

v. 8   JEAN HENRI D'ANGLEBERT (1628?–1691), *Pièces de clavecin,* ed. Marguerite Roesgen-Champion.

v. 9   JEAN-JOSEPH CASSANEA DE MONDOVILLE (1711–1772), *Pièces de clavecin en sonates,* ed. Marc Pincherle.

v. 10   *Le manuscrit de musique polyphonique du trésor d'Apt (XIVe– XVe siècle),* ed. Amédée Gastoué.

v. 11–12   FRANÇOIS-ADRIEN BOIELDIEU (1775–1834), *Sonates pour piano,* ed. G. Favre.

v. 13   *Premier livre d'orgue de Gilles Jullien* [1653–1703], ed. Norbert Dufourcq.

v. 14   *Troisième livre d'orgue de Guillaume-Gabriel Nivers* [1632–1714], ed. N. Dufourcq.

V. 15   *Les chansons à la Vierge de Gautier de Coinci* [1177/8–1236], ed. Jacques Chailley.

V. 16   *Airs de cour pour voix et luth (1603–1643)*, ed. André Verchaly.

V. 17   *Anthologie du motet latin polyphonique en France (1609–1661)*, ed. Denise Launay.
           Works by EUSTACHE DU CAURROY (1549–1609), JACQUES MAUDUIT (1557–1627), GUILLAUME BOUZIGNAC, HENRY DU MONT (1610–1684), *et al.*

97

Sources for the History of Polish Music (Zrodla do historiimuzyki Polskiej). The extant monuments of Polish music from its beginnings to the end of the 18th century.

Includes commentary in English

V. 1   *Polish dances from the Vietoris Codex.*

V. 2   *Polish dances from the lute tablatures: Waisselius (1592), Hainhofer (1603–4), Fabricius (1605–8), Arpinus (17th c.), Vallet (1615), Dluforaj (1619), Stobeus (ca. 1640).*

V. 3   JAKÓB GOŁABEK (*d.* 1789), *Symphonies 1 in D, 2 in D, 3 in C.*

V. 4   J. GOŁABEK, *Partita for wind instruments.*

V. 5   JAN WAŃSKI (*b.* 1762), *2 symphonies from opera overtures: in D from "The shepherd by the Vistula; in G from "The peasant".*

V. 6   *Polish dances from the collection of Anna Szirmay-Keczer (17th c.).*

V. 7   GRZEGORZ GERWAZY GORCZYCKI (*ca.* 1664–1734), *Completorium.*

98

Torchi, Luigi, L'Arte Musicale in Italia. Milano, Ricordi, 1897–1908.

V. 1   *Composizioni sacre e profane a più voci, secoli XIV, XV e XVI.*
           Works by JAN GERO (1518?–1583?), FRANCESCO CORTECCIA (1504–1571), GIOVANNI ANIMUCCIA (*ca.* 1500–1571), BAL-

DASSARE DONATO (*ca.* 1530–1603), VINCENZO RUFFO (*ca.* 1510–1587), ANNIBALE ZOILO (*ca.* 1537–1592), PIETRO VINCI (*ca.* 1535–1584), ALESSANDRO STRIGGIO (*ca.* 1535–*ca.* 1595), CLAUDIO MERULO (1533–1604), *et al.*

v. 2   *Composizioni sacre e profane a più voci, secolo XVI.*
Works by GIOVANNI MARIA NANINI (1545–1607), ANDREA GABRIELI (*ca.* 1510–1586), GIOVANNI GABRIELI (1557–1612), LUCA MARENZIO (1553–1599), ORAZIO VECCHI (1550–1605), ACHILLE FALCONE.

v. 3   *Composizioni per organo o cembalo, secoli XVI, XVII, e XVIII.*
Works by GEROLAMO CAVAZZONI (*ca.* 1500–1560), A. GABRIELI, C. MERULO, GEROLAMO FRESCOBALDI (1583–1643), MICHELANGELO ROSSI (*ca.* 1600–*ca.* 1660), ADRIANO BANCHIERI (1563–1634), GIOVANNI MARIA TRABACI (1575–1647), DOMENICO ZIPOLI (1688–1726), *et. al.*

v. 4   *Composizioni a più voci, secolo XVII.*
Madrigals by CARLO GESUALDO (*ca.* 1560–1613), MARCO DA GAGLIANO (*ca.* 1575–1642), PIETRO EREDIA [HEREDIA] (*d.* 1648), CLAUDIO MONTEVERDI (1567–1643); *Benedictus* by GAGLIANO; *I fidi amanti* by GASPARE TORELLI; *L'Amfiparnasso* by VECCHI; *La Pazzia senile* by BANCHIERI.

v. 5   *Composizioni ad una e più voci, secolo XVII.*
GIACOMO CARISSIMI (1605–1674), Mass excerpts; STEFANO LANDI (*ca.* 1590–*ca.* 1655), excerpts from *S. Alessio;* VIRGILIO MAZZOCCHI (1597–1646), cantata; Anonymous, *Daniele* (oratorio); *et al.*

v. 6   *La musica scenica, secolo XVII.*
JACOPO PERI (1561–1633), *L'Euridice;* MONTEVERDI, *Combattimento di Tancredi e Clorinda, Il ballo delle ingrate.*

v. 7   *Musica instrumentale, secolo XVII.*
Works by BIAGIO MARINI (*d.* 1665), GIOVANNI BATTISTA BASSANI (*ca.* 1567–1612), MARCO UCCELLINI (*ca.* 1610–after 1677), MARTINO PESENTI (*ca.* 1600–1647).

99

Tudor Church Music, ed. Percy C. Buck, Edmund H. Fellowes, A. Ramsbotham, R. R. Terry, Sylvia Townsend Warner. 1923–1948.

100

Van Ockeghem tot Sweelinck. Nederlandse Muziekgeschiedenis in Voorbeelden, ed. A. Smijers. Vereniging voor Nederlandse Muziekgeschiedenis [2nd ed.], Amsterdam, 1949–

7 sections *(Aflevering)* have been issued so far, paged continuously. A composer index follows.

Composer, composition.	Afl.	Page
AGRICOLA, ALEXANDER (1450–1506).		
D'ung aultre amer (3 versions).	IV	101ff.
Tout a par moy	IV	107
ARCADELT, JACOB (*ca.* 1540–*after* 1567)		
Io mi rivolgo indietro	VII	227
BARBIREAU, JACOB (*d.* 1491)		
Osculetur me osculo oris sui	II	40

BASIRON, PHILIPPE (*fl. early* 15th c.)
D'un aultre amer   I   30

BRUMEL, ANTOINE (*d. ca.* 1505)
Lauda Sion   VI   161
Mater patris et filia   V   138

BUSNOIS, ANTONIUS (*d.* 1492)
Anima mea liquefacta est   I   22
Corps digne/ Dieu quel mariage   I   27
Kyrie L'homme armé   I   13
Quant j'ay au cueur   VI   185
Regina coeli   I   16

CARON (*fl. late* 15th c.)
Missa L'homme armé: Agnus Dei   II   33

COMPERE, LOYSET (*ca.* 1450–1518)
Lourdault, lourdault   IV   119
Missa L'homme armé: Kyrie   IV   113
O bone Jesu   IV   116
Se mieulx ne vient d'amours   IV   121

CRAEN, NICOLAAS (*d.* 1507)
Si ascendero in caelum   IV   111

DEPRES, JOSQUIN (*ca.* 1450–1521)
Adieu mes amours (4 voices)   V   156
Benedicta es coelorum regina   V   146
L'homme armé   V   155
Missa L'homme armé super voces musicales: Kyrie   V   131
Missa Mater Patris: Kyrie   V   135
Petite camusette   V   158
Victimae paschali laudes   V   140

GOMBERT, NICHOLAS (*ca.* 1490–*ca.* 1556)
Homo erat in Jerusalem   VII   230

HAYNE VAN GHIZEGHEM (*fl.* 1453–1472)
De tous biens playne   V   144

HELLINCK, LUPUS (*ca.* 1495–1541)
Missa Christus resurgens: Kyrie   VII   223

ISAAC, HEINRICH (*ca.* 1450–1517)
Dona di dentro/Dammene un poco/Fortuna d'un gran

Tenebrae factae sunt	VI	178
Verbum caro factum est	VI	174

Venice, Fondazioni G. Cimi, see **A 25, Collana...**

Veröffentlichungen der Musikbibliothek Paul Hirsch see **A 47, Hirsch...**

101

The Wellesley Edition, Jan La Rue, director. Wellesley College, 1950–

v. 1   JOHN JENKINS (1592–1678), *Fancies and ayres,* ed. Helen Joy Sleeper.

v. 2   HUBERT LAMB, *Six scenes from the Protevangelion.*

v. 3   *The Dublin virginal manuscript* [Dublin, Trinity College, Ms. D. 3.30], ed. John Ward.

v. 4   JOSEPH HAYDN (1732–1809), *Three Divertimenti,* ed. J. La Rue.

v. 5   *The Italian cantata I: Antonio Cesti (1623–1669),* ed. David Burrows.
　　　　See also v. 7.

v. 6   *Fifteenth century basse dances (Brussels Bibl. Roy. Ms 9085, collated with Michel Toulouze's L'art et instruction de bien danser),* ed. James L. Jackman.

v. 7   The Italian cantata II: [*Alessandro*] *Stradella* [*ca.* 1645–1682], ed. Owen Jander.

v. 8   *The Bottegari lute book* [Modena Ms C 311, dated 1574], ed. Carol MacClintock.

v. 9   Not yet published.

v. 10   JOHN JENKINS (1592–1678), *Three-part fancy and ayre divisions for two trebles and a bass to the organ,* ed. Robert Austin Warner.

Yale University, Collegium Musicum, see **A 26, Collegium...**

SECTION B

SETS AND SERIES DEVOTED
TO ONE COMPOSER

1

ABEL, KARL FRIEDRICH, 1723–1787

1. Complete works   2. Thematic catalog

1. *Kompositionen,* gesammelt, neueingerichtet und herausgegeben von
Walter Knape. Cuzhaven 1, Verlag des Herausgebers Walter Knape.
This set consists of photostatic copies of the editor's ms.
Introduction/critical notes for each v. are in separate leaflets. The
abbreviation WK presumably stands for part B of item 2 below.
Proposed v. are listed in parentheses.

Series A. *45 Sinfonien* (WK Sammelordnung 1–45)

> v. 1   *6 Sinfonien op. 1* (nos. 1–6)
>
> v. 2   *6 Sonfonien op. 4* (nos. 7–12)
>
> v. 3   *6 Sinfonien op. 7* (nos. 13–18)
>
> v. 4   *6 Sinfonien op. 10* (nos. 19–24)
>
> v. 5   *6 Sinfonien op. 14* (nos. 25–30)
>
> v. 6   *6 Sinfonien op. 17* (nos. 31–36)
>
> v. 7   *5 Sinfonien op. 17* (nos. 37–41)
>
> v. 8   *Sinfonien nr. 42–45*

Series B. *13 Konzerte* (WK Sammelordnung 46–60)

> v. 1   *Flöten-Konzerte op. 6 nr. 1–6; Violoncello-Konzert*
>   (nos. 46–52)
>   [The cello concerto is paged separately]
>
> v. 2   *Klavier-Konzerte op. 11, nr. 1–6* (nos. 53–58)
>   "Supplement Band 10" (i.e. suppl. to Ser. B v. 2).
>   *Violoncello-konzert in C-dur (WK no. 60)*

[145]

Series C. v. 11–12 *(sic)*, in 1.   Quartette (WK nos. 61–76)

(Series D. 18 strings trios, WK 79–96 = v. 13–14)

(Series E. 24 sonatas, WK 97–120)

2.   WALTER KNAPE, *Der Sinfoniker Karl Friedrich Abel.* Teil A: *Biographie, Werk, Stil-Betrachtung;* Teil B: *Thematisch-bibliographisches Verzeichnis der Kompositionen*

2

AGRICOLA, ALEXANDER, *ca.* **1446–***ca.* **1506**

Opera omnia, ed. Edward E. Lerner. *Corpus mensurabilis musicae* [**A 28**], series 22. 5 v. proposed.

v. 1   Masses: *Le serviteur, Malheur me bat, Je ne demande, In myn Zyn*

v. 2   Masses: *Paschalis, Primi toni, Secundi toni, Sine nomine.* Mass sections.

v. 3   Lamentations, hymns, magnificat

v. 4   Motets and *contra facta*

3

ARCADELT, JACOB, *ca.* **1514–***after* **1557**

Opera omnia, ed. Albert Seay. *Corpus mensurabilis musicae* [**A 28**], series 31. About 12 v. proposed.

v. 1   Masses: *Noe, noe, Ave regina coelorum, De beata virgine*

v. 3   Madrigals, Book 2

v. 4   Madrigals, Book 3

v. 5   Madrigals, Book 4

v. 6   Madrigals, Book 5

v. 8   Chansons, I

v. 9   Chansons, II

4

ASOLA, GIOVANNI MATTEO, 1524–1609

Opera omnia, ed. Giuseppe Vecchi. *Antiquae musicae italicae: Monumenta Veronensia* [**A 9**], v. 2.

[Series 1] *Madrigalia*

V. I   *Madrigali a due voci accommodati da cantare in Fuga
(1587)*. [In preparation]

V. 2   *Le Vergini a tre voci, Libro primo (1571)*

5
BACH, JOHANN SEBASTIAN, 1685-1750

1-2. Complete works   3-4. Cantata indices   5. Thematic catalog   *ML 134.B1A25*
6. Yearbook 7-9. Other series

040.21
1.   *Werke*. Leipzig, Bach-Gesellschaft, 1851-99, 1926. Unchanged reprint
M3.B2B (Edwards, Ann Arbor), 1947. Reprint in reduced size announced for
ca. 1968 by Gregg Press.

> Common abbreviation: BGA. Called "Bach Gesellschaft edition".
> The volumes of this set are numbered by *Jahrgang*. In addition to
> the Jg., or v. no., many (but not all) of the v. have a separate series or
> category numbering, shown below. Further, v. 47 is also *Veröffentli-*
> *chungen der Neuen Bachgesellschaft,* Jg. 28/1.

Chamber music, instrumental

V. I = V. 9		V. 5 = V. 21/2
V. 2 = V. 17		V. 6 = V. 27/1
V. 3 = V. 19		V. 7 = V. 31/3
V. 4 = V. 21/1		V. 8 = V. 43/1

Chamber music, vocal

V. I = V. 11/2	V. 3 = V. 29
V. 2 = V. 20/2	V. 4 = V. 34

Church cantatas

V. I = V. I	V. 11 = V. 23
V. 2 = V. 2	V. 12 = V. 24
V. 3 = V. 5/1	V. 13 = V. 26
V. 4 = V. 7	V. 14 = V. 28
V. 5 = V. 10	V. 15 = V. 30
V. 6 = V. 12/2	V. 16 = V. 32
V. 7 = V. 16	V. 17 = V. 33
V. 8 = V. 18	V. 18 = V. 35
V. 9 = V. 20/1	V. 19 = V. 37
V. 10 = V. 22	V. 20 = V. 41

Clavier works

v. 1 = v. 3
v. 2 = v. 13/2, v. 45 (revised)   v. 4 = v. 36
v. 3 = v. 14   v. 5 = v. 42

Organ works

v. 1 = v. 15   v. 3 = v. 38
v. 2 = v. 25/2   v. 4 = v. 40

In place of a listing of contents by volume, the following alphabetical
listing is offered. There is a detailed thematic INDEX in v. 46, covering
the entire set except for cantatas 1–120 (which are indexed in v. 27/2),
and v. 47. For a complete listing of cantatas see Bach items 3–4 below.

Die Kunst der Fuge	25/1, 47
Magnificat	11/1
Mass, b minor	6
Masses, other	8
Motets	39
Musical offering	31/2
Organ works, miscellaneous	15, 38
Orgelbüchlein	25/2
Partitas, harpsichord	3
Partitas, violin solo	27/1
Passion, St. John	12/1
Passion, St. Luke	45/2
Passion, St. Matthew	4
Preludes and fugues, organ	15
Sanctus (4 separate)	11/1
Sonatas, flute	9, 43
Sonatas, organ	15
Sonatas, trio	9
Sonatas, violin/cello solo	27/1
Sonatas, violin and harpsichord	9
Suites, cello solo	27/1
Suites: French, English	13/2, 45
Suites, orchestra	31/1
Trauer Ode	13/3
Wilhelm Friedemann Bach: Clavierbüchlein	45
Well-tempered Clavier	3

2.   *Neue Ausgabe sämtlicher Werke,* herausgegeben von Johann-Sebastian-Bach-Institut Göttingen und vom Bach-Archiv, Leipzig. Kassel, Bärenreiter.

The following listing gives the entire proposed publication plan. For clear differentiation, v. not yet published are given English titles and placed in parentheses.

N.B. The critical notes are published separately in small format, numbered corresponding to the series and v. numbers of the set.

Series I.   Cantatas. [Arranged according to the liturgical calendar. For an index see Bach items 3–4 below]

v.   1   *Adventskantaten,* ed. Alfred Dürr, Werner Neumann
Contents: 61, 36, 62, 132

v. 2   *Kantaten zum 1. Weihnachtstag,* ed. A Dürr
Contents: 63, 197a, 110, 91, 191

(v. 3   Cantatas for the second and third days of Christmas
and the Sunday after Christmas)

v. 4   *Kantaten zu Neujahr und zum Sonntag nach Neujahr,*
ed. W. Neumann
Contents: 190, 41, 16, 171, 143, 153

(v. 5   Cantatas from Epiphany to the second Sunday after
Epiphany

(v. 6   Cantatas for the third and fourth Sundays after
Epiphany)

v. 7   *Kantaten zu den Sonntagen Septuagesimae und Sexua-
gesimae,* ed. W. Neumann
Contents: 144, 84, 92, 18, 181, 126

(v. 8   Cantatas for *Estomihi* Sunday through Palm Sunday)

(v. 9   Cantatas for Easter)

v. 10   *Kantaten zum 2. und 3. Ostertag,* ed. A Dürr
Contents: 66, 6, 134, 145, 158

(v. 11   Cantatas for *Quasimodogeniti* Sunday through *Jub-
ilate*)

v. 12   *Kantaten zum Sonntag Cantate bis zum Sonntag
Exaudi,* ed. A. Dürr

v. 13   *Kantaten zum 1. Pfingsttag,* ed. Dietrich Kilian
Contents: 172, 59, 74, 34

v. 14   *Kantaten zum 2. und 3. Pfingsttag,* ed. A. Dürr,
Arthur Mendel
Contents: 173, 68, 174, 184, 175

v. 15   *Kantaten zum Trinitatisfest und zum 1. Sonntag nach
Trinitatis,* ed. A. Dürr, Robert Freeman, James
Webster
Contents: 165, 194, 176, 129, 75, 20, 39

(v. 16   Cantatas for the second and third Sundays after
Trinity)

(v. 17   Cantatas for the fourth through sixth Sundays after
Trinity)

v. 18   *Kantatem zum 7. und 8. Sonntag nach Trinitatis,*
ed. A. Dürr, Leo Treitler
Contents: 54, 186, 107, 187, 136, 178, 45

(v. 19   Cantatas for the ninth and tenth Sundays after Trinity)

(v. 20   Cantatas for the 11th and 12th Sundays after Trinity)

v. 21   *Kantaten zum 13. und 14. Sonntag nach Trinitatis,*
ed. W. Neumann
Contents: 77, 33, 164, 25, 78, 17

(v. 22   Cantatas for the 15th Sunday after Trinity)

(v. 23   Cantatas for the 16th and 17th Sundays after Trinity)

(v. 24   Cantatas for the 18th and 19th Sundays after Trinity)

(v. 25   Cantatas for the 20th and 21st Sundays after Trinity)

(v. 26   Cantatas for the 22nd and 23d Sundays after Trinity)

v. 27   *Kantaten zum 24.–27. Sonntag nach Trinitatis,* ed.
A. Dürr
Contents: 60, 26, 90, 116, 70, 140

(v. 28   Cantatas for Lady day)

(v. 29   Cantatas for St. John's day)

(v. 30   Cantatas for Michaelmas)

(v. 31   Cantatas for Reformation day and Dedication of an
organ)

(v. 32   Cantatas for council election)

v. 33   *Trauungskantaten,* ed. Frederick Hudson
Contents: 196, 34a, 120a, 197, 195

(v. 34   Cantatas for funerals and various occasions)

v. 35   *Festmusiken für die Fürstenhäuser von Weimar, Weis-
senfels und Köthen,* ed. A. Dürr
Contents: 208, 134a, 173

v. 36   *Festmusiken für das Kurfürstlich-Sächsische Haus, I,*
ed. W. Neumann
Contents: 213, 214, 206

v. 37   ———, II
Contents: 207a, 215

v. 38   *Festmusiken zu Leipziger Universitätsfeiern,* ed. W.
Neumann
Contents: 205, 207, 198, 36b

(v. 39   Festival cantatas for Leipzig council and school
ceremonies; homage cantatas for nobles and burghers)

v. 40   *Hochzeitskantaten und weltliche Kantaten verschiedener
Bestimmung,* ed. W. Neumann
Contents: 202, 216, 210, 204, 201, 211

(v. 41   Cantatas of doubtful authenticity)

Series II.   Masses, Passions, and Oratorios

v. 1   *Missa Symbolum Niceum, Sanctus, Osanna, Benedictus, Agnus Dei et Dona nobis pacem, später genannt:
Messe in h-Moll, BWV 232,* ed. Friedrich Smend

(v. 2   Masses and separate mass movements)

v. 3   *Magnificat 243a, 243,* ed. A Dürr

(v. 4   St. John Passion)

(v. 5   St. Matthew and St. Mark Passions)

v. 6   *Weihnachts-Oratorium BWV 248,* ed. Walter Blankenburg

(v. 7   Easter and Ascension oratorios)

(v. 8   Arrangements of other composers' works)

(v. 9   Works of doubtful authenticity)

Series III.   Motets, chorales, songs

v. 1   *Motetten, BWV 225–30, 118,* ed. Konrad Ameln

(v. 2   Chorales and songs)

(v. 3   Works of doubtful authenticity)

Series IV.   Organ works

    (v.   1   Chorale settings I)

    v.   2   *Die Orgelchoräle aus der Leipziger Originalhandschrift,*
        ed. Hans Klotz
        Contents: BWV 651–668, 651a–656a, 658a–668a,
        769, 769a

    v.   3   *Die einzeln überlieferten Orgelchoräle,* ed. H. Klotz
        Contents: BWV 690–91, 694–701, 703–4, 706,
        709–15, 717–18, 720–22, 724–38, 741, 722a, 729a,
        732a, 735a, 738a, *O Lamm Gottes unschuldig (man.)*

    v.   4   *Dritter Teil der Clavier-Übung,* ed. M. Tessmer
        Contents: BWV 552 (*Praeludium und Fuge* Es-dur),
        BWV 669–89, 802–5

    (v.   5   Preludes, toccatas and fugues, I)

    v.   6   *Präludien, Toccaten, Fantasien und Fugen II (und
        Frühfassungen und Varianten zu I und II,* ed. D. Kilian
        Contents: BWV 564, 570, 573–5, 565–6, 568, 578,
        569, 551, 563, 579, 545a, 574a-b, 532a, 549a, 533a,
        535a–6a, 543a

Series V.   Clavier and lute works
The plan of this series and the next have been changed since the prospectus was issued, so only v. actually published are listed.

    v.   4   *Die Klavierbüchlein für Anna Magdalena Bach von
        1722 und 1725,* ed. Georg von Dadelson
        Contents: BWV 82, 299, 508–18, 515a, 573, 691,
        728, 812–17, 827, 830, 841, 846/1, 988/1, 991,
        BWV Anh. 113–13, 117a, 177b, 118–133

    v.   5   *Klavierbüchlein für Wilhelm Friedemann Bach,* ed.
        Wolfgang Plath
        Contents: BWV 691, 772–801, 824, 836–7, 841–3,
        846a, 847–51, 853–4, 855a, 856–7, 924, 924a,
        925–32, 953, 994

Series VI.   Chamber music

    v.   1   *Werke für Violine,* ed. Günter Hausswald, Rudolf
        Gerber

Contents: Sonatas, partitas for violin solo BWV
1001–6; Sonatas for violin and continuo BWV 1021,
1023; Sonatas for violin and harpsichord BWV 1014,
1019

v. 3 *Werke für Flöte,* ed. Hans-Peter Schmitz
Contents: Partita, flute solo BWV 1013; Sonatas
1034–5, 1030, 1032, 1039

Series VII. Orchestral works

v. 1 *Vier Overtüren (Orchester-Suiten) in C-dur, h-moll,
D-dur, D-dur BWV 1066–1069,* ed. Heinrich Besseler

v. 2 *Sechs Brandenburgische Konzerte, BWV 1046–1051
und Urfassung des Concerto I (Sinfonia F-dur BWV
1046a),* ed. H. Besseler

Series VIII. Canons, Musical offering, Art of fugue

(v. 1 Canons and Musical offering)

(v. 2 The art of the fugue)

Supplement: Bach documents

v. 1 *Schriftstücke von der Hand Johann Sebastian Bachs,*
ed. Werner Neumann, Hans-Joachim Schulze

3. Numerical listing of Bach cantatas, giving the v. no. of their appearance
in items 1–2 above. An alphabetical index follows. Nos. appearing in
parentheses are of doubtful authenticity.

Number, title	BGA	New, Ser. 1
1. Wie schön leuchtet	1	
2. Ach Gott vom Himmel	1	
3. Ach Gott wie manches	1	
4. Christ lag in Todesbanden	1	
5. Wo soll ich fliehen hin	1	
6. Bleib' bei uns	1	10
7. Christ unser Herr	1	
8. Liebester Gott, wann werd' ich sterben	1	
9. Es ist das Heil	1	
10. Meine Seel' erhebt den Herren	1	16
11. Lobet Gott in seinen Reichen	2	

12. Weinen, Klagen	2	
13. Meine Seufzer	2	
14. Wär Gott nicht mit uns	2	
(15. Denn du wirst meine Seele)	2	
16. Herr Gott, dich loben wir	2	4
17. Wer Dank opfert	2	21
18. Gleich wie der Regen	2	7
19. Es erhub sich ein Streit	2	
20. O Ewigkeit	2	15
21. Ich hatte viel Bekümmernis	5/1	
22. Jesus nahm zu sich die Zwölfe	5/1	
23. Du wahrer Gott	5/1	
24. Ein ungefärbt Gemüte	5/1	
25. Es ist nichts Gesundes	5/1	21
26. Ach wie flüchtig	5/1	27
27. Wer weiss, wie nahe	5/1	
28. Gottlob! Nun geht das Jahr	5/1	
29. Wir danken dir, Gott	5/1	
30. Freue dich, erlöste Schar	5/1	
30a. Angenehmes Wiederau	5/1,34	
31. Der Himmel lacht	7	
32. Liebster Jesu, mein Verlangen	7	
33. Allein zu dir	7	21
34. O ewiges Feuer	7	13
34a. ———, incomplete version	41	33
35. Geist und Seele	7	
36. Schwingt freudig euch empor	7	1
36a. Steigt freudig in die Luft	7,34	
36b. Die Freude reget sich	34	38
36c. Schwingt freudig euch empor	34	1
37. Wer da glaubet	7	12
38. Aus tiefer Not	7	
39. Brich dem Hungrigen dein Brot	7	15
40. Dazu ist erschienen	7	
41. Jesu, nun sei gepreiset	10	4
42. Am abend aber desselbigen Sabbaths	10	12
43. Gott fähret auf mit Jauchzen	10	12
44. Sie werden euch in den Bann	10	
45. Es ist dir gesagt	10	18
46. Schauet doch und sehet	10	
47. Wer sich selbst erhöhet	10	

48.	Ich elender Mensch	10	
49.	Ich geh' und suche	10	
50.	Nun ist das Heil	10	
51.	Jauchzet Gott	12/2	
52.	Falsche Welt	12/2	
(53.	Schlage doch)	12/2	
54.	Widerstehe doch der Sünde	12/2	18
55.	Ich armer Mensch	12/2	
56.	Ich will den Kreuzstab	12/2	
57.	Selig ist der Mann	12/2	
58.	Ach, Gott, wie manches Herzeleid	12/2	
59.	Wer mich liebet	12/2	13
60.	O Ewigkeit	12/2	27
61.	Nun komm, der Heiden Heiland	16	1
62.	[same]	16	1
63.	Christen, ätzet diesen Tag	16	2
64.	Sehet, welch eine Liebe	16	
65.	Sie werden aus Saba	16	
66.	Erfreut euch	16	10
67.	Halt im Gedächtnis	16	
68.	Also hat Gott die Welt geliebt	16	14
69.	Lobe den Herrn	16	
70.	Wachet, betet	16	27
71.	Gott ist mein König	18	
72.	Alles nur nach Gottes Willen	18	
73.	Herr, wie du willt	18	
74.	Wer mich liebet	18	13
75.	Die Elenden sollen essen	18	15
76.	Die Himmel erzählen	18	
77.	Du sollst Gott, deinen Herren, lieben	18	21
78.	Jesu, der du meine Seele	18	21
79.	Gott, der Herr, ist Sonn' und Schild	18	
80.	Ein feste Burg	18	
80a.	Alles, was von Gott geboren	18	
81.	Jesus schläft	20/1	
82.	Ich habe genug	20/1	
83.	Erfreute Zeit	20/1	
84.	Ich bin vergnügt	20/1	7
85.	Ich bin ein guter Hirt	20/1	
86.	Wahrlich, wahrlich	20/1	12
87.	Bisher habt ihr nichts gebeten	20/1	12

88. Siehe, ich will viel Fischer aussenden	20/1	
89. Was soll ich aus dir machen	20/1	
90. Es reifet euch	20/1	27
91. Gelobet seist du	22	2
92. Ich hab in Gottes Herz	22	7
93. Wer nur den lieben Gott	22	
94. Was frag' ich nach der Welt	22	
95. Christus, der ist mein Leben	22	
96. Herr Christ, der ein'ge Gottes-Sohn	22	
97. In allen meinen Taten	22	
98. Was Gott tut	22	
99. Was Gott tut	22	
100. Was Gott tut	22	
101. Nimm von uns, Herr	23	
102. Herr, deine Augen sehen	23	
103. Ihr werdet weinen	23	
104. Du Hirte Israel	23	
105. Herr, gehe nicht ins Gericht	23	
106. Gottes Zeit	23	
107. Was willst du dich betrüben	23	18
108. Es ist euch gut	23	12
109. Ich glaube, lieber Herr	23	
110. Unser Mund sei voll Lachens	23	2
111. Was mein Gott will	24	
112. Der Herr ist mein getreuer Hirt	24	
113. Herr Jesu Christ, du höchstes Gut	24	
114. Ach, lieben Christen	24	
115. Mache dich, mein Geist, bereit	24	
116. Du Friedefürst	24	27
117. Sei Lob und Ehr'	24	
118. O Jesu Christ, mein's Lebens Licht	24	
119. Preise, Jerusalem	24	
120. Gott, man lobet dich	24	
120a. Herr Gott, Beherrscher	41	33
121. Christum wir sollen loben	26	
122. Das neugebor'ne Kindelein	26	1
123. Liebster Immanuel	26	
124. Meinen Jesum lass' ich nicht	26	
125. Mit Fried' und Freud'	26	
126. Erhalt' uns, Herr	26	7
127. Herr Jesu Christ, wahr'r Mensch	26	

4.   Alphabetical table of cantatas, giving BWV no.

Falsche Welt	52
Ein feste Burg	80
Die Freude reget	36b
Freue dich	30
Der Friede sei mit dir	158
Gedenke, Herr	217
Geist und Seele	35
Gelobet sei der Herr	129
Gelobet seist du	91
Dem Gerechten muss das Licht	195
Geschwinde, geschwinde	201
Gleich wie der Regen	18
Gloria in excelsis Deo	191
Gott, der Herr	79
Gott, der Hoffnung	218
Gott fähret auf	43
Gott ist mein König	71
Gott ist unsre Zuversicht	197
Gott, man lobet dich	120
Gott soll allein mein Herze haben	169
Gott, wie dein Name	171
Gottes Zeit	106
Gottlob! Nun geht das Jahr zu Ende	28
Halt im Gedächtnis	67
Hercules auf dem Scheidewege	213
Herr Christ, der ein'ge Gottes-Söhn	96
Herr, deine Augen	102
Der Herr denket an uns	196
Herr, gehe nicht ins Gericht	105
Herr Gott, Beherrscher	120a
Herr Gott, dich loben	16, 130
Der Herr ist mein getreuer Hirt	112
Herr Jesu Christ, du höchstes Gut	113
Herr Jesu Christ, wahr'r Mensch	127
Herr, wie du willt	73
Ein Herz, das seinen Jesus	134
Herz und Mund	147
Die Himmel erzählen	76
Der Himmel lacht	31
Himmelskönig, sei willkommen	182

Schleicht, spielende Wellen	206
Schmücke dich	180
Schweigt stille	211
Schwingt freudig	36, 36c
Sehet, wir geh'n hinauf	159
Sei Lob und Ehr'	117
Selig ist der Mann	57
Sie werden aus Saba	65
Sie werden euch in den Bann	44, 183
Siehe, es hat überwunden	219
Siehe, ich will viel Fischer aussenden	88
Siehe zu	179
Singet dem Herrn	190
So du mit deinem Munde	145
Steigt freudig	36a
Der Streit zwischen Phoebus und Pan	201
Süsser Trost	151
Tönet, ihr Pauken!	214
Tritt auf die Glaubensbahn	152
Tue Rechnung!	168
Ein ungefärbt Gemüte	24
Uns ist ein Kind geboren	142
Unser Mund sei voll Lachens	110
Vereinigte Zweitracht	207
Vergnügte Ruh'	170
Von der Vergnügsamkeit	204
Wachet auf	140
Wachet, betet	70
Wär Gott nicht mit uns	14
Wahrlich, wahrlich	86
Warum betrübst du dich	138
Was frag ich	94
Was Gott tut	98, 99, 100
Was mein Gott will	111
Was mir behagt	208
Was soll ich aus dir machen	89
Was willst du	107
Weichet nur, betrübte Schatten	202
Weinen, Klagen	12
Wer da glaubet	37

Wer Dank opfert	17
Wer mich liebet	49, 74
Wer nur den lieben Gott	93
Wer sich selbst erhöhet	47
Wer sucht die Pracht	221
Wer weiss	27
Widerstehe doch der Sünde	54
Wie schön leuchtet	1
Wir danken dir	29
Wir müssen durch viel Trübsal	146
Wo gehest du hin?	166
Wo Gott der Herr	178
Wo soll ich fliehen hin?	5
Wohl dem, der sich auf seinen Gott	139
Die Zeit, der Tag	134a
Zerreisset, zersprenget	205
Der zufriedengestellte Aeolus	205

5. Wolfgang Schmieder, *Thematisches-systematisches Verzeichnis der musikalischen Werke von Johann Sebastian Bach. Bach-Werke-Verzeichnis (BWV).* Leipzig, Breitkopf & Härtel, 1950.

6. *Bach-Jahrbuch,* herausgegeben von der neuen Bachgesellschaft, 1904–   .Jg. 1–36 (1904–39), were reprinted, unchanged in 1965–6. INDICES: Ten year cumulative indices in Jg. 11 (1914), 21 (1924) and 31 (1934). Less detailed 50 year index in Jg. 50 (1963–4), plus tables of contents of the first 50 v.

The v. have three different numbering systems: there is always a date given; from v. 6 on there is a *Jahrgang* no.; all v. through 1961 also carry a different v. no. as part of the *Veröffentlichungen der neuen Bachgesellschaft.* The following table shows the correlation of these numbering systems.

Jg.	Date	Veröff. no.
[1]	1904	5/3
[2]	1905	6/3
[3]	1906	7/3
[4]	1907	8/3
[5]	1908	9/5

Jg.	Date	Veröff. no.
6	1909	10/4
7	1910	11/2
8	1911	12/2
9	1912	13/4
10	1913	14/2
11	1914	15/2
12	1915	16/3
13	1916	17/4
14	1917	18/3
15	1918	19/1
16	1919	20/2
17	1920	21/2
18	1921	22/2
19	1922	23/2
20	1923	24/2
21	1924	25/3
22	1925	26/3
23	1926	27/2
24	1927	28/3
25	1928	29/3
26	1929	30/3
27	1930	31/3
28	1931	32/1
29	1932	33/1
30	1933	34/3
31	1934	35/2
32	1935	36/1
33	1936	37/1
34	1937	38/1
35	1938	39/1
36	1939	40/1
37	1940–48	47
38	1949–50	51 *(sic)*
39	1951–2	52
40	1953	53
41	1954	54
42	1955	55

Jg.	Date	Veröff. no.
43	1956	56
44	1957	57
45	1958	58
46	1959	59
47	1960	60
48	1961	61
49	1962	
50	1963–4	
51	1965	
52	1966	

This series contains the following articles of about 100 pages or longer:

Jg. 11 GEORG SCHÜNEMANN, "Johann Christoph Friedrich Bach", pp. 45–165

Jg. 15 HANS LUEDTKE, "Seb. Bachs Choralvorspiele", pp. 1–96

Jg. 21 WOLFGANG GRASER, "Bachs 'Kunst der Fuge'", pp. 1–105

Jg. 24 MARC-ANDRÉ SOUCHAY, "Das Thema in der Fuge Bachs", pp. 1–103

Jg. 25 FRIEDRICH SMEND, "Bachs Matthäus-Passion", pp. 1–95

Jg. 28 HERMANN SIRP, "Die Thematik der Kirchenkantaten J. S. Bachs in ihren Beziehungen zum protestantischen Kirchenlied", pp. 1–51; Part 2 in Jg. 29, pp. 51–114

Jg. 44 ALFRED DÜRR, "Zur Chronologie der Leipziger Vokalwerke J. S. Bachs", pp. 5–162

7. Societas Bach internationalis (Internationale Bachgesellschaft). *Jahresgaben*
   Various publishers; published irregularly
   1956. WALTER REINHART, *Die Aufführung der Johannes-Passion von J. S. Bach und deren Probleme*

1958.   PAUL MIES, *Die geistlichen Kantaten Johann Sebastian Bachs und den Hörer von Heute,* ∨1. Teil. [See 1959, 1964, 1966 below]

1959. ✓ 2. Teil [See 1958]

1960.   RUDOLF STEGLICH, *Tanzrhythmen in der Musik Johann Sebastian Bachs*

1964.✓ MIES [See 1958], *3. Teil,* including table of contents for the first three parts

1966.   MIES [See 1958], [*4. Teil*]

1967.   FRIEDRICH BLUME, *Der junge Bach*

8.   *Tübinger Bach-Studien,* ed. Walter Gerstenberg. 1953–

v. 1   GEORG VON DADELSON, *Bermerkungen zur Handschrift Johann Sebastian Bachs, seiner Familie und seines Kreises*

v. 2–3 (bound together) PAUL KAST, *Die Bach-Handschriften der Berliner Staatsbibliothek*

v. 4–5 (bound together) G. VON DADELSON, *Beiträge zur Chronologie der Werke Johann Sebastian Bachs*

v. 6   Finke-Hecklinger, Tanzcharaktere . . .

9.   *Faksimile-Reihe Bachscher Werke und Schriftstücke,* hrsg. Bach-Archiv, Leipzig [Werner Neumann, gen. ed.]. Kassel, Bärenreiter, 1955–

v. 1   *Entwurf einer wohlbestallten Kirchenmusik vom 23. August, 1730*

v. 2   *Originalstimmensatz der Kantate "Wär Gott nicht mit uns diese Zeit"*

v. 3   *Brief an den Jugendfreund Georg Erdmann vom 28. Oktober 1730*

v. 4   *Sonata a Cembalo obligato e Travers solo*

v. 5   *Das wohltemperierte Clavier (Teil I)*

v. 6   *Vier Eingaben an den Rat der Stadt Leipzig . . . August 1736*

v. 7   *Passio Domini nostri Jesu Christi secundum Evangelistam Matthaeum*

✓ v. 8   *O holder Tag, erwünschte Zeit. Hochzeitskantate BWV*
        210

9-11

[10 *Bach-Dokumente* = *Supplement* series of Bach item 2 above]

MLHIO
81 B23

6
BANCHIERI, ADRIANO, 1568–1634

Opera omnia, ed. Giuseppe Vecchi. *Antiquae Musicae Italicae: Monumenta Bononiensia* [**A 6**], v. 12

[Series 1: *Madrigalia cum tribus vocibus*]
      (1.   *La pazzia senile* [in preparation])
      2.   *Il metamorfosi musicale*

7
BARBIREAU, JACOB, *fl. from* 1448, *d.* 1491

Opera omnia, ed. Bernhard Meier. *Corpus mensurabilis musicae* [**A 28**], series 7. Complete in 2 v.

(+)M3
.337

v. 1   Masses

v. 2   Motet, chansons, Lieder

8
BEETHOVEN, LUDWIG VAN, 1770–1827

1–3. Complete works   4. List of works   5. Thematic catalog   6–8. Yearbooks   9. Other series

    N.B.   The works of Beethoven without opus numbers might be cited by four different and mutually exclusive numbering systems, depending on the age and nationality of the source. First, they may simply be cited by their location in item 1 below. Second, they may be cited by Grove numbers, which can be found most conveniently in the first through fourth editions of Grove's *Dictionary of Music and Musicians,* where they appear in consecutive order in the list of works at the end of the Beethoven article. (Grove numbers are also still found in the fifth edition, but are divided among categories of compositions.) Third, they may be cited by Hess numbers. (Hess = item 4 below. Actually Hess has made three different numberings, but they are correlated in item 4. Hess has numbered only works which do not appear in item 1 below.) Fourth, they may be cited according to the numbering of Kinsky (item 5 below), where they are given the prefix WoO. A Kinsky *Anhang* no. denotes a work that is doubtful or spurious. The following listing supplies Kinsky numbers in items 1 and 2.

1. *Werke.* Vollständige kritisch durchgesehene überall berechtigte Ausgabe. Leipzig, Breitkopf & Härtel, 1862–1888
   Reprint ed. 1949 (Edwards, Ann Arbor); another reprint has been announced by Kalmus for 1967–8.

Originally issued in separate sections bearing Arabic numbers: 1–311, omitting nos. 104, 199–200, and adding 17a, 36a, 70a, 111a and 207a–9. The sections were further organized in 25 series. Both section and series numbers run consecutively through the entire set. However, some series are divided into volumes, numbered separately within each series: these v. nos. vary between the old bound set and the reprint of Edwards, and possibly the new reprint will offer more variety. Therefore only the series and sections are given below.

Series 1. Symphonies

1. op.21
2. op.36
3. op.55 "Eroica"
4. op.60
5. op.67
6. op.68 "Pastoral"
7. op.92
8. op.93
9. op.125

Series 2. Other large orchestral works

10. op.91 *(Wellingtons Sieg)*
11. op.43 *(Die Geschöpfe des Prometheus)*
12. op.84 *(Egmont)*
13–17a. WoO 3, 2a, 24, 7, 8, 14 (Marches, dances)

Series 3. Overtures

18. op.62 *(Coriolanus)*
19. op.138 *(Leonore 1)*

20. *(Leonore 2)*
21. *(Leonore 3)*
22. op.115 *(Namensfeier)*
23. op.117 *(König Stefan)*
24. op.124 *(Weihe des Hauses)*
25. op.43 *(Prometheus)*
26. op.72 *(Fidelio)*
27. op.84 *(Egmont)*
28. op.113 *(Ruins of Athens)*

Series 4. Violin and orchestra

29. op.61 *(Concerto)*
30. op.40 *(Romance)*
31. op.50 *(Romance)*

Series 5. Chamber music for 5 or more instruments [without piano]

32. op.20 (septet)
33. op.81b (sextet)
34. op.29 (quintet)
35. op.137 (fugue, quintet)
36. op.4 (quintet arr. from op.103)
36a. op.104 (quintet arr. from op.1 no.3)

Series 6. String quartets

37–42. op.18:1–6
43–5.   op.59:1–3 "Rasumowsky"
46. op.74
47. op.95
48. op.127
49. op.130
50. op.131
51. op.132
52. op.135
53. op.133 "Grosse fuge"

Series 7. String trios

54. op.3
55–7.   op.9:1–3
58. op.8

Series 8. Chamber music for winds

59. op.103 (octet)
60. WoO 25 (*Rondo,* sextet)
61. op.71 (sextet)
62. op.25 (trio)
63. op.87 (trio)
64. WoO 64 (variations, *"Là ci darem")*

Series 9. Piano and orchestra

65. op.15 (Concerto 1)
66. op.19 (Concerto 2)
67. op.37 (Concerto 3)
68. op.58 (Concerto 4)
69. op.73 (Concerto 5, "Emperor")
70. op.56 (Triple concerto)
70a. WoO 58 (Cadenzas for Mozart K.466)
71. op. 80 *(Chorfantasie)*
72. WoO 6 *(Rondo)*
73. op.61 (Violin concerto arr. piano)

Series 10. Piano quartets and quintets

74. op.16 (quintet, piano and winds)
75-7. WoO 36 (3 piano quartets)
78. op.16 (arr. piano quartet)

Series 11. Trios with piano

79–81. op.1:1–3
82–3. op.70:1–2
84. op.97 "Archduke"
85. WoO 39
86. WoO 38
87. op.121a
88. op.44
89. op.11
90.
91. op.38 (arr. of Septet op.20)

Series 12. Piano and violin

92–4. op.12:1–3
95. op.23
96. op.24 ("Spring" sonata)

     97–9. op.30:1–3
     100. op.47 ("Kreutzer" sonata)
     101. op.96
     102. WoO 41 *(Rondo)*
     103. WoO 40 (Variations, "Si vuol ballare")

Series 13. Piano and cello

     105–6. op.5:1–2
     107. op.69
     108–9. op.102:1–2
     110. WoO 45 (Variations, theme by Händel)
     111. op.66 (Variations, theme by Mozart)
     111a. WoO 45 (Variations, theme by Mozart)

Series 14. Piano and wind instruments

     112. op.17 (Horn sonata)
     113–14. op.105 (Flute/violin variations)
     115–19. op.107 (Flute/violin variations, National themes)

Series 15. Works for piano, 4 hands

     120. op.6 (Sonata)
     121. op.45 (3 marches)
     122. WoO 67 (Variations, theme by Waldstein)
     123. WoO 75 (Variations)

Series 16. Piano sonatas

     124–6. op.2:1–3
     127. op.7
     128–30. op.10:1–3
     131. op.13 *"Pathétique"*
     132–3. op.14:1–2
     134. op.22
     135. op.26
     136–7. op.27:1–2 (no.2 = "Moonlight")
     138. op.28 "Pastoral"
     139–41. op.31:1–3
     142–3. op.49:1–2 (Sonatinas)
     144. op.53 "Waldstein"
     145. op.54
     146. op.57 *"Appassionata"*
     147. op.78

148. op.79 (Sonatina)
149. op.81a *"Les adieux, l'absence et le retour"*
150. op.90
151. op.101
152. op.106 *"Hammerklavier"*
153. op.109
154. op.110
155. op.111
156–8. WoO 47
160–61. *Anh.5*

Series 17. Piano variations

162. op.34 (original theme)
163. op.35 (Theme from *Prometheus*)
164. op.76 (Theme from *Die Ruinen von Athen*)
165. op.120 (Theme by Diabelli)
166. WoO 63 (Theme by Dressler)
167–8. WoO 69–70 (Themes by Paisiello)
169. WoO 68 (Theme by Haibel)
170. WoO 71 (Theme by Wranitzky)
171. WoO 72 (Theme by Grétry)
172. WoO 73 (Theme by Salieri)
173. WoO 75 (Theme by Winter)
174. WoO 76 (Theme by Süssmayr)
175. WoO 66 (Theme by Dittersdorf)
176. WoO 77 (*"Leichte"*, G major)
177. WoO 64 (on a Swiss air)
178. WoO 65 (Theme by Righini)
179. WoO 78 ("God save the king")
180. WoO 79 ("Rule, Britannia")
181. WoO 80 (Original theme, c minor)
182. *Anh.10*

Series 18. Smaller piano pieces

183. op.33 *(Bagatelles)*
184. op.39 *(Preludes)*
185–6. op.51:1–2 *(Rondos)*
187. op.77 *(Fantasie)*
188. op.89 *(Polonaise)*
189. op.119 *(Bagatelles)*
190. op.126 *(Bagatelles)*

191. op.129 *(Rondo a capriccio)*
192. WoO 57 *(Andante favori)*
193. WoO 82 *(Menuet)*
194. WoO 10 *(Menuets)*
195. WoO 55 *(Prelude)*
196. WoO 49 *(Rondo)*
197. WoO 15
198. WoO 11

Series 19. Sacred music

203. op.123 *(Missa solemnis)*
204. op.86 *(Mass in C)*
205. op.85 *(Christus am Ölberge)*

Series 20. Dramatic works

206. op.72 *(Fidelio)*
207–207a. op.113–14 *(Die Ruinen von Athen)*
207b. op.117 *(König Stephan)*
207c. WoO 97 *(Es ist vollbracht)*
207d. WoO 94 *(Germania)*

Series 21. Cantatas

208. op.136 *(Der glorreiche Augenblick)*
209. op.112 *(Meeresstille und glückliche Fahrt)*

Series 22. Arias with orchestra

210. op.65 *(Ah, perfido)*
211. op.116 *(Tremate)*
212. op.121b *(Opferlied)*
213. op.122 *(Bundeslied)*
214. op.118 *(Sanft wie du lebtest)*

Series 23. Songs with piano

215. op.32 *(An die Hoffnung)*
216. op.46 *(Adelaide)*
217. op.48:1–6 (poems by Gellert)
218. op.52:1–8
219. op.75:1–6
220. op.82
221. op.83:1–3 (poems by Goethe)

222. op.88 *(Das Glück der Freundschaft)*
223. op.94 *(An die Hoffnung)*
224. op.98:1–6 *(An die ferne Geliebte)*
225. op.99
226. op.100
227. op.128
228–9. WoO 107–8
230–31. WoO 121–2
232. WoO 117
233. WoO 126
234. WoO 129
235. WoO 132
236–8. WoO 137–9
238. WoO 146
240. WoO 143
241. WoO 142
242. WoO 147
243. WoO 140
244. WoO 148
245. WoO 145
246. WoO 149
247. WoO 150
248. WoO 136
249. WoO 123
250. WoO 134
251. WoO 124
252. WoO 133
253. WoO 118
254. WoO 135
255. WoO 104
256. WoO 159, 161–4, 166, 172, 176, 178–85, 187, 191
        194 (canons)

Series 24. Songs with piano and strings

257. op.108 (Scottish songs)
258. WoO 154 (Irish songs)
259. WoO 157 (Folk songs)
260. WoO 156 (Scottish songs)
261. WoO 152 (Irish songs)
262. WoO 153 (Irish songs)
263. WoO 155 (Welsh songs)

Series 25. Supplement

2. *Supplement zur Gesamtausgabe,* herausgegeben von Willy Hess. Wiesbaden, Breitkopf & Härtel, 1950–
   This set (which should not be confused with Series 25 above), follows the numberings of item 4 below.

   v. 1 *Mehrstimmige italienische Gesänge ohne Begleitung*

   v. 2 *Gesänge mit Orchester*

   v. 3 *Werke für Soloinstrumente und Orchester*

   v. 4 *Werke für Orchester*

   v. 5 *Lieder und Gesänge mit Klavierbegleitung, Kanons und musikalische Scherze*

   v. 6 *Kammermusik für Streichinstrumente*

   v. 7 *Kammermusik für Blasinstrumente; Kammermusik für Bläser und Streicher; Werke für ein mechanisches Laufwerk*

v. 8   *Original-Klavierauszüge eigener Werke*

v. 9   *Klavierwerke, Kammermusikwerke mit Klavier*

v. 10 Not yet published

v. 11 *Leonore* (1805 version), part 1

v. 12 same, part 2

3.   *Beethoven Werke,* herausgegeben vom Beethoven-Archiv Bonn, unter
     Leitung von Joseph Schmidt-Görg. München, G. Henle. 1961–

   The proposed general plan of this set is given below in its major
   divisions *(Abteilungen),* but the only individual v. listed are those
   which have actually appeared (early 1970).

Abt. 1   *Symphonien*

Abt. 2   *Andere Orchesterwerke*

Abt. 3   *Werke für ein und mehrere Soloinstrumente mit Orchester*
   v. 1   *Konzert C-dur für Klavier, Violine und Violoncello mit
           Begleitung des Orchesters, Opus 56,* ed. Bernard Van
           der Linde

Abt. 4   *Kammermusik mit Klavier*

   v. 1   *Klavierquintett und Klavierquartette,* ed. Siegfried
           Kross
           Contents: op.16 (2 versions); WoO 36:1–3

   v. 3   *Klaviertrios,* ed. Friedhelm Klugmann
           Contents: Op.44, op.121a, WoO 37–9, op. 38,
           trio arranged from Symphony 2, and 2 unnumbered
           trios

Abt. 5   *Duos mit Klavier*

Abt. 6   *Kammermusik ohne Klavier*

   v. 3   *Streichquartette I,* ed. Paul Mies
           Contents: Op.18:1–6, first version of op. 18:1,
           and quartet arr. from piano sonata op.14:1

   v. 4   *Streichquartette II,* ed. Paul Mies
           Contents: Op.59:1–3, Op.74, Op.95

   v. 6   *Streichtrios und Streichduo,* ed. Emil Platten
           Contents: Op. 3, 8, 9:1–3, WoO 32

Abt. 7   *Werke für Klavier*

    v. 1   *Werke für Klavier zu vier Händen,* ed. Hans Schmidt
        Contents: op.6, op.45:1–3, WoO 67, WoO 74
        (2 versions), op.134 (arr. of op.133)

    v. 5   *Variationen für Klavier,* ed. Joseph Schmidt-Görg
        Contents: WoO 63 (2 versions), WoO 64–6, 68–73,
        75–80; op.34–5, op.76, op.120, *Anh.*10

Abt. 8   *Geistliche Chorwerke*

Abt. 9   *Dramatische Werke*

Abt. 10   *Kantaten und Gesänge mit Orchester*

Abt. 11   *Mehrstimmige Gesänge ohne Begleitung*

Abt. 12   *Lieder und Gesänge mit Trio-Begleitung*

Abt. 13   *Lieder mit Klavier*

Abt. 14   *Nachtrag*

Catalogs of Compositions

N.B. There are many catalogs of Beethoven's works, but only the two most
recent and comprehensive are cited here. See also the note before 1 above.

4.   Willy Hess, *Verzeichnis der nicht der Gesamtausgabe veröffentlichten
    Werke Ludwig van Beethovens. Wiesbaden, Breitkopf,* 1957.

5.   Georg Kinsky, *Das Werk Beethovens. Thematisch-Bibliographisches
    Verzeichnis seiner sämtlichen vollendeten Kompositionen.* Nach dem
    Tode des Verfassers abgeschlossen und herausgegeben von Hans Halm.
    München, G. Henle, 1955–.

Yearbooks

6.   *Beethovenjahrbuch,* ed. Theodor von Frimmel. München, 1908–9
    Only 2 v. published. V. 1 has no table of contents or index, but there
    is an index of both v. in v. 2.

7.   *Neues Beethoven-Jahrbuch,* begründet und herausgegeben von Adolf
    Sandberger. 1924–1942
    10 v. published. Each v. includes a survey of Beethoven bibliography
    of its date.

8.   *Beethoven-Jahrbuch (Veröffentlichungen des Beethovenhauses in Bonn.
    Neue Folge, Zweite Reihe),* 1953–

v. I   (1953–4). Ernst August Ballin "Beethoven-Schriftum von 1938–1952", pp. 109–244.
A classified bibliography of 2011 items, with index of names

v. 2   (1955–6). Includes current bibliography

v. 3   (1957–8). Includes current bibliography

v. 4   (1959–60).

v. 5   (1961–64). Includes current bibliography

v. 6   (1965–68). Hans Schmidt "Verzeichnis der Skizzen Beethovens", pp. 7–127
Includes current bibliography

Other series

9.   *Veröffentlichungen des Beethovenhauses in Bonn*. Neue Folge. Im Auftrag des Vorstandes herausgegeben von Professor Dr. Joseph Schmidt-Görg. 1954–

Erste Reihe. *Beethoven Skizzen und Entwürfe* [Facsimiles] transcriptions

v. I³⁴   *Drei Skizzenbücher zur Missa solemnis: 1. Ein Skiz-* no
zenbuch der Jahre 1819/20, ed. J. Schmidt-Görg

v. 2¹⁵   *Ein Skizzenbuch zur Chorfantasie op.80 und zu anderen Werken*, ed. Dagmar Weise

Zweite Reihe. *Beethoven-Jahrbuch* (see item 8 above)

Dritte Reihe. *Beethoven: Ausgewählte Hss. in Faksimile-Ausgabe*

v. I   *Entwurf einer Denkschrift an das Appellationsgericht in Wien von 18. Feburar 1820*, ed. Dagmar Weise

v. 2   *Klaviersonate in C-dur op.53 "Waldsteinsonate"*

v. 3   *Dreizehn unbekannte Briefe an Josephine Gräfin Deym, geb. Brunsvik . . .* ed. J. Schmidt-Görg

Vierte Reihe. *Schriften zur Beethovenforschung*

v. I   J. SCHMIDT-GÖRG, *Beethoven: die Geschichte seiner Familie*

v. 2   (1957). PAUL MIES, *Textkritische Untersuchungen bei Beethoven*

MLHIO.B46683

V. 3   (1958). LUDWIG MISCH, *Die Faktoren der Einheit in der Mehrsätzigkeit der Werke Beethovens*

MLHIO .B42.B8

V. 4   (1967). L. MISCH, *Neue Beethoven-Studien und andere Themen*

MLHIO .B43563

v. 5

(*)M3
.B48
folio

9
BENEVOLI, ORAZIO, 1605–1672

Opera omnia (Monumenta liturgiae polychoralis Sanctae Ecclesiae Romanae). Tridenti, Societas universalis Sanctae Ceciliae, 1966–
The entire proposed scheme of this set is shown below, but at present (mid–1968) only v. 1, nos. 1–3 and v. 2, nos. 1,3 have appeared.

v. 1   *Missarum XVI vocum tomus I*
    ✓ no.1   *Missa sine nomine*
    ✓ no.2   *Missa Victoria*
    ✓ no.3   *Missa Benevola*

v. 2   *Missarum XVI vocum tomus II*
    ✓ no.1   *Missa Tira corda*   *no.2 Missa si deus pro nobis quis contra nos*
    ✓ no.3   *Missa In diluvio aquarum multarum*

v. 3   *Missarum XVI vocum tomus III*

v. 4   *Missae XII vocum*   *1 Angelus Domini*

v. 5   *Missae X vocum*

v. 6   *Missae IX, VIII et V vocum*

✓ v. 7   *Missa Salisburgensis* [in facsimile]   *+ Missa Bruxellensis*

v. 8   *Psalmi XXIV et XVI vocum*

v. 9   *Psalmi XIV et XII vocum*

v. 10   *Psalmi X et IX vocum*

v. 11   *Psalmi VIII vocum*

v. 12   *Antiphonae, Motecta et Varia*

v. 13   *Catalogus thematicus et bibliographicus, cum adnotationibus criticus ad opera omnia et singula*

10
BERLIOZ, HECTOR, 1803–1869

1–2. Complete works   3. Index

1. *Werke*, herausgegeben von Charles Malherbe und Felix Weingartner. Leipzig, Breitkopf & Härtel, 1900–1907

Commentary in French, German and English. For an INDEX of this set see item 3 below

v. 1   *Symphonies I*
Contents: *Symphonie fantastique, Symphonie funèbre et triomphale*

v. 2   *Symphonies II*
Contents: *Harold en Italie*

v. 3   *Roméo et Juliette*

v. 4   *Overtures I*
Contents: *Waverly, Franc-Juges, King Lear, Rob Roy*

v. 5   *Overtures II*
Contents: *Benvenuto Cellini, Carnaval Romain, Corsair, Béatrice et Bénédict, Les Troyens*

v. 6   *Smaller instrumental works*
Contents: *Rêverie et Caprice, Marche funèbre pour la dernière scène d'Hamlet, et al.*

v. 7   *Sacred vocal works I*
Contents include *Requiem*

v. 8   *Sacred vocal works II*

Contents include *Te Deum*

v. 9   *Sacred vocal works III*
Contents: *L'enfance du Christ*

v. 10   *Secular cantatas I*
Contents: *La révolution Grecque, 8 scènes de Faust*

v. 11–12 (in 1). *Secular cantatas II*
Contents: *La damnation de Faust*

v. 13   *Secular cantatas III*
Contents: *Lélio, Le 5 Mai, L'impériale*

v. 14   *Works for chorus and orchestra*

v. 15   *Arias for 1 or 2 voices with orchestra*

v. 16   *Arias for mixed voices with piano*

v. 17   *Arias for solo voice with piano*

v. 18   *Arrangements*

v. 19–20   *Béatrice et Bénédict*

2.   *Hector Berlioz. New edition of his complete works,* issued by the Berlioz centenary committee, London, in association with the Calouste Gulbenkian Foundation, Lisbon. Chairman, Wilfred Mellers
      The entire proposed plan of this edition is given. At present (mid–1968), only v. 2, 5, and 19 have been published

Series 1.   Operas

       v.   1   *Benvenuto Cellini*

       √v. 2   *Les Troyens,* ed. Hugh MacDonald
                 In 2 parts: v. 2a, acts 1–2; v. 2b, acts 3–4
                          v. 2c suppl. √
       v.   3   *Béatrice et Bénédict*

       v.   4   *Les Francs Juges; La nonne sanglante*

Series 2.   Secular works

       √ v. 5   *La révolution Grecque; Huit scènes de Faust*

       v.   6   *Prix de Rome cantatas*

       v.   7   *Lélio*

       v.   8   *La damnation de Faust*

Series 3.   Sacred works

       v.   9   *Grand messe des morts*

       √√v. 10   *Te Deum*

       v. 11   *L'enfance du Christ*

Series 4.   Miscellaneous vocal works

       v. 12   Chorus and orchestra

       √v. 13   One, two and three voices and orchestra

v. 14   Chorus and piano

v. 15   One, two and three voices and piano

Series 5.   Symphonies

✓ v. 16   *Symphonie fantastique*

v. 17   *Harold en Italie*

v. 18   *Roméo et Juliette*

✓ v. 19   *Grande symphonie funèbre et triomphale,* ed. Hugh McDonald

Series 6.   Orchestral and instrumental works

v. 20   Overtures

v. 21   Other orchestral and instrumental works

Series 7.   Supplement

v. 22   Arrangements of works by other composers

v. 23   Addenda, works of doubtful authenticity, sketches &

v. 24   Berlioz and his world in contemporary pictures

v. 25   A documentary biography

L13+3.
B5M9   *An alphabetical index to Hector Berlioz Werke,* edited by the bibliography committee of the New York chapter, Music Library Association. (*MLA Index series,* no.2)

11

BERWALD, FRANZ, 1796–1868 See (*Monumenta Musica Svecicae*
33

Sämtliche Werke, ed. Ingmar Bengtsson, Nils Castegren, Folke Lindberg, Stig Walin, Bo Waldner. (*Monumenta Musica Svecicae* **A 67,** series 2) English commentary included. The entire proposed plan of this set is given; at present (mid–1968), only v. 3, 11, and 18 have been published.

Orchestral works

v. 1   *Symphonie sérieuse*

v. 2   *Symphonie capricieuse*

v. 3   *Symphonie singulière,* ed. Herbert Blomstedt

v. 4   *Symphonie in E flat*

v. 5   *Violin concerto*

v. 6   *Piano concerto*

v. 7   *Konzertstück, and other works for solo and orchestra*

v. 8   *Tone poems I (Die Schlacht bei Leipzig, Elfenspiel, Ernste und heitere Grillen)*

v. 9   *Tone poems II (Erinnerungen an die norwegischen Alpen, Bayaderen-Fest, Wettlauf)*

v. 10   *Opera overtures and ballet music*

Chamber music

v. 11   *String quartets,* ed. Nils Castegren, Lars Frydén, Erling Lommäs

v. 12   *Septet*

v. 13   *Piano quartet with winds, piano quintet*

v. 14   *Piano trios*

v. 15   Other chamber music

v. 16   Piano music

Vocal works

v. 17   *Estrella di Soria*

v. 18   *Aline, Drottningen av Golconda (The Queen of Golconda),* ed. Folke Lindberg

v. 19   *Jag gär i kloster*

v. 20   *Modehandlerskan*

v. 21–2 Other vocal works

v. 23   Songs with piano accompaniment

v. 24   Chorales and chorale arrangements

Supplement

v. 25   Additional music, sketches, arrangements &

*M3
B72

Boccherini, Luigi. Le opere complete di Luigi Boccherini. [A cura di Pina Carmirelli] . Rome, Istituto Italiano per la Storia della musica, 1970—
  v. 1 Quintetti
  v. 2 Quintetti

12
BÖHM, GEORG, 1661–1733

ML *Sämtliche Werke.* Veröffentlichungen des Kirchenmusikalischen Instituts der Evangelisch-Lutherischen Landeskirche in Sachsen am Landeskonservatorium der Musik zu Leipzig. Leipzig, Breitkopf & Härtel, 1927, 1953

v. 1–2   *Klavier- und Orgelwerke,* ed. Johannes Wolgast
New edition by Gesa Wolgast in 1953 in 2 v. V. 1: Free compositions and suites; v. 2: compositions on chorales

13
BRAHMS, JOHANNES, 1833–1897

1. Complete works   2. Thematic catalog

1. *Sämtliche Werke.* Ausgabe der Gesellschaft der Musikfreunde in Wien. Herausgegeben von Hans Gál und Eusebius Mandyczewski. Leipzig, Breitkopf & Härtel, 1927–8.

ML483
.199

An unchanged reprint (Edwards, Ann Arbor), appeared in 1947, and a second reprint, making minor corrections and adding the *Ophelia Lieder* (discovered in 1935) was issued by Breitkopf & Härtel in 1964.

v. 1   *Symphonien für Orchester I*

v. 2   *Symphonien für Orchester II*

v. 3   *Overtüren und Variationen für Orchester*

v. 4   *Serenaden und Tänze für Orchester*

v. 5   *Konzerte für Violine und Violoncello*

v. 6   *Klavierkonzerte*

v. 7   *Kammermusik für Streichinstrumente*

v. 8   *Klavier-Quintett und -Quartette*

v. 9   *Klavier-Trios*

v. 10   *Klavier-Duos*
Contents: violin, cello, clarinet sonatas

v. 11   *Werke für zwei Klaviere zu vier Händen*

v. 12   *Werke für ein Klavier zu vier Händen*

v. 13	*Klaviersonaten und Variationen*

v. 14	*Kleinere Klavierwerke*
Contents: op.4, op.10, op.39, op.76, op.79, op.116–119

v. 15	*Studien und Bearbeitungen für Klavier*
Contents: Etudes, works without opus no., cadenzas &

v. 16	*Orgelwerke*

v. 17	*Chorwerke mit Orchester I*
Contents: *Ein deutsches Requiem, op.45*

v. 18	*Chorwerke mit Orchester II*
Contents: *Triumphlied, op.55; Rinaldo, op.50*

v. 19	*Chorwerke mit Orchester III*
Contents: *Alto rhapsody, op. 53; Schiksalslied, op. 54;*
Nänie, op.82; Gesang der Parzen, op.89; Ave Maria, op.12;
Begräbnisgesang, op.13; op.17; Schubert arrangements.

v. 20	*Mehrstimmige Gesänge mit Klavier oder Orgel*
Contents: *23. Psalm, op.27; Geistliches Lied von Flemming,*
op.30; Quartets op.31, 64, 92, 112; Liebeslieder, op.52, 65;
Zigeunerlieder op.103; Tafellied op.93b; Kleine Hoch-
zeitskantate

v. 21	*Mehrstimmige Gesänge ohne Begleitung*
Contents: For mixed chorus: *Marienlieder, op.22; Motets,*
op.29, 74, 110; Fest- und Gedenkssprüche, op.109; Gesänge,
op.43, 104; Lieder, op.62, 93a; Deutsche Volkslieder; Dem
dunkeln Schoss; Töne lindernder Klang; canons. For women's
chorus: *Geistliche Chöre, op.37; Lieder und Romanzen,*
op.44; op.113; canons. For men's chorus: *op.41*

v. 22	*Duette mit Klavierbegleitung*
Contents: *op.20, op.28, op.61, op.66, op.75*

v. 23	*Einstimmige Lieder mit Klavierbegleitung I*
Contents: *op.3, op.6, op.7, op.14, op.19, op.32, op.33*

v. 24	———, II
Contents: *op.43, op.46, op.47, op.48, op.57, op.58, op.59,*
op.63

v. 25	———, III

Contents: *op.69, op.70, op.71, op.72, op.84, op.85, op.86, op.91, op.94, op.95, op.96, op.97*

v. 26 ⟋   ———, IV

Contents: *op.105, op.106, op.107, op.121, Mondnacht, Regenlied, 8 Zigeunerlieder, Folk songs, Ophelia Lieder*

L 1342.   Joseph Braunstein, *Thematic catalog of the collected works of Brahms.*
73A22   Ars musica press, 1956

14

BRASSART, JOHANNES *(fl. from* **1431,** *d. ca.* **1450***)*
Opera omnia, ed. Keith E. Mixter. *Corpus mensurabilis musicae* **(A 28),** ser. 35. 2 v. proposed

v. 1   Mass sections

15

BRUCKNER, ANTON, 1824–1896

Kritische Gesamtausgabe, herausgegeben von der Generaldirektion der Österreichischen Nationalbibliothek und der Internationalen Bruckner-Gesellschaft.

There are two sets of this title and auspices, neither complete. The earlier, dating from 1930, was edited by Robert Haas and Alfred Orel. The second, still in progress, is edited by Leopold Nowak. The following alphabetical list shows the location of works actually published in the two sets. Symphonies are in the original versions unless otherwise stated.

Cat. Sep.   ✱ M 3. B 8944

Title	Hass/ Orel v.	Nowak v.
Intermezzo in D (string quintet)		13/2
Mass no. 1 in d		16
Mass no. 2 in e (1869)	13	
—— 1892 version M 2010. B78 Emin.		17/2
Mass no. 3 in f M 2010. B78 F mm.	14	18
Missa solemnis in B♭	15	
Psalm 150		20/6

Title	Hass/ Orel v.	Nowak v.
Quartet, string, in c		12
Quintet, string, in F		13/2
Requiem	15	14
Symphony no. 1 in c, Linz version	1	1
—— Vienna version	1	
Symphony no. 2 in c	2	
—— 1877 version		2
Symphony no. 3 in d, 1889 version		3/3
Symphony no. 4 in E♭, "Romantic",		
2nd version	4	4
3d version: Finale	4	
Symphony no. 5 in B♭	5	5
Symphony no. 6 in A	6	6
Symphony no. 7 in E *(✳)M1001.B78 no.7*	7	7
Symphony no. 8 in c, "Apocalyptic"	8	
—— 1890 version		8
Symphony no. 9 in c *(✳)M1001.B78 no.9*	9	9
Te Deum, 1884 version		19

16
✳✳M3
.B78

BRUMEL, ANTOINE, *ca.* **1475–***ca.* **1520**

Opera omnia, ed. Barton Hudson. *Corpus mensurabilis* musicae **(A 28)**, ser. 5.

✓v. 1   ✓part 1.   *Missa L'homme armé*
              ✓part 2.   *Missa Je nay dueul*
✓. 3-4

17

BUXTEHUDE, DIETRICH, 1637–1707

Werke, herausgegeben von der Oberleitung der Glaubensgemeinde Ugrino ... unter Leitung von Willibald Gurlitt. Klecken, Ugrino, 1925–

Only the following volumes, edited by Gottlieb Harms and Helmar Trede, were published. They have been reprinted unchanged (*ca.* 1960?), and a continuation is proposed but has not yet started.

✓ v. 1   *Siebzehn Kirchenkantaten für eine Sopranostimme (nr.1–17)*

✓ v. 2   *Drei Kirchenkantaten für eine Altstimme; Vier Kirchenkantaten für eine Tenorstimme; Drei Kirchenkantaten für eine Bassstimme; Trauermusik (nr.18–28)*

✓ v. 3   *Dreizehn Kirchenkantaten für zwei Singstimmen (nr.29–41)*

✓ v. 4   *Missa brevis; Motette Benedicam Dominum (nr.42–3).* NACHWEISE ZU BAND 1–4

✓ v. 5   *Elf Kirchenkantaten und eine Aria für drei Singstimmen (nr.44–55)*

✓ v. 6   *Neun Kirchenkantaten (nr.56–64)*

✓ v. 7   *Elf Kirchenkantaten und eine Aria für drei Singstimmen und Instrumente (nr.65–76)*

✓ v. 8   *Neun Kirchenkantaten (nr.65–73)*

18
BYRD, WILLIAM, 1543/3–1623

The collected vocal works of William Byrd, ed. Edmund H. Fellowes. London, Stainer & Bell, 1937–

In the course of publication the set was enlarged to include Byrd's instrumental works, and in later v. the title omits the word *vocal.* This set is in the process of appearing in revised editions.

v. 1   *Masses, Cantiones sacrae (1575)*

v. 2   *Cantiones sacrae (1589),* rev. ed. by Thurston Dart

v. 3   *Cantiones sacrae (1591),* rev. ed. by T. Dart

v. 4   *Gradualia (1605), part 1*

v. 5   *Gradualia (1605), parts 2–3*

v. 6   *Gradualia (1607), part 1*

v. 7   *Gradualia (1607), part 2*

v. 8   *Motets for three, four and five voices*

v. 9   *Motets of six, eight and nine voices*

v. 10   *English liturgical music*

v. 11   *English anthems*

M3.B99 v. 12   *Psalmes, sonets and songs (1588),* rev. ed. by Philip Brett

M3.B99 v. 13   *Songs of sundrie natures (1589),* rev. ed. by P. Brett

M3.B99 v. 14   *Psalmes, songs ·and sonnets (1611),* rev. ed. by T. Dart

M3.B99 v. 15   *Songs*

v. 16   *Additional madrigals, canons and rounds*

M3.B99 v. 17   *Chamber music for strings*

v. 18   *Keyboard works, part 1*

v. 19   *Keyboard works, part 2*

v. 20   *Keyboard works, part 3*

CABANILLES, JUAN, 1644–1712

Opera omnia. See **A 14,** v. 4, v. 8, v. 13, v. 17.

19
CABEZÓN, ANTONIO DE, 1500–1566

Collected works, ed. Charles Jacobs. *The Institute of Mediaeval Music:
Collected Works* **(A 51),** v. 4
  no. 1. *Duos, Kyries, variations*
  v. 1-2

20
CARISSIMI, GIACOMO, 1605–1674

Instituto Italiano per la Storia della Musica **(A 53),** *Monumenti 3*

a.   Oratorios

          v. 1   *Historia di Job; Historia di Ezechia,* ed. Carlo dall'
                        Argine, Frederico Ghisi, Roberto Lupi

          v. 2   *Historia di Abraham et Isaac; Vir frugi et pater
                        familias,* ed. Lino Bianchi

          v. 3   *Historia di Baltazar,* ed. L. Bianchi

          v. 4   *Judicium extremum,* ed. L. Bianchi

v. 5   *Historia divitis (Dives malus),* ed. L. Bianchi

v. 6   *Tolle, sponsa; Historia dei pellegrina di Emmaus,* ed. L. Bianchi

v. 7   *Daniele,* ed. L. Bianchi

v. 8   *Oratorio della SS.^ma Vergine,* ed. L. Bianchi

b.   Masses and motets

v. I   *Missa a 3 voce e basso continuo; Hodie Simon Petrus; Cum reverteretur,* ed. L. Bianchi

c.   Cantatas

v. I   *Dunque degl' horti miei; Ahi non torna; Serenata "I naviganti" (Sciolto havean),* ed. Bianchi

13.C29   Caron, Philippe   v. I   Institute of Medieval Music.

21

CARVER, ROBERT, 1487–*after* 1546

Collected works, ed. Denis Stevens. *Corpus mensurabilis musicae* **(A 28),** ser. 16. 3–5 v. proposed

✓ v. I   *2 motets*

22

CHAIKOVSKII, PETER IL'ICH, 1840–1893

1. Complete works   2. Thematic catalog

1.   *Polnoe sobranie sochinenii.* [Moscow, State Music Publishing Co.], 1940–   . This set, edited by a group of Russian musicians and published in Moscow, has all titles, commentary etc. in Russian only. Most works with orchestra are presented in full score and also in a separate volume with the orchestra part arranged for piano. In this set, most of the piano arrangements (some for four hands) were made by Chaikovskii. The set is not yet complete; the following alphabetical list includes only works published so far. The letters a and b refer to separately bound books.

Title, description	Full score v.	Arr. v.
Andante and finale op.29 (completed by S. I. Taniev (piano and orch.)	62 ✓	62 ✓
Capriccio italien, op.45 (orch.)	25	50a ✓
Le caprice d'Oxane (opera) = *Cherevichki*		
Cantatas	27	33
Charodeika (opera)	8a, b	40a, b ✓
Cherevichki, op.14 (opera)	7a, b	39 ✓
Concert fantasy, op.56 (piano and orch.)	29	46b ✓
Concertos, piano, nos. 1–2, op.23–4	28	46a ✓
Concerto, piano, no. 3, op.75	29	
Concerto, violin, op.35	30a	55a ✓
Coronation march (= Festive March, orch.)	25	50b ✓
Dmitri the pretender (incidental music)	14 ✓	
1812 overture, op.49 (orch.)	25	
Elegy for I. V. Samarin (string orch.)	26	
The enchantress (opera) = *Charodeika*		
Eugene Onegin, op.24 (opera)	4	36 ✓
Fatum (Fate), op.77 (symphonic poem)	22 ✓	
Festive march (= Coronation march, orch.)	25	50b ✓
Folk songs: arrangements and transcriptions	61 ✓	
Francesca da Rimini, op.32 (Fantasia, orch.)	24	
Hamlet, op.67 (Overture-fantasia, orch.)	26	
Iolanthe (Iolanta), op.69 (opera)	10	42
Joan of Arc (opera) = *Orleanskaia deva*		
Jurists' march (= March solonelle, orch.)	26	
Kusnez Vakula (= Vakula the blacksmith, another version of *Cherevichki,* opera)		35
Lebedinoie osero (= Swan lake, ballet)	11a, b ✓	56
The Maid of Orleans (opera) = *Orleanskaia deva*		
Marche Slave, op.81 (orch.)	24	50b ✓
March solonelle (= Jurists' march, orch.)	26	
Mandragora (opera fragment): excerpts	2	
Manfred symphony, op.58	18 ✓	48
Mozartiana (Suite no. 4, orch.)	20	
The nutcracker (Schelkunchik, ballet)	13a, b	54
Ondine (Undine, opera): excerpts	2	
Oprichnik (opera)	3a, b	34

Title, description	Full score v.	Arr. v.
Orleanskaia deva (*Joan of Arc*, opera)	5 ✓	37 ✓
Overture in c (orch.)	21 ✓	
Overture in F, 2 versions (orch.)	21 ✓	
Overture on the Danish national hymn, op.15 (orch.)	22 ✓	50a ✓
overtures, other, *see* individual titles		
Oxana's caprice (opera) = Cherevichki		
Pezzi capriccioso, op.62 (cello and orch.)	30b	55b ✓
Piano works, op.4–21 (1868–1873)	51b	
Pique dame (*Picovaia dama*), op.68 (opera)	9a-c	41
Quartets, string	31	
The queen of spades (opera) = Pique dame		
Romeo and Juliet (*Overture-fantasia*, orch.), 2 versions	23	
Romeo and Juliet (vocal duet with orch., finished by S. I. Taniev)	62 ✓	
Schelcunchik (*Nutcracker*, ballet)	13a.b	54
Serenade for small orchestra for the name day of N. Rubinstein	24	
Serenade for strings, op.48	20	50b ✓
Serenade melancholique, op.26 (violin and orch.)	30a	55a ✓
Sextet, strings, op.70 (*Souvenir de Florence*)	32b ✓	
Slavonic march (*Marche Slave*), op.81 (orch.)	27	50b
Sleeping beauty, op.66 (*Spiaschaia crassaviza*, ballet)	12a-d	57 ✓
The slippers (opera) = Cherevichki		
The snow maiden (*Snegurochka*), op.12 (incidental music)	14 ✓	33
The sorceress (opera) = Charodeika		
Souvenir de Florence, op.70 (string sextet)	32b ✓	
The storm, op.76 (Overture, orch.)	21 ✓	
Suite no. 1, op.43 (orch.)	19a	49
Suite no. 2, op.53 (orch.)	19b	49
Suite no. 3, op.55 (orch.)	20	49
Suite no. 4, op.61 "Mozartiana" (orch.)	20	
Swan lake (*Lebedinoie osero*, ballet)	11a,b ✓	56
Symphony no. 1, op.15 "Winter day dreams"	15a ✓	

Title, description	Full score v.	Arr. v.
Symphony no. 2, op.17 "Little Russian", 2 versions	15b	47
Symphony no. 3, op.29 "Polish"	16a	
Symphony no. 4, op.36	16b	
Symphony no. 5, op.64	17a	
Symphony no. 6, op.74 "Pathétique"	17b	
Symphony, "Manfred", op.58	18	48
The tempest, op.24 (Fantasia, orch.)	24	
Tcharodeika (opera) = *Charodeika*		
Tcherevichki (opera) = *Cherevichki*		
Trio, op.50 (piano, violin, cello)	32a	
Undine (Ondine, opera): excerpts	2	
Vakula the blacksmith see *Kusnez Vakula*		
Valse-scherzo, op.34 (violin and orch.)	30a	55a
Variations on a rococo theme, op.31 (cello and orch.)	30b	55b
Voyevoda, op.3 (opera)	1a-c	1 suppl.
Voyevoda (incidental music for play)	14	
Voyevoda, op.78 (symphonic ballad)	26	
Waltz-scherzo, op.34 (violin and orch.)	30a	55a

2. Boris Petrovich Iürgenson, *Catalogue thématique des oeuvres de P. Tschaikowsky*. New York, Russian American music publishers, 1947

23
CHOPIN, FREDERYK FRANCISZEK, 1810–1849

1. Complete works   2–3. Yearbooks   3. Monograph series   4. Bibliography   5. Catalog

1. *Complete works*, according to the autographs and original editions with critical commentary, ed. Ignacy J. Paderewski [Ludwig Bronarski, Joseph Turczyński]. Warsaw, 1949–
Includes English commentary, titles.

v. 1   *Preludes*

v. 2   *Etudes*

v. 3   *Ballades*

v. 4   *Impromptus*

v. 5   *Scherzos*

v. 6   *Sonatas*

v. 7   *Nocturnes*

v. 8   *Polonaises*

v. 9   *Waltzes*

v. 10   *Mazurkas*

v. 11   *Fantasia, Berceuse, Barcarolle*

v. 12   *Rondos*

v. 13   *Concert allegro, Variations*

v. 14   *Concertos 1–2* (2 piano score. See v. 19–20)

v. 15   *Works for piano and orchestra* (2 piano score. See v. 21)

v. 16   *Chamber music*

v. 17   *Songs*

v. 18   *Minor works*

v. 19   *Piano concerto in e minor, no. 1, op.11* (full score)

v. 20   *Piano concerto in f minor, no. 2, op.21* (full score)

v. 21   *Works for piano and orchestra* (full score)

v. 22–7   Orchestral parts for v. 19–21

Yearbooks

2.   *Chopin Jahrbuch*. Internationale Chopin-Gesellschaft, Wien, ed. Franz Zagiba. Zürich, Amalthus. 2 v. (1956, 1963).

3.   *Rocznik Chopinowski (Annales Chopin)*. Towarzystwo Fryderyka Chopina. Polskie Wydawnictwo Muzyozne. [gen. ed. Józef M. Chomiński]   *Ceased with v. 8.*

From v. 3, this series is multilingual, and articles in Pólish have résumés in another language, usually French.

v. 1   (1956). All in Polish. Includes Chopin bibliography 1945–55.

v. 2   (1958). = v. 1 translated into other languages, mostly French

v. 3   (1958)

v. 4	(1959)

v. 5	(1960). Zofia Chechlińska, "Ze studiów nad Źródłami do Scherz F. Chopina", pp. 82–194; French résumé pp. 195–200

v. 6	(1965). Contains book review section

4.	*Biblioteka Chopinowska* pod redakcja Mieczyslawa Tomaszewskiego Przypsy opracowali Franciszek German i Jadwiga Ilnicka. Kraków, 1960–

v. 1	JAN KLECZYŃSKI, *Owykonywaniu dzieł Chopina, Wyd 1*

v. 2	M. TOMASZEWSKI, *Kompozytorzy polsçy o Fryderyku Chopinie: antologia, Wyd 2*

v. 3	FRANZ LISZT, *Fryderyk Chopin, Wyd 1*

v. 4	LUDWIK BRONARSKI, *Szkice Chopinowskie, Wyd 1*

v. 5/1	FERDYNAND HOESICK, *Chopin, Zyue i twóczośé*

v. 5/2	same, v. 2: *Purzswe lata w Paryzy, George Sand*

v. 6	Not published?

v. 7	EDMUND SŁUSZKIEWICZ, *Wiersze o Chopinie, antologia i bibliografia*

5.	Edward Bronisław Sydow, *Bibliografia F. F. Chopina.* Warszawa, 1949. *Supplement,* 1954
	Complete bibliography from 1818

6.	Maurice J. E. Brown, *Chopin. An index of his works in chronological order.* London, Macmillan, 1960

24
CLEMENT, JACOB, *known as* **CLEMENS NON PAPA,** *ca.* **1510–1555?**

Opera omnia, ed. K. Ph. Bernet Kempers. *Corpus mensurabilis musicae* **(A 28),** ser. 4. 21 v. proposed

v. 1	*Masses: Misericorde, Virtute magna, En espoir, Ecce quam bonum*

v. 2	*Psalms (Souterliedekens)*

✓ v. 3   *Motets*

✓ v. 4   *2 sets of Magnificats*

✓ v. 5   *Masses: Spes salutis, Gauda lux Donatiane, Languir my fault*

✓ v. 6   *Masses: Pastores quidnam vidistis, Caro mea, Jay veu le cerf*

✓ v. 7   *Masses: A la fontaine, Quam pulchra es, Panis quem ego dabo,
                 Or combien est*

✓ v. 8   *Missa defunctorum, Kyrie Paschale, Credo*

✓ v. 9   *Motets*

✓ v. 10   *Chansons*

✓ v. 11   *Chansons*

✓ v. 12–15   *Motets*

   v, 17-19

25
COMPÈRE, LOYSET, *ca.* 1450–1518

Opera omnia, ed. Ludwig Finscher. *Corpus mensurabilis musicae* **(A 28),**
ser. 15. 6 v. proposed

✓ v. 1   *All the Masses and Mass sections*

✓ v. 2–4   *Motets*

26
CORELLI, ARCANGELO, 1653–1713

1. Complete works   2. Thematic catalog

1. *Les oeuvres,* revues par J. Joachim et F. Chrysander. London, Augener.
1888–1891

   v. 1   *Sonate da chiesa a tre, op.1–2*

   v. 2   *Sonate da chiesa a tre, op.3–4*

   v. 3   *6 sonate a violino e violone e cembalo, op.5*

   v. 4   *Concerti grossi, op.6, no. 1–6*

   v. 5   *Concerti grossi, op.6, no. 7–12*

**ML410
.C78R5**

2. Thematic catalog is included in Mario Rinaldi, *Archangelo Corelli*. Milano, Curci, 1953, pp. 474–501

27
CORNELIUS, PETER, 1824–1874

**M.414
.20**

Musikalische Werke. Erste Gesamtausgabe im Auftrage seiner Familie herausgegeben von Max Hesse und Waldemar von Baussnern. Leipzig, Breitkopf & Härtel, 1905–6

v. 1   *Einstimmige Lieder mit Klavier*

v. 2   *Mehrstimmige Gesänge und Chöre*

v. 3   *Der Barbier von Bagdad*

v. 4   *Der Cid*

v. 5   *Gunlöd,* completed by von Baussnern [Excerpts in (*)M.414.21]

28
COUPERIN, FRANÇOIS, 1668–1733

**M.482
.750**

1. Complete works   2. Thematic catalog

1. *Oeuvres complètes,* publiées par un groupe de musicologues sous la direction de Maurice Cauchie. Paris, Éditions de l'Oiseau-lyre, 1932–3. There is an INDEX of all harpsichord works in v. 5

v. 1   *Oeuvres didactiques,* ed. Paul Brunold
           Contents: *Règle pour l'accompagnement, L'art de toucher le clavecin*

v. 2   *Musique de clavecin I,* ed. M. Cauchie
           Contents: *Pièces de clavecin, premier livre, 1713 (Ordres 1–5)*

v. 3   *Musique de clavecin II,* ed. M. Cauchie
           Contents: *Second livre de pièces de clavecin, 1716 (Ordres 6–12)*

v. 4   *Musique de clavecin III,* ed. M. Cauchie
           Contents: *Troisième livre de pièces de clavecin, 1722 (Ordres 13–19)*

v. 5   *Musique de clavecin IV,* ed. M. Cauchie
       Contents: *Quatrième livre de pièces de clavecin, 1730
       (Ordres 20–27).* Title index of harpsichord works

v. 6   *Musique d'orgue consistantes en deux messes,* ed. Paul Brunold

v. 7   *Musique de chambre I,* ed. André Schaeffner
       Contents: *Concerts royaux, 1722 (nos. 1–4)*

v. 8   *Musique de chambre II,* ed. A. Schaeffner
       Contents: *Les goûts-réunis ou nouveaux concerts, 1724
       (nos 5–15)* .

v. 9   *Musique de chambre III,* ed. Amédée Gastoué
       Contents: *Suites et sonades I. Les nations (Ordres 1–4)*

v. 10 *Musique de chambre IV,* ed. A Gastoué
       Contents: *Suite et sonades II. L'apothéose de Corelli,
       L'apothéose de Lully, Pièces de violon avec la basse chiffré,
       Sonades inédites (La Steinquerque, La sultane, La superbe)*

v. 11 *Musique vocale I,* ed. P. Brunold, André Tessier
       Contents: Secular vocal music; sacred vocal music I:
       *Laudate pueri, Quatre versets, Sept versets (1704), Sept
       versets (1705), Motet de Ste. Suzanne*

v. 12 *Musique vocale II,* ed. P. Brunold
       Contents: *Elévations, motets divers, Leçons de ténèbres*

2.   Maurice Cauchie, *Thematic catalog of the works of François Couperin.*
     Monaco, Lyrebird Press, 1949

29
DE PRES, JOSQUIN, *ca.* 1450–1521

1. Complete works   2. List of works

1.   *Werken,* uitgegeven door A. Smijers. Vereeniging vor Nederlandse
     Musiekgeschiedenis. Amsterdam, Alsbach, 1925–
     This set is still in progress, under the editorship of M. Antonowycz
     and W. Elders. Many of the pre-war issues have been reprinted
     since the 1950's, some under the title *Opera omnia.* The set has an
     abundance of numbering systems. Starting with the smallest division,
     each composition is numbered individually within the appropriate

*** M.482. 64*

In each case give Class of work (Mass, Motet, etc), Deel & Bundel no. (Mass.no.= Bundel).

one of four categories: Masses, Mass sections, motets, and secular works. A second numbering system is by *Aflevering,* which numbers the entire set consecutively in the order in which each *Aflevering* was published. A third system is the numbering according to *Bundel,* which numbers each *Aflevering* within one of the four categories named above. Finally there is a *Deel* (volume) numbering which becomes apparent only after a sufficient number of *Bundel* in each category have been issued. The music pagination for each *Deel* is continuous, but the critical notes at the beginning of each *Bundel* are paged separately and individually for each *Bundel*. The set is listed below in alphabetical order for each of the four categories. All four numbering systems are shown, except in the Mass category, in which the Mass no. and the *Bundel* no. are identical. Only works actually published are included. Titles in parentheses are those listed as doubtful or spurious works in item 2 below.

Give Mass no. & Deel no.

Title	no. voices	Afl. no.	Mass no.	Deel v.no. in Mass series
Ad fugam	4	28	14	3
Allez regretz	4	43	20	4
Ave maris stella	4	15	6	2
Da pacem	4–6	34	19	4
Di dadi	4–5	29	15	3
D'ung aultre amer	4	23	11	2
Faisant regretz	4	27	13	3
Fortuna desperata	4	13	4	1
Gaudeamus	4	12	3	1
Hercules dux Ferrariae	4–6	17	7	2
La sol fa re mi	4	2	2	1
L'ami Baudichon	4	20	9	2
L'homme armé sexti toni	4–6	14	5	1
L'homme armé super voces musicales	4	—	1	1
Malheur me bat	4	19	8	2
Mater patris	4	26	12	3
Pange lingua	4	33	18	4
Sine nomine	4	32	17	3
Una musque de Buscaya	4	22	10	2

MASS SECTIONS *Bd. in Deel 4 Missen 18-20* 19 20

Title	no. voices	item no.	Afl. no.	Bdl. no.	V. no. in series
Gloria De beata Virgine	4	1	44	1	1 4
Credo	4	4	50	2	1 4
(Credo)	4	5	50	2	1 4
Credo [Ciaschun me crie]	4	6	50	2	1 4
Credo De tous biens	4	2	44	1	1 4
(Credo Vilayge)	4	3	44	1	1 4
Sanctus De passione	4	7	50	2	1 4

MOTETS

Bdl. *Deel*

Title	no. voices	item no.	Afl. no.	Bdl. no.	V. no. in series
Absolve quaesumus/ Requiem	6	82	49	23	5
Alma redemptoris/Ave regina	4	21	7	4	1
Alma redemptoris mater	4	38	21	8	2
Ave Christe immolate	4	76	46	20	5
Ave Maria . . . virgo serena	4	1	2	1	1
Ave Maria . . . virgo serena	6	1a	2	1	1
Ave Maria . . . benedicta	4	2	2	1	1
(Ave maris stella)	4	94	52	25	5
Ave noblissima creatura	6	34	18	7	2
Ave regina (Alma redemptoris)	4	21	7	4	1
Ave verum corpus	2–3	12	4	2	1
Ave verum corpus	5	80	45	22	5
(Beata quorum remissae)	5	62	40	16	4
Benedicite omnia opera	4	53	37	13	3
Benedicta es caelorum regina	6	46	35	11	3
Caeli ennarrunt gloria Dei	4	61	39	15	3
Cantate Domino	5	72	45	19	5
Christum ducem	4	4	2	1	1
Christus mortuus est	6	87	51	24	5
De profundis clamavi	4	47	35	11	3
(De profundis clamavi)	4	91	52	25	5
De profundis clamavi	5	90	51	24	5

Give Deel 4 Bundel nos.

Title	no. voices	item no.	Afl. no.	Bdl. no.	v. no. in series
(Deus in nomine tuo)	4	44	25	10	2
(Deus pacis reduxit)	4	57	38	14	3
Domine Dominus noster	5	89	51	24	5
Domine exaudi	4	92	52	25	5
Domine ne in furore	4	39	2	8	2
Domine ne in furore	4	59	39	15	3
Domine ne projicias me	4	64	40	16	4
Domine non secundum peccata	2–4	13	4	2	1
Dominus regnavit	4	65	41	17	4
Ecce Maria genuit	4	9	2	1	1
Ecce tu pulchra es	4	30	16	6	2
Factus est autem	4	16	6	3	1
Gaude virgo	4	23	7	4	1
Germinavit radix Jesse	4	8	2	1	1
Homo quidam	5	28	9	5	1
Huc me sydereo	6	32	16	6	2
Illibata Dei virgo nutrix	5	27	9	5	1
In Domine confido	4	73	45	19	5
In exitu Israel	4	51	36	12	3
In illo tempore assumpsit	4	79	48	22	5
In illo tempore stetit	6	55	38	14	3
In principio erat verbum	4	56	38	14	3
Inter natos mulierum	6	84	49	23	5
Inviolata, integra	5	42	25	10	2
Jubilate Deo omnis terra	4	66	41	17	4
Laudate pueri	4	68	42	18	4
Lectio actuum apostolorum	4	41	24	9	2
Levavi oculos meos	4	70	42	18	4
Liber generationis	4	15	6	3	1
Magnificat quarti toni	4	78	47	21	5
Magnificat tertii toni	4	77	47	21	5

Dee L

Title	no. voices	item no.	Afl. no.	Bdl. no.	v. no. in series
Magnus es tu	4	19	6	3	1
Memor esto	4	31	16	6	2
Miribilia testimonia tua	4	69	42	18	4
Miserere mei, Deus	5	37	21	5	2
Misericordias Domini	4	43	25	10	2
Missus est Gabriel angelus	4	17	6	3	1
Missus est Gabriel angelus	5	40	24	9	2
Mittit ad virginum	4	3	2	1	1
Nesciens mater virgo	5	71	45	19	5
(Nunc dimittis)	4	93	52	25	5
O admirabile commercium	4	5	2	1	1
(O bone et dulcis Domine)	4	18	6	3	1
O bone et dulcissime Jesu	4	96	52	25	5
O Domine Jesu Christe	4	10	4	2	1
O virgo prudentissima	6	45	35	11	3
O virgo virginum	6	83	49	23	5
Paratum cor meum	4	67	41	17	4
Pater noster	6	50	36	12	3
Planxit autem David	4	20	6	3	1
Praeter rerum serium	6	33	18	7	2
Quando natus est	4	6	2	1	1
Qui habitat in adjutorio altissimi	4	32	37	13	3
Qui velatus facie fuisti	4	11	4	2	1
(Qui regis Israel intende)	5	63	40	16	4
Requiem	5	29	9	5	1
Responde mihi	4	75	46	20	5
Responsum acceperat Simeon	6	85	49	23	5
Rubum quem viderat Moyses	4	7	2	1	1
Salve regina	5	48	35	11	3
Salve regina	4	95	52	25	5
(Sancti Dei omnes)	4	74	46	20	5

Deel *(handwritten)*

Title.	no. voices	item no.	Afl. no.	Bdl. no.	v. no. in series
Sic Deus dilexit mundum	6	86	51	24	5
Stabat mater	5	36	21	8	2
Stetit autem Salomon	4	58	39	15	3
(Tribulatio et angustia)	4	54	37	13	3
Tu solus qui facis miribilia	4	14	4	2	1
Usquequo Domine	4	60	39	15	3
Ut Phebi radiis	4	22	7	4	1
Veni sancte spiritus	6	49	36	12	3
Verbum caro factum est	5	88	51	24	5
Victimae paschali laudes	4	26	9	5	1
Victimae paschali laudes	6	81	48	22	5
Virgo prudentissima	4	25	9	5	1
Virgo salutiferi	5	35	18	7	2
Vultum tuum deprecabuntur	4	24	7	4	1

SECULAR WORKS — *Give Deel & Bundel no.* *(handwritten)*

Title.	no. voices	item no.	Afl. no.	Bdl. no.	v. no. in series
A l'eure que ie vous p.x.	4	41	53	4	2
Adieu mes amours	4	35	53	4	2
(Allegez moy)	6	14	5	2	1
Baisiez moy	4	20a	5	2	1
(Baisiez moy)	6	20	5	2	1
Bergerette Savoyenne	4	36	53	4	2
Cela sans plus	3	44	53	4	2
(Cent mille regretz)	5	26	8	3	1
Cueur langoreulx	5	1	3	1	1
Cueurs desolez	5	32	8	3	1
(Cueurs desolez)	5	28	8	3	1
De tous biens playne (arr. from H. van Gizeghem; also Hayne version)	4	49b	53	4	2
Deploration de J. Okeghem (Nymphes des bois)	5	22	5	2	1
Doleur me bat	5	18	5	2	1

Deel

Title	no. voices	item no.	Afl. no.	Bdl. no.	v. no. in series
Du mien amant	5	23	5	2	I
En non saichant	5	9	3	I	I
Faulte d'argent	5	15	5	2	I
(Fortuna desperata, arr. from Busnois; also Busnois version)	3	48b	53	4	2
Fortune destrange plummage/Pauper sum ego	3	46	53	4	I
Instrumental: Ile fantazies	3	43	53	4	2
Incessament livré suis	5	6	3	I	I
(Incessament mon povre cueur)	5	27	8	3	I
J'ay bien cause	6	33	8	3	I
Je me complains	5	11	3	I	I
Je ne me puis tenir	5	31	8	3	I
Je sey bien dire	4	38	53	4	2
La bernardina	3	42	53	4	2
La plus de plus	3	45	53	4	I
L'amye a tous	5	25	3	I	I
Ma bouche rit	6	19	5	2	I
Mi larés vous	5	34	8	3	I
Mille regretz	4	24	8	3	I
N'esse pas ung grant desplasir	5	8	3	I	I
Nimphes, nappés	6	8	3	I	I
Nymphes des bois (Deploration)	5	22	5	2	I
Parfons regretz	5	3	3	I	I
Petite camusette	6	17	5	2	I
Plaine de dueil	5	4	3	I	I
Plus n'estes ma maitresse	4	30	8	3	I
Plus nulz regretz	4	29	8	3	I
Plusieurs regretz	5	7	3	I	I
Pour souhaitter	6	10	3	I	I

Deel

Title	no. voices	item no.	Afl. no.	Bdl. no.	v. no. in series
Que vous madame/In pace	3	47	53	4	I
Recordans de my segnora	4	39	53	4	I
Regretz sans fin	6	5	3	I	I
Se conge prens	6	12	3	I	I
Tenez moys en voz bras	6	13	5	2	I
Una musque de Buscaya	4	37	53	4	I
(Vous l'aurez)	6	16	5	2	I
(Vous ne l'aurez pas)	6	2	3	I	I

**ML410
D367 07

2.   A complete list of works is found in Helmuth Osthoff, *Josquin Desprez.*
Tutzing, Hans Schneider, 1962–65, v. 2, pp. 203–301.

**M.404
.77

30

DITTERS VON DITTERSDORF, KARL, 1739–1799

Ausgewählte Orchesterwerke. Zur Centenarfier des Todestages Dittersdorf
1799, 31. Oktober, 1899 herausgegeben von Josef Liebeskind. Leipzig,
Gebrüder Reineke, 1899–1904

Series 1   [Program symphonies on Ovid's *Metamorphoses*]

    v.   1   *Die vier Weltalter (Les quatre âges du monde)*

    v.   2   *Der Sturz Phaëtons (La chute de Phaeton)*

    v.   3   *Verwandlung Actaeons in einen Hirsch (Actéon changé en cerf)*

    v.   4   *Die Rettung der Andromede durch Perseus (Andromède sauvée par Persée)*

    v.   5   *Verwandlung der lycischen Bauern in Frösche (Les paysans changés en grenouilles)*

    v.   6   *Die Versteinerung des Phineus und seiner Freunde (Phinée avec ses amis changés en rochers)*

Series 2.   [Other orchestral works]

    v.   7   *Sinfonie in F*

v. 8   *Sinfonie in E^b*

v. 9   *Overture zu dem Oratorium "Esther"; Musique pour
un petit ballet en forme d'une contredanse*

v. 10 *Divertimento: "Il combattimento dell'umane passione"*

v. 11 *Carnaval, ou La redoute*

31
DUFAY, GUILLAUME, *ca.* 1400–1474

Opera omnia, ed. Heinrich Besseler. *Corpus mensurabilis musicae* **(A 28),**
ser. I
> This series began under the editorship of Guillaume de Van, who edited
> v. 1 (motets), v. 2 part 1 *(Missa sine nomine),* and v. 2 part 2 *(Missa
> Sancti Jacobi).* Later a re-edition of these v. (with the separate parts of
> v. 2 combined with other masses in a single volume, as listed below)
> by Besseler was published.

v. 1   *Motets, complete*

v. 2   *Masses*
          Contents: *Missa sine nomine, Missa Sancti Jacobi, Missa
          Sancti Antonii Viennensis, Missa Caput, Alleluia Veni sancti
          spiritus, Missa La mort de Saint Gothard*

v. 3   *Masses*
          Contents: *Missa Se le face ay pale, Missa L'homme armé,
          Missa Ecce ancilla Domini, Missa Ave regina*

v. 4   *The remaining Mass music*

v. 5   *Mass sections*

v. 6   *Complete secular works*

32
DVORAK, ANTON, 1841–1904

1. Complete works   2. Thematic catalog

1. *Souborne vydani del Antonina Dvoraka.* Spolecnost Antonina Dvoraka.
    Praha, Actia, 1956–
    Editorial board: Otakar Šourek, František Bartoš, Jan Hanus, Jiri
    Berkovec, Jarmil Burghauser, Antonin Čubr, Ladislav Láska, Antonin
    Pokorný, Karel Šolc. Title pages and commentary in Czechoslovakian,

German, English and French. The entire proposed plan is given below;
v. not yet published are in parentheses.

Series 1.   *Theatrical works*

    (v. 1)   *Alfred*

    (v. 2)   *King and charcoal burner* (1871 version)

    (v. 3)   ——— (1874, 1887 versions)

    (v. 4)   *The stubborn lovers*

    (v. 5)   *Vanda*

    (v. 6)   *The cunning peasant*

    (v. 7)   *Dimitri* (1883 version)

    (v. 8)   ——— (1894 version)

    (v. 9)   *Incidental music to Samberk's "Josef Kajetan Tyl"*

    v. 10   *The Jacobin, op.84,* ed. F. Bartoš
        In 2 parts: 1, acts 1–2; 2, act 3, notes.

    (v. 11)   *Kate and the Devil*

    v. 12   *Rusalka, op.114,* ed. J. Burghauser

    (v. 13)   *Armida*

Series 2.   *Oratorios, cantatas, Mass*

    v. 1   *Stabat mater, op.58,* ed. A Čubr

    (v. 2)   *The spectre's bride*

    v. 3   *St. Ludmilla, op.71,* ed. Antonin Sychra
        In 3 parts: 1, nos. 1–17; 2–3 (bound together),
        nos. 18–45

    v. 4   *Requiem, op.89,* ed. Čubr, Bartoš, Burghauser

    (v. 5)   *Hymns, Evening songs, Ode op.115*

    (v. 6)   *Psalm 149, Te Deum, Biblical songs*

    (v. 7)   *Mass in D* (1st version with organ)

    (v. 8)   *Mass in D* (2nd version with orchestra)

Series 3.   *Orchestral works*

v. 1   *Symphony no. 1 in c (The bells of Zlonice)*, ed. Bartoš

v. 2   *Symphony no. 2 in B^b, op.4*, ed. Bartoš

v. 3   *Symphony no. 3 in E^b, op.10*, ed. Bartoš

v. 4   *Symphony no. 4 in d, op.13 (1874)*, ed. Bartoš

v. 5   *Symphony no. 5* [old no. 3] *in F, op.76*, ed. Bartoš

v. 6   *Symphony no. 6* [old no. 1] *in D, op.60*, ed. Bartoš

v. 7   *Symphony no. 7* [old no. 2] *in d, op.70*, ed. Bartoš

v. 8   *Symphony no. 8* [old no. 4] *in G, op.88*, ed. Bartoš

v. 9   *Symphony no. 9* [old no. 5, *New World*] *in e, op. 95*, ed. Šourek

v. 10   *Piano concerto in g, op.33*, ed. Berkovec, Šolc

v. 11   *Violin concerto in a, op.53*, ed. Burghauser

v. 12   *Cello concerto in b, op.104*, ed. Bartoš

v. 13   *Four overtures*, ed. Pokorný, Šolc, Bartoš, Čubr
         Contents: *Hussite overture, In nature's realm, Carnival, Othello*

v. 14   *Three symphonic poems*, ed. Čubr, Pokorný, Šolc
         Contents: *The water goblin, The noon witch, The golden spinning wheel*

v. 15   *Two symphonic poems*, ed. Pokorný, Šolc
         Contents: *The wild dove, A hero's song*

v. 16   *Serenades, op.22 in E, op.44 in d*, ed. Šourek, Bartoš

v. 17   *Two suites*, ed. Bercovec, Šolc
         Contents: *Bohemian suite, Suite in A*

v. 18   *Rhapsodies, op.14, op.45*, ed. Pokorný, Šolc

v. 19   *Slavonic dances, op.46*, ed. Burghauser

v. 20   *Slavonic dances, op.72*, ed. Burghauser

(v. 21) *Legends*

v. 22   *Symphonic variations op.78, Scherzo capriccioso, op.66,* ed. Bartoš, Berkovec, Šolc

(v. 23)   *Romance op.11, Mazurek op.49* for violin and and orchestra; *Silent woods, Rondo* for cello and orchestra

(v. 24)   *Entr'acts from the year 1867, Notturno op. 40, Festival march op.54, Vanda overture, Polonaise in E^b, Prague waltzes, Polka in E^b*

Series 4   *Chamber music*

(v. 1)   Works for violin and piano: *Romance op.11, Ballade op.15, Mazurek op.49, Notturno op.49, Sonata op.57, Romantic pieces op.75, Sonatina op.100*

(v. 2)   *Cello concerto* with piano accompaniment

(v. 3)   Works for cello and piano: *Polonaise in A, Rondo op.94, Slavonic dance op.46:8, Silent woods op.68:5*

(v. 4)   Trios: *Terzetto op.74, Miniatures op.75a, Gavotte*

(v. 5)   String quartets I: *op.2, op.9, op.12, and 3 without opus no.*

(v. 6)   String quartets II: *op.16, op.80, op.34, op.51. 2 waltzes from op.54, movement in F*

(v. 7)   String quartets III: *op.61, Cypresses, op.96 (American), op.105, op.106*

(v. 8)   String quintets and sextet: *quintets op.1, op.77, op.97; sextet op.48*

v. 9   Piano trios: *op.21, op.26, op.65, op.90 (Dumky),* ed. Pokorný, Šolc, Bartoš, Čubr

v. 10   Piano quartets: *op.23, op.87, Bagatelles op.47,* ed. Pokorný, Šolc, Bartoš

v. 11   Piano quartets: *op.5, op.81,* ed. Burghauser, Šolc, Čubr

Series 5   *Piano works*

(v. 1)   Piano solo I: *Polka in E^b, Minuets op.28, Scottish* *dances op.41, Dumka op.35, Tema con variazioni op.36, Silhouettes op.8, 2 furiants op.42*

(v. 2)   Piano solo II: *op.52, Waltzes op.54, Eclogues op.52, Mazurka op.56, Album leaves*

(v. 3)   Piano solo III: *Impromptu, Humoresque in F ♯, Dumka and furiant op.12, 2 little pearls, Poetic tone pictures op.85*

v. 4   Piano solo IV: *Suite in a, Humoresques op.101, Lullaby and capriccio,* ed. Šolc, Šourek

· v. 5   Piano 4 hands: *Slavonic dances op.46, 72,* ed. Burghauser

v. 6   Piano 4 hands: *Legends op.59, From the Bohemian forest op.68,* ed. Bartoš, Pokorný, Šolc, Čubr

Series 6   *Vocal music*

(v. 1)   Solo songs I: *Songs to words by E. Krásnohorská, The orphan op.5, 4 Serbian songs op.6, 6 songs from Dvŭr Králové Ms op.7, Evening songs op.3, 9, 11, Ave Maria, Ave maris stella, Hymnus ad laudes, 3 modern Greek songs op.50, Gypsy songs op.55*

(v. 2)   Solo songs II: *2 songs to folk poems, In folk style op.73, 4 songs op.82, Love songs op.83, Biblical songs op.99, Lullaby, Song from "The blacksmith of Lešetín"*

v. 3   Duets: *Moravian duets op.20, 32, 38, O sanctissima,* ed. Čubr

(v. 4)   Choruses: *In nature's realm, op.63 &*

2.   Jarmil Burghauser. *Antonín Dvořák. Thematic catalogue, bibliography, survey of his life and work.* Praha, 1960
   In Czechoslovakian, English, German

33
FAYRFAX, ROBERT, *ca.* **1464–1521**

Collected works, ed. Edwin B. Warren. *Corpus mensurabilis musicae* **(A 28),** ser. 17

⁄ V. 1   *Masses*

√v. 2   *Magnificat, motets, Mass sections, lute fragments*

√v. 3   *Secular works*

34
FESTA, CONSTANZO, *ca.* 1490–1545

Opera omnia, ed. Alexander Main. *Corpus mensurabilis musicae* (**A 28**), ser. 25. About 10 v. proposed

v. 1   *All the Mass music*

v. 2   *All the Magnificats*

35
FREDERICK II, KING OF PRUSSIA, 1712–1786

Friedrich des Grossen Musikalische Werke, ed. Philipp Spitta. Leipzig, Breitkopf & Härtel, 1889

There is a recent reprint of this set by Da Capo Press. In it the v. are numbered differently:

reprint v. 1 = original v. 1–2 combined
reprint v. 2 = original v. 3
reprint v. 3 = solo flute parts for all v.

v. 1   *Sonaten für Flöte und Klavier nr. 1–12*

v. 2   ———, nr. 13–25

v. 3   *Konzerte für Flöte, Streichorchester und Generalbass. Abteilung 1: Partitur, Abteilung 2: Bearbeitung für Flöte und Klavier*

36
FRESCOBALDI, GIROLAMO, 1583–1644

1–2. Complete works for keyboard

1.   *Orgel- und Klavierwerke.* Gesamtausgabe nach dem Urtext herausgegeben von Pierre Pidoux. Kassel, Bärenreiter, 1949–

v. 1   *23 Fantasien und Canzoni alla Francese*

v. 2   *12 Capricci, 10 Ricercari und 8 Canzoni*

v. 3   *12 Toccaten, Partitien sopra l'aria delle romanesca*

v. 4   *11 Toccaten, 6 Canzonen, 3 Hymnen, 3 Magnificat, Madrigal,
Aria, 5 Gagliarden, 6 Correnten*

v. 5   *Fiori musicali*

2.   *Opere per organo e cembalo,* ed. Fernando Germani. Roma, Edizioni
De Santis, 1951–

v. 1   *Toccate (dal I libro) con l'aggiunta dell'Arte Organica di Constanzo Antegnati [1549–1624] e altri scritti dell' epocha*

v. 2   *Toccate (dal II libro) con l'aggiunta della Toccata per organo
(dal Codice Chigiano esistente nella Biblioteca Vaticana)*

v. 3   *Fiori musicali di diverse composizioni: Toccate, Kyrie, Canzoni,*
(8051. 1554)   *Capricci e Ricercari, in partitura ... Opera XII. Revisione
conforme all' edizione originale del 1635 ...*

37
FUX, JOHANN JOSEPH, 1660–1741

1. Complete works   2, 3. Lists of compositions
N. B. Fux's compositions may be cited by K. nos., from item 2 below;
or by E. numbers, from the article on Fux in Eitner's *Quellenlexikon.*

13
F97   1.   *Sämtliche Werke,* herausgegeben von der Johann-Joseph-Fux Gesellschaft. Graz, 1959–

Series 1.   Masses and Requiem

v. 1   *Masses- De carnival, Sexti toni irregularis*

Series 2.   Litanies, vespers, compline music, Te Deum

v. 1   *Te Deum, E.37,* ed. Istován Kecskeméti

Series 3.   Smaller sacred works

v. 1   *Motetten und Antiphonen K.162, 167, 173, 176, 185–7,
205–8, E.80,* ed. H. Federhofer, Renate Federhofer-
Königs

Series 4.   Oratorios

v. 1   *La fede sacrilega nella morte del precursor S. Giovanni*

Battista, K.291 (1741), ed. Hugo Zelzer, Leopold Ergens

Series 5.   Operas

    v. 1   Julo Ascanio, Re d'Alba, K.304, ed. H. Federhofer, L. Ergens

    v. 2   Pulcheria, K.303, ed. H. Federhofer, Wolfgang Suppan, L. Ergens

Series 6.   Instrumental music

    v. 1   Werke für Tasteninstrumente, ed. Friedrich Wilhelm Riedel

Series 7.   Theoretical and pedagogical works

    v. 1   Gradus ad Parnassum (facsimile), ed. Alfred Mann

2. Ludwig, Ritter von Köchel, *Johann Joseph Fux, Hofcompositor und Hofkapellmeister der Kaiser Leopold I., . . . Joseph I. und Karl VI. von 1698–1740.* Wien, 1872
    Includes thematic catalog

3. Andreas Liess, *Johann Joseph Fux, ein Steirischer Meister des Barock. Nebst einem Verzeichnis neuer Werkfunde.* Wien, 1948

38
GABRIELI, GIOVANNI, 1557–1612

Opera omnia, ed. Denis Arnold. *Corpus mensurabilis musicae* (**A 28**), ser. 12. About 10 v. proposed

    v. 1   Concerti (1587); Sacrae symphoniae (1597), first part

    v. 2   Sacrae symphoniae (1597), completion

    v. 3   Sacrae symphoniae (1615), first part

    v. 4   Sacrae symphoniae (1615), second part

39
GAFURIO, FRANCHINO, 1451–1522

Opera omnia, ed. Ludwig Finscher. *Corpus mensurabilis musicae* (**A 28**), ser. 10

✓ v. 1   *Masses: De carnival, Sexti toni irregularis*

✓ v. 2   *Masses: Omnipotens genitor, Sanctae Catherinae, De tous biens pleine, O clara luce, Sine nomine, Brevis primi toni*

See also **A 10,** v. 1–5

40
GESUALDO, CARLO, PRINCE OF VENOSA, 1560–1615

1. Complete works   2. Index of madrigals

1. *Sämtliche Werke,* ed. Wilhelm Weismann, Glenn E. Watkins. Hamburg, Ugrino.
   The secular works are ed. by Weismann, sacred by Watkins.

v. 1   *Sämtliche Madrigale für fünf Stimmen . . . 1613* [Book 1]

v. 2   ———, Book 2

v. 3   ———, Book 3

v. 4   ———, Book 4

v. 5   ———, Book 5

v. 6   ———, Book 6

v. 7   *Responsoria et alia ad officium hebdomadae sanctae spectantia (1611)*

v. 8   *Sacrae cantiones* [5 voices]

v. 9   ——— [6–7 voice]
            Includes Stravinsky completions of missing parts

v. 10   *Instrumental Werke, Psalmen, Canzonetten*

2.   Alphabetical index of madrigals

Title	Book/v.
A voi, mentre il mio cor	4
Ahi, dispietata e cruda	3
Ahi, disperata vita	3
Ahi, già mi discoloro	4
Ahi, troppo saggia nell'errar	1

Title	Book/v.
Al l'apparir di quelle luci ardenti	2
Al mio gioir il ciel si fa sereno	6
Alme d'amor rubelle	6
Amor, pace non chero	1
Ancide sol la morte	6
Ancidetemi pur, grievi martiri	3
Ancor che per amarti	6
Arde il mio cor	4
Ardita Zanzaretta	6
Ardo per te, mio bene	6
Asciugate i begli occhi	5
Baci soavi e cari	1
Bella Angioletta	1
Beltà, poiche t'assenti	6
Candida man	2
Candido e verde fiore	6
Caro, amoroso neo	2
Che fai meco, mio cor	4
Che sentir dove il petto mio	2
Chiaro risplender suole	6
Come esser può ch'io viva	1
Cor mio, deh, non piangete	4
Correte, amanti, a prova	5
Crudelissima doglia	3
Dalle odorate spoglie	2
Danzan le Ninfe oneste	1
Deh, come invan sospiro	6
Deh, coprite il bel seno	5
Deh, se già fu crudele	3
Del bel de'bei, vostri occhi	3
Dolce spirto d'amore	3
Dolcissima mia vita	5
Dolcissimo sospiro	3
Donna, se m'ancidete	3
Dunque non m'offendete	4
E quella arpa felice	2
Ecco, morirò dunque	4
Ed ardo e vivo	3

Title	Book/v.
Felice primavera	I
Felicissimo sonno	5
Frenò Tirsi il desio	I
Gelo ha madonna il seno	I
Gia piansi nel dolore	6
Gioite voi col canto	5
Hai rotto e sciolte e spento	2
In più leggiadro velo	2
Invan dunque o crudele	4
"Io parto" e non più dissi	6
Io pur respiro in così gran dolore	6
Io tacerò ma nel silenzio mio	4
Itene, o miei sospiri	5
Languisce al fin	5
Languisco e moro	3
Luci serene e chiare	4
Ma se avverrà ch'io moia	2
Ma se tale hà costei	2
Ma tu, cagion	5
Madonna, io ben vorrei	I
Mentre gira costei	4
Mentre madonna il lasso fianco posa	I
Mentre, mia stella, miri	I
Meraviglia d'amore	3
Mercè grido piangendo	5
Mille volte il dì moro	6
Moro, e mentre sospiro	4
Moro, lasso, al mio duolo	6
Moro o non moro	3
Nè tien face o saetta	2
Non è, questa la mano	2
Non mai non cangerò	2
Non mirar, non mirare	I
Non mi toglia il ben mio	2
Non t'amo, o voce ingrata	3
O come è gran martire	2
O dolce mio martire	I

Title	Book/v.
O dolce mio tesoro	6
O dolorosa gioia	5
O mal nati messaggi	3
O mio soave ardore	2
O sempre crudo amore	4
O tenebroso giorno	5
O voi, troppo felici	5
Occhi del mio cor vita	5
Or, che in gioia	4
Poichè l'avida sete	5
Qual fora, donna	5
Quando di lui la sospirata vita	4
Quando ridente e bella	6
Quanto ha di dolce amore	I
Quel "no" crudel che la mia speme anchise	6
Questa crudele e pia	4
Questi leggiadri odorosetti fiori	I
Resta di darmi noia	6
Se chiudete nel core	4
Se così dolce è il duolo	2
Se da sì nobil mano	I
Se la mia morte brami	6
Se per lieve ferita	2
Se piange, la donna del mio core oimè	3
Se tu fuggi, io non resto	5
Se vi duol il mio duolo	5
Se vi miro pietoso	3
Sento che nel partire	2
Sì gioioso mi fanno i dolor miei	I
S'io non miro non moro	5
Il sol, qual or più splende	4
Son sì belle le rose	I
Sospirava il mio core	3
Sparge la morte al mio Signor nel viso	4
Tall'or sano desio	4
T'amo, mia vita	5

Title	Book/v.
Tirsi morir volea	I
Tu m'uccidi, o crudele	5
Tu piangi, o Filli mia	6
Tu segui, o bella Clori	6
Veggio, sì, dal mio sole	3
Vogli, mia luce	4
Voi volete ch'io mora	3
Volan quasi farfalle	6

41

GHISELIN, JOHANNES, *called* **VERBONNET,** *fl.* **1491–1535**

Opera omnia, ed. Clytus Gottwald. *Corpus mensurabilis musicae* **(A 28),** ser. 23. 4 v. proposed

✓ V. 1   *All the motets*

✓ V. 2   *Masses: La belle se siet, De les armes, Marayge*

✓ V. 3   *Masses: Gratieuse, Je nay dueul, Ghy syt die wertste boven al*

✓ v. 4

42

GIACOBBI, GIROLAMO, 1567–1629

Opera omnia. ed. V. Gibelli, J. P. Roba. *(Antiquae musicae italicae: monumenta bononiensia 5)* See **A 5**

V. 1   *Motecta multiplici vocum numero concinenda*
             1. *Motecta cum quinque vocibus*

43

GLINKA, MIKHAIL IVANOVICH, 1804–1857

Polnoe sopranie sochinenii. [Moscow, State Music Publishers, 1955–] This set is similar in format and organization to the complete works of Chaikovskii **(B 22),** q.v., except that fewer piano arrangements of orchestral works are included.

Title/medium	v.no.
Andante cantabile and rondo (orch.)	1
Chorus works with orchestra	8
Divertimento brilliante on Bellini's "La Sonambula"	
(string sextet)	4
——— arr. 2 piano	5
Ivan Sussanin (= A life for the Tsar, opera)	
full score	12
vocal score	13
Kamarinskaya (orch.)	2
A life for the Tsar *see* Ivan Sussanin	
Moldavanka and the Gypsy (aria and chorus)	7
Night in Madrid (= Recuerdas de Castilla, orch.)	2
Overture in D	1
Overture in g	1
Piano solo works	6
Piano 4 hands, 2 piano works	5
Polonaise in E (orch.)	2
Prince Kholmsky, incidental music	7
Quartets, string	3
Recuerdos de Castilla (= Night in Madrid, orch.)	2
Romances (songs)	10
Russlan and Ludmilla (opera), full score	14
Septet (oboe, basoon, horn, 2 violins, cello, bass)	3
Serenade on motives from Donizetti's Anna Bolena	
(piano, harp, bassoon, horn, viola, cello, bass)	4 suppl.
Sestetto originale in E^b (piano, strings)	4
Sonata (viola and piano)	4
Songs with orchestra	8
Songs with piano	10
Symphony on Russian themes	1
Trio pathétique (piano, clarinet, bassoon)	4
Valse-fantaisie (orch.)	2
Vocal ensemble with piano	9
Vocal works with orchestra	8
Vocalises	11
Waltz-fantasy (orchestra)	2

44
GLUCK, CHRISTOPH WILLIBALD, RITTER VON, 1714–1787

1. Complete works   2. Thematic catalog   3. Bibliography   4. Yearbook

1. *Sämtliche Werke.* Herausgegeben im Auftrage des Instituts für Musikforschung, Berlin mit Unterstützung der Stadt Hannover. Begründet von Rudolf Gerber. Kassel, Bärenreiter, 1951–

Abt. 1   *Musikdramen*

       v. 1   *Orfeo ed Euridice (Wiener Fassung von 1762),* ed. H. Abert, L. Finscher
            cf. v. 6 below

       v. 4   *Paride ed Elena,* ed. Rudolf Gerber

       v. 6   *Orphée et Euridice (Pariser Fassung von 1774),* ed. L. Finscher
            cf. v. 1 above

       v. 7   *Alceste (Pariser Fassung von 1776),* ed. R. Gerber

       v. 10   *Echo et Narcisse,* ed. R. Gerber

       v. 11   *Iphigenie auf Tauris (Deutsche Fassung, 1781, von Alxinger und Gluck),* ed. Gerhard Croll

Abt. 2   *Tanzdramen*

       v. 1   *Don Juan/Semiramis,* ed. Richard Engländer

Abt. 3   *Italienische Opere serie und Opernserenaden*

       v. 8   *Il Re Pastore,* ed. B. Somfai

       v. 17   *La Cinesi,* ed. G. Croll

       v. 18   *La Danza,* ed. G. Croll

Abt. 4   *Französische komische Opern*

       v. 1   *L'Ile de Merlin ou le monde renversé,* ed. Günter Hausswald

       v. 5   *L'Ivrogne corrigé (1760),* ed. Franz Rühlmann

       v. 7   *La rencontre imprévue,* ed. Herald Heckmann

Abt. 5   *Instrumental- und Vokalmusik*

v. 1   *Triosonaten für 2 Violinen und Basso continuo,* ed. Friedrich-Heinrich Neumann

2. Alfred Wotquenne, *Thematisches Verzeichnis der Werke von Chr. W. v. Gluck (1774–1785).* Leipzig, Breitkopf & Härtel, 1904

3. Cecil Hopkinson, *A Bibliography of the works of C. W. von Gluck 1714–1787.* London, 1959

− 4. *Gluck-Jahrbuch,* ed. Hermann Abert. Leipzig, Breitkopf & Härtel, 1915–1918. 4 v. published

45
GOMBERT, NICHOLAS, *ca.* **1490**–*after* **1556**

Opera omnia, ed. Joseph Schmidt-Görg. *Corpus mensurabilis musicae* **(A 28),** ser. 6. About 12 v. proposed

✓ v. 1   *Masses: Da pacem, Sancta Maria, Beati omnes, Je suis deshé-ritée*

✓ v. 2   *Masses: Media vita, Sur tous regretz, Filomena, Forseulement*

✓v. 3   *Masses: Quam pulchra es, Tempore paschali; Credo (8 v.)*

✓ v. 4   *Magnificats*

✓v. 5   *Motets*

✓v. 6   *Motets*

✓ v. 7   *Motets*

46
GOUDIMEL, CLAUDE, *ca.* **1505–1572**

Oeuvres complètes, publiées par Henri Gagneben, Rudolf Häusler et Eleanor Lawry sous la direction de Luther A. Dittmer et Pierre Pidoux. *Institute of Medieval Music, Brooklyn, N.Y. Collected works* **(A 52),** III

✓ v. 1   *Premier livre des psaumes en forme de motets (1557),* ed. H. Gagnebin

✓ v. 2   *Second livre des psaumes en forme de motets (1559),* ed. E. Lawry

v. 9   *Les 150 psaumes (1564, 1565),* ed. P. Pidoux

v. 10   *Les 150 psaumes (1568, 1580),* ed. P. Pidoux

47
GRAUPNER, CHRISTOPH, 1683–1760

Ausgewählte Werke, herausgegeben in Verbindung mit der Stadt Darmstadt von Friedrich Noack. Kassel, Bärenreiter

v. 1   *Sinfonia, D-dur*

v. 2   *Overtüre, E-dur*

v. 3   *Konzert, c-moll, für Fagott oder Violoncello*

v. 4   *Konzert, A-dur, für Violine*

48
GRÉTRY, ANDRÉ ERNEST MODEST, 1741–1813

Collection complète des oeuvres de Grétry. Publiée par le Gouvernement Belge. Leipzig, Breitkopf & Härtel, 1884–1936
Despite the title this set consists only of operas, which are listed alphabetically below.

Title	v.no.
L'amant jaloux (1774)	21
L'ami de la maison (1771)	38
L'amitié à l'épreuve (1770)	42–3
Amphitryon (1788)	33–4
Anacréon chez Polycrate (1797)	7–8
Andromaque (1780)	36–7
Aucassin et Nicolette (1780)	32
La caravane du Caire (1784)	22–3
Céphale et Procris (1775)	3–4
Clarice et Belton (Le prisonnier anglais, 1787)	48–9
Colinette à la cour (1782)	15–16
Le comte d'Albert (1796)	26
Delphis et Mopsa (1803)	41

Denys le tyran (1794)   28
Les deux avares (1770)   20
La double épreuve (Colinette à la cour, 1782)   15–16
Elisca (1799)   39
L'embarras des richesses (1782)   11–12
Emilie (1781)   47
✓L'épreuve villageoise (1784)   6
Les événements imprévus (1777)   10
La fausse Magie (1775)   25
Guillaume Tell (1791)   24
Le Huron (1768)   14
Le jugement de Midas (1778)   17
Lisbeth (1797)   44
Lucile (1769)   2
Le Magnifique (1773)   31
Les mariages Samnites (1786)   35
✓Les méprises par ressemblance (1786)   5
✓ Panurge (1785) *v. 19 only*   19, 23
Pierre le Grand (1790)   40
Le prisonnier anglais (1787)   48–9
Raoul Barbe-bleue (1789)   18
✓ Richard Cœur-de-lion (1784)   1
Le rival confident (1788)   45
✓La rosière de Salency (1774)   30
La rosière républicaine (1793)   29
Le sylvain (1770)   27
Le tableau parlant (1769)   9
✓Théodore et Pauline (L'épreuve villageoise, 1784)   6
Les trois âges de l'opéra (1778)   46
Zémire et Azor (1771)   13

GUERRERO, FRANCISCO, 1527–1599

Opera omnia, see *Monumentos de la musica española* **(A 72),** v. 16, 19

49
GUILLAUME DE MACHAUT, *ca.* 1300–1377

1–2. Complete works

1. *Musikalische Werke,* ed. Friedrich Ludwig. Leipzig, Breitkopf &
    Härtel, 1928, 1954.

The first 3 v. of this set originally appeared as Jg.1:1, 3:1, and 4:2 respectively, of the set *Publikationen älterer Musik* **(A 87)**. In 1954 these v. were reprinted and v. 4, ed. by Heinrich Besseler from notes left by Ludwig was added.

v. 1   *Balladen, rondeaux und virelais*

v. 2   *Einleitung*

v. 3   *Motetten*

v. 4   *Messe und lais*   Lack

M2   2. *The works of Guillaume de Machaut*, ed. Leo Schrade.
ₒ377P6   This set is composed of v. 2–3 of *Polyphonic music of the fourteenth century* **(A 85)**

v. 2   *Lais, complainte, chanson royale, motets nos. 1–16*

v. 3   *Motets nos. 17–24, Mass, double hoquet, ballades, rondeaux, virelais*

3. Opera. Rome, American Institute of Musicology in Rome, (Corpus Mensurabilis musicae 2)
M3
.89

50
HÄNDEL, GEORG FRIEDRICH, 1685–1759

1–2. Complete works   3–4. Yearbooks   5. Bibliography

₃₁₃·¹1. *Werke*. Ausgabe der Deutschen Händelgesellschaft. Leipzig, Breitkopf & Härtel, 1859–1895
        Called "Händel Gesellschaft edition" and "Chrysander edition". This set was reprinted around 1965 by Gregg Press in small size volumes. The reprint does not use the v. nos. of the original set, and furthermore combines some v. together which are not consecutive in the original set. The following alphabetical list takes account of the titles used in the bound reprint set.

Title	v.no.
Aci, Galatea e Polifemo (serenata, 1708, 1732)	53
Acis and Galatea (Pastoral, *ca.* 1720) Bound w/ v.18	3
Admeto (opera, 1709)	73
Agrippina (opera, 1709)	57
Alceste (masque, 1740)	46b
Alcina (opera, 1735)	86

Title	v. no.
Alessandro (opera, 1720)	72
Alexander Balus (oratorio, 1747)	33
Alexander's feast (ode, 1736)	12
L'allegro, il pensieroso ed il moderato (oratorio, 1740).	
Bound with Acis and Galatea in reprint edition	6
Almira (opera, 1704)	55
Anthem, funeral, on death of Queen Caroline (1737). Bound	
with Utrecht Te Deum in reprint edition Bd. w/v. 14	11
Anthems, v. 1 (Chandos anthems, 3 voice, 1716–18)	34
Anthems, v. 2 (Chandos anthems, 4 voice, 1716–18)	35
Anthems, v. 3 (O praise the Lord, Wedding anthems, Dettingen	
anthem, Foundling hospital anthem)	36
Anthems, coronation (1727) Bd. w/v. 11	14
Arianna (opera, 1734)	83
Ariodante (opera, 1734)	85
Arminio (opera, 1736)	89
Atalanta (opera, 1736)	87
Athalia (oratorio, 1733)	5
Belshazzar (oratorio, 1737)	19
Berenice (opera, 1737)	90
Birthday ode for Queen Anne (1713)	46a
Brockes' Passion (1716). Bound with Passion according	
to St. John in reprint edition Bound w/v. 9	15
Cantatas, solo Italian (Reprint title: Italian cantatas for	
solo voice and bass)	50–51
Cantatas, Italian, with instrumental accompaniment	52–3
Chandos anthems (1716–18, 3 voice) and Chandos anthems	
(4 voice) (Reprint title: Anthems v. 1–2)	35
The choice of Hercules (musical interlude, 1750) Bound with	
Ode to St. Cecilia in reprint Bd. w/ v. 3	18
Concerti grossi, op.6 (1739)	30
Concertos, oboe, op.3, and Concerto in C (1736), 4 early	
concertos (Reprint title: Instrumental concerti)	21
Concertos, organ (1738 &) (Reprint title: Organ concerti)	28
Concertos in F and D, Double concertos in E^b and F	
(Reprint title: Orchestral music)	47
Coronation anthems (1727)	14
Deborah (oratorio, 1733)	29

Title	v. no.
Deidamia (opera, 1740)	94
Dettingen Te Deum (1743) *Bd. w/v. 31*	25
Duetti e terzetti (1707/8, 1741/5) (Reprint title: Italian duets and trios)	32 = *32ª*
Esther (oratorio), first version: Haman and Mordecai (*ca.* 1720)	40
Esther (oratorio, 1732)	41
Ezio (opera, 1732)	80
Faramundo (opera, 1732)	91
Fireworks music (1749) (Reprint title: Orchestral music)	47
Flavio (opera, 1723)	67
Floridante (opera, 1721)	65
Funeral anthem on the death of Queen Caroline (1737) Bound with Utrecht Te Deum in reprint	11
Giulio Cesare (opera, 1723)	68
Guistino (opera, 1738–40)	93
Haman and Mordecai (masque, *ca.* 1700) (Reprint title: Esther, first version)	40
Harpsichord music (Reprint title: Keyboard music)	2
Imeneo (opera, 1738–40)	93
Instrumental concerti *see* Concerto	
Instrumental music (a reprint title comprising organ music and miscellaneous works)	48
Israel in Egypt (oratorio, 1738)	16
Italian cantatas for solo voice and bass	50–51
Italian cantatas with instrumental accompaniment	52–53
Italian duets and trios	32
Jephtha (oratorio, 1751)	44
—— facsimile of Ms (not in reprint ed.)	97
Joseph (oratorio, 1742)	42
Joshua (oratorio, 1747)	17
Judas Maccabeus (oratorio, 1746)	22
Julius Caesar = Giulio Cesare	
Latin church music	38
Lotario (opera, 1729)	77
Messiah (oratorio, 1741)	45
Muzio Scevola, act 3 (opera, 1721)	64
Oboe concertos (Reprint title: Instrumental concerti)	21

Title	v. no.
Occasional oratorio (1746)	43
Ode to St. Cecilia (1739)	23
Odes, other, *see* individual titles	
Orchestral music (Reprint title comprising Water music, Royal fireworks music, Concertos in F, D, and Double concertos)	47
Organ concertos	28
Organ music (Reprint title: Instrumental music)	48
Orlando (opera, 1732)	82
Ottone (opera, 1722)	66
Partenope (opera, 1730)	78
Passion according to St. John (1704) Bd. w/ v. 15	9
Passion oratorio = Passion, words by B. H. Brockes (1716). Bound with Passion according to St. John in reprint ed.	15
Il pastor fido (opera, first version, 1712)	59
———, (second version, 1734) (Bound together with first version in reprint ed.)	84
Poro (opera, 1731)	79
Psalms (chorus) (Reprint title: Latin church music)	38
Radamisto (opera, 1720)	63
La resurrezione (oratorio, 1708)	39
Riccardo (opera, 1727)	74
Rinaldo (opera: first version, 1711, and second version, 1731) (Bound separately in reprint)	58
Rodelinda (opera, 1725)	70
Roderigo (opera, 1707)	56
Royal fireworks music (1749) (Reprint title: Orchestral music)	47
St. John Passion	9
Samson (oratorio, 1741)	10
Saul (oratorio, 1738)	13
Scipione (opera, 1726)	71
Semele (oratorio, 1743)	7
Serse (opera, 1727)	92
Silla (opera, 1714). Bound with Roderigo in reprint ed.	61
Siroe (opera, 1714)	75
Solomon (oratorio, 1748)	26
Sonate da camera	27
Suites, harpsichord	2

Title	v. no.
Susanna (oratorio, 1748)	1
Tamerlano (opera, 1724)	69
Te Deums, 3 (*ca.* 1714–1727) (Reprint title: Three Te Deums.	
Does not include Dettingen or Utrecht Te Deums, q.v.)	37
Terpsichore (prologue, 1734) (Not in reprint)	84
Theodora (oratorio, 1749)	8
Tolomeo (opera, 1728)	76
Il trionfo del tempo e della verità (oratorio, 1708, 1737)	24
The triumph of time and truth (oratorio, 1757) Bound	
with Il trionfo . . . in reprint	20
Utrecht Te Deum and Jubilate (1713) Bd. w/v. 25	38 v. 31 ?
Vocal pieces, miscellaneous (Not in reprint)	96
Water music (1715) (Reprint title: Orchestral music)	47

Xerxes = Serse

1a. *Supplement,* ed. F. Chrysander.

v. 1   Dionigi Erba (*fl.* 1692–1695), *Magnificat*

v. 2   Francesco Antonio Urio (*fl.* 1690–1706), *Te Deum*

v. 3   Alessandro Stradella (1642–1682), *Serenata, "Qual prodigio ch'io miro"*

v. 4   Giovanni Clari (1677–1754), *Duetti e terzetti a diverse voci (1720)*

v. 5   Gottlieb Muffat (1690–1770), *Componimenti musicali*

v. 6   Reinhard Keiser (1674–1739), *Octavia*

2. *Hallische Händel-Ausgabe.* Herausgegeben von der Georg-Friedrich-Händel-Gesellschaft. Kassel, Bärenreiter, 1955–   . [Gen. eds. Max Schneider, Rudolf Steglich)

Serie 1.   *Oratorien und grosse Kantaten*

v. 1   *Das Alexander-Fest oder Die Macht der Music. Ode zu Ehren der heiligen Cäcilia,* ed. Konrad Ameln

v. 2   *Passion nach dem Evangelisten Johannes,* ed. Karl Gustav Fellerer

v. 6   *Ode for the birthday of Queen Anne,* ed. Walther Siegmund-Schultze

v. 7   *Passion nach B. H. Brockes,* ed. Felix Schröder

v. 13   *Saul,* ed. Percy M. Young

v. 16   *L'Allegro, il penseroso ed il moderato,* ed. James S and Martin V. Hall

v. 17   *The Messiah,* ed. John Tobin

v. 28   *Susanna,* ed. Bernard Rose

v. 31   *The choice of Hercules,* ed. W. Siegmund-Schultze

Serie 2.   *Opern*

v. 14   *Julius Caesar,* ed. Frieder Zschoch

v. 26   *Ezio,* ed. F. Zschoch

v. 32   *Ariodante,* ed. W. Siegmund-Schultze

v. 39   *Xerxes,* ed. Rudolf Steglich

Serie 3.   *Kirchenmusik*

v. 1   *"Dixit Dominus Domino meo", Psalm 109 (Vulgata. Nach Luthers Zählung Ps. 110),* ed. Eberhard Wenzel

Serie 4.   *Instrumentalmusik*

v. 1   *Klavierwerke I: Die acht grossen Suiten,* ed. R. Steglich

v. 2   *Orgelkonzerte I: op.4, nr. 1–6,* ed. Karl Matthaei

v. 3   *Elf Sonaten für Flöte . . . und bezifferten Bass,* ed. Hans-Peter Schmitz

v. 4   *Sechs Sonaten für Violine und bezifferten Bass,* ed. Johann Philipp Hinnenthal

v. 10   *Triosonaten op.5:1–7,* ed. Walter Serauky, Siegfried Flesch, Max Schneider

v. 11   *Sechs Concerti grossi, op.3:1–6,* ed. Frederick Hudson

v. 13   *Wassermusik und Feuerwerksmusik,* ed. Hans Ferdinand Redlich

v. 14   *Zwölf Concerti grossi, op.6:1–12,* ed. Adolf Hoffman, H. F. Redlich

3. *Händel-Jahrbuch.* Im Auftrage der Händel-Gesellschaft herausgegeben von Rudolf Steglich. Leipzig, Breitkopf & Härtel, 1928–1933. 6 v.

v. 2 (1929). Bruno Flögel, "Studien zur Arientechnik in den
Opern Händels", pp. 50–156

4. *Händel-Jahrbuch.* Im Auftrag der Georg-Friedrich-Händel-Gesellschaft herausgegeben von Max Schneider und Rudolf Steglich. Leipzig,
Deutscher Verlag, 1955–
This series started with a double numbering system: the 1955 v.
was labeled both v. 1 and v. 7 (as continuation of item 3 above).
The latter system was abandoned after 1958 (v.4/10). Thus far
1 v. per year has been issued, but v. 7/8 (1961/2) and v. 10/11 (1964/5)
each appeared as a single issue.
v. 1 (1955). Bibliography 1933–54; record list 1952–54.

5. Konrad Sasse, *Händel-Bibliographie.* Leipzig, Deutscher Verlag,
[2nd ed.] 1967

51
HASSLER, HANS LEO, 1564–1612

Sämtliche Werke. Veröffentlichung der Gesellschaft für Bayerische Musikgeschichte in München, herausgegeben von C. Russell Crosby, Jr.
In this set, v. 1–6 are re-issues of v. from other sets, v. 7–8 are new,
and v. 9–12 are proposed but not yet published.

v. 1 = DDT **(A 33)**, v. 2

v. 2 = DTB **(A 31)**, v. 9

v. 3 = DTB v. 20

v. 4 = DDT v. 7

v. 5 = DDT v. 24

v. 6 = DDT v. 25

v. 7   *Psalmen und geistliche Gesänge (1607)*

v. 8   *Psalmen und geistliche Gesänge (1608)*

(v. 9–10) *Ungedruckte Vokalwerke*

(v. 11)   *Lustgarten und ungedruckte Instrumentalwerke*

(v. 12)   *Orgelwerke* [might be DTB v. 7]

52
HAYDN, JOSEPH, 1732-1809

1-2. Complete works 3-4. Symphonies 5. Thematic catalog 6-7. Yearbooks

1.   *The complete works: critical edition.* General editor Jens Peter Larsen. Boston, Vienna, The Haydn Society Inc. 1950ff. [ceased publication]

Series 1.   *Symphonies*

    v. 5   *Symphonies no. 50–57,* ed. Helmut Schultz

    v. 9   *Symphonies no. 82–87,* ed. H. C. Robbins Landon
          Includes thematic list of all symphonies

    v. 10   *Symphonies no. 88–92,* ed. H. C. Robbins Landon

Series 23   *Masses*

    v. 1   *Masses 1–4,* ed. Carl Maria Brand
          Includes thematic list of all Masses. Contents:
          1. *Missa brevis in F;* 2. *Missa in honorem beatis-simae verginis Mariae;* 3. *Missa Sanctae Caeciliae;* 4. *Missa Sancti Nicolai*

2.   *Joseph Haydn Werke,* herausgegeben vom Joseph Haydn Institut, Köln, unter der Leitung von Georg Feder. München, G. Henle, 1958– The *Kritische Berichte* are published separately, numbered the same as the music volumes

Series 1.   *Symphonies*

    v. 4   *Sinfonien 1764 und 1765,* ed. Horst Walter
          Contents: nos. 21–24, 28–31

    v. 6   *Sinfonien 1767–1772,* ed. C.-G. Stellan Mörner
          Contents: nos. 35, 42, 45–7, 49

    v. 7   *Sinfonien 1773 und 1774,* ed. Wolfgang Stockmeier
          Contents: nos. 50, 54–7

    v. 17   *Londoner Sinfonien, 3. Folge,* ed. H. Walter
          Contents: nos. 99–101

    v. 18   *Londoner Sinfonien, 4. Folge,* ed. Hubert Unverricht
          Contents: nos. 102–4

Series 4. *Die sieben letzten Worte unseres Erlösers am Kreuze: Orchesterfassung*, ed. H. Unverricht

Series 12 *String quartets*

  v. 2 *Streichquartette "op.9" und "op.17"*, ed. Georg Feder

Series 14. *Baryton trios*

  v. 2 *Barytontrios nr. 25–48*, ed. H. Unverricht

  v. 3 *Barytontrios nr. 49–72*, ed. H. Unverricht

  v. 4 *Barytontrios nr. 73–96*, ed. H. Unverricht

  v. 5 *Barytontrios nr. 97–126*, ed. Michael Härting, Horst Walter

Series 18. *Piano sonatas*

  v. 3 *Klaviersonaten, 3. Folge.*, ed. G. Feder
         Contents: Hob.XVI:33–4, 40–43, 48–52

Series 23. *Masses*

  v. 2 *Messen nr. 5–8*, ed. H. C. Robbins Landon
         Contents: 5. *Missa brevis St^i Johannis de Deo (Kleine Orgelmesse)*; 6. *Missa Cellensis (Mariazellermesse)*; 7. *Missa in tempore belli (Paukenmesse)*; 9. *Missa St^i Bernardi von Offida (Heiligmesse)*

  v. 3 *Messen nr. 9–10*, ed. Günter Thomas
         Contents: 9. *Missa in angustiis (Nelsonmesse)*; 10. *Missa, "Theresienmesse"*

  v. 4 *Messe nr. 11: "Schöpfungsmesse" 1801*, ed. Irmgard Becker-Glauch

  v. 5 *Messe nr. 12: "Harmoniemesse" 1802*, ed. Friedrich Lippmann

Series 25. *Operas*

  v. 2 *La canterina: intermezzo in musica, 1766*, ed. Dénes Bartha

  v. 3 *Lo speziale, dramma giocoso ... 1765*, ed. Helmut Wirth

v. 5   *L'infedeltà delusa: burletta per musica . . . 1773,* ed.
D. Bartha, Jenö Vécsey

v. 6:1 *L'incontro improvviso: dramma giocosa per musica . . .*
1775, ed. H. Wirth [Act 1]

v. 6:2 ——— [Acts 2–3]

v. 10   *La Fedeltà premiata, Dramma pastorale giocoso . . .*
1780, ed. Günter Thomas

v. 12   *Armida: dramma eroico, 1783,* ed. Wilhelm Pfannkuch

Series 28. *Oratorios*

v. 1:1 *Il ritorno di Tobia (1775/84),* ed. Ernst Fritz Schmid
[*Parte prima*]

v. 1:2   ——— [*Parte secunda*]

v. 2   *Die sieben letzten Worte unseres Erlösers am Kreuze:*
Vokalfassung, ed. H. Unverricht

Series 29. *Solo songs*

v. 1   *Lieder für eine Singstimme mit Begleitung des Klaviers,*
ed. Paul Mies

Series 30. *Mehrstimmige Gesänge,* ed. P. Mies

Series 31. *Kanons,* ed. Otto Erich Deutsch

Series 32. *Arrangements of folk songs*

v. 1   *Volksliedbearbeiten nr. 1–100: Schottische Lieder,* ed.
Karl Geiringer

3.   *Critical edition of the complete symphonies in pocket scores, with forward
and notes on each symphony,* ed. H. C. R. Landon

v. 1   *Symphonies 1–12*

v. 2   *Symphonies 13–27*

v. 3   *Symphonies 28–40*

v. 4   *Symphonies 41–49*

v. 5   *Symphonies 50–57*

v. 6   *Symphonies 58–65*

v. 7   *Symphonies 66–73*

v. 8   *Symphonies 74–81*

v. 9   *Symphonies 82–87*

v. 10   *Symphonies 88–92, Sinfonia concertante*

v. 11   *Symphonies 93–98*

v. 12   *Symphonies 99–104*

4.   List of old numbers and titles of symphonies

Abschied	45
La chasse	73
The clock	101
Il distrato	60
Drum roll	103
Farewell	45
Feuer	59
Hornsignal	31
L'imperiale	53
Lamentatione	26
Laudon	69
The London symphony	104
London symphonies, old nos:	
1	97
2	93
3	94
4	98
5	95
6	96
7	104
8	103
9	102
10	99
11	101
12	100
Lucavec	1
Maria Theresia	48
Le matin	6
Merkur (Mercury)	43

Le midi	7
Military	100
Miracle	96
L'ours	82
Oxford	92
Paris symphonies, old nos:	
1	82
2	83
3	84
4	85
5	86
6	87
7	88
8	89
9	90
10	92
11	91
La passione	49
Paukenschlag	94
Paukenwirbel	103
The philosopher *(Der Philosoph)*	22
La poule	83
La reine (also: *La reine de France)*	85
La Roxelane	63
Salomon symphonies = London symphonies	
The schoolmaster	55
Le soir	8
Surprise	94
Trauer	44

5. Anthony van Hoboken, *Joseph Haydn: Thematisch-bibliographisches Werkverzeichnis.* Mains, B. Schott's Söhne. v. 1, 1957 (Instrumental music)
   Abbreviation: Hob.

6. *Haydn Yearbook.* Editorial staff: Herta Singer, Karlheinz Füssl, H. C. Robbins Landon. Bryn Mawr, Theodore Presser, 1962–
   In English and German, with English summaries of the German articles and *vice versa.* Each v. includes reviews of music, books and records.

v. 1   (1962). Janos Harich, "Das Repertoire des Opernkapell-
          meisters Joseph Haydn in Estzterházsa (1780–1790)", pp.
          9–107 (English summary pp. 108–10)

v. 2   (1963–4)

v. 3   (1965)

v. 4   (1968)

v. 5   (1968). *The diaries of Joseph Carl Rosenbaum, 1770–1829,*
          ed. Else Radant

7.   *Haydn-Studien.* Veröffentlichungen des Joseph Haydn Instituts, Köln,
     herausgegeben von Georg Feder, 1965–
     The v. appear in *Heften,* 4 to a v., published irregularly. There is an
     index in v. 1

v. 1   (1965–7)

v. 2:1–2 (1969)

53
JANNEQUIN, CLÉMENT, *ca.* 1475–*ca.* 1560

Chansons polyphoniques, ed. A. Tillman Merritt, François Lesure

v. 1   *Période Bordelaise, 1505–1531*

v. 2   *Période Angevine, 1533–1537*

v. 3   *Période Angevine, 1540–1545*

v. 4   *Période Angevine, fin; Période Parisienne, début*

54
LASSO, ORLANDO DI, 1532?–1594

1–2. Complete works   3. Index of Masses   4. List of works

1.   *Sämtliche Werke.* [Ed. Franz Xaver Haberl, Adolf Sandberger]
     Leipzig, Breitkopf & Härtel, 1894–
     This edition was never completed, but is more or less continued by
     item 2 below. Although it is not organized by series, the v. fall into
     clear categories and are so arranged below. The *Magnum opus* was
     edited by Haberl, the secular works by Sandberger.

Magnum opus musicum. Lateinische Gesänge für 2, 3, 4, 5, 6, 7, 8, 9, 10 u.
12 Stimmen

v. 1 [2, 3, and 4 voices]
v. 3 [4–5 voices]
v. 5 [5 voices]
v. 7 [5 voices]
v. 9 [5 voices]
v. 11 [5–6 voices]
v. 13 [6 voices]
v. 15 [6 voices]
v. 17 [6 voices]
v. 19 [6, 7 and 8 voices]
v. 21 [8, 9, 10 and 12 voices]

An alphabetical title INDEX of all 11 v. of the *Magnus opus* in this set
is in the Lassus article in the 5th ed. of Grove's *Dictionary of Music and*
Musicians.

Polyphonic chansons

v. 12, v. 14, v. 16. INDEX of all chansons in v. 16; also in Grove's as
above.

Polyphonic Lieder

v. 18, v. 20. INDEX of all Lieder in v. 20, also in Grove's.

Madrigals

v. 2 [from publications of 1555, 1557]
v. 4 [from publications of 1565, 1567]
v. 6 [from publications of 1587]
v. 8 [from publications of 1569, 1583]
v. 10 [from publications of 1555, 1581].
INDEX of all madrigals in v. 10, also in Grove's.

2. *Sämtliche Werke, neue Reihe.* Académie Royale de Belgique, Bayerische
    Akademie der Wissenschaften. Kassel, Bärenreiter

v. 1   *Lateinische Motetten, französische Chansons und italienische*
              Madrigale aus wiedergefundenen Drucken 1559–1588, ed.
              Wolfgang Boetticher

v. 2   *Die vier Passionen,* ed. Kurt von Fischer

v. 3   *Messen 1–9: Messen der Drucke Venedig 1570 und München 1570,* ed. Siegfried Hermelink

v. 4   *Messen 10–17: Messen des Druckes Paris 1577,* ed. S. Hermelink

v. 5   *Messen 18–23: Messen der Drucke Paris 1577 und Nürnberg 1581,* ed. S. Hermelink

v. 6   *Messen 24–29: Messen des Druckes München 1589,* ed. S. Hermelink

v. 7   *Messen 30–35: Messen aus Einzel- und Sammeldrucken 1570–1588,* ed. S. Hermelink

v. 8   *Messen 36–41: Messen der Drucke Paris 1607 und München 1610,* ed. S. Hermelink

3.   Index of Masses in item 2 above

Title	no. voices	Herme- link no.	v. no.
Amar donna	5	25	6
Amor ecco collei	6	38	8
Beatus qui intellegit	6	35	7
Bella Amfitrit' altera	8	37	8
Certa fortiter	6	39	8
Congratulamini mihi	6	34	7
Credidi propter	5	9	3
De Feria	4	14	4
Deus in adiutorium	6	41	8
Dittes maistresse	5	24	6
Dixit Joseph	6	36	8
Domine secundum actum meum	5	32	7
Doulce memoire	4	10	4
Ecce nunc benedicite	6	40	8
Entre vous filles	5	22	5
Frére Thibault	4	4	3
Iager	4	13	4
Ie ne menge poinct de porcq	4	1	3
Il me suffit	4	21	5

In die tribulationis	5	27	6
In te Domine speravi	6	19	5
Ite rime dolenti	5	6	3
La la maistre Pierre	4	2	3
Laudate Dominum	4	30	7
Le berger et la bergère	5	5	3
Locutus sum	6	33	7
O passi sparsi	4	12	4
Pilons pilons lorge	4	3	3
Pro Defunctis	4	15	4
Pro Defunctis	5	29	6
Puis que j'ay perdu	4	11	4
Qual donna attende	5	26	6
Quand' io penso al martiri	4	31	7
Scarco di doglia	5	7	3
Sidus ex claro	5	8	3
Surge propera	6	17	4
Susanne un iour	5	16	4
Tous les regretz	6	18	5
Veni in hortum meum	5	23	5
Vinum bonum	8	20	5

---

4. A detailed listing of the sources for di Lasso's works will be found in
    Wolfgang Boetticher, *Orlando di Lasso und seine Zeit, 1532–1594,
    Band I: Monographie.* Kassel, Bärenreiter, 1958., pp. 729–838. This
    book also contains an alphabetical list of compositions indicating
    doubtful and spurious works and *contrefacta*, pp. 945–80.

55
LECHNER, LEONHARD, *ca.* 1553–1606

Werke. Im Auftrag der neuen Schütz-Gesellschaft herausgegeben von
Konrad Ameln. Kassel, Bärenreiter, 1954–

v. 1   *Motectae sacrae quatuor, quinque et sex vocum 1575,* ed. Ludwig Finscher

v. 3   *Newe teutsche Lieder mit vier und fünff Stimmen 1577,* ed. Uwe Martin

v. 4   *Sanctissimae virginis Mariae Canticum, secundum octo vulgares tonos, quatuor vocibus 1578,* ed. Walter Lipphardt

v. 8   *Liber missarum sex et quinque vocum adjunctis aliquot Introitibus in praecipia festa 1584,* ed. W. Lipphardt

v. 9   *Newe lustige teutsche Lieder nach Art der Welschen Canzonen 1586–1588,* ed. Ernst Fritz Schmid

v. 12   *Historia der Passion und Leidens unser einigen Erlösers und Seligmachers Jesu Christi 1593,* ed. K. Ameln

56
LISZT, FRANZ, 1811–1886

Sämtliche Werke, herausgegeben von der Franz-Liszt-Stiftung. Leipzig, Breitkopf & Härtel, 1907–1936

   Reprinted in reduced size by Gregg Press, 1966. Includes English commentary. Missing v. nos. below were never issued.

[Series 1]   Orchestral works

v. 1   Symphonic poems: *Ce qu'on entend sur la montagne; Tasso, Lamento e trionfo*

"   v. 2   Symphonic poems: *Le triomphe funèbre du Tasso* [from *Trois odes funèbres*]; *Orpheus; Les préludes*

"   v. 3   Symphonic poems: *Prometheus; Mazeppa*

"   v. 4   Symphonic poems: *Festklänge; Héroïde funèbre (Heldenklage)*

"   v. 5   Symphonic poems: *Hungaria; Hamlet*

"   v. 6   Symphonic poems: *Hunnenschlacht; Die Ideale*

"   v. 7   *A symphony to Dante's "Divina commedia"*

"   v. 8–9 *A Faust symphony*

"   v. 10   *Two episodes from Lenau's "Faust": 1. Der nächtliche*

> *Zug   2. Der Tanz in der Dorfschenke [Mephisto waltz no. 1];   2nd Mephisto waltz; Von der Wiege bis zum Grabe [Du berceau jusqu'à la tombe]*

※ M.480.188
      „   v. 11   *Künstlerfestzug zur Schillerfeier 1859; Festmarsch zur Goethejubiläumsfeier; Festvorspiel; Huldigungsmarsch*

      „   v. 12   *Trois odes funèbres* [nos. 1–2; see v. 2 above for no. 3]; *Ungarischer Marsch zur Krönungsfeier ... 1867; Ungarischer Sturmmarsch; Vom Fels zum Meer (Deutscher Siegesmarsch)*

      „   v. 13   Works for piano and orchestra: *Malediction; Concerto no. 1 in E♭; Concerto no. 2 in A; Totentanz*

[Series 2]   Piano works
※※ M.480.188
      „   v. 1–3 *Etudes*

      „   v. 4   *Album d'un voyageur*

      „   v. 5   *Harmonies poétiques et religieuses; Apparitions; Fantaisie romantique ...; Tre sonetti del Petrarca (1st version); Venezia e Napoli*

      „   v. 6   *Années de pélerinage 1–3*

M3.L66 L7 1966 v. 7–9 Shorter piano works

      „   v. 10   Dances &

      „   v. 12   *Hungarian Rhapsody*

[Series 3̶5̶]   Sacred vocal works

M3.L66 L7 1966 v. 3   *Missa quattuor vocum ad aequales concinente organo* [2nd version]; *Missa choralis, organo concinente; Requiem*
      „   v. 4   *Psalmen*
      „   v. 5   *Cantico del sol di San Francesco d'Assisi; Cantantibus organis; An den heiligen Franziskus von Paula; Domine salvum fac regem; Hymne de l'enfant; In domum domini ibimus; Inno a Maria vergine*

      „   v. 6–7 Shorter choral works

Series 7
[~~Series 4~~]   Songs and arias

M3.L66 L7 1966 v. 1   25 songs and arias 1843–8

M3.L66L7 1966   v.   2   48 songs and arias 1850–60

          ''   v.   3   38 songs and arias 1860–83

[Series 5]   *Freje Bearbeitungen.* Arrangements for piano

M3,L66L7 1966
F.3 .   v.   1   Works of Wagner *also on* **M.480.188 *Ser. 3 no.1*

   ''   v.   2–3 Beethoven symphonies

M3   *New Liszt Edition   see   Monuments file*
L772

57
LUDFORD, NICHOLAS, *ca.* 1480–*ca.* 1542

Collected works, ed. John D. Bergsagel. *Corpus mensurabilis musicae* **(A 28),**
ser. 27. 3 v. proposed

v. 1   *Lady Masses*

58
LULLY, JEAN-BAPTISTE, 1632–1687

Ouevres complètes, publiées sous la direction de Henri Prunières. Paris,
La Revue musicale, 1930–
     Never completed. The v. are in unnumbered series.

Les opéras

          v. 1   *Cadmus et Hermione*

          v. 2   *Alceste*

          v. 3   *Amadis*

Les ballets

          v. 1   *Ballet du temps; Ballet des plaisirs; Ballet de l'Amour
                     malade*

          v. 2   *Ballet d'Alcidiane; Ballet des gardes; Ballet de Xerxes*

Les comédies-ballets

          v. 1   *Le mariage forcé; L'amour médecin*

          v. 2   *Les plaisirs de l'île enchantée; La pastorale comique; Le
                     Sicilien; Le grand divertissement royal de Versailles*

Les motets

> v. 1   *Miserere mei Deus*
>
> v. 2   *Plaude, laetare, Gallia; Te Deum laudamus; Dies irae*

MACHAUT, GUILLAUME DE *see* GUILLAUME DE MACHAUT

59
MAHLER, GUSTAV, 1860–1911

Sämtliche Werke: kritische Gesamtausgabe, herausgegeben von der Internationalen Gustav Mahler Gesellschaft, Wien. Berlin, Wiesbaden, Bote & Bock, 1960–

> v. 4   *Symphonie nr. 4,* ed. Erwin Ratz
>
> v. 5   *Symphonie nr. 5,* ed. E. Ratz
>
> v. 6   *Symphonie nr. 6,* ed. E. Ratz
>
> v. 7   *Symphonie nr. 7,* ed. E. Ratz
>
> v. 9   *Das Lied von der Erde,* ed. E. Ratz
>
> v. 11a   *Adagio aus der Symphonie nr. 10,* ed. E. Ratz

60
MENDELSSOHN-BARTHOLDY, FELIX, 1809–1847

1–2. Works   3. Thematic catalog

1.   *Werke.* Kritische durchgesehene Ausgabe von Julius Reitz. Leipzig, Breitkopf & Härtel, 1874–77

> Serie 1   *Symphonien*
>
> Serie 2   *Overtüren*
>
> Serie 3   *Marsch für Orchester, op. 108*
>
> Serie 4   *Violinkonzert*
>
> Serie 5   *Oktett und 2 Quintette*
>
> Serie 6   *Streichquartette*

Serie 7   *Werke für Blasinstrumente*

Serie 8   *Werke für Pianoforte und Orchester*

Serie 9   *Werke für Pianoforte und Saiteninstrumente*

Serie 10   *Werke für Pianoforte zu 4 Händen*

Serie 11   *Werke für Pianoforte allein*

  v. 1   [op.5, 6, 7, 14, 15, 16, 28]

  v. 2   [op.33, 35, 54, 72, 82, 83]

  v. 3   [op.104–6, 117–19]

  v. 4   [*Songs without words*]

Serie 12   *Orgelwerke* Bound with Series 10

Serie 13   *Oratorien*

  v. 1   *Paulus*

  v. 2   *Elias*

  v. 3   *Christus*

Serie 14   *Geistliche Gesangwerke*

 Abt. A.   *Für Solostimmen, Chor und Orchester*

  v. 1   *Psalmen 115, 42, 93, 114, 98*

  v. 2   *Lobgesang: Symphonie-Kantate, op.52*

  v. 3   *Lauda Sion op.73; Hymne für Altstimme op.96; Tu es Petrus op.111; Verleih uns Frieden*

 Abt. B.   *Für Solostimme, Chor und Orgel*

 Abt. C.   *Für Solostimme und Chor ohne Begleitung*

Serie 15.   Grössere weltliche Gesangwerke

  v. 1   *Antigone, op.55*

  v. 2   *Athalia, op.74*

  v. 3   *Oedipus in Kolonos, op.93*

  v. 4   *Sommernachtstraum, op.61*

   v. 5 *Walpurgisnacht*

   v. 6 *Festgesänge, op.119–20*

   v. 7 *Die Hochzeit des Comacho, op.10*

   v. 8 *Heimkehr aus der Fremde, op.89*

   v. 9 *Loreley, op.98*

   v. 10 *Konzertarie "Infelice", op.94*

Serie 16. *Lieder für Sopran, Alt, Tenor und Bass*

Serie 17. *Lieder und Gesänge für 4 Männerstimmen*

Serie 18. *Lieder und Gesänge für 2 Stimmen mit Pianoforte-Begleitung*

Serie 19. *Lieder und Gesänge für 1 Stimme mit Pianoforte-Begleitung*

2. *Leipziger Ausgabe der Werke Felix Mendelssohn Bartholdys,* herausgegeben von der Internationalen Felix-Mendelssohn-Gesellschaft Basel. Leipzig, Deutscher Verlag für Musik, Mainz, B. Schott's Söhne

  The object of this edition is to publish works not included in item 1. Of the projected set listed below, only Serie 2, v. 4–5 have been published so far.

Serie 1. *Orchesterwerke*

Serie 2. *Konzerte und Konzertstücke*

M1010.M452C6
1960

   v. 4 *Konzert für zwei Klaviere und Orchester E-dur,* ed. K. Koehler

   v. 5 *Konzert für zwei Klaviere und Orchester As-dur,* ed. K. Koehler

Serie 3. *Kammermusikwerke*

Serie 4. *Klavier- und Orgelwerke*

Serie 5. *Bühnenwerke*

Serie 6. *Geistliche Vokalmusik*

Serie 7. *Weltliche Vokalmusik*

Serie 8. *Supplement* [Documentary biography, Pictorial biography, Thematic catalog, Drawings and water colors of M.]

3. *Thematisches Verzeichnis der im Druck erschienenen Compositionen von Felix Mendelssohn-Bartholdy.*
Leipzig, Breitkopf & Härtel [3d ed.] 1882

61
MONTE, PHILIPPE DE, 1521–1603

1. Works   2. List of works

1. *Opera,* ed. Charles Van den Borren, Georges van Doorslaer. Bruges, Desclée, 1927–1939
   The contents of this set (which does not comprise de Monte's *complete* works) are not organized by series, but for convenience are so presented below. All the Masses were ed. by Van den Borren; the other works by van Doorslaer. All parody Masses include the model for the parody in the same v., as noted.

Masses

v. 1 *Missa Inclina cor meum* (with de Monte motet)

v. 3 *Secunda missa sine nomine*

v. 4 *Missa O altitude divitarium* (with de Rore motet)

v. 5 *Missa Ultimi miei sospiri* (with Verdelot madrigal)

v. 7 *Missa sine nomine*

v. 8 *Missa Ancor che col partire* (with de Rore madrigal)

v. 9 *Missa Reviens vers moi* (with de Monte chanson)

v. 10 *Missa Nasce la pena mia* (with Striggio madrigal)

v. 11 *Prima missa sine nomine*

v. 13 *Missa de Requiem*

v. 14 *Missa La dolce vista* (with de Monte madrigal)

v. 16 *Missa quaternis vocibus*

v. 18 *Missa sex vocum*

v. 21 *Missa super Cara la vita mia* (with Wert madrigal)

v. 23 *Missa Quando lieta sperai* (with de Rore madrigal)

v. 24   *Missa Cum sit omnipotens rector Olympi* (with de Monte motet)

v. 26   *Missa Aspice Domine* (with van Berchem motet)

v. 30   *Missa sine nomine*

v. 31   *Missa sine nomine*

Magnificat

v. 12   *Canticum magnificat*

Motets

v. 2   *Motettum "O bone Jesu"*

v. 15   *Collectio decem motettorum 5–6–7 et 8 vocum*

v. 17   *Liber septimus motettorum cum quinque vocibus*

v. 22   *Liber quartus motettorum quinque vocum*

Madrigals

v. 6   *Madrigalium spiritualium cum sex vocibus liber primus (1583)*

v. 19   *Liber quartus madrigalium quatuor vocum (1581)*

Chansons

v. 20   *Collectio decem carminum gallicorum alias chansons françaises*

Arrangements of de Monte's works for lute

v. 25   *Cantiones ad testudinii usum accommodate*
Includes vocal versions of madrigals

2.   Georges van Doorslaer, *La vie et les oeuvres de Philippe de Monte.* Bruxelles. Lamertin, 1921 *(Académie royale des sciences, des lettres et des beaux-arts de Belgique. Classe des beaux-arts. Mémoires, 1:4)*

62
MONTEVERDI, CLAUDIO, 1567–1643

1. Complete works   2. Index to complete works

1. *Tutte le opere,* nuovamente date in luce da G. Francesco Malipiero. Asolo, 1926–42.

    Unchanged reprint in the 1960's by Universal

    v. 1   *Il primo libro de madrigali a 5 voci (1587)*

    v. 2   *Il secondo libro de madrigali a 5 voci (1590)*

    v. 3   *Il terzo libro de madrigali a 5 voci (1592)*

    v. 4   *Il quarto libro de madrigali a 5 voci (1603)*

    v. 5   *Il quinto libro de madrigali a 5 voci (1605)*

    v. 6   *Il sesto libro de madrigali a 5 voci (1614)*

    v. 7   *Il settimo libro de madrigali a 1, 2, 3, 4, e 6 voci con altri generide canti (1619)*

    v. 8   *Madrigali guerrieri, et amorosi, libro ottavo . . . 1638*
                 1. Canti guerrieri
                 2. Canti amorosi

    v. 9   *Madrigalie canzonette a due e tre voci (1651)*

    v. 10   *Canzonette a tre voci (1584); Scherzi musicali (I: 1607, II: 1632)*

    v. 11   *Orfeo (1607); Arianna (1608); Maddalena (1617)*

    v. 12   *Il ritorno d'Ulisse in patria (1611)*

    v. 13   *L'incoronazione di Poppea (1642)*

    v. 14/1   *Sacrae cantiuncula (1582); Sanctissimae virgini missis senis vocibus (1610)*

    v. 14/2   *Musica religiosa I (1610)*

    v. 15/1   *Musica religiosa II (Selva morale e spirituale I, 1640)*

    v. 15/2   *Musica religiosa II (Selva morale e spirituale II)*

    v. 16   *Musica religiosa III (Missae e psalmi)*

2. An alphabetical index to Claudio Monteverdi Tutte li opere, ed. by the bibliography committee of the New York chapter MLA. *(Music Library Association Index series* no. 1)

MORALES, CRISTÓBAL DE

See *Monumentos de la musica española* **(A 72),** v. 11 for full listing

63
MOUTON, JEAN, *d.* 1522

Opera omnia, ed. Andrew Minor. *Corpus mensurabilis musicae* **(A 28)**, ser. 43. 10 v. proposed

v. 1   *Masses: Alleluia, Alma redemptoris mater, Benedictus Dominus Deus; motet Benedictus Dominus Deus by Fevin*

64
MOZART, WOLFGANG AMADEUS, 1756–1791

1–2. Complete works   3. Thematic catalog   4. Handbook/bibliography
5–10. Yearbooks and other series

⋇⋇ M. 315.1   1.   *Werke.* Kritisch durchgesehene Gesamtausgabe. Leipzig, Breitkopf & Härtel, 1877 ff.

In the following listing of the contents of this set, only K. numbers (K. = item 3 below) are given for most works. In parentheses following each K. no. as stated in the set is given the new K. no. (if any) according to the 6th ed. of K. It should be noted that a K. Anh. no. *in parentheses* indicates a spurious or doubtful work. A name following a K. Anh. no. in parentheses is that of the actual composer. An INDEX of this set by K. no. is provided on pp. 466–73 of item 4 below, this set being cited as no. 2320.

Series 1.   *Messen*

v.   1   *Nr. 1–8:* K. 49 (47d), 65 (61a), 66, 139 (47a), 167, 192 (186f), 194 (186h), 220 (196b)

v.   2   *Nr. 9–15:* K. 257, 258, 259, 262 (246a), 275 (272b), 317, 337

Series 2.   *Litanien und Vespern, nr. 1–7:* K. 109 (74e), 125, 195 (186d), 243, 193 (186g), 321, 339

Series 3.   *Kleinere geistliche Gesangwerke mit Begleitung des Orchesters*

v.   1   *Kyries, antiphons &], nr. 1–16:* K. 33, 89 (73k), 322, 323, 341 (368a), 20, 47, 85 (73s), 86 (73v), 108 (74d), 127, 276 (321b), 141 (66b), 142 (Anh. C 3.04), 197 (Anh. C. 3.05), 343 (336c)

v.   2   *[Offertories, motets, hymns &], nr. 17–31:* K. 34, 72 (74 f), 93 (Anh. A 22, J. A. K. G. Reutter), 117 (66a),

143 (73a), 165 (158a), 177/342 (Anh. C 3.09), 198 (Anh. C 3.08), 222 (205a), 260 (248a), 273, 277 (272a), 326 (Anh. A 4, J. E. Eberlin), 327 (Anh. A 10, Q. Gasparini), 618

Series 4. [*Cantatas and oratorios*]

Abt. 1 *Kantaten nr. 1–3:* K. 42 (35a), 471, 623

Abt. 2 *Oratorien: Betulia liberata* K. 118 (74c), *Davidde penitente* K. 469

Series 5. *Opern*

v. 1   *Die Schuldigkeit des ersten Gebotes,* K. 35

v. 2   *Apollo und Hyacinthus,* K. 38

v. 3   *Bastien und Bastienne,* K. 50 (46b)

v. 4   *La finta semplice,* K. 51 (46a)

v. 5   *Mitridate, rè di Ponto,* K. 87 (74a)

v. 6   *Ascanio in Alba,* K. 111

v. 7   *Il sogno di Scipione,* K. 126

v. 8   *Lucio Silla,* K. 135

v. 9   *La finta giardiniera,* K. 196

v. 10   *Il rè pastore,* K. 208

v. 11   *Zaide,* K. 344 (336b)

v. 12   *Thamos, König in Ägypten,* K. 345 (336a)

v. 13   *Idomeneo, rè di Creta,* K. 366

v. 14   *Ballettmusik zur Oper Idomeneo,* K. 367

v. 15   *Die Entführung aus dem Serail,* K. 384

v. 16   *Der Schauspieldirektor,* K. 486

v. 17   *Le nozze di Figaro,* K. 492

v. 18   *Don Giovanni,* K. 527

v. 19   *Così fan tutte,* K. 588

v. 20   *Die Zauberflöte,* K. 620

v. 21   *La clemenza di Tito,* K. 621

v. 22   *Overtüren* [from v. 1–10, 13, 15–21 above]

Series 6.   *Arien, Duette, Terzette und Quartette*

v. 1   *Nr. 1–23:* K. 21 (19c), 23, 36 (33i), 70 (61c), 77 (73e),
78 (73b), 79 (73d), 83 (73p), 88 (73c), 146 (317b),
209, 210, 217, 255, 256, 272, 294, 295, 316 (300b),
368, 369, 374, 383

v. 2   *Nr. 24–47:* K. 416, 418, 419, 420, 431 (425b), 432
(421a), 436, 437, 479, 480, 505, 512, 513, 528, 538,
539, 541, 549, 578, 582, 583, 584, 612, 625 (592a)

Series 7.   *[Songs and canons]*

Abt. 1   *Lieder und Gesänge nr. 1–40:* K. 52 (46c), 53 (47e),
147 (125g), 148 (125h), 149 (125d), 150 (125e), 151
(125 f), 152 (210a), 307 (284d), 308 (295b), 349 (367a),
350 (Anh. C 8.48), 351 (367b), 390 (340c), 391 (340b),
392 (340a), 441, 468, 472, 473, 474, 476, 483, 484,
506, 517, 518, 519, 520, 523, 524, 529, 530, 531, 532,
579, 596, 597, 598, 619

Abt. 2   *Kanons, nr. 41–61:* K. 228 (515b), 229 (382a), 230
(382b), 231 (382c), 232 (509a), 233 (382d), 234 (382e),
347 (382f), 348 (382g), 507, 508, 553–562

Series 8.   *Symphonien*

v. 1   *Nr. 1–21:* no. 1 K. 16; no. 2 K. 17 (Anh. C 11.02),
no. 3 K. 18 (Anh. A 51, K. F. Abel), no. 4 K. 19,
no. 5 K. 22, no. 6 K. 43, no. 7 K. 45, no. 8 K. 48,
no. 9 K. 73, no. 10 K. 74, no. 11 K. 84 (73q), no. 12
K. 110 (75b), no. 13 K. 112, no. 14 K. 114, no. 15 K. 124
no. 16 K. 128, no. 17 K. 129, no. 18 K. 130, no. 19
K. 132, no. 20 K. 133, no. 21 K. 134

v. 2   *Nr. 22–34:* no. 22 K. 162, no. 23 K. 181 (162b),
no. 24 K. 182 (173dA), no. 25 K. 183 (173dB), no.26
K. 184 (161a), no. 27 K. 199 (161b), no. 28 K. 200
(189k), no. 29 K. 201 (186a), no. 30 K. 202 (186b),
no. 31 K. 297 (300a), no. 32 K. 318, no. 33 K. 319,
no. 34 K. 338

v. 3 *Nr. 35–41:* no. 35 K. 385, no. 36 K. 425, no. 37 K. 444
(Introduction K. 425a; rest by M. Haydn), no. 38
K. 504, no. 39 K. 543, no. 40 K. 550, no. 41 K. 551

Series 9. *[Kassationen, Serenaden, Divertimenti]*

Abt. 1 *Kassationen und Serenaden nr. 1–14:* K. 63, 99 (63a),
100 (62a), 101 (250a), 185 (167a), 203 (189b), 204
(213a), 239, 250 (248b), 286 (269a), 320, 361 (370a),
375, 388 (384a) [n.b. *Eine kleine Nachtmusik,* K.
525 is in Series 13]

Abt. 2 *Divertimenti nr. 15–31:* K. 113, 131, 166 (159d),
186 (159b), 187 (Anh. C 17.12), 188 (240b), 205 (167a),
213, 240, 247, 251, 252 (240a), 253, 270, 287 (241H),
289 (271g), 334 (320b)

Series 10. *Märsche und kleine Stücke für Orchester, nr. 1–21:* K. 189
(167b), 214, 215 (213b), 237 (189c), 248, 249, 290 (167AB),
335 (320a), 408 (383e, 385a, 383F), 121 (207a), 409 (383f),
477 (479a), 522, 292 (196c), 410 (484d), 411 (484a), 356 (617a),
617, 608, 616, 445 (320c)

Series 11. *Tänze für Orchester, nr. 1–24;* K. 568, 585, 599, 601, 604,
509, 536, 567, 571, 586, 600, 602, 605, 123 (73g), 267 (271c),
461 (448a), 462 (448b), 463 (448c), 510 (Anh. C 13.02), 535,
587, 603, 609, 610

Series 12. *Konzerte für ein Saiten- oder Blasinstrument und Orchester*

Abt. 1 *Violinkonzerte nr. 1–10:* K. 207, 211, 216, 218, 219,
261, 269 (261a), 373, 190 (186E), 364 (320d)

Abt. 2 *Konzerte für ein Blasinstrument und Orchester, 11–20:*
K. 191 (186a), 299 (297c), 313 (285c), 314 (285d),
315 (285e), 412 (386b), 417, 447, 495, 622

Series 13. *Quintette für Streichinstrumente, nr. 1–9:* K. 174, 406 (516b),
407 (386c), 515, 516, 581, 593, 614, 525

Series 14. *Streichquartette, nr. 1–30:* K. 80 (73f), 155 (134a), 156 (134b),
157–159, 160 (159a), 168–173, 387, 421 (417b), 428 (421b),
458, 464, 465, 499, 575, 589, 590, 136 (125a), 137 (125b),
138 (125c), 546, 285, 298, 370 (368b)

Series 15. *Duos und Trio für Streichinstrumente, nr. 1–4:* K. 423, 424,
487 (496a), 563

Series 16. *Klavierkonzerte*

    v.   1   *Nr. 1–8:* K. 37, 39–41, 175, 238, 242, 246

    v.   2   *Nr. 9–16:* K. 271, 365 (316a), 413 (387a), 414 (385p),
            415 (387b), 449, 450, 451

    v.   3   *Nr. 17–21:* K. 453, 456, 459, 466, 467

    v.   4   *Nr. 22–28:* K. 482, 488, 491, 503, 537, 595, 382

Series 17. *Klavier-Quintette, -Quartette und -Trios*

    Abt. 1   *Klavier-Quintette und -Quartette nr. 1–3:* K.452, 478,
            493

    Abt. 2   *Klavier-Trios nr. 4–11:* K. 254, 442, 496, 498, 502,
            542, 548, 564

Series 18. *Sonaten für Klavier und Violine*

    v.   1   *Nr. 1–23:* K. 6–15, 26–31, 55–61 (Anh. C 23.01–.07)

    v.   2   *Nr. 24–45:* K. 296, 301 (293a), 302 (293b), 303 (293c),
            304 (300c), 305 (293d), 306 (300l), 372, 376 (374d),
            377 (374e), 378 (317d), 379 (373a), 380 (374f), 402
            (385e), 403 (385c), 404 (385d), 454, 481, 526, 547, 359
            (374a)

Series 19. *Werke für Klavier zu 4 Hände und für 2 Klaviere, nr. 1–8:*
            K. 357 (497a), 358 (186c), 381 (123a), 497, 521, 501,
            426, 448 (375a)

Series 20. *Sonaten und Fantasien für Klavier, nr. 1–21:* K. 279 (189d),
            280 (189e), 281 (189f), 282 (189g), 283 (189h), 284 (205b),
            309 (284b), 310 (300d), 311 (284c), 330 (300h), 331 (300i),
            332 (300k), 333 (315c), 457, 545, 570, 576, 394 (383a), 396
            (385f), 397 (385g), 475

Series 21. *Variationen für Pianoforte nr. 1–15:* K. 24–5, 179 (189a),
            180 (173c), 264 (315d), 265 (300e), 352 (374c), 353 (300f),
            354 (299a), 398 (416e), 455, 460 (454a), 500, 573, 613

Series 22. *Kleinere Stücke für Pianoforte, nr. 1–18:* K. 1, 2, 4, 5, 94 (73h),
            355 (576b), 485, 494, 511, 399 (385i), 401 (374e), 3, 312 (590d),
            533, 236 (588b), 540, 574, 624 (626a)

Series 23. *Sonaten für Orgel mit Begleitung, nr. 1–15:* K. 67 (41h),

68 (41i), 69 (41k), 144 (124a), 145 (124b), 212, 224 (241a), 225 (241b), 244–5, 274 (271d), 278 (271a), 328 (317c), 329 (317a), 336 (336d)

Series 24. *Wiederaufgefundene, unbeglaubigte und unvollendete Werke*

    v. 1 *Nr. 1–7: Requiem* K. 626, *6 Symphonien:* K. 75, 76 (42a), 81 (73l), 95 (73n), 96 (111b), 97 (73m)

    v. 2 *Kleinere Orchesterstücke nr. 7a–18:* (Anh. C 14.01), K. 102 (213c), 120 (111a), 163 (141a), Anh. 10 (299b), 291 (Anh. A 52, M. Haydn), 32, 65a (61b), 122 (73t), 363, 106 (588a), 606, 607 (605a), 446 (416d), 268 (Anh. C 14.04), 293 (416f), 371

    v. 3 *Konzerte; Kammermusik und Klavierwerke, nr. 21a–27a:* K. Anh. 56 (315f), 46 (370a), Anh. 91 (516c), 266 (271f), 395 (300g), 153 (375f), 154 (385k), 400 (372a), 534, 594. [*Masses, vocal works, miscellany*] *nr. 28–63:* K. 115 (166d), 427 (417a), Anh. 21 (Anh. A 2, J. Eberlin), 44 (73u), 91 (186i), 116 (90a), 221 (Anh. A 1, J. Eberlin), 337, 429 (468a), 422, 430 (424a), 71, 119 (382h), 178 (417e), 389 (384A), 433 (416c), 434 (480b), 435 (416b), 438, 440 (383h), 580, 82 (730), 393 (385b), Anh. 5 (571a), (562c), 232 (509a), 23, (73i), 98 (Anh. C 11.04), 164 (130a), 487 (496a), 452 (375b, 295a, 439b), Anh. 216 (Anh. 11.03)

2. *Neue Ausgabe sämtlicher Werke.* Herausgegeben von der Internationalen Stiftung Mozarteum, Salzburg. Kassel, Bärenreiter
   This set is organized by Series and by *Werkgruppe* (Wg.) numbers, both of which systems run consecutively throughout the set. Within each Wg., further subdivision may be made into *Abteilung* (Abt.), and/or *Band* (v.), which are numbered separately. The following listing gives first the proposed overall outline of the entire set, then a detailed listing of the v. actually published by 1968. As in the listing of the preceding set, K. nos. in parentheses are those of the 6th ed. (item 3 below). In this set the critical notes are published separately, with numbering corresponding to the music v.

Series 1. Sacred vocal works
    Wg. 1. Masses, Requiem
        Abt. 1. Masses
        Abt. 2. Requiem

     Wg.   2.   Litanies, vespers
               Abt.   1.   Litanies
               Abt.   2.   Vespers

     Wg.   3.   Smaller sacred works

     Wg.   4.   Oratorios, sacred *Singspiele,* cantatas

Series   2.   Theatrical works

     Wg.   5.   Operas and *Singspiele*

     Wg.   6.   Music for plays, pantomimes, ballets

     Wg.   7.   Arias, scenes, ensembles and choruses with orchestra

Series   3.   Songs and canons

     Wg.   8.   Songs with piano or mandolin

     Wg.   9.   Part songs with piano, with wind instruments, and a cappella

     Wg.   10.   Canons

Series   4.   Orchestral works

     Wg.   11.   Symphonies

     Wg.   12.   Cassations, serenades and divertimenti [but see also ser. 7]

     Wg.   13.   Marches and dances for orchestra
               Abt.   1.   Dances
               Abt.   2.   Marches

Series   5.   Concertos

     Wg.   14.   For one or more string, wind or plucked string instruments and orchestra

     Wg.   15.   For one or more pianos and orchestra with [original] cadenzas

Series   6.   Church sonatas

     Wg.   16.   Sonatas for organ and orchestra

Series   7.   Ensemble music for larger groups of performers

     Wg.   17.   Divertimenti and serenades for 6 to 13 wind instruments

Wg. 18. Divertimenti for 6 and 7 string and wind instruments

Series 8.   Chamber music

Wg. 19. String quintets and quintets with wind instruments
Abt. 1. String quintets
Abt. 2. Quintets with wind instruments

Wg. 20. String quartets and quartets with one wind instrument

Wg. 21. Trios and duos for strings and winds

Wg. 22. Quintets, quartets and trios with piano and with glass harmonica
Abt. 1. Quintets and quartets with piano and with glass harmonica
Abt. 2. Piano trios

Wg. 23. Sonatas and variations for piano and violin

Series 9.   Piano music

Wg. 24. Works for 2 pianos and for piano 4 hands

Abt. 1.   Works for 2 pianos
Abt. 2.   Works for piano 4 hands

Wg. 25. Sonatas, fantasies, rondos for piano

Wg. 26. Variations for piano

Wg. 27. Single pieces for piano, for glass harmonica and for mechanical organ

Series 10.   Supplement

Wg. 28. Arrangements, completions and altered versions of works by other composers
Abt. 1. Händel
Abt. 2. Other composers

Wg. 29. Works of doubtful authenticity

Wg. 30. Studies, sketches, &

Wg. 31. Appendices to all series

Wg. 32. Iconography

Wg. 33. Facsimiles of Mozart's handwriting

Wg. 34. Documentary biography

Wg. 35. Index and concordance

Series 1. *Geistliche Gesangwerke*

Wg. 1. *Messen und Requiem*
Abt. 1. *Messen*

v. 1   *Messen* K. 49 (47d), 139 (47a), 65 (61a), 66, 140 (Anh. C 1.12), ed. Walter Senn

Abt. 2. *Requiem,* K. 626, ed. Leopold Nowak
Teilband 1. *Fragment Mozarts*
Teilband 2. *Fragment Mozarts mit den Ergänzungen von Eybler und Süssmayr*

Wg. 2. *Litaneien, Vespern*
Abt. 1. *Litaneien* K. 109 (74e), 125, 195 (186d), 243, ed. Hellmut Federhofer, Renate Federhofer-Königs

Abt. 2. *Vespern und Vesperpsalmen* K. 193 (186g), 321, 339, 321a, ed. Karl Gustav Fellerer, Felix Schröder

Wg. 3. *Kleinere Kirchenwerke,* K. 34, 47, 117 (66a), 141 (66b), 143 (73a), 85 (73s), 86 (73v), 108 (74d), 72 (74f), 127, 165 (158a), 198 (Anh. C 3.08), 222 (205a), 260 (248a), 277 (272a), 273, 276 (321b), 618, ed. H. Federhofer

Wg. 4. *Oratorien, geistliche Singspiele und Kantaten*

v. 1   *Die Schuldigkeit des 1. Gebots,* K. 35, ed. Franz Giegling

v. 2   *Betulia liberata,* K. 118 (74c), ed. Luigi Ferdinando Tagliavini

v. 4   *Kantaten,* K. 42 (35a), 146 (317b), 471, 619, 623, 429 (468a), ed. F. Giegling

Series 2. *Bühnenwerke*

Wg. 5. *Opern und Singspiele*

v. 1   *Apollo und Hyacinth,* K. 38, ed. Alfred Orel

v. 4   *Mitradate, rè di Ponto*, K. 87 (74a),
ed. L. F. Tagliavini

v. 5   *Ascanio in Alba*, K. 111, ed. L. F. Tagliavini

v. 10   *Zaide (Das Serail)*, K. 344 (336b), ed.
Friedrich Heinrich Neumann

v. 13   *L'oca del Cairo*, K. 422, ed. F. H. Neumann

v. 15   *Der Schauspieldirektor*, K. 486, ed.
Gerhard Croll

v. 17   *Il dissoluto punito ossia il Don Giovanni*,
K. 527, ed. Wolfgang Plath, Wolfgang
Rehm

v. 19   *Die Zauberflöte*, K. 620, ed. A. Orel

v. 20   *La clemenza di Tito*, K. 621, ed. F. Giegling

Wg. 6.   *Musik zu Schauspielen, Pantomimen, Balletten*

v. 1   *Chöre und Zwischenaktmusiken zu Thamos,
König in Ägypten*, K. 345 (336a), ed.
Herald Heckmann

v. 2   *Musik zu Pantomimen und Balletten*, K.
Anh. 10 (K. 299b), K. 300, 367, ed. H.
Heckmann

Wg. 7.   *Arien, Szenen, Ensembles und Chöre mit Orchester*

v. 1   K. 21 (19c), 23, 78 (73b), 79 (73d), 36 (33i),
70 (61c), 88 (73c), 77 (73e), 82 (73o),
83 (73p), 74b, 209, 210, 217, 152 (210a),
ed. Stefan Kunze

v. 2   K. 255, 256, 272, 294, 295, 486a (295a),
316 (300b), 368, 369, 374, ed. S. Kunze

Series 3.   *Lieder und Kanons*

Wg. 8.   *Lieder mit Klavier:* K. 53 (47e, 43b), 147 (125g),
148 (125h), 307 (284d), 308 (295b), 349 (367a),
351 (367b), 392 (340a), 391 (340b), 390 (340c),
468, 472–4, 476, 506, 343 (336c), 517–20, 523–4,
529–31, 552, 596–8 *et al.*, ed. Ernst August Ballin

Series   4.   *Orchesterwerke*

    Wg.   11.   Sinfonien

        v.   3   *Sinfonien,* K. 128–30, 132–4 [= nos. 16–21], 141a, ed. Wilhelm Fischer

        v.   4   *Sinfonien,* K. 162, 181 (162b), 182 (173dA), 183 (173dB), 184 (161a), 199 (161b), 200 (189k) [= nos. 22–28], ed. Hermann Beck.

        v.   5   *Sinfonien* K. 201–2 (186a–b) [= nos. 29–30], overture to K. 196 [*La finta giardiniera;* overture also found separate as K. 121 (207a)], K. 297 (300a) [= no. 31], overture to K. 208 [*Il rè pastore;* overture also found separate as K. 102 (213c)], ed. H. Beck

        v.   7   *Sinfonien nach den Serenaden* K. 204 (213a), 250 (248b), 320, ed. Günter Hausswald

        v.   9   *Sinfonien K. 543, 550 (1. und 2. Fassung), 551* [nos. 39–41], ed. H. C. Robbins Landon

    Wg.   12.   *Kassationen, Serenaden und Divertimenti für Orchester*

        v.   2   *Serenaden* K. 113, 131, 186/185 (167b/a), ed. G. Hausswald

        v.   3   *Serenaden,* K. 237/203 (189c/b), 215/204 (213b/a), 239, ed. G. Hausswald

        v.   6   *Serenaden* K. 525, 136–8 (125a–c), Anh. 69 (525a), Anh. 223c (Anh. A 50), ed. Karl Heinz Füssl, Ernst Fritz Schmid

    Wg.   13.   *Märsche und Tänze für Orchester*

        Abt.   1.   *Tänze*

        v.   1   *Tänze,* K. 65a (61b), 103 (61d), 104 (61e), 105 (61f), 61h, 123 (73g), 122 (73t),

164 (130a), 176, 101 (250a), 267 (271c);
Klavierfassungen: 12 *Duette aus* K. 103
(61d), 61g, 11, 94 (73h), Kontretänze für
Graf Czernin (no K. no.), K. 315a (315g),
ed. Rudolf Rivers

Series 5.   *Konzerte*

Wg. 15.   *Konzerte für ein oder mehrere Klaviere und Orchester
mit (original) Kadenzen*

v.   5   *Klavierkonzerte* K. 453, 456, 459, ed. Eva
and Paul Badura-Skoda

v.   6   *Klavierkonzerte* K. 466, 467, 482, ed. Hans
Engel, Horst Heussner

v.   7   *Klavierkonzerte* K. 488, 491, 503, ed.
Hermann Beck

v.   8   *Klavierkonzerte.* K. 537, 595, 386, *Fragmente und Skizzen,* ed. W. Rehm

Series 6.   *Kirchensonaten*

Wg. 16.   *Sonaten für Orgel und Orchester,* K. 67 (41h),
68 (41i), 69 (41k), 144 (124a), 145 (124b), 212,
224 (241a), 225 (241b), 244–5, 263, 274 (271d),
278 (271e), 328 (317c), 329 (317a), 336 (336d);
Fragmente K. 124A, 124c (Anh. C 16.01, L. Mozart), ed. Minos E. Dounias

Series 8.   *Kammermusik*

Wg. 19.   *Streichquintette und Quintette mit Blasinstrumenten*

Abt. 1.   *Streichquintette* K. 174, 515, 516, 406
(516b), 593, 614, ed. Ernst Hess, E. F.
Schmid
Abt. 2.   *Quintette mit Bläsern,* K. 407 (386c), 581,
Fragmente, ed. E. F. Schmid

Wg. 20.   *Streichquartette und Quartette mit einem Blasinstrument*

Abt. 1.   *Streichquartette*

v.   1   K. 80 (73f), 155 (134a), 156 (134b),

157–9, 160 (159a), 168–73, ed. K. H.
Füssl, W. Plath, W. Rehm

v. 2   K. 387, 421 (417b), 458, 428 (421b), 464,
465, ed. Ludwig Finscher

v. 3   K. 499, 575, 589, 590, *Entwürfe und Fragmente,* ed. L. Finscher

Abt. 2.   *Quartette mit einem Blasinstrument* K.
285, 285a, Anh. 171 (K. 285b), 298, 370
(368b), ed. Jaroslav Pohanka

Wg. 22.   *Quintette, Quartette und Trios mit Klavier und mit
Glasharmonika*

Abt. 1.   *Quartette und Quintette mit Klavier und
mit Glasharmonika,* K. 478, 493, 452, 617,
161a, ed. H. Federhofer

Abt. 2.   *Klaviertrios* K. 10–15, 254, 496, 498, 502,
542, 548, 564, 442, ed. W. Plath, W. Rehm

Wg. 23.   *Sonaten und Variationen für Klavier und Violine*

v. 1   *Sonaten* K. 6–9, 26–31, 301–3 (293a–c),
304 (300c), 305 (293d), 306 (300e), 296,
378 (317d), ed. Edvard Reeser

v. 2   *Sonaten* K. 379 (373a), 376 (374d), 380
(394f), 454, 481, 526, 547, 372, 403 (385c),
404 (385d), 402 (385e), 396 (385i); Variationen K. 359 (374a), 360 (374b), *Fragmente und Frühfassungen,* ed. E. Reeser

Series 9.   *Klaviermusik*

Wg. 24.   *Werke für zwei Klaviere und für Klavier zu vier
Händen*

Abt. 1.   *Werke für zwei Klaviere* K. 448 (375a),
426 *und Fragmente,* ed. E. F. Schmid

Abt. 2.   *Werke für Klavier zu vier Händen* K. 19d,
381 (123a), 358 (186c), 497, 501, 521,
357 (497a), ed. W. Rehm

Wg. 26.   K. 24, 25, 180 (173c), 179 (189a), 354 (299a),

265 (300e), 353 (300f), 264 (315d), 352 (374d), 398 (416e), 455, 500, 573, 613, *Fragmente,* ed. Kurt von Fischer

Series 10.   *Supplement*

Wg. 28.   *Bearbeitungen, Ergänzungen und Übertragungen fremder Werke*

   Abt. 1.   *Bearbeitungen von Werken Georg Friedrich Händels*

      v. 2   *Der Messias* K. 572, ed. Andreas Holschneider

      v. 3   *Das Alexander-Fest* K. 591, ed. A. Holschneider

   Abt. 2.   *Bearbeitungen von Werken verschiedener Komponisten. Klavierkonzerte K. 37, 39–41, 107 und Kadenzen Mozarts zu fremden Klavierkonzerten,* ed. Walter Gerstenberg, E. Reeser

Wg. 30.   *Studien und nicht zugewiesene Skizzen und Entwürfe*

      v. 1   *Thomas Attwood's Theorie und Kompositionen bei Mozart,* ed. Erich Hertzmann, Cecil B. Oldman, Daniel Heartz, Alfred Mann

Wg. 32.   *Mozart und seine Welt in zeitgenössischen Bildern,* by Maximillian Zenger, Otto Erich Deutsch

Wg. 34.   *Mozart, die Dokumente seines Lebens,* by Otto E. Deutsch

      This was translated into English by Eric Blom, Peter Branscombe and Jeremy Noble and published as a separate book by the Stanford University Press (1965) under the title *Mozart, A documentary biography.*

3.   Ludwig, Ritter von Köchel, *Chronologisch-thematisches Verzeichnis sämtlicher Tonwerke Wolfgang Amadé Mozarts.* Sechste Auflage, bearbeitet von Franz Giegling, Alexander Weinmann, Gerd Sievers. Wiesbaden, Breitkopf & Härtel

   Common abbreviations: K., KV

**ML 410
.M9 S365
1962**

4. Otto Schneider und Anton Algatsky, *Mozart-Handbuch: Chronik-Werk-Bibliographie*. Wien, Brüder Hollinek, 1962
   Includes indexed bibliography of 3871 items

5. *Mittheilungen für die Mozart-Gemeinde in Berlin*, hrsg. von Rudolph Genée. 1895–1925
   Appeared in *Heften* annually, grouped into v. as follows: Heft 1–10 (1895–1900) = v. 1; Heft 11–22 (1900–06) = v. 2; Heft 23–32 (1907–11) = v. 3; Heft 33–43 (1912–14, 1919–25) = v. 4. There is an INDEX for Heft 1–20 in v. 2 and cumulative tables of contents in v. 3 and 4. There is also a *Supplement* (1906) of music and facsimiles

ML410
.M9 A11

6. *Mozart-Jahrbuch*, hrsg. von Hermann Abert. Jg. 1 (1923), Jg. 2 (1924), Jg. 3 (1929).
   Includes book reviews, bibliographical lists

ML410
.M9 N25

7. *Neues Mozart-Jahrbuch*, hrsg. von Erich Valentin. 3 v. (1941–3)

ML 5
.M617

8. *Mozart-Jahrbuch*, hrsg. von der Internationalen Stiftung Mozarteum. 1950–

   Jg. 1–10   (1950–59) 1 v. each
   Jg. 11   (1960–61)
   Jg. 12   (1962/3)
   Jg. 13   (1964)
   Jg. 14   (1965/6)
   From Jg. 3 (1952) contains current bibliography lists.

9. *Acta-Mozartiana*. Mitteilungen der deutschen Mozart-Gesellschaft, hrsg. von Erich Valentin

10. *Internationalen Stiftung Mozarteum: Schriftenreihe*, 1966–

see Kardex
ML410
.M9 B15
      v. 1   Carl Bär, *Mozart: Krankheit, Tod, Begräbnis*
      v. 2–4 rec'd.

**64 A
MUSORGSKII, MODEST PETROVICH, 1839–1881**
XX M3
M85

Sämliche Werke, ed. Paul Lamm. Moskau, Staatsmusikverlag, 1928–1939

This set originally appeared in many short sections, and was never completed. In 1969, Kalmus of New York issued an unaltered reprint of the set as it stood in 1931, but with some additions of Lamm editions of Musorgskii not included in the original set. The Kalmus reprint does not include a volume of the complete solo piano works which appeared in 1939. New volume numbers are assigned to the reprint. The following listing gives the original volume numbers first, followed by the Kalmus numbers in parentheses.

v. 1:1	(v. 1)	*Szene in der Schenke aus der Oper "Boris Godunov"* (orch. score)
v. 1:2	(v. 1)	*Szene bei Kromy aus der Oper "Boris Godunov"* (orch. score)
	(v. 2)	*Boris Godunov* (piano score)
	(v. 3:1)	*Boris Godunov: Prolog und 1. Aufzug* (orch. score)
	(v. 3:2)	———: *II Aufzug* (orch. score)
	(v. 3:3)	———: *III Aufzug* (orch. score)
	(v. 3:4)	———: *IV Aufzug* (orch. score)
v. 2	(v. 4)	*Chowanschtschina* (piano score; completed by B. V. Assafiev)
v. 3:1	(v. 5)	*Der Jahrmarkt zu Sorotschinzi* (piano score)
v. 3:2	(v. 6)	——— (orch. score)
v. 4:3	(v. 7)	*Mlada: Marktszene, Zug der Fürstin und Priester* (2 piano & voice score)
v. 5:1–2	(v. 8)	*Jugendlieder: Sammlung von Liedern und Gesängen* Contents: O mein Sternlein; Frohe Stunde; Düster und feucht war der Abend; Hab viel Schlösser; Gevet; Sag', o sag'; Ihr nennet Fieberwahn; Rauhe Winde wehn; Doch könnt ich dich im Leben noch einmal wiedersehn; Ach, warum blickt dein Auge; Lied des Harfenspielers; König Saul; Nacht; Kallistrat; Der Verstossene; Schlafe ein; Lied des Balearers; Ogni sabato
v. 5:3	(v. 9)	*Lieder und Gesänge* Contents: Meines Herzens Sehnsucht; Ich wollt'

meine Schmerzen ergössen; Hopak; Aus meinen
Tränen spriessen; Jungfer Sawischna; O, du
Säufer; Der Seminarist

v. 5:4   (v. 10)   *Lieder und Gesänge*
Contents: Hebräisches Lied; Die Elster; Nach
Pilzen; Bauernfest; Der Spassvogel; Der Zie-
genbock; Der Klassiker; Auf dem Berge; Das
Waisenkind; Wiegenlied Jerjemuschkas; Kinder-
liedchen; Abendliedchen; Der Vergessene

v. 5:5   (v. 11)   *Der Schaukasten*

v. 5:6   (v. 12)   *Die Kinderstube*

v. 5:7   (v. 13)   *Ohne Sonne*

v. 5:8   (v. 14)   *Lieder und Gesänge*
Contents: Die Unbegreifliche; Es rollt kein
Donner; Schweigend durchflog eine Seele;
Hochmut; Wer sah einen Burschen am Spinnrad
sitzen?; Es vergessen sich; Vision; Wanderer;
Lied des Mephistopheles; Am Dnjepr

v. 5:9   (v. 15)   *Lieder und Tänze des Todes*

v. 7:1   (v. 16)   (Kalmus title: *Six works for orchestra)*
Feierlicher Marsch (orch.)

v. 7:2   (v. 16)   *Marfa's Lied* (voice, orch.)

v. 7:3   (v. 16)   *Nacht* (voice, orch.)

v. 7:4   (v. 16)   *Scherzo* (orch.)

v. 7:5   (v. 16)   *Intermezzo in modo classico* (orch.)

v. 7:6   (v. 16)   Hopak (voice, orch.)

v. 8:2   (v. 17)   *Tableaux d'une exposition, pour piano*

              (v. 18)   *Feierlicher Marsch* (piano 4 hands)

v. 8:3   (v. 18)   *Scherzo* (arr. for piano 4 hands by D. Kabalewsky)

v. 8:4   (v. 18)   *Intermezzo* (arr. for piano 4 hands by D. Kabalewsky

In addition to the above, published by 1931, a v. 8 containing all the solo
piano works was issued in 1939; not in the reprint.

65
OBRECHT, JACOB, *ca.* 1453–1505

1–2. Complete works

1. *Werken,* uitgegevwn dor Prof. Dr. Johannes Wolf. Vereeniging voor Nord-Nederlands Musiekgeschiedenis. Leipzig, Breitkopf & Härtel, 1908–1921

> The numbering systems of this set are like those of DePres **(B 29)**, q.v. Its 30 *Aflevering* are organized as follow:
> Masses: see index below
> Motets
> Afl. 2 = *Motetten 1* (nos. 1–4)
> Afl. 4 = *Motetten 2* (nos. 5–10)
> Afl. 8 = *Motetten 3* (nos. 11–15)
> Afl. 30 = *Motetten 4* (nos. 16–22)
>
> Secular works
> Afl. 15–16

Mass title	Mass no.	Afl.	Mass v.
Adieu mes amours	14	19	4
Ave regina coelorum	12	17	3
Beata viscera	21	27	5
Caput	18	23–4	4
Carminum	16	21	4
Forseulement	22	29	5
Fortuna desperata	3		1
Kyrie, Gloria		3	
Credo-Agnus		5	
Graecorum	2	3	1
Je ne demande	1	1	1
L'homme armé	20	26	5
Malheur me bat	4	6	1
Maria zart	7	10	2
O quam suavis est	10	13	3
Petrus apostolus	13	18	3
Salva diva parens	5	7	1
Sancto Martino	8	11	2
Schoen lief	17	22	4

Mass title	Mass no.	Afl.	Mass v.
Si dedero	9	12	3
Sicut spina rosum	11	14	3
sine nomine	15	20	4
sine nomine	19	25	5
sine nomine	23	29	5
Sub tuum prasidium	6	9	2

2.   *Opera omnia*. Editio altera quam edendam curavit Vereniging vor Nederlandse Muziekgeschiedenis

        This is a new edition of item 1 and preserves the numbering of the v. and individual items, but abandons the *Aflevering* numbering system. Each v. is instead divided into fascicles. This edition was started by A. Smijers and is now edited by M. van Crevel.

v. 1   *Missae*, ed. Smijers

        Fasc. 1 *Missa Je ne demande*
        Fasc. 2 *Missa Graecorum*
        Fasc. 3 *Missa Fortuna desperata*
        Fasc. 4 *Missa Malheur me bat*
        Fasc. 5 *Missa Salve diva parens*

[v. ?]   *Missae*, ed. M. van Crevel. Introduction and critical notes in English

        Fasc. 6 *Missa Sub tuum praesidium*
        Fasc. 7 *Missa Maria Zart*

v. 2   *Motetti*, ed. Smijers

        Fasc. 1 *Salve regina, Salve crux arbor vita, Haec Deum caeli*
        Fasc. 2 *Factor orbis, Laudemus nunc Dominus, Ave regina caelorum*

66
OCKEGHEM, JOHANNES, *ca.* 1430–1495

Collected works, ed. Dragan Plamenac. American Musicological Society, 1947–59

v. 1   *Masses I–VIII.* Second, corrected edition (The first edition
was Jg. 1:1 of *Publikationen älterer Musik* [**A 87**])
1. *Missa quarti toni* (3 v.)   2. *Missa sine nomine* (3 v.)
3. *Missa Au travail suis* (4 v.)   4. *Missa cuiusvis toni* (4 v.)
5. *Missa De plus en plus* (4 v.)   6. *Missa Ecce ancilla Domini*
(4 v.) 7. *Missa L'homme armé* (4 v.) 8. *Missa Ma maitresse*
(4 v.)

v. 2   *Masses and Mass sections IX–XVI*
9. *Missa mi-mi* (4 v.)   10. *Missa prolationum* (4 v.)   11.
Missa Caput (4 v.)   12. *Credo sine nomine* (4 v.)   13. *Missa
Fors seulement* (5 v.)   14. *Missa sine nomine* (5 v.)   15.
Requiem   16. Doubtful authorship (Ockeghem or Cornelis
Heyns), *Missa Pour quelque paine*

67
PALESTRINA, GIOVANNI PIERLUIGI DA, 1525–1594

1. Complete works   2. Index of Masses   3. Index of motets   4. Monograph series

1.   *Le opere complete.* Roma, Fratelli Scalera, 1939–[*ca.* 1965]
Referred to as "Casimiri edition" to distinguish it from the older
"Haberl edition" which it supersedes. The latter is fully indexed in
Karl Gustav Fellerer, *Palestrina: Leben und Werke* (zweite . . .
Ausgabe. Düsseldorf, Schwann, 1960), which also includes an index
to the present set through v. 27. The Masses and motets of the
present set are indexed in items 2–3 below.

v. 1   *Il libro primo delle Messe a 4, 5, e 6 voci (1554, 1591),* ed.
Raffaele Casimiri

v. 2   *Il libro dei Madrigali a 4 voci (1596, 1554, 1561),* ed. Casimiri

v. 3   *Il libro primo dei Motetti a 4 voci (1590),* ed. Casimiri

v. 4   *Il libro secondo delle Messe a 4, 5, e 6 voci (1567, 1600),* ed.
Casimiri

v. 5   *Il libro primo dei Motetti a 5, 6, e 7 voci (1600),* ed. Casimiri

v. 6   *Il libro terzo delle Messe a 4, 5, e 6 voci (1570),* ed. Casimiri

v. 7   *Il libro secondo dei Motetti a 5, 6, e 8 voci (1573),* ed. Casimiri

v. 8   *Il libro terzo dei motetti a 5, 6, e 7 voci (1575)*

v. 9   *Il libro primo dei madrigali (spirituali) a 5 voci (1581, 1566–1576)*, ed. Casimiri

v. 10   *Il libro quarto delle messe a 4 e 5 voci (1582)*, ed. Casimiri

v. 11   *Il libro secondo dei motetti a 4 voci (1604) ; Il libro quarto dei motetti a 5 voci (1588)*, ed. Casimiri

v. 12   *Il libro quinto dei motetti a 5 voci (1588)*, ed. Casimiri

v. 13   *Le lamentazioni a 4, 6, e 8 voci (1589)*, ed. Casimiri

v. 14   *Inni di tutto l'anno a 4, 5, e 6 voci (1590)*, ed. Casimiri

v. 15   *Il liber quinto delle messe a 4, 5, e 6 voci (1590)*, ed. Casimiri

v. 16   *Magnificat a 4, 5, 6, e 8 v. (1591)*, ed. Casimiri

v. 17   *Offertori di tutto l'anno a 5 voci (1593)*, ed. Lavinio Virgili

v. 18   *Le messe di Mantova (I)*, ed. Knud Jeppesen

v. 19   *Le messe di Mantova (II)*, ed. K. Jeppesen

v. 20   *Le litanie a (3), 4, 5, 6, e 8 voci (1600)*, ed. Lino Bianchi

v. 21   *Il libro sesto delle messe a 4, 5, e 6 voci (1594, 1596, Mss)*, ed. L. Bianchi

v. 22   *Il libro secondo dei madrigali spirituali a 5 voci (Priego alla B. Vergine, 1594)*, ed. Bianchi

v. 23   *Il libro settimo delle messe a 4 e 5 voci (1594, 1605, 1609, Mss)*, ed. Bianchi

v. 24   *Il libro ottavo delle messe a 4, 5, e 6 voci (1599, 1609, Mss)*, ed. Bianchi

v. 25   *Il libro nono delle messe a 4, 5, e 6 voci (1599, 1609, Mss)*, ed. Bianchi

v. 26   *Messa Tu es Petrus a 18 voci in tre cori*, ed. Bianchi

v. 27   *Il libro decimo delle messe a 4, 5, e 6 voci (1600 &)*, ed. Bianchi

v. 28   *Il libro decimoprimo delle messe a 4, 5, e 6 voci (1600, Mss)*, ed. Bianchi

v. 29   *Il libro decimosecondo delle messe a 4, 5, e 6 voci (1601, Mss)*, ed. Bianchi

v. 30   *Le messe a 8 voci (1585, 1601, Mss),* ed. Bianchi

v. 31   *Il libro secondo dei madrigali a 4 voci (1589),* ed. Bianchi

2. Index of Masses in item 1

Title	no.voices	v.no.
Ad coenam agni	5	1
Ad fugam	4	4
Aeterna Christi munera	4	15
Alma redemptoris	6	28
Ascendo ad patrem	5	29
Aspice Domine	5	4
Assumpta est Maria	6	25
Ave Maria	4	23
Ave Maria	6	21
Ave regina	4	25
Beatae Mariae virginis (3 settings)	5	18
Beatus Laurentius	5	24
Brevis	4	6
Confitebor tibi	8	30
De beata virgine	4	4
De beata virgine	6	6
De feria	4	6
Descendit angelus	4	28
Dies sanctificatus	4	21
Dilexi quoniam	5	21
Dum complerentur	6	24
Dum esset summus pontifex	4	24
Ecce ego Joannes	6	24
Ecce sacerdos magnus	4	1
Emendemus in melius	4	23
Eripe me de inimicis	5	10
Fratres ego enim accepi	8	30
Fugam, ad	4	4
Gabriel archangelus	4	1
Già fu chi m'ebbe cara	4	27
Hodie Christus natus est	8	30

Title	no. voices	v. no.
Iam Christus astra ascendat	4	15
Illumina oculos meos	6	27
In duplicibus minoribus (2 settings)	5	18
In festis apostolorum (2 settings)	5	19
In illo tempore	4	27
In maioribus duplicibus	4	23
In semiduplicibus maioribus (2 settings)	5	19
In te, Domine, speravi	4	21
In te, Domine, speravi	6	25
Inviolata	4	4
Io mi son giovanetta (Primi toni)	4	6
Iste confessor	4	15
Jam = Iam		
Je suis déshéritée (sine nomine)	4	19
Jesu nostra redemptio (Missa tertia)	4	10
Lauda Sion (Missa prima)	4	10
Laudate Dominum	8	30
L'homme armé (Missa quarta)	4	10
L'homme armé	5	6
Memor esto	5	24
Nasce la gioia mia	6	15
Nigra sum	5	15
O admirabile commercium	5	24
O magnum mysterium (Missa quarta)	5	10
O regem coeli	4	1
O rex gloriae	4	24
O sacrum convivium	5	24
O virgo simul et mater	5	27
Octavi toni	6	28
Panem nostrum	5	27
Panis quem ego dabo	4	15
Papae Marcelli	6	4
Pater noster	4	27
Petra sancta	5	27
Pope Marcellus	6	4
Prima (Lauda Sion)	4	10

Title	no. voices	v. no.
Primi toni (Io mi son giovanetta)	4	6
Primi toni (Missa secunda)	4	10
Pro defunctis	5	1
Qual è il più grand' amor	5	29
Quam pulchra es	4	21
Quando lieta sperai	5	28
Quarta (L'homme armé)	4	10
Quarta (O magnum mysterium)	5	10
Quem dicunt homines	4	24
Regina coeli	4	29
Regina coeli	5	28
Repleatur os meum	5	6
Requiem	5	1
Sacerdos et pontifex	5	23
Sacerdotes Domini	6	24
Salve regina	5	28
Salvum me fac	5	4
Sanctorum meritis	4	23
Secunda (primi toni)	4	10
Sicut lilium inter spinas	5	15
Sine nomine	4	4
Sine nomine (Mantua Ms.)	4	19
Sine nomine (Je suis déshéritée)	4	21
Sine nomine	5	25
Sine nomine	6	1
Sine titule	6	28
Spem in alium	4	6
Te Deum laudamus	6	25
Tertia (Jesu nostra redemptio)	4	10
Tu es pastor ovium	5	23
Tu es Petrus	6	28
Tu es Petrus	18	26
Ut re mi fa sol la	6	6
Veni creator spiritus	6	25
Veni sponsa Christi	4	25
Vestiva et colli	5	25
Viri Galilei	6	29

Virtute magna   4   I

3.   Index of motets and other works with Latin texts in item i above.

Title	no.voices	v.no.
A solis ortus cardine	4	14
Accepit Jesus calicem	6	8
Ad coenam agni providi	4	14
Ad Dominum cum tribularer	4	11
Ad preces nostras	4	14
Ad te levavi	4	11
Ad te levavi	5	17
Adjuro vos	5	11
Adoramus te	4	11
Aegypte, noliflere	5	12
Afferentur regi	5	17
Afflige opprimentes nos	5	8
Alleluia: Tulerunt Dominum	5	5
Alma redemptoris mater	4	11
Ambula, sancte Dei	5	12
Angelus Domini	5	8
Angelus Domini	5	17
Anima me turbata est	4	11
Anima nostra	5	17
Apparuit caro suo Joanni	5	12
Ardens est cor meum	5	12
Ascendit Deus	5	17
Ascendit Deus	6	5
Ascendo ad patrem	5	7
Assumpta est	5	17
Aurea luce	4	14
Ave Maria	4	3
Ave Maria	4	11
Ave Maria	5	8
Ave Maria	5	17
Ave maris stella	4	14
Ave regina coelorum	4	11
Ave regina coelorum	5	12
Ave regina coelorum	8	8
Ave trinitatis sacrarium	5	12

Title	no. voices	v. no.
Beata Barbara	6	7
Beatae Mariae Magdalenae	5	5
Beatus Laurentius	4	3
Beatus Laurentius	5	5
Beatus vir qui suffert	4	3
Benedicam Dominum	5	17
Benedicite gentes	5	17
Benedicta sit	4	3
Benedicta tu	6	7
Benedictus es	5	17
Benedictus sit Deus	5	17
Benedixisti, Domine	5	17
Biduanis ac triduanis	5	8
Bonum est confiteri	5	17
Canite tuba in Sion	5	7
Cantate Domine	6	7
Cantantibus organis	5	8
Caput ejus	5	11
Caro mea	5	8
Christe qui lux es	4	14
Christe redemptor omnium	4	14
Circuire possum (by P.'s son Angelo)	5	7
Coenantibus illis	5	7
Columna es immobilis	6	8
Commissa mea ravesco	4	11
Conditor alme siderum	4	14
Confessio et pulchritudo	5	17
Confirma hoc, Deus	5	17
Confitebor tibi	5	17
Confitebor tibi	8	7
Confitebor tibi (by P.'s son Rodolfo)	5	7
Confitebuntur coeli	5	17
Confitemini Domino	4	11
Congratulamini mihi	4	3
Congrega, Domine	5	8
Constitues eos	5	17
Corona aurea	5	7

Title	v. no. voices	v. no.
Crucem sanctam	5	5
Cum ortus fuerit sol	6	8
Cum pervenisset beatus Andreas	5	5
De profundis	5	17
Decus morum, dux minorum	5	14
Deficiant peccatores	6	7
Derelinquat impius	5	7
Descendi in hortum meum	5	11
Deus, Deus meus	5	17
Deus enim firmavit	5	17
Deus qui dedisti legem	5	5
Deus qui ecclesiam tuam	6	8
Deus tu convertens	5	17
Deus tuorum militum	3–5	14
Deus tuorum militum	3–4	14
Dextera Domini	5	17
Dies sanctificatus	4	3
Diffusa est gratia	5	17
Dilectus meus descendit	5	11
Dilectus meus mihi	5	11
Doctor bonus	4	3
Doctor egregie Paule	4	14
Domine, convertere	5	17
Domine Deus, in simplicitate	5	17
Domine Deus, qui conteris	5	8
Domine, in auxilium	5	17
Domine, in virtute tua	8	7
Domine pater (by P.'s brother Silla)	5	7
Domine, praevenisti	5	7
Domine, quando veneris	4	11
Domine, secundum actum meum	5	12
Dominus Jesus	5	7
Dum aurora finem daret	4	3
Dum complerentur	6	5
Dum ergo essent	6	5
Duo utera tua	5	11
Ecce merces sanctorum	5	12

Title	no. voices	v. no.
Ecce nunc benedicite	4	11
Ecce tu pulcher es	5	11
Ego enim sum Dominus	6	7
Ego rogabo patrem	5	7
Ego sum panis vivus	4	11
Ego sum panis vivus	5	5
Eja ergo	4	11
Eja ergo	5	12
Elegerunt apostoli	5	17
En gratulemur hodie	3–4	14
Erat Joannes in deserto	5	8
Et introeuentes in monumentum	5	8
Et omnes angeli	6	5
Exaltabo te	5	17
Exaudi Domine	4	3
Exi cito	5	7
Excita, Domine	6	7
Exspectans exspectavi	5	17
Exultet coelum laudibus	4–5	14
Exultate Deo	5	12
Fasiculus myrrae	5	11
Fuit homo	4	3
Fuit homo	5	8
Fundamenta eius	4	11
Gaude, Barbara	5	7
Gaude, praesul optime	5	8
Gaude, quia meruisti	5	7
Gaude, virgo gloriosa	4	11
Gaude, virgo gloriosa	5	12
Gaudent in coelis	4	3
Gloriosam mortem	6	7
Gloriosi principes	4	11
Guttur tuum	5	11
Haec dies	4	11
Haec dies	6	8
Heu mihi	4	11

Title	no. voices	v. no.
Hic est discipulis ille	5	5
Hic est vere Martyr	4	3
Hierusalem, cito veniet	6	7
Hodie beata virgo	4	3
Hodie beata virgo	5	5
Hodie Christus natus est	8	8
Hodie nata est	5	5
Homo quidam	5	7
Hostias Herodes impie	3,6	14
Hujus abtentu	4	14
Hymnus canoris personet	4	14
Illumina oculos meos	5	17
Immittet angelus	5	17
Improperium	5	17
In diebus illis	4	3
In hac cruce (by P.'s son Angelo)	5	7
In illo tempore	5	7
In omnem terram	5	17
In te speravi	5	17
Inclytae sanctae virginis Catherinae	5	8
Introduxit me rex	5	11
Inveni David	5	17
Iste confessor	4,5	14
Iste est qui ante Deum	4	3
Isti sunt viri sancti	4	3
Iu . . see Ju. . .		
Jesu corona virginum	4,5	14
Jesu, nostra redemptio	4,6	14
Jesus junxit se	4	3
Jubilate Deo omnis terra	5	8
Jubilate Deo omnis terra	5	17
Jubilate Deo omnis terra	8	8
Jubilate Deo universa terra	5	17
Judica me, Deus	6	8
Justitiae Domini	5	17
Justorum animae	5	17
Justus ut palma	5	17

Title	no. voices	v. no.
Laetamini in Domino	5	17
Laetus Hyperboreum	5	12
Laeva ejus	5	11
Lamentationes		13
Lapidabant Stephanum	4	3
Lapidabant Stephanum	5	5
Lauda anima mea	5	17
Lauda mater ecclesia	4	14
Lauda Sion	4	3
Lauda Sion	8	8
Laudate Dominum omnes gentes	8	7
Laudate Dominum qui	5	17
Laudate nomen ejus	5	8
Laudate pueri	8	7
Laudibus summis	4,5	14
Litanies		20
Loquebantur	4	3
Lucis creator optime	3,5	14
Magna est gloria ejus	8	7
Magne pater Augustine	4,5	14
Magnificats		16
Magnum haereditatis mysterius	4	3
Magnus sanctus Paulus	4	3
Manifesto vobis veritatem	5	8
Manus tuae	5	12
Maria virgo	7	5
Meditabor	5	17
Memor esto	5	7
Mensis Augusti	5	14
Mihi autem	5	17
Miserere nostri	4	11
Misso Herodes speculatore	4	3
Nativitas tua	4	3
Nigra sum	5	11
Nisi ego abiero	5	12
Nos autem gloriari	4	3
Notas facite in populis	8	7

Title	no. voices	v. no.
Numquid Sion dicet	4	11
Nunc dimittis (by P.'s brother Silla)	6	7
Nunc juvat celsi	4	14
O admirabile commercium	5	5
O Antoni eremita	5	5
O beata et benedicta	5	5
O beatum pontificem	5	5
O beatum virum	5	5
O bone Jesu	6	8
O Domine Jesu Christe	6	5
O lux beata trinitas	4	14
O lux et decus Hispaniae	5	8
O magnum mysterium	6	5
O patruo	5	12
O quam metuendus est	5	8
O quantus luctus	4	3
O rex gloriae	4	3
O sacrum convivium	5	7
O singulare praesidium	5	8
O vera summa	5	5
O virgo simul et mater	5	7
Omnipotens sempiterne Deus	5	8
Oravi ad Dominum	5	17
Orietur stella	5	12
Osculetur me	5	11
Pange lingua	4,5	14
Panis quem ego dabo	5	5
Parce mihi, Domine	5	12
Paries quidem filium	5	5
Pater noster	5	8
Paucitas dierum	5	12
Pax vobis	5	8
Peccantem me quotidie	5	7
Peccavi, quid faciam	5	12
Peccavimus	5	12
Perfice gressus meos	5	17

Title	no. voices	v. no.
Petrus beatus	4	14
Populum humilem	5	17
Postquam autem	6	8
Posuisti Domine	5	17
Precatus est Moyses	5	17
Prima lux surgens	4-5	14
Proles coelo prodiit	4-5	14
Puer qui natus est	5	5
Pueri Hebraeorum	4	11
Pulchra es amica mea	5	11
Pulchra es, O Maria	6	5
Pulchrae sunt genae tuae	5	11
Quae est ista	4	3
Quae est ista	5	11
Quam pulchra es	5	11
Quam pulchri sunt	4	3
Quam pulchri sunt	5	5
Quam pulchri sunt	5	11
Quem vidistis, pastores	6	5
Quia vidiste me, Thoma	4	11
Quicumque Christum quaeritis	4	14
Quid habes, Hester	5	8
Quis sicut Dominus	8	7
Quodcumque ligaveris	6	5
Quodcumque ligaveris	6	7
Quocumque vinclis	4	14
Recordare mei	5	17
Reges Tharsis	5	17
Rex gloriose martyrum	4	14
Rex Melchior	5	12
Rex pacificus	6	8
Rorate coeli	5	7
Sacerdotes Domini	5	17
Saggitae potentis acutia	4	11
Salvator mundi	4	3
Salve regina	4	11

Title	no. voices	v. no.
Salve regina	5	12
Salvete flores martyrum	4	14
Sancta et immaculata	6	7
Sancte Paule apostole	5	5
Sancte praesul Nicolae	5	8
Sanctificavit Dominus	5	8
Sanctificavit Moyses	5	17
Sanctorum meritis	3–4	14
Scapulis suis	5	17
Secundum multitudinem	6	7
Senex puerum portatat	5	5
Si ambulavero	5	17
Si ignoras te	5	11
Sic Deus dilexit mundum	5	12
Sicut cervus	4	11
Sicut in olocaustis	5	17
Sicut lilium inter spinas	5	5
Sicut lilium inter spinas	5	11
Sitivit anima mea	4	11
Solve, jubente Deo	6	5
Sperunt in te	5	17
Stellam quam viderant Magi	5	5
Stetit angelus	5	17
Sub tuum praesidium	4	11
Super flumina Babylonis	4	11
Super flumina Babylonis	5	17
Surgam et circuibo civitatem	5	11
Surge, amica mea	5	11
Surge, illuminare, Hierusalem	8	8
Surge, Petre	5	12
Surge, propera	4	3
Surge, propera	5	11
Surge, sancte Dei	5	12
Surrexit pastor bonus	4	11
Susanna, ab improbis	6	8
Suscipe verbum	5	5

Title	no. voices	v. no.
Tempus est	5	12
Terra tremuit	5	17
Tibi, Christe, splendor patris	4	14
Tollite jugum meum	4	3
Tota pulchra es	5	11
Tradent enim vos	5	8
Trahe me	5	11
Tribularer, si nescirem	6	7
Tribulationes civitatum	5	12
Tribus miraculis	4	3
Tristes erant apostoli	3,5	14
Tu, Domine	5	8
Tu es Petrus	5	17
Tu es Petrus	6	7
Tu es Petrus	7	5
Tu quae genuisti	4	11
Tui sunt coeli	5	17
Unus ex duobus	5	5
Urbs beata Jerusalem	4,5	14
Ut queant laxis	4,5	14
Valde honorandus est	4	3
Veni creator spiritus	4,5	14
Veni, dilecte mi	5	11
Veni, Domine	6	7
Veni sancte spiritus	8	8
Veni sponsa Christi	4	3
Venit Michael archangelus	5	5
Veritas mea	5	17
Vexilla regis prodeunt	3,5	14
Videns secundus	5	12
Vidi te, Domine	5	8
Vidi turbam magnam	6	5
Vineam meam non custodivi	5	11
Vir erat in terra	5	17
Virgo prudentissima	7	5

Title	no. voices	v. no.
Viri Galilaei	6	5
Vox dilecti mei	5	11
Vulnerasti cor meum	5	11

4. *Collana di studi Palestriniani.* Roma, Centro di Studi Palestriniani.

v. 1   EMILIO FERRACCI, *Il Palestrina. Documenti di vita, problemi
         e prospettive d'arte*

v. 2   ERMENGILDO PACCAGNELLA, *La formazione del linguaggio
         musicale*
         Parte I. Il canto gregoriano
         Parte II. J. S. Bach
         Parte III. Palestrina

68
PERGOLESI, GIOVANNI BATTISTA, 1710–1736

Opera omnia, ed. F. Caffarelli. Roma, Gli amici della musica da camera
(Palazzo Doria Pamphili), 1939–1942
   This set is unreliable, especially in that it includes works not by Pergolesi
while omitting others which probably are by Pergolesi. It should be used
only in conjunction with more recent lists of works such as are given in
MGG or Grove's (5th ed.). Two useful articles discussing this set in par-
ticular are Frank Walker's "Two centuries of Pergolesi forgeries and
misattributions", and Charles Cudworth's "Some notes on the instrumental works attributed to Pergolesi" (both in *Music and Letters* XXX
[1949], pp. 297, 321 respectively).
   The set was reprinted in 1943 by Bärenreiter with the volumes numbered
differently, the random order of the Italian set being organized into work
categories. The following alphabetical list of the contents of the set gives
the Italian v. no. first followed by the Bärenreiter v. no.

Ariano in Siria (opera)	14	II:3
Arie da camera	22	I:5
Cantate	10	I:4
Concerto a cinque	21	I:1

Concertos, flute	21	I:1
Concertos, string instruments	7	I:3
La contadina astuta (opera buffa)	11:2	III:4
Dies irae	26	V:3
Flaminio (opera buffa)	12	III:3
Le frate'nnamorato (opera buffa)	2	III:3
Il geloso schernito (opera buffa)	3	III:1
Gugliemo d'Aquitania (oratorio)	4	IV:2
Livietta e Tracollo (opera buffa)	11:3	III:4
Il maestro di musica (opera buffa)	25	III:2
Mass in F (double chorus, orch.)	6	IV:5
Mass in F	18	IV:8
Mass in D	15:2	IV:6
Masses (4 voice), Mass fragments	23	IV:3
Miserere (Psalmus 50)	13	V:2
La morte di S. Giuseppe (oratorio)	1	IV:1
Motets	17:1	V:5
Olimpiade (opera)	24	II:4
Opera fragments	19	II:5
Il prigioniero superbo (opera)	20	II:2
Psalms (see also *Miserere*)	8	V:1
Requiem	16	IV:4
Salustio (opera)	9	IV:1
Salve regina	15:1	V:4
La serva padrona (opera buffa)	11:1	III:4
Sinfonia (cello, basso continuo)	21	I:1
Sonatas, keyboard	21	I:1
Sonatas, solo and basso continuo	21	I:1
Sonatas, trio	5	I:2
Stabat mater	26	V:3
Suites, harpsichord	21	I:1
Super flumina	17:2	V:5

69
PIPELARE, MATTHAEUS, *fl. ca.* **1497–1500**

Opera omnia, ed. Ronald Cross. *Corpus mensurabilis musicae* **(A 28),** ser. 34

V. 1   *Chansons, motets*

V. 2   *Credo de Sancte Johanne evangelisti; Masses: De feria, Dixit Dominus nihil tulerites, Floruit egregius infans, Fors seulement*

v. 3   Masses: *Joannes Christe care/Ecce puer meus, L'homme armé, Mi-mi, Sine nomine (Segovia-Jena), Sine nomine (Vienna)*

69A
PORTA, COSTANZO, 1529?–1601

Opera omnia, nunc edita transcriptione Presb. Syri Cisilino, cura P. Joannis M. Luisetto O.F.M. Padua, Biblioteca Antoniana, 1964–

v. 1   *Motecta quatuor vocum*

v. 2   *Motecta quinque vocum, liber primus*

v. 3   *Motecta quinque vocum, liber secundus*

v. 4–9   Not yet published

v. 10   *Missae tres ineditae: Missa ducalis; Missa Da pacem; Missa mortuorum*

70
PRAETORIUS, MICHAEL, 1571–1621

Gesamtausgabe des musikalischen Werkes, herausgegeben von Friedrich Blume, Arnold Mendelssohn, Wilibald Gurlitt. Berlin, Georg Kallmeyer Verlag, 1928–1941 [Index 195–   ]

v. 1   *Musae Sionae (1605–1610), I. 8-stimmige Choralmotetten,* ed. Rudolf Gerber

v. 2   ———— *II: Choralmotetten in mehrchöriger Besetzung,* ed. R. Gerber

v. 3   ———— *III: Choralmotetten zu 8–12 Stimmen,* ed. Hans Hoffmann

v. 4   ———— *IV: Choralmotetten in mehrchöriger Besetzung,* ed. Herbert Birtner

v. 5   ———— *V: Choralmotetten in kleinerer Besetzung,* ed. Friedrich Blume, Hans Költzsch

v. 6   ———— *VI: Schlichte 4-stimmige Choralsätze,* ed. Fritz Reusch

v. 7–8   ———— *VII–VIII: Schlichte 4-stimmige Choralsätze,* ed. F. Blume

v. 9   ———— *IX: 2–3-stimmige Choralbearbeitungen,* ed. F. Blume

v. 10   *Musarum Sioniarum Motectae et Psalmi Latini (1607),* ed. R. Gerber

v. 11   *Missodia Sionia (1611),* ed. F. Blume

v. 12   *Hymnodia Sionia (1611),* ed. R. Gerber

v. 13   *Eulogodia Sionia (1611),* ed. H. Birtner

v. 14   *Megalynodia Sionia (1611),* ed. Hermann Zenck

v. 15   *Terpsichore (1612),* ed. Günther Oberst

v. 16   *Urania (1613),* ed. F. Blume

v. 17   *Polyhymnia Caduceatrix et Panegyrica (1619),* ed. W. Gurlitt

v. 18   *Polyhymnia Exercitatrix (1620),* ed. F. Blume

v. 19   *Puercinium (1621),* ed. Max Schneider

v. 20   *Kleinere Einzelwerke,* ed. Walther Engelhardt

v. 21   GENERALREGISTER, ed. W. Engelhardt

PUJOL, JOANNIS

Opera omnia see **A 14,** v. 3, v. 7

71
PURCELL, HENRY, 1659–1695

1. Complete works   2. Thematic catalog

M3   1.   Works. The Purcell Society. London, Novello, 1876–
.P93   This series progressed slowly until 1928, by which date 26 v. had
+   been published. There was no further activity until 1956, when it was
M3   announced that the series would be continued and that some,
.P94   perhaps all of the first 26 v. would be re-issued with revisions where
               necessary. At present, the set has reached v. 32, and v. 9 *(Dioclesian)*
               and v. 17 *(Sacred music III)* have appeared in revised editions.
               V. 13b has never been issued. In the following alphabetical list of
               contents, the individual titles of anthems are not included, as they
               are indexed in the set (v. 32).

Title	v.no.
Abdelazar (1690)	16
Amphitryon (1690)	16
Anthems	13a, 14, 17, 28–30, 32
Arise, my muse (Birthday ode for Queen Mary, 1690)	11
Aureng-Zebe (1692?)	16
Birthday odes for Queen Mary:	
Now does the glorious day appear (1689)	11
Arise, my muse (1690)	11
Welcome, welcome, glorious morn (1691)	11
Love's goddess sure (1692)	24
Celebrate this festival (1693)	24
Come, ye sons of art (1694)	24
Bonduca (1695)	16
Cantatas, secular, solo	25
The Canterbury guests (1694)	16
Catches	22
Celebrate this festival (Birthday ode for Queen Mary, 1693)	24
Celestial music (1689)	27
Circe (1685?)	16
Cleomenes (1692)	16
Come, ye sons of art (Birthday ode for Queen Mary, 1694)	24
The comical history of Don Quixote (1694–5)	16
Dido and Aeneas (1689)	3
Dioclesian (1690)	9
Distressed innocence (1690)	16
The double dealer (1693)	16
The double marriage	16
Duets, secular vocal	22
Duke of Gloucester's birthday ode, "Who can from joy refrain" (1695)	4
The English lawyer	16
The fairy queen (1692)	12
Fantasias	31
The fatal marriage (1694)	20
The female virtuosos (1693)	20
Fly, bold rebellion (1683)	15
A fool's preferment (1688)	20
From hardy climes (1683)	27

Title	v. no.
From these serene and rapturous joys (1684)	18
The Gordian knot untied (1691)	20
Great parent, hail (1694)	27
Hail, bright Cecilia (Ode for St. Cecilia's day, 1692)	8
Hark, Damon	27
Hark how the wild musicians sing	27
Harpsichord music	6
Henry II (1692)	20
The history of King Richard II (1681)	20
In a deep vision's intellectual scene	27
In nomines (instrumental)	31
The Indian emperor (1691)	20
The Indian queen (1695)	19
Instrumental ensembles without continuo	31
King Arthur (1691)	26
The knight of Malta	20
Laudate Ceciliam (Ode for St. Cecilia's day, 1683)	10
The Libertine (1692?)	20
Love triumphant (1694)	20
Love's goddess sure (Birthday ode for Queen Mary, 1692)	24
The maid's last prayer (1693)	20
The marriage-hater match'd (1692)	20
The married beau (1694)	20
Masque in Timon of Athens (1694)	2
The massacre of Paris	20
The mock marriage (1695)	20
Now does the glorious day appear (Birthday ode for Queen Mary, 1689)	11
Ode on St. Cecilia's day, "Hail, bright Cecilia" (1692)	8
Ode on St. Cecilia's day, "Laudate Ceciliam" (1683)	10
Ode on St. Cecilia's day, "Raise the voice" (1683?)	10
Ode on St. Cecilia's day, "Welcome to all the pleasures" (1683)	10
Oedipus (1692)	21
Of old when heroes (Yorkshire feast song, 1689)	1
The old bachelor (1693)	21
Organ music	6
Oroonoko (1695)	21
Part-songs, 3 voice, secular	22

Title	v. no.
Pausanias (1695)	21
Raise the voice (Ode for St. Cecilia's day, 1683?)	10
Regulus (1692)	21
The Richmond heiress (1693)	21
The rival sisters (1695)	21
Rounds	22
Rule a wife and have a wife (1693)	21
Services, Anglican	23
Sir Anthony Love (1690)	21
Sir Barnaby Whigg (1681)	21
Sonatas of three parts (1683)	5
Sonatas of four parts (1697)	7
Songs, sacred	30
Songs, secular (other than those for plays)	25
Sophonisba (1685?)	21
Sound the trumpet (1687)	18
The Spanish friar (1694–5)	21
The summer's absence (1682)	15
Swifter, Isis, swifter flow (1681)	15
Te Deum and Jubilate (1694)	23
The Tempest (1695?)	19
Theodosius (1680)	21
Timon of Athens, masque (1694)	2
Tyrannic love (1694)	21
The virtuous wife	21
We reap all the pleasure	27
Welcome songs:	
Welcome, Viceregent (1680)	15
Swifter, Isis, swifter flow (1681)	15
What shall be done (1682)	15
The summer's absence (1682)	15
Fly, bold rebellion (1683)	18
Why, why are all the muses mute? (1685)	18
Ye tuneful Muses (1686)	18
Sound the trumpet (1687)	18
Welcome, Viceregent (1680)	15
Welcome, welcome, glorious morning (Birthday ode for Queen Mary, 1691)	11

Title	v. no.
What shall be done (1682)	15
Who can from joy refrain? (Duke of Gloucester's birthday ode, 1695)	4
Why, why are all the muses mute (1685)	18
The wives' excuse (1691)	21
Ye tuneful muses (1686)	18
Yorkshire feast song, "Of old when Heroes" (1689)	1

2. Franklin B. Zimmerman, *Henry Purcell, 1659–1695. An analytical catalogue of his music.* London, Macmillan, 1963.

72
RAMEAU, JEAN-PHILIPPE, 1683–1764

Oeuvres complètes. Publication faite sous la direction de C. Saint-Saëns. Paris, Durand, 1895–1913

A reprint of this set has been announced by Broude Bros., New York.

v. 1	*Pièces de clavecin*
v. 2	*Musique instrumentale*
v. 3	*Cantates à 1 et 2 voix*
v. 4	*Motets, Iᵉ série*
v. 5	*Motets, IIᵉ série*
v. 6	*Hippolyte et Aricie* (1733)
v. 7	*Les Indes galantes* (1735)
v. 8	*Castor et Pollux* (1737)
v. 9	*Les fêtes d'Hébé* (1739)
v. 10	*Dardanus* (1739)
v. 11	*La princesse de Navarre* (1745); *Les Fêtes de Ramire* (1745); *Nélée et Myrthis; Zéphire* (ca. 1754)
v. 12	*Platée* (1745)
v. 13	*Les fêtes de Polymnie* (1745)
v. 14	*Le temple de la Gloire* (1745)
v. 15	*Les fêtes de l'Hymen et de l'Amour* (1747)

v. 16   *Zaïs* (1748)

v. 17/1   *Pygmalion* (1748); *Les surprises de l'amour* (1748)

v. 17/2   *Anacréon* (1754), *Les Sybarites* (1753)

v. 18   *Naïs* (1749)

73
REGIS, JOHANNES, *ca.* 1430–1485

Opera omnia, ed. Cornelis W. H. Lindenburg. *Corpus mensurabilis musicae*
(A 28), ser. 9. Complete in 2 v.

v. 1   *Masses*

v. 2   *Motets, chansons*

74
RENER, ADAM, 1485–1520

*Collected works. The Institute of mediaeval music, Brooklyn, N.Y.: Collected
works* **(A 52)**, v. 2.

v. 1   *The motets*

75
RIMSKII-KORSAKOV, NIKOLAI ANDREYEVICH, 1844–1908

[Complete works]. [Moscow, State Music Publishers, 1948–]. This set
is the same in format and organization as the works of Chaikovskii **(B 22)**,
q.v. Only works published so far are listed below

Title	full score v.	arr. v.
Antar (*Symphony no. 2;* 2 versions)	17a, b	
Boyarina Vera Sheloga (opera)	8	36
Cantatas	24	44
Capriccio Español (orch.)	21	

Title	full score v.	arr. v.
Chamber music with piano	28	
Chamber music without piano	27	
Chorus works	46b	
Christmas eve (*Noch piered Rozhdiestvom*, opera)	5a, b	33
Concert fantasy on Russian themes, op. 33 (violin, orch.)	26	48
Concerto, clarinet and band, in E*ᵇ*	25	
Concerto, piano and orch., op.30	26	48
Concerto, trombone and band	25	
Conte féerique (orch.)	20	
Le coq d'or (*Solotoi Pietuschok*, opera)	15a–c	43
The czar's bride (*Zarskaia nievessta*, opera)	9a, b	37
Duets, vocal	46a	
Fairy tale (orch.)	20	
Fantasy on Serbian themes (orch., 2 versions)	19b	
Folk songs, op.24	47	
The golden cockerel (*Solotoi pietuschok*, opera)	15a–c	43
The invisible city of Kitezh (*Skasaniie o nevidimom gradie Kitezh*, opera)	14a, b, sup.	42
Kastchei the immortal (*Kaschtchei bessmertnii*, opera)	12	40
The legend of the invisible city of Kitezh (*Skasaniie o nevidimom gradie Kitezh*, opera)	14a, b, sup.	42
The maid of Pskov (*Pskovitianka*, opera)	1	29a
May night (*Maiskaia noch*, opera)	2a, b	30
Mazurka on Polish folk themes (Violin, orch.)	26	48
Mlada (opera-ballet)	4a, b	32
Mlada, act 3, orchestral excerpts	4 sup.	
Mozart and Salieri (opera)	7	35
The night before Christmas (*Noch piered Rozhdiestvom*, opera)	5a, b	33
A night in May (*Maiskaia noch*, opera)	2a, b	30
Noch piered Rozhdiestvom (opera)	5a, b	33
Oriental suite (*Symphony no. 3*)	17a, b	
Overture on Russian themes, 2 versions	20	
Pan Voyevoda (opera)	13a, b	41
Piano works	49	

Title	full score v.	arr. v.
Pskovitianka (opera)	1	29a
Quartets, string	27	
Quintet, piano and winds	28	
Romances (songs)	45	
Russian folk songs, op.24	47	
Sadko (opera)	6a–c	34
Sasaniie (Fairy tale, orch.)	20	
Skasaniie o nevidimom gradie Kitezh (opera)	14a, b, sup.	42
Skaska o Zarie Saltanie (opera)	10a, b	38
Scheherezade (orch.)	22	
Serbian fantasy (orch.)	19b	
Serenade (cello, orch.)	26	48
Servilia (opera)	11a, b	39
Sextet, strings	27	
Sinfonietta, op.31	20	
The snow maiden (*Snegurochka,* opera)	3a, b	31a, b
Solotoi pietuschok (opera)	15a, c	43
Songs	45	
Symphony no. 1	16	
Symphony no. 2 "Antar"	17a, b	
Symphony no. 3 "Oriental suite"	18	
The tale of the invisible city of Kitezh (*Skasaniie o nevidimom gradie Kitezh,* opera)	14a, b, sup.	42
The tale of Tsar Saltan (*Skaska o Zarie Saltanie,* opera)	10a, b	38
Trios, vocal	46a	
The Tsar's bride (*Zarskaia nievessta,* opera)	9a, b	37
Variations on a theme of Glinka (oboe and band)	25	
Vera Sheloga (opera)	8	36
Vocal duets, trios	46a	
Zarskaia nievessta (opera)	9a, b	37

76
RORE, CIPRIANO DE, 1516–1565

Opera omnia, ed. Bernhard Meier. *Corpus mensurabilis musicae* **(A 28),** ser. 14. 9–10 v. proposed.

✓v. 1–3   *Motets*
　v. 4, 6
✓v. 7   *Masses*

77
ROTA, ANDREA, *ca.* 1553–1597

Opera omnia, ed. Giuseppe Vecchi. *Antiqua musicae italicae: Monumenta Bononiensia* **(A 6)**, v. 4. Only v. 3, part 1 published at present.

v. 1   *Motectorum liber primus (1584)*

v. 2   *Motectorum liber secundus (1595)*

v. 3   *Missarum liber primus (1595)*
          1. *Missa "Qual'è piu grand'amore"*

78
RUFFO, VINCENZO, *ca.* 1510–1587

Opera omnia, ed. Giuseppe Vecchi. *Antiquae musicae italicae: Monumenta Veroniensia* **(A 9)**, v. 1

1. *Missae . . . 3a missae quatuor concinatae ad ritum concilli Mediolani*

79
SCARLATTI, DOMENICO, 1685–1757

Opere complete per clavicembalo, ed. Alessandro Longo. 10 v., supplement, and separate thematic index. Milan, New York, Ricordi, 1947–1951
The sonatas in this set are arranged 50 per volume, with 45 in the supplement. This edition is the source for L. nos. often used with Scarlatti sonatas. Cf. Ralph Kirkpatrick, *Domenico Scarlatti* (Princeton, Princeton University Press, 1953), which supplies K. nos. for the sonatas, based on chronological and other considerations.

80
SCHEIDT, SAMUEL, 1587–1634

Gesamtausgabe, herausgegeben von Christhard Mahrenholz und Gottfried Harms im Auftrage der Ugrino Gemeinschaft, Hamburg. 1923–1953

B 80   Scheidt, Samuel : 1

v. 1   *Tabulatur-Buch, Görlitz (1650)*, ed. Harms

v. 2   *Ludi musici (Paduana, Galliarda, Couranta, Alemande, Intrada, Canzonetto), Hamburg, 1621* [Part 1], ed. Harms

v. 3   ————, [Part 2]

v. 4   *Cantiones sacrae, Hamburg, 1620*, ed. Harms

v. 5   *Unedierte Werke für Tasteninstrumente*, ed. Harms

v. 6   *Tabulatura nova, Hamburg, 1624, Teil I und II*, ed. Mahrenholz

v. 7   ————, *Teil III und Kritischer Bericht*, ed. Mahrenholz

v. 8   *Geistliche Konzerte, Teil I. Hamburg, 1631*, ed. Mahrenholz

v. 9   ————, *Teil II. Halle, 1634*, ed. Mahrenholz, Adam Adrio

v. 10   ————, *Halle, 1635, Teil III: 1*, ed. Adrio

v. 11   ————, ————, *Teil III: 2*, ed. Adrio

v. 12   ————, *Leipzig, 1640, Teil IV*, ed. Erika Gessner

v. 13   *70 Symphonien auf Concerten Manir*, ed. Mahrenholz, Hermann Keller

81
SCHEIN, JOHANN HERMANN, 1586–1630

Neue Ausgabe sämtlicher Werke, herausgegeben von Adam Adrio. Kassel, Bärenreiter
  The entire proposed plan of this set is given; at present only v. 1, 2, and 9 have appeared.

v. 1   *Israelsbrünnlein, 1629. Geistliche Madrigale zu 5 Stimmen und Generalbass*, ed. Adrio

v. 2   *Cantional oder Gesangbuch Augsburgischer Konfession 1627 und 1645. Choralsätze für 4 und 5 Stimmen, teilweise mit Generalbass*, ed. Adrio
     In 2 parts

v. 3   *Cymbalum Sionium sive Cantiones sacrae, 1615*

v. 4   *Opella nova: Erster Teil Geistlicher Concerten, 1618*

v. 5   *Opella nova: Ander Teil Geistlicher Concerten, 1626*

v. 6   *Venuskränzlein . . . oder neue weltliche Lieder, 1609; Studen-*
           tenschmaus, 1626

v. 7   *Musica boscareccia. Waldliederlein I. bis III. Teil, 1621,*
           1626 und 1628

v. 8   *Diletti pastorali. Hirtenlust, 1624*

v. 9   *Banchetto musicale, 1617,* ed. Dieter Krickeberg

v. 10   *Geistliche und weltliche Gelegenheitswerke (1617 bis 1630)*

82
SCHÖNBERG, ARNOLD, 1874–1951

1. Complete works   2. Thematic catalog

M3 1. *Gesamtausgabe,* unter dem Patronat der Akademie der Künste,
S36   Berlin. Editors: Joseph Rufer, R. Hoffman, R. Kolisch, L. Stein,
folio   E. Steuermann. Mainz, B. Schott's Söhne; Wien, Universal Edition
        AG, 1966–
        The editors of this set initially issued a detailed plan for the set.
        The 2 v. which have appeared so far, however, show that the plan
        has been considerably modified, both as to contents of individual
        volumes and to their numbering in the set. Therefore only the v.
        which have actually appeared are listed below. The overall scheme
        is that each v. is to appear in 2 forms: Series A, containing completed
        final versions, and Series B, containing early versions, sketches,
        and editorial commentary. There are to be 9 category divisions in
        each series: 1. Songs and canons   2. Piano and organ music   3.
        Stage works   4. Orchestral works   5. Choral works   6. Instru-
        mental concertos   7. Chamber music   8. Orchestrations   9. Parer-
        ga; but the v. numbers are evidently to run consecutively throughout
        each series, regardless of the category divisions.

Series A.

I. *Lieder und Kanons*

        v. 1   *Lieder mit Klavierbegleitung,* ed. Josef Rufer

II. *Klavier und Orgelmusik*

v. 4   *Werke für Klavier zu zwei Händen,* ed. E. Steuermann und Reinhold Brinkmann

2. Joseph Rufer, *The works of Arnold Schoenberg. A catalogue of his compositions, writings and painting,* translated by Dika Newlin. London, Faber and Faber, 1962. (Originally publ. as *Das Werk Arnold Schönbergs,* Kassel, Bärenreiter, 1959)

83
SCHUBERT, FRANZ PETER, 1797–1828

1–2. Complete works   3. Thematic catalog

1. *Kritisch durchgesehene Gesammtausgabe* [Editors included J. Brahms, E. Mandyczewski, Ignaz Brill *et al.*] Leipzig, Breitkopf & Härtel, 1884–1895
   This set has been reprinted by Dover with the original 21 series in 39 v. combined to make 19 v. The listing below gives both the original and the reprint numbering, with titles in English, as in the reprint. Reprint v. nos. are in parentheses to distinguish them from the v. into which the original series were divided.

(v. 1)	Series 1	*Symphonies*
	v. 1	Nos. 1–4
	v. 2	Nos. 5–8 [old numbering]
	Series 2	*Overtures and other orchestral music*
(v. 2)	Series 3	*Octet*
	Series 4	*String quintet*
	Series 4	*String quintet*
	Series 5	*String quartets*
	Series 6	*String trio*
(v. 3)	Series 7	*Piano quintet, piano quartet, piano trios*
	Series 8	*Piano and one [other] instrument*
(v. 4)	Series 9	*Piano, 4 hands*
	v. 1	*Marches*

	v. 2	*Overtures, sonatas, rondos, variations*
	v. 3	*Divertissements, polonaises, fantasies &*
(v. 5)	Series 10	*Sonatas for piano solo*
	Series 11	*Fantasy, impromptus and other pieces for piano solo*
	Series 12	*Dances for piano solo*
(v. 6)	Series 13	*Masses*
	Series 14	*Smaller sacred works*
(v. 7)	Series 15	*Dramatic works*
	v. 1	*Des Teufels Lustschloss*
	v. 2	[Operettas]: *Der vierjährige Posten, Fernando, Die beiden Freunde von Salamanka*
(v. 8)	v. 3	*Die Zwillingsbrüder* [incidental music], *Die Ver-schworenen, Die Zauberharfe* [incidental music]
(v. 9)	v. 4	*Rosamunde* [incidental music]
	v. 5	*Alfonso und Estrella*
(v. 10)	v. 6	*Fierrabras*
(v. 11)	v. 7	[*Unfinished operas*]: *Claudine von Villa Bella, Der Spiegelritter, Die Bürgschaft, Adrast. Aria and duet for Hérold's Das Zauberglöckchen* [*La clochette*]
(v. 12)	Series 16	*Music for men's chorus*
	Series 17	*Music for women's chorus*
	Series 18	*Music for mixed chorus*
	Series 19	*Songs and cantatas for 2 and 3 voices*
(v. 13)	Series 20	*Songs for 1 voice*
	v. 1	1811–July 1815
(v. 14)	v. 2	August 1815–December 1816
(v. 15)	v. 3	1817–1818

         v. 4   *1819–1821*

(v. 16)   v. 5   *1822 to Die schöne Müllerin, 1823*

         v. 6   *Between Die schöne Müllerin and Winterreise*

(v. 17)   v. 7   *From Die Winterreise to Schwanengesang, 1827–1828*

         v. 8   *Supplement to songs*

(v. 18)   Series 21   *General supplement of instrumental and vocal music*

(v. 19)   Commentary, and INDEX

2. *Neue Ausgabe sämtlicher Werke,* herausgegeben von der internationalen Schubert-Gesellschaft. Kassel, Bärenreiter
   The entire proposed plan of this set is given below. At present (mid-1968) only Series 8 v. 5 and series 5, Wg. 1, v. 1 have appeared.

Series 1   *Kirchenmusik*

         Wg. 1   *Messen*
         Wg. 2   *Kleinere kirchenmusikalische Werke*

Series 2   *Bühnenwerke*

Series 3   *Mehrstimmige Gesänge*

         Wg. 1 *für gemischte Stimmen*

              a. *mit Orchesterbegleitung*
              b. *mit Klavierbegleitung*
              c. *ohne Begleitung*

         Wg. 2 *für Männerstimmen*
              a. *mit Begleitung meherer Instrumente*
              b. *mit Klavierbegleitung*

         Wg. 3 *für Frauenstimmen mit Klavierbegleitung*

Series 4   *Lieder*

[The following volumes have been announced for early publication. A wg. no., if any, is not stated]

         v. 6   *Einzelne Lieder (D. 5, 7, 10, 23, 39, 42, 44, 50, 59, 76–78, 111),* ed. Walter Dürr

v. 7   *Einzelne Lieder (D. 95–159)*, ed. W. Dürr

Series 5   *Orchesterwerke*

Wg. 1 *Sinfonien*

v. 1 *Sinfonien nr. 1–3 (D. 82, 125, 200)*, ed. Arnold Feil, Christa Landon

Wg. 2 *Ouvertüren und andere Orchesterwerke*

Series 6   *Kammermusik*

[The following v. has been announced for early publication]

v. 1   *Oktett F-dur op.166 (D. 803), Nonett (Eine kleine Trauermusik) für Bläser (D. 79), Minuett und Finale in F für 8 Bläser (D. 72)*, ed. A. Feil

v. 2   *Streichquartette*

v. 3   *Streichquartette*

v. 4   *Streichtrios*

v. 5   *Kammermusik mit Klavier*
a.   *Quintet, Quartett und Trios*
b.   *Für Klavier und ein Instrument*

Series 7   *Klaviermusik*

Wg. 1 *zu vier Händen*

Wg. 2 *zu zwei Händen*
a.   *Sonaten*
b.   *Fantasien, Impromptus und Verwandtes*
c.   *Tänze*

Series 8   *Supplement*

v. 1   *Bearbeitungen, Incerta*

v. 2   *Studien*

v. 3   *Nachträge*

v. 4   *Liedertexte*

v. 5   OTTO DEUTSCH, *Schubert. Die Dokumente seines Lebens*

This is an enlarged and revised ed. of Deutsch's *Schubert, a documentary biography* (London, 1946), which in turn was a revision of Deutsch's *Franz Schubert: die Dokumente seines Lebens und Schaffens* (Munich, 1913–14) 2 v.

3. OTTO ERICH DEUTSCH, *Schubert. Thematic catalog of all his works in chronological order*. In collaboration with Donald R. Wakeling, London, Dent, 1951
   Abbreviation: D.

84
SCHÜTZ, HEINRICH, 1585–1672

1–2. Complete works　3. Catalog of works　4. Periodical

1. *Neue Ausgabe sämtlicher Werke,* herausgegeben von der neuen Schütz-Gesellschaft. Kassel, Bärenreiter
   This set, still in progress, is being issued in two forms: first, with each v. as listed below bound together; second, as pamphlets containing single works or small groups of short works. The latter often appear over quite a period of time, long before the former. Details concerning the separate pamphlets are not given below. V. which have started separate pamphlets but are not yet complete are listed in parentheses. SWV = item 3 below

v. 1　*Historia der Geburt Jesu Christi SWV 435,* ed. Friedrich Schöneich

v. 2　*Die sieben Worte Jesu Christi am Kreuz SWV 478; Die Lukas-Passion SWV 480; Die Johannes-Passion SWV 481; Die Mattäus-Passion SWV 479,* ed. Bruno Grusnik, Wilhelm Kamlah, Fritz Schmidt

v. 3　*Historia der Auferstehung Jesu Christi SWV 50,* ed. Walter Simon Huber

v. 4　*Musikalische Exequien SWV 279–281,* ed. Schöneich

v. 5　*Geistliche Chormusik 1648 SWV 369–397,* ed. Kamlah

v. 6　*Der Psalter in vierstimmigen Liedsätzen nach Cornelius Beckers Dichtungen SWV 97–256,* ed. Walter Blankenburg

v. 8   *Cantiones sacrae 1625 I–XX SWV 53 bis 72*, ed. Gottfried
           Grote

v. 9   —————— *XXI–XL SWV 73–93*, ed. Grote

v. 10   *Kleine geistliche Konzerte 1636–9 I: Für Frauen- und Männer-
           stimmen SWV 282–290, 293–296, 300, 306–314, 317–320, 324*,
           ed. Wilhelm Ehmann

v. 11   —————— *II: Für 2–4 gemischte Stimmen SWV 282, 292, 297–
           299, 301–304, 315–316, 321–323, 325–332*, ed. Ehmann

v. 12   —————— *III: Für 5 gemischte Stimmen SWV 395, 333–337, 94*,
           ed. Ehmann

v. 13   *Symphonia sacrae I: nr. 1–10 SWV 257–266*, ed. Rudulf
           Gerber

v. 14   —————— *I: nr. 11–20 SWV 267–274, 276–277*, ed. R. Gerber,
           Gerhard Kirchner

v. 15   —————— *II: nr. 1–12 SWV 341–352*, ed. Werner Bittinger

v. 16   —————— *II: nr. 13–22 SWV 353–362*, ed. Bittinger

(v. 17)   —————— *II: nr. 23–27 SWV 363–367*, ed. Bittinger

v. 22   *Italienische Madrigale (Venedig 1611) SWV 1–19*, ed. Hans
           Joachim Moser

(v. 37)   *Weltliche Lieder und Madrigale SWV 434, 52, 368, 96, 419,
           440–42, 278, 438, 451–2, Anh. 1*, ed. Bittinger

2.   *Stuttgarter Ausgabe sämtlicher Werke*, herausgegeben von Günter
     Graulich, Paul Horn [*et al.*]. Stuttgart, Hänssler, 1967–
     The entire proposed plan of this edition is given below, but at present
     only v. 1–2 have appeared. The publisher has announced the inten-
     tion of completing the set by 1972.   *Revised pub. plan in*
Sacred music
                                            Notes XXIX : 4, p. 789

Series A.   *The oratorios and passions*

new numbering
   v. 16   v. 1   *The Christmas story SWV 436a, 435, 435b* [3 versions]

   v. 17   v. 2   *The passions: St. Matthew SWV 479, St. Luke SWV
                     480, St. John SWV 4812, 481* [2 versions]

   4   v. 3   *The resurrection story SWV 50* [3 parts]

new #

v, 8   v. 4   *The German Requiem [Musikalische Exequien], op.7,*
SWV 279–281

Series B.   *Collections of works*

v. 2-3   v. 5–8 *The psalms of David, 1619, op.2, SWV 22–47*

v. 5   v. 9–10 *Cantiones sacrae, 1625, op. 4, SWV 53–93*

6   v. 11   *Becker psalter I, 1628, op.5, early version, SWV 97a–*
256a

?   v. 12   *Becker psalter II, 1661, final version, SWV 97–256*

7   v. 13   *Symphoniae sacrae I, op.6, 1629, SWV 257–276*

9   v. 14   *Kleine geistliche Konzerte I, op.8, 1636, SWV 282–*
305, and 94

10   v. 15   *Kleine geistliche Konzerte II, op.9, 1639, SWV 306–*
337

11   v. 16–18 *Symphoniae sacrae II, op.10, 1647, SWV 341–367*

12   v. 19   *Geistliche Chormusik, op.11, 1648, SWV 369–397*

13-14 v. 20–23 *Symphoniae sacrae III, op.12, 1650, SWV 398–418*

15 v. 24   *Twelve sacred songs, op.13, 1657, SWV 420–431*

Series C.   *Works not belonging to any collection*

18 ⎰ v. 25   *Works in 1–5 parts*
      ⎱ v. 26   *Works in 6–7 parts*

19 ⎰ v. 27   *Works in 9–10 parts*
      ⎱ v. 28   *Works in 11–21 parts*

Secular music

1   v. 29   *Italian madrigals, op.1, 1611, SWV 1–19*

20.? ⎰ v. 30   *Opitz madrigals*
       ⎱ v. 31   *Remaining secular works*

Supplement

21? ⎰ v. 32   *(Suppl. 1)   Works ascribed to Schütz*
      ⎱ v. 33   *(Suppl. 2)   Letters, deeds, documents*

v. 34   (Suppl. 3)   Book of pictorial illustrations:
        Heinrich Schütz and his era

v. 35   (Suppl. 4)   *The performance of the music of Heinrich
        Schütz*

v. 36   (Suppl. 5) *Addenda and any newly discovered works*

3.   Werner Bittinger, *Schütz-Werke Verzeichnis (SWV)*, Kassel, Bären-
     reiter, 1960

4.   *Saggitarius. Beiträge zur Erforschung und Praxis alter und neuer Kirchen-
     musik,* herausgegeben von der Internationalen Heinrich-Schütz-
     Gesellschaft. Kassle, Bärenreiter, 1966–

85
SCHUMANN, ROBERT, 1810–1856

1. Complete works   2. Thematic catalog   3. Yearbook   4. Index

1.   *Sämtliche Werke,* herausgegeben von Clara Schumann. Leipzig,
     Breitkopf & Härtel, 1879–1893

Ser.   1   *Symphonien für Orchester nr. 1–4*

Ser.   2   *Overtüren für Orchester*

Ser.   3   *Konzerte und Konzertstücke für Orchester*

Ser.   4   *Werke für Streichinstrumente: 3 Streichquartette*

Ser.   5   *Werke für Pianoforte und andere Instrumente*

       v. 1   *Quintett und Quartett*

       v. 2   *Trios*

       v. 3   *Duos*

Ser.   6   *Werke für Pianoforte zu 4 Händen*

Ser.   7   *Werke für Pianoforte zu 2 Händen*

       v. 1   *Op.1–8*

       v. 2   *Op.9–13*

       v. 3   *Op.14–19*

v. 4   *Op.20–23, 26, 28, 32*

v. 5   *Op.56, 58, 68, 72, 76, 82*

v. 6   *Op.99, 111, 124, 126, 133*

Ser. 8   *Werke für Orgel*

Ser. 9   *Grössere Gesangwerke mit Orchester*

v. 1   *Paradies und die Peri, op.50; Adventlied, op.71*

v. 2   *Genoveva*

v. 3   *Op.84, 93, 98b, 108*

v. 4   *Op.115, 116, 136, 139*

v. 5   *Op.140, 143, 144*

v. 6   *Messe, op.147; Requiem, op.148*

v. 7   *Scenen aus Goethe's Faust*

Ser. 10   *Mehrstimmige Gesangwerke mit Pianoforte*

v. 1   *Für 2 Singstimmen*

v. 2   *Für 3 und mehrere Singstimmen*

Ser. 11   *Werke für Männerchor*

Ser. 12   *Werke für Soprano, Alt, Tenor, und Bass*

Ser. 13   *Werke für eine Singstimme und Pianoforte*

v. 1   *Liederkreis op.24, Myrthen op.25, op.27, 29, 30, 31,*
        35, 36

v. 2   *Op.37, Liederkreis op.39, op.40, Frauenliebe und*
        Leben op.42, op.45, Dichterliebe op.48, op.49, 51, 53

v. 3   *Op.57, 64, 77, 79, 83, 87, 89, 90, 96*

v. 4   *Op.98a, 104, 106–7, 117–18, 122, 126–7, 135, 142,*
        Soldatenlied

Ser. 14   *Supplement*

2.   *Thematisches Verzeichnis sämtlicher im Druck erschienen Werke.*
Leipzig, Breitkopf & Härtel, 1860; reprinted for H. Baron, 1966

3. *Sammelbände der Robert-Schumann-Gesellschaft.* Leipzig, Deutscher Verlag für Musik. 1961–

4. See **C 50**, v. 6–7

86
SENFL, LUDWIG, *ca.* 1490–1542/3

Sämtliche Werke, herausgegeben von der Schweizerischen Musikforschenden Gesellschaft in Verbindung mit dem Schweizerischen Tonkünstler-Verein

The first 4 v. appeared as part of *Das erbe deutscher Musik* (**A 43**), cited as EDM below

v. 1   (EDM v. 5). *Messen,* ed. Edwin Löhrer, Otto Ursprung

v. 2   (EDM v. 10). *Deutsche Lieder, I. Teil: Lieder aus handschriftlichen Quellen bis etwa 1533,* ed. Arnold Geering, Wilhelm Altwegg

v. 3   (EDM v. 13). *Motetten, I. Teil: Gelegenheitsmotetten und Psalmvertonungen,* ed. Walter Gerstenberg

v. 4   (EDM v. 15). *Deutsche Lieder, II. Teil: Lieder aus Hans Otts Liederbuch von 1534,* ed. Geering, Altwegg

v. 5   *Deutsche Lieder, III. Teil: Lieder aus gedruckten Liederbüchern,* ed. Geering, Altwegg

v. 6   *Deutsche Lieder, IV. Teil; italienische, französische und lateinische Lieder und Gesänge; lateinische Oden,* ed. Geering, Altwegg

v. 7   *Instrumental-carmina; Lieder in Bearbeitungen,* ed. Geering, Altwegg

87
SWEELINCK, JAN PIETERSZOON, 1562–1621

Werken, uitgegeven dor de Vereeniging vor Nederlandsche Muziekgeschiedenis. 1894–1921; 1943–

This set is being re-issued in revised and supplemented editions, only the first 3 v. of which have yet appeared.

v. 1   *Werken voor Orgel en Clavicimbel,* ed. Max Seiffert. 2nd ed. by Alfons Annegarn

v. 1 suppl. (separate v.) ed. A. Annegarn

v. 2   *Cinquante psaumes de David (Premier livre, 1604),* ed. R. Lagas

v. 3   *Livre second des psaumes de David (1613),* ed. R. Lagas

v. 4   *Het derde boek der psalmen* [*1614*], ed. M. Seiffert

v. 5   *Het vierde boek der psalmen* [*1621*], ed. M. Seiffert

v. 6   *Cantiones sacrae* [*1619*], ed. B. van Sigtenhorst Meyer

v. 7   *De "chansons",* ed. M. Seiffert

v. 8   *De "Rimes françoises et italiennes",* ed. M. Seiffert

v. 9   *Verschellende Gelegenheids-Compositiën,* ed. M. Seiffert

v. 10   *"Composition-Regeln Herrn M. Johan Peterssen Sweling",* ed. Hermann Gehrmann. In German.

88
TELEMANN, GEORG PHILIPP, 1681–1767

1. Complete works 2. Periodical

1. *Musikalische Werke.* Herausgegeben in Auftrag der Gesellschaft für Musikforschung. Kassel, Bärenreiter

v. 1   *Zwölf methodische Sonaten für Querflöte (Violine) und Basso continuo,* ed. Max Seiffert

v. 2   *Der harmonische Gottesdienst. 72 Solokantaten . . . Hamburg 1725/23, Teil 1: Neujahr bis Reminiscere,* ed. Gustav Fock, M. Seiffert

v. 3   ———, *Teil 2: Oculi bis 1. Pfingsttag*

v. 4   ———, *Teil 3: 2. Pfingsttag bis 16. Sonntag nach Trinitatis*

v. 5   ———, *Teil 4:17. Sonntag nach Trinitatis bis Sonntag nach Weihnachten*

v. 6   *Kammermusik ohne Generalbass: Zwölf Fantasien für Quer-*

flöte; Zwölf Fantasien für Violine 1735; Drei Konzerte für vier Violinen, ed. Günter Hausswald

v. 7   *Kammermusik ohne Generalbass: Sechs Sonaten 1. Folge . . . Sechs Sonaten 2. Folge, für zwei Querflöten,* ed. G. Hausswald

v. 8   *Kammermusik ohne Generalbass: Sechs Sonaten op.2 (1727) für zwei Querflöten oder Violinen; Sechs Sonaten op.5 (1738) für zwei Querflöten oder Violinen,* ed. G. Hausswald

v. 9   *Sechs Suiten für Querflöte, Violine und Basso continuo,* ed. Johann Philipp Hinnenthal

v. 10   *Sechs ausgewählte Ouverturen für Orchester mit vorwiegend programmatischen Überschriften,* ed. Friedrich Noack

v. 11   *Sechs Konzerte für Querflöte, cembalo . . . ,* ed. J. P. Hinnenthal

v. 12   *Tafelmusik I,* ed. J. P. Hinnenthal

v. 13   *Tafelmusik II,* ed. J. P. Hinnenthal

v. 14   *Tafelmusik III,* ed. J. P. Hinnenthal

v. 15   *Lukas-Passion 1728,* ed. Hans Hörner, Martin Ruhnke

v. 16   *Lukas-Passion 1744,* ed. H. Hörner, M. Ruhnke

v. 18   *Zwölf Pariser Quartette I: nr. 1–6,* ed. Walter Bergmann

v. 19   ———— *II: nr. 7–12*

v. 20   *Der geduldige Socrates. Oper in 3 Akten,* ed. Bernd Baselt

2.   *Hamburger Telemann-Gesellschaft: Veröffentlichung.* Hamburg, H. Sikorski, 1968–

v. 1   ERICH VALENTIN, *Telemann in seiner Zeit. Versuch eines geistesgeschichtlichen Porträts*

v. 2   BERTHA ENGELHARD, *Takt und Tempo: Studien über die Zusammenhänge von Takt und Tempo*

89
TINCTORIS, JOHANNES, 1446–1511

Opera omnia, ed. Fritz Feldman. *Corpus mensurabilis musicae* (A 28), ser. 18

v. 1   *Mass dedicated to Ferdinand, King of Sicily and Aragon*

VAET, JAKOB

See DTO (A 32), v. 98, 100, 103–4, 108–9, 113–14, 116

90
VERDELOT, PHILIPPE, *d. ca.* 1540

Opera omnia, ed. Anne-Marie Bragard. *Corpus mensurabilis musicae* (A 28), ser. 28

v. 1   *Masses, hymns*

91
VICTORIA, TOMAS LUIS DE, 1549–1611

Opera omnia, ed. Felipe Pedrell. Leipzig, Breitkopf & Härtel, 1902–1913

1. This set has been reprinted verbatim in reduced size by Gregg Press, with the original 8 v. bound in 4.

2. A revised edition by Higinio Anglés has started to appear in *Monumentos Musica Española* (A 72). Victoria v. 1–3 = MME v. 24–26

3. Organization of set:
    Magnificats: v. 3
    Masses: v. 2, 4, 6, 8
    Motets: v. 1, 5, 7, 8
    Commentary: v. 8

4. Indices: In Victoria article in Grove's *Dictionary of Music and Musicians* (3d, 4th & 5th eds.) and in *An alphabetical index to Thomas Luis de Victoria Opera omnia,* ed. by the Bibliography Committee of the New York chapter of MLA (*Music Library Association Index Series,* no. 5)

92
VIVALDI, ANTONIO, *1678–1741*

1. Complete instrumental works   1A. Conversion table of Fanno nos. to v. nos. 1B. Alphabetical index of distinctive titles and opus numbers
2–5. Thematic catalogs

I. *Opere strumentali.* Direzione artistica di Gian Francesco Malipiero. Milan, Ricordi, 1948–

Each v. of this set consists of the score of a single composition. 475 v. were published by the end of 1968; evidently the entire set is to consist of 530 v. according to the Fanna catalog (item 2 below), which also can serve as an index to the set. Since the arrangement of v. is completely random, the following listing observes the order of v. according to their Fanna nos. The F. no. is at the left, followed by the set v. no., the key of the piece (capital letters are major keys; small letters are minor keys), and, if necessary, the instrumentation.

1A. Conversion table of F. nos. to v. nos.

F.I: Concertos for one or more violins
    (The no. of violins, if more than 1, is stated in parentheses)

1 = 1 : B^b	28 = 82 : d
2 = 4 : c	29 = 83 : B^b
3 = 13 : C	30 = 84 : D
4 = 15 : E	31 = 85 : C
5 = 16 : A	32 = 86 : B^b
6 = 27 : g (2)	33 = 87 : F
7 = 29 : E	34 = 88 : F (3)
8 = 31 : D	35 = 89 : D (2)
9 = 38 : E^b	36 = 92 : g
10 = 37 : D	37 = 93 : e
11 = 45 : d	38 = 96 : b
12 = 48 : c (2)	39 = 100 : A
13 = 55 : C ("in due cori")	40 = 107 : B^b (2)
14 = 60 : c (2)	41 = 108 : D (2)
15 = 64 : B^b	42 = 111 : B^b (2)
16 = 65 : g	43 = 112 : C (2)
17 = 66 : F	44 = 116 : C (2)
18 = 68 : D	45 = 117 : D
19 = 69 : D	46 = 120 : C
20 = 70 : F	47 = 122 : C
21 = 74 : d	48 = 123 : E
22 = 76 : E	49 = 124 : G
23 = 77 : g	50 = 125 : b
24 = 78 : F	51 = 126 : A
25 = 79 : f	52 = 127 : g
26 = 80 : E^b	53 = 128 : a
27 = 81 : C	54 = 129 : A

55 = 130:B^b	96 = 202:G
56 = 131:d	97 = 203:D
57 = 132:B^b (2)	98 = 207:g (2)
58 = 133:c	99 = 208:B^b (2)
59 = 134:B^b (4)	100 = 209:d (2)
60 = 136:B^b ("in due cori")	101 = 210:E^b (2)
61 = 140:a (2)	102 = 227:E^b
62 = 141:D ("in due cori")	103 = 228:G
63 = 145 B^b (2)	104 = 229:A
64 = 156:G	105 = 230:c
65 = 157:B^b	106 = 245:A
66 = 158:F	107 = 247:G
67 = 160:C	108 = 253:g
68 = 162:C	109 = 254:E^b
69 = 163:B^b	110 = 255:G
70 = 164:e	111 = 256:C
71 = 165:F	112 = 257:g
72 = 166:E	113 = 258:d
73 = 167:C	114 = 259:C
74 = 168:e	115 = 260:b
75 = 169:E^b	116 = 261:D
76 = 170:B^b	117 = 262:B^b
77 = 171:b	118 = 284:B^b
78 = 172:B^b	119 = 265:d
79 = 173:c	120 = 286:D
80 = 174:D	121 = 291:B^b
81 = 175:g	122 = 292:g
82 = 178:g	123 = 293:A
83 = 179:b	124 = 294:D
84 = 180:E	125 = 295:g
85 = 181:C (2)	126 = 296:d
86 = 183:B^b	127 = 297:E
87 = 186:G	128 = 301:F
88 = 187:F	129 = 302:D
89 = 188:D	130 = 303:F
90 = 191:A	131 = 304:E^b
91 = 192:G	132 = 305:D
92 = 193:E^b	133 = 306:D
93 = 194:C	134 = 307:D
94 = 195:C	135 = 311:C
95 = 199:B^b	136 = 312:D

137 = 313 : A

138 = 314 : D

139 = 319 : g (1 + 3 "per eco")

140 = 322 : C

141 = 323 : A

142 = 324 : d

143 = 325 : d

144 = 326 : b

145 = 327 : E

146 = 328 : C

147 = 329 : g

148 = 330 : A

149 = 331 : D

150 = 332 : B^b

151 = 333 : d

152 = 334 : g

153 = 335 : D

154 = 336 : d

155 = 339 : A

156 = 340 : E^b

157 = 342 : C (2)

158 = 343 : D

159 = 344 : A (2)

160 = 345 : D

161 = 346 : F

162 = 347 : D

163 = 348 : B^b

164 = 349 : E^b

165 = 351 : g

166 = 352 : E^b

167 = 357 : F

168 = 358 : G

169 = 376 : C

170 = 377 : B^b

171 = 378 : b

172 = 379 : C

173 = 408 : G

174 = 409 : e (4)

175 = 410 : A (2)

176 = 411 : a

177 = 413 : a (2)

178 = 414 : D

179 = 417 : E

180 = 418 : B^b

181 = 419 : e

182 = 420 : G

183 = 421 : a

184 = 422 : A

185 = 423 : g

186 = 424 : C

187 = 425 : d

188 = 426 : F

189 = 427 : c

190 = 428 : D

191 = 429 : G

192 = 436 : g

193 = 437 : E^b

194 = 438 : g

195 = 439 : D

196 = 440 : e

197 = 441 : d

198 = 443 : C

199 = 444 : g

200 = 445 : a

201 = 446 : F

202 = 447 : B^b

203 = 449 : G

204 = 450 : B^b

205 = 451 : F

206 = 452 : D

207 = 453 : D

208 = 459 : e

209 = 460 : G

210 = 461 : c

211 = 462 : g

212 = 463 : d

213 = 465 : C

214 = 466 : B^b

215 = 479 : F

216 = 480 : e

217 = 481 : C

218 = 482 : D

219 = 483:B♭   228 = 497:D
220 = 484:e   229 = 498:b
221 = 485:A   230 = 499:B♭
222 = 486:D (2)   231 = 502:E♭
223 = 487:A   232 = 508:C
224 = 489:A   233 = 511:B♭
225 = 494:D   234 = 513:D
226 = 495:C   235 = 514:B♭
227 = 496:A   236 = 519:a

F.II: Concertos for viola d'amore

1 = 189:A
2 = 196:d
3 = 197:d
4 = 198:d
5 = 337:D
6 = 341:a

F.III: Concertos for one or more cellos

1 = 19:c   15 = 234:g
2 = 61:g (2)   16 = 235:D
3 = 204:C   17 = 243:F
4 = 205:a   18 = 244:a
5 = 206:B♭   19 = 317:G
6 = 211:C   20 = 500:D
7 = 212:d   21 = 521:a
8 = 218:C   22 = 522:G
9 = 219:b   23 = 523:d
10 = 220:a   24 = 524:d
11 = 221:F   25 = 525:B♭
12 = 231:G   26 = 526:g
13 = 232:a   27 = 527:c
14 = 253:F

F.IV: Concertos for violin with other bowed string instruments

1 = 26:G (2 v, 2 vc)   7 = 406:D (4 v, vc)
2 = 35:B♭ (v, vc)   8 = 407:g (2 v, vc)
3 = 53:C (v, vc)   9 = 412:F (4 v, vc)
4 = 99:D (2 v, 2 vc)   10 = 415:b (4 v, vc)
5 = 135:F (v, vc)   11 = 416:d (2 v, vc)
6 = 146:A (v, vc)

F.V: Concertos for mandolin

    I = 98:C
    2 = 104:g (2)

F.VI. Concertos for one or more flutes, or piccolo
    N.B. In addition to the works listed below, v. 360 also contains a
    flute concerto in G. Its no. in the score is given as F.VI:12, a no.
    also assigned to a flute concerto in F listed below, in v. 454. However,
    the Fanna thematic catalog calls the former F.XII:49.
        Concertos in F.VI are for 1 flute unless otherwise stated.

I = 46:F	9 = 152:a (picc)
2 = 101:C (2 fl)	10 = 153:D
3 = 102:D	11 = 159:c
4 = 105:C (picc)	12 = 454:F
5 = 110:C (picc)	13 = 455:g
6 = 138:G	14 = 456:D
7 = 148:a	15 = 457:G
8 = 151:G	16 = 458:G

F.VII. Concertos for one or more oboes

I = 2:d	10 = 279:D
2 = 14:F	11 = 283:C
3 = 139:C (2)	12 = 315:F
4 = 222:C	13 = 316:a
5 = 215:a	14 = 442:B^h
6 = 216:C	15 = 448:B^h
7 = 217:C	16 = 488:F
8 = 263:a (2)	17 = 520:C
9 = 264:d (2)	

F.VIII. Concertos for bassoon

I = 12:B^b	10 = 119:a
2 = 28:a	11 = 214:g
3 = 34:C	12 = 223:a
4 = 47:C	13 = 224:C
5 = 67:d	14 = 225:c
6 = 71:a	15 = 236:F
7 = 72:a	16 = 237:C
8 = 109:F	17 = 238:C
9 = 118:C	18 = 239:C

19 = 240:F	29 = 275:G
20 = 266:F	30 = 276:G
21 = 267:C	31 = 277:C
22 = 268:F	32 = 278:F
23 = 269:g	33 = 281:C
24 = 270:B^h	34 = 282:C
25 = 271:F	35 = 298:B^h
26 = 272:C	36 = 299:B^h
27 = 273:E^h	37 = 300:G
28 = 274:C	

F.IX: Concerto for two trumpets

    1 = 97:C

F.X: Concertos for two horns

    1 = 91:F
    2 = 121:F

F.XI: Concertos and sinfonias for strings

1 = 5:A	23 = 185:C
2 = 6:F	24 = 190:B^h
3 = 7:B^h	25 = 200:C
4 = 8:A	26 = 201:a
5 = 9:B^h	27 = 226:g
6 = 11:g	28 = 241:F
7 = 22:b	29 = 242:F
8 = 30:c	30 = 246:D
9 = 32:c	31 = 251:d
10 = 36:d	32 = 252:G
11 = 49:G	33 = 287:g
12 = 50:B^h	34 = 288:F
13 = 56:e	35 = 289:f
14 = 59:F	36 = 290:G
15 = 113:D	37 = 308:C
16 = 114:D	38 = 309:C
17 = 115:g	39 = 310:g
18 = 161:E	40 = 321:G
19 = 176:d	41 = 361:G
20 = 177:c	42 = 464:D
21 = 182:g	43 = 492:e
22 = 184:A	44 = 493:C

il not be published

45 = 505:G	49 = 512:G
46 = 506:C	50 = 515:E
47 = 507:C	51 = 516:F
48 = 509:C	52 = 518:b

F.XII: Concertos for various combinations of instruments

The works in this category fall into two groups: those in which the solo instruments are accompanied by string orchestra and a keyboard instrument, and those which are accompanied either by *basso continuo* (b.c.) or not at all. Those without orchestra are given an asterisk below.

An error on the title page of no. 7 gives its F. no. as VIII instead of XII.

```
  1 = 33:C (2 ob, 2 cl)
  2 = 10:C (2 ob, 2 cl)
  3 = 25:g (2 fl, 2 ob, 2 bn, v)
 *4 = 23:g (fl, ob, bn)
  5 = 33:g (fl/v, bn)
 *6 = 40:g (fl, ob, v, b.c.)
 *7 = 39:D (fl, v, vc/bn)
 *8 = 41:g (fl, v, bn, b.c./or 2 v, vc, b.c.)
 *9 = 42:D (fl, ob, v, bn, b.c.)
 10 = 43:F (2 ob, bn, 2 hn, v)
*11 = 44:a (fl, 2 v, b.c.)
 12 = 51:B♭ (ob, e.h., v, 2 va, vc)
*13 = 52:G (fl, ob, bn, b.c.)
 14 = 54:C (2 fl, 2 ob, 2 cl, bn, 2 v)
*15 = 62:D (2 v, lute, b.c.)
 16 = 73:B♭ (ob, v)
 17 = 90:C (2 fl, 2 ob, bn, 2 v)
 18 = 94:F (2 ob, bn, 2 hn, v)
 19 = 95:d (v, organ)
*20 = 103:g (fl, ob, v, bn, b.c.)
*21 = 106:F (fl, v, bn, b.c.)
 22 = 137:e (vc, bn)
 23 = 142:C (2 fl, ob, e.h., 2 tpt, v, 2 va)
*24 = 143:C (fl, ob, v, bn, b.c.)
*25 = 144:D (fl, ob, v, bn, b.c.)
*26 = 147:F (fl, ob, v, bn, b.c.)
*27 = 149:D (fl, v, bn, b.c.)
 28 = 150:F (fl, ob, bn)
```

*29 = 154:D (fl, ob, v, bn, b.c./ or 3 v, bn, b.c.)
*30 = 155:C (fl, ob, 2 v, b.c.)
 31 = 213:d (2 fl, 2 ob, bn, 2 v)
*32 = 248:F (2 ob, viola d'amore, bn, 2 hn, b.c.)
 33 = 249:g (2 fl, 3 ob, bn, v)
 34 = 250:C (ob, 2 v)
 35 = 265:F (ob, v)
 36 = 280:G (ob, hn)
 37 = 318:(2 fl, 2 e.h., hn, 2 mandolins, 2 theorboes, vc)
 38 = 320:d (viola d'amore, lute)
 39 = 338:F (2 ob, bn, 2 hn, v)
 40 = 350:F (2 ob, bn, 2 hn, v)
 41 = 353:F (v, organ)
*42 = 354:d (fl, v, bn, b.c.)
*43 = 355:D (fl, v, b.c.)
 44 = 359:B^h (2 fl, 2 ob, bn)
 45 = 362:D (2 ob, bn)
 46 = 363:F (2 hn, bn)
 47 = 380:D (2 ob, 2 hn, v, 2 organs)
 48 = 381:A (4 fl, 4 v)
 49 = 360:G (fl; see note under F.VI above)
 50 = 510:D (2 ob, v)

F.XIII: Sonatas for one or two violins

1 = 17:G (2)	18 = 383:e (2)
2 = 24:B^h (2)	19 = 384:C (2)
3 = 57:F (2)	20 = 385:E (2)
4 = 58:F (2)	21 = 386:F (2)
5 = 356:g	22 = 387:D (2)
6 = 364:D	23 = 388:E^h (2)
7 = 365:d	24 = 389:d (2)
8 = 366:C	25 = 390:A (2)
9 = 367:d	26 = 391:B^h (2)
10 = 368:c	27 = 392:b (2)
11 = 369:C	28 = 393:d (2)
12 = 370:A	29 = 394:g
13 = 371:G	30 = 395:A
14 = 372:c	31 = 396:d
15 = 373:g	32 = 397:F
16 = 374:B^h	33 = 398:b
17 = 382:g (2)	34 = 399:C

35 = 400:c	43 = 432:B^b
36 = 401:G	44 = 433:b
37 = 402:e	45 = 434:B^b (2)
38 = 403:f	46 = 435:g (2)
39 = 404:D	47 = 491:F
40 = 405:a	48 = 528:C (2)
41 = 430:F	49 = 529:G
42 = 431:A	

F.XIV: Cello sonatas

1 = 473:B^b	6 = 478:B^b
2 = 474:F	7 = 503:a
3 = 475:a	8 = 504:B^b
4 = 476:B^b	9 = 530:g
5 = 477:e	

F.XV: Sonatas for wind instruments

1 = 18:a (fl)
2 = 375:c (ob)
3 = 490:C (fl)
4 = 501:F (fl)
5 = 517:d (fl)

F.XVI: Sonatas for various combinations of instruments

1 = 20:c (v, vc, b.c.)
2 = 21:E^b (2 v, va, b.c.)
3 = 63:C (v, lute, b.c.)
4 = 75:g (v. lute, b.c.)
5 = 467:C (musetta/hurdy-gurdy/fl/ob/v, b.c.)
6 = 468:C (same)
7 = 469:G (same)
8 = 470:A (same)
9 = 471:C (same)
10 = 472:g (same)

1B.   Alphabetical index of works with identifying titles, descriptions, or opus numbers, giving the F. no.

"The a minor violin concerto"	I:176
Al santo sepulcro	XI:8; XVI:2
Alla rustica	XI:11
Amoroso, l'	I:127

2. [Antonio Fanna], *Antonio Vivaldi (1678–1741). Catalogo numerico-tematico delle opere strumentali.* Milan, Ricordi, 1968.
    Includes correlation of nos. with no. 4 below, and supersedes no. 2 B.

2B. [Antonio Fanna], *Antonio Vivaldi: Indice tematico di 200 opere strumentali.* Milano, Ricordi, 1955

3. MARIO RINALDI, *Catalogo numerico tematico delle compositioni di Antonio Vivaldi.* Roma, Editrice cultura moderna, 1945

4. MARC PINCHERLE, *Antonio Vivaldi et la musique instrumentale. Tome II: Inventaire thématique.* Paris, Fleury, 1958

5. LEONORE CORAL, *A concordance of the thematic indexes to the instrumental works of Antonio Vivaldi. (Music Library Association Index Series, no. 4)*
    Correlates items 2B–4

93
WALTER [WALTHER], JOHANN, 1496–1570

Sämtliche Werke, herausgegeben von Otto Schröder. Kassel, Bärenreiter

v. 1   *Geistliche Gesangbüchlein, Wittenberg 1551. Teil 1: Deutsche Gesänge,* ed. O. Schröder, Max Schneider

v. 2   ——— Teil 2: *Cantiones latinae*

v. 3   *Geistliches Gesangbüchlein Wittenberg. Lieder und Motetten, die nur 1524, 1525 und 1544 im Wittenbergischen Gesangbüchlein enthalten oder in Handschriften und Drucken verstreut sind,* ed. Schröder, Schneider

v. 5   *Cantiones septem vocum (Psalm 118, Psalm 120), 1544 und 1545, und Magnificat octo tonorum quatuor, quinque et sex vocibus senae 1557,* ed. M. Schneider

v. 6   *Das Christlich Kinderlied D. Martini Lutheri "Erhalt uns, Herr", aufs neu in sechs Stimmen gesetzet und mit etlichen schönen christlichen Texten, lateinischen und deutschen Gesängen gemehrt, 1566. Dichtungen (nicht vertont). Zweifelhafte und unechte Werke.* REGISTER

94
WERT, GIACHES DE, 1536–1596

Opera omnia, ed. Carol MacClintock and Melvin Bernstein. Corpus mensurabilis musicae **(A 28),** ser. 24. 12 v. proposed.

v. 1   *Madrigals of 1558*

v. 2   *Madrigals of 1561*

v. 3   *Madrigals of 1563*

v. 4   *Madrigals of 1567*

v. 5   *Madrigals of 1571*

v. 6   *Madrigals of 1577*

v. 7   *Madrigals of 1581*

95
WILLAERT, ADRIANO, *ca.* 1485–1562

Opera omnia, ed. H. Zenck and Walter Gerstenberg. *Corpus mensurabilis musicae* **(A 28),** ser. 3. About 15 v. proposed.
    An earlier edition of v. 1 appeared as Jg. 9 of *Publikationen älterer Musik* **(A 87).**

√ v. 1   *Motets, 4 voice,* ed. Zenck

√v. 2   *Motets, 4 voice,* ed. Zenck

√v. 3   *Motets, 5 voice,* ed. Zenck

√v. 4   *Motets, 6 voice,* ed. Zenck

√v. 5   *Motets of Musica nova, 4–7 voice,* ed. Gerstenberg

  v. 6

√v. 7   *Hymns*

√v. 8   Madrigals of the *Musica nova,* ed. Gerstenberg

v. 13

96
WOLF, HUGO, 1860–1903

Kritische Gesamtausgabe. Herausgegeben von der Internationalen Hugo-Wolf-Gesellschaft unter Leitung von Hans Jancik mit Unterstützung des Bundesministeriums für Unterricht und der Steiermärkischen Landesregierung. Kassel, Bärenreiter

v. 1   *53 Lieder auf Gedichte von Eduard Mörike*

v. 15   *Kammermusik*

v. 17   *Italienische Serenade für Orchester*

SECTION C

MUSIC LITERATURE

MONOGRAPH AND FACSIMILE SERIES

1

Accademia Chigiana, Siena. *Quaderni.* Siena, Ticci editore, 1940–

Some few v. of this series are not concerned with music, as noted below.

.V8 2 A4 v. 1   Olga Rudge, *Lettere e dediche de Antonio Vivaldi*

v. 2   [not about music]

v. 3   Guido Agosti, *Osservazioni intorno alla tecnica pianistica*

v. 4   Matteo Glinski, *La prima staglione lirica italana all'estero (1628)*

v. 5   Mario Rinaldi, *La data di nascita di Antonio Vivaldi*

v. 6   E. J. Luin, *Fortuna e influenza della musica di Pergolesi in Europa*

v. 7   [not about music]

v. 8   Giuseppe Schena, *Musica e religione*

v. 9   [not about music]

v. 10   M. Rinaldi, *Il problema degli abbellimenti nell'Op. V di Corelli*

v. 11   [not about music]

v. 12   E. A. Mario, *Francesco Paolo Tosti*

v. 13   O. Rudge, *Facsimile di un autografo di Antonio Vivaldi*

v. 14   [not about music]

v. 15   Antonio Bruers, *Facsimile del Concerto funebre di Antonio Vivaldi*

v. 34   F. SCHLITZER, *Antonio Sacchini. Schede e appunti per una sua storia teatrale*

v. 35   F. SCHLITZER, *Rossiniana. Contributo all'epistolario di G. Rossini*

v. 36   ALESSANDRO RASELLI, *L'Accademia Musicale Chigiana MCMXXXII–MCMLVI*

v. 37   F. SCHLITZER, *Circostanze della vita di Gaspare Spontini. Con lettere inedite*

v. 38   O. RUDGE, *"Ricordanze" di Guido Chigi Saracini*

v. 39   F. SCHLITZER, *Rossini e Siena, e altri scritti Rossiniana (con lettere inedite)*

v. 40   FRANK WALKER, *Arrigo Boito. Lettere inedite e poesie giovanili*

v. 41   VITO FRAZZI, *I vari sistemi del "Linguaggio musicale"*

2
Accademia musicale Chigiana, *Settimane musicali Senesi.*

Firenze, Case editrice Leo S. Olschki. 1939–1963

In 1964, changed to a periodical: *Chigiana. Rassegna annuale di studi musicologi* **(D 10)**

v. 1   *Antonio Vivaldi. Note e documenti sulla vita e sulle opere*

v. 2   *Gli Scarlatti (Alessandro, Francesco, Pietro, Domenico, Giuseppe). Note e documenti sulla vita e sulle opere*

v. 3   *La scuola Veneziana (Secoli XVII–XVIII). Note e documenti*

v. 4   *Giovanni Battista Pergolesi (1710–1736). Note e documenti*

v. 5   *Baldassaro Galuppi detto "Il Buranello" (1706–1785). Note e documenti*

v. 6   ANTONIO BRUERS, *La rivendicazione di Antonio Vivaldi*

v. 7   FRANCO SCHLITZER, *Goethe e Cimarosa. Con un'appendice di note bio-bibliografiche* [Also in **C 1**, v. 23]

v. 8   *Giuseppe Verdi. Scritti di autori vari*

v. 9   F. SCHLITZER, *Tommaso Traetta, Leonardo Leo, Vincenzo Bellini. Notizie e documenti*

⁹⁰ ⁷ ₅₃	v. 10	*La scuola Romana: G. Carissimi, A. Cesti, M. Marazzoli*
⁴ᴸ³⁹⁰ ³⁸⁶⁸ ₁₉₅₄	v. 11	*Musicisti Toscani. Scritti di autori vari,* ed. F. Schlitzer
ᴸ³⁹⁰ ₃₅₈ ₁₉₅₅	v. 12	*Musicisti Toscani. Scritti di autori vari,* ed. Adelmo Damerini, F. Schlitzer
ᴹᴸ³⁹⁰ ᴅ₃₅	v. 13	*Musicisti della Scuola Emiliana,* ed. A. Damerini, Gino Roncaglia
	v. 14	*Immagini esotiche nella musica italiana,* ed. A. Damerina, G. Roncaglia
ᴸ³⁹⁰ ᴅ₃₅₄	v. 15	*Musicisti Lombardi e Emiliani,* ed. A. Damerini
	v. 16	*Musicisti Piedmontesi e Liguri,* ed. A. Damerini, G. Roncaglia
ᴹᴸ²⁹⁰ ᴅ₃₄	v. 17	*I Grandi anniversari del 1960 e la musica sinfonica e da camera nell'Ottocento in Italia,* ed. A. Damerini, G. Roncaglia
⁶⁴ ₀₂₄ ₁₉₆₁	v. 18	*Volti musicali di Falstaff,* ed. Damerini, Roncaglia
₂₉₀ ᴅ₂₉ ₁₉₆₂	v. 19	*Musiche italiane rare e vive da Giovanni Gabrieli,* ed. Damerini, Roncaglia
ᴸ²⁹⁰ ₁ ꜰ₃	v. 20	*Le celebrazioni del 1963 e alcune nuove indagini sulla musica dei secoli XVIII e XIX,* ed. Mario Fabbri

3

The American Musicological Society, *Studies and Documents*

v. 1   Ockeghem, *Collected works.* See **B 66**

v. 2   Dunstable, *Collected works.* See **A 76**, v. 8

v. 3   See v. 1 above

v. 4   Joseph Kerman, *The Elizabethan madrigal, a comparative study*

The American Musicological Society: Bulletin, Papers, Journal, see Section **D 2**

4

Antiquae musicae italicae bibliotheca: Scriptores (see **A 5**)

Series 1.   *Mensurabilis musicae tractatuli*

V. I   Anonymi, *Capitulum de semibrevibus*
GUIDONIS FRATRIS, *Ars musice mensurate*
Anonymi, *Fragmentum de mensuris*
PETRI DE AMALFIA, *Compendium artis motectorum Marchecti*
Anonymi, *Tractatulus de figuris et temporibus*
Anonymi, *Musice compilatio*
Anonymi, *De modo accipiendo*
Anonymi, *Fragmentum de proportionibus*
ed. F. Alberto Gallo

Series 3.   *Prosdocimi de Beldemandis: Opera*

V. I   *Expositiones tractatus pratice cantus mensurabilis magistri Johannis de Muris,* ed. F. A. Gallo

Series 4.   *Franchini Gafuri*

V. I   *Extractus parvus musicae ex cod. Par. Palat. 1158* [in preparation], ed. F. A. Gallo

Series 5.   GIOVANNI SPATARO, *Utile e breve regulo di canto (dal ms. Londin. British Museum Add. 4920),* ed. G. Vecchi
Also serves as V. 2:2 of *Antiqua musicae italicae bibliotheca: Monumenta Bononiensia* **(A 6)**

5
Antiqua musicae italicae bibliotheca: Subsidia didascalica (see A 5)

V. I   L. CERVELLI, *Contributi alla storia degli strumenti musicali in Italia: Rinascimento e Barocco.* Bologna, Tamari

6
Antiqua musicae italicae bibliotheca: Subsidia historica (see A 5)

Series A.   *Medioevo e Rinascimento*

V. I   Not yet published

V. 2   UGO SESINI, *Monumenti di teoria musicale tra Umanesimo e Rinascimento,* ed. G. Vecchi. Bologna, Tamari

Series B.   *Età Barocca e Moderna*

    v. 1   Not yet published

    v. 2   N. MORINI, *L'Accademia Filarmonica di Bologna I:
         Fondazione e vicende storiche,* ed. G. Vecchi. Bologna,
         Tamari

7
Antiquae musicae italicae: Subsidia theorica

    v. 1   Not yet published

    v. 2   F. ALBERTO GALLO, *La teoria della notazione in Italia dalla
         fine del XIII all'inizio del XV secolo.* Bologna, Tamari

Austria see **Oesterreich**

8
Beiträge zur Mittelrheinischen Musikgeschichte. Herausgegeben von der
Arbeitsgemeinschaft für mittelrheinischen Musikgeschichte. Amster-
dam, Heuwekemeyer, 1962–

    v. 1   ALBERT DUNNING, *Joseph Schmitt. Leben und Kompositionen
         des Eberbacher Zisterziensers und Amsterdamer Musikver-
         legers (1734–1791)*

    v. 2   FRANZ BÖSKEN, *Die Orgeln der evangelischen Marienstifts-
         kirche in Lich*

    v. 3   ADAM GOTTRON, *Arnold Rucker, Orgelmacher von Seligenstadt*

    v. 4   ERNST FRITZ SCHMID, *Die Orgeln von Amorbach, eine Musik-
         geschichte des Klosters*

    v. 5   GUSTAV BERETHS, *Die Musikpflege am Kurtrierischen Hofe zu
         Koblenz-Ehrenbreitstein* [1652–1802]

    v. 6   FRANZ BÖSKEN, *Quellen und Forschungen zur Orgelgeschichte
         Mittelrheins. Band 1: Mainz und Vororte, Rheinhessen, Worms
         und Vororte*

    v. 7   Not yet published?

[332]   C 8   Beiträge zur Mittelrheinischen Musikgeschichte : 8

v. 8   ELISABETH NOACK, *Musikgeschichte Darmstadts vom Mittel-
           alter bis zur Goetheszeit*

v. 9   ARNO LEMKE, *Jacob Gottfried Weber, Leben und Werk.
           Ein Beitrag zur Musikgeschichte des mittelrheinischen Raumes*

v. 10   HERBERT UNVERRICHT, *Die beiden Hoffstetter. Zwei Kompo-
           nistenporträts mit Werkverzeichnissen*

9
Beiträge zur Musikforschung, herausgegeben von Max Schneider. Berlin,
      1935–

v. 1   WALTER SERAUKY, *Musikgeschichte der Stadt Halle* [v. 1,
           part 1]
           v. 1 part 2 = v. 6 below; v. 2 part 1 = v. 7; v. 2 part 2 = v. 8

v. 2   WILHELM TWITTENHOFF, *Die musiktheoretischen Schriften
           Joseph Riepels (1709–1782) als Beispiel einer anschaulichen
           Musiklehre*

v. 3   ERNST ZELLER, *Der Erfurter Organist Johann Heinrich Buttstädt
           (1668–1728)*

v. 4   HELLMUT LUDWIG, *Marin Mersenne und seine Musiklehre*

v. 5   JOHANNES SCHÄFER, *Nordhäuser Orgelchronik. Geschichte der
           Orgelwerke in der tausendjährigen Stadt Nordhausen am Harz*

v. 6–8   See v. 1
   6-7

10
Beiträge zur Rheinischen Musikgeschichte. Herausgegeben von der Arbeitsgemeinschaft für rheinische Musikgeschichte. Köln, Staufen, 1952–

v. 1   *Beiträge zur Musikgeschichte der Stadt Düsseldorf,* ed. Karl
           Gustav Fellerer *et al.*

v. 2   HEINRICH HÜSCHEN, *Das Cantuagium des Heinrich Eger von
           Kalkar (1328–1408)*

v. 3   WILLI KAHL, *Studien zur Kölner Musikgeschichte des 16. und
           17. Jahrhunderts*

v. 38   FRIEDRICH BEURHAUS (1536–1609), *Musicae rudimenta (Dortmund 1581)* [cf. v. 31]

v. 39   K. W. NIEMÖLLER, *Kirchenmusik und reichsstädtische Musikpflege im Köln des 18. Jahrhunderts*

v. 40   GERHARD STEFFEN, *Johann Hugo von Wilderer (1670–1724), Kapellmeister am kurpfaelzischen Hofe zu Düsseldorf und Mannheim*

v. 41   GÜNTHER KASPERSMEIER, *Wilhelm Dyckerhoff (1810–1881) und seine Kompositionslehre*

, v. 42   HEINZ BLOMMER, *Anfänge und Entwicklung des Männerchorwesens am Niederrhein*

v. 43   *Rheinische Musiker, 1. Folge,* ed. K. G. Fellerer
2. Folge = v. 53; 3. Folge = v. 58, 62; 4. Folge = v. 64 (with cumulative index); 5. Folge = v. 69

v. 44   *Musik im Raume Remscheid,* ed. K. G. Fellerer

v. 45   RUDOLF POHL, *Die Messen des Johannes Mangon* [*before 1550–ca. 1577?*]

v. 46   REINER KIRCHRATH, *Theatrum musicae, das ist Kurze und gründlich erklärte Verfassung der Aretinischer und Gregorienischer Singkunst. Köln am Rheine 1782,* ed. Fellerer (facsimile)

v. 47   FRIEDRICH BEURHAUS, *Erotematum musicae libri duo, Nürnberg 1580.* (facsimile; cf. v. 38)

v. 48   See v. 28

v. 49   BERT VOSS, *August von Othegraven [1864–1920]. Leben und Werke*

v. 50   K. W. NIEMÖLLER, *Die Musica figurativa des Melchior Schanppecher [fl. 1496–1506]*

v. 51   *Richard Strauss und Franz Wüllner im Briefwechsel,* ed. Dietrich Kämper

v. 52   *Professor Fellerer zum 60. Geburtstag,* ed. Herbert Drux, K. W. Niemöller, Walter Thoene

v. 53   See v. 43

11
Berliner Studien zur Musikwissenschaft. Veröffentlichungen des Musikwissenschaftlichen Instituts der Freien Universität Berlin, herausgegeben von Adam Adrio. Berlin, Merseburger, 1959–

publikation in der ersten Hälfte des 16. Jahrhunderts. 2 **Bde.**: Bd. 1. *Studie;* Bd. 2. *Bibliographie*

v. 12   MARIANNE HENZE, *Studien zu den Messenkompositionen Johannes Ockeghems*

v. 13   WOLFGANG NITSCHKE, *Studien zu den Cantus-Firmus-Messen Guillaume Dufays*
Music examples = v. 13/2

v. 14   JÜRGEN GRIMM, *Das neue Leipziger Gesangbuch des Gottfried Vopelius (Leipzig, 1682)*

v. 15   LEO KARL GERHARTZ, *Die Auseinandersetzungen des jungen Giuseppe Verdi mit dem literarischen Drama*

12
Berner Veröffentlichungen zur Musikforschung, herausgegeben von Ernst Kurth, 1927–

Series 2 (1951–   ) called *Publikationen der Schweizerischen Musikforschenden Gesellschaft*

v. 1   MAX ZULAUF, *Die Harmonik Johann Sebastian Bachs*

v. 2   LUCIE DIKENMANN-BALMER, *Tonsystem und Kirchentöne bei Johannes Tinctoris*

v. 3   M. ZULAUF, *Der Musikunterricht in der Geschichte des Bernischen Schulwesens von 1528–1798*

v. 4   PAUL DIKENMANN, *Die Entwicklung der Harmonik bei A. Skrjabin*

v. 5   GEORG BIERI, *Die Lieder von Hugo Wolf*

v. 6   RUDOLF VON TOBEL, *Die Formenwelt der klassischen Instrumentalmusik*

v. 7   FRITZ DE QUERVAIN, *Der Chorstil Henri Purcells*

v. 8   EUGEN THEILE, *Die Chorfugen Johann Sebastian Bachs*

v. 9   CHRISTO OBRESCHKOV, *Das bulgarische Volkslied*

v. 10   EDITH SCHNAPPER, *Die Gesänge des jungen Schubert*

MT100
.S683G5

v. 13   REINHARD GERLACH, *Don Juan und Rosenkavalier. Studien zu Idee und Gestalt . . . im Werk Richard Strauss*

v. 14   PIERRE M. TAGMANN, *Archivalische Studien zur Musikpflege am Dom von Mantua (1500–1627)*

ML410
.V32 R8

v. 15   RAIMUND RÜEGGE, *O. Vecchis geistliche Werke*

ML410
.M 36786
.1971 b

v. 23   *Billeter, Die Harmonik bei Frank Martin*

13
ML120
.I 84

Bibliotheca musicae. Collana di cataloghi e bibliografie. Milano, 1962–

✓ v. 1   *Assisi. La capella della basilica di S. Francesco. Catalogo del fondo musicale nella biblioteca communale di Assisi,* ed. Claudio Sartori

ML 120
.I8 54 ✓

v. 2   *Lucca. Biblioteca del seminario. Catalogo delle musiche del fondo antico,* ed. E. Maggini

ML 136
.L88S4

v. 3   *Roma. Biblioteca Corsiniana e dell'Accademia dei Lincei. Catalogo del fondi Chiti e Corsiniani,* ed. A. Bertini

ML 120
.I8 54

✓ v. 4   *Genova, Biblioteca dell'Instituto musicale "Nicolò Paganini". Catalogo del fondo antico,* ed. S. Pintacuda

ML136
.P4189

✓ v. 5   *Placenza. Archivio del Duomo. Catalogo del fondo musicale,* ed. F. Bussi

14
Bibliotheca musicae Bononiensis. Bologna, Arnaldo Forni.
This series consists of facsimiles and reprints.

Section I. *Bibliografia, cataloghi, etc.*

v. 1   G. GASPERINI, N. PELICELLI, *Catalogo delle opere musicali, teoriche o pratiche, manoscritte o stampate . . . Città di Parma e di Reggio Emilia.* Parma, 1911

v. 2   P. LODI, *Catalogo delle opere musicali. Città di Modena, Biblioteca Estense.* Parma, 1923

v. 3   LUIGI FRANCESCO VALDRIGHI, *Nomocheliurgografia antica e moderna, ossia Elenco di Fabbricatori di strumenti armonici, con note esplicative e documenti estratti dall'Archivio di Stato di Modena.* Modena, 1884

v. 4   T. WEIL, *I Codici musicali Contarinini del secolo XVII nella R. Biblioteca di S. Marco in Venezia.* Venezia, 1888

v. 5   E. COLOMBANI, *Catalogo della collezione d'autografi lasciata alla R. Accademia Filarmonica di Bologna da M. Masseangeli.* Bologna, 1896

v. 6   PETER LICHTENTHAL (1780–1853), *Dizonaria e bibliografia della musica.* Milano, 1826–36. 4 v.

v. 7   [EDOUARD FÉTIS], *Catalogue de la Bibliothèque de F. J. Fétis acquise par l'Etat Belge.* Bruxelles, 1877

v. 8   HUGO RIEMANN, *Notenschrift und Notendruck. Bibliographisch-Typographische Studie.* Leipzig, 1896

Section II. *Teoria.*

v. 1   LUDOVICO ZACCONI, *Prattica di musica utile et necessaria . . .* Venezia, 1592

v. 2   L. ZACCONI, *Prattica di musica, seconda parte . . .* Venezia, 1622

v. 3   BARTOLOMEO RAMIS DE PAREIA, *Musica practica.* Bologna, 1482

v. 4   NICOLÒ BURZIO, *Musices opusculum.* Bologna, 1487

v. 5   FRANCHINO GAFFURIO, *Theorica musice.* Milano, 1492

v. 6   F. GAFFURIO, *Practica musice.* Milano, 1496

v. 7   F. GAFFURIO, *De harmonia musicorum instrumentorum opus.* Milano, 1518

v. 8   PIETRO AARON, *Libri tres de institutione harmonica.* Bologna, 1516

v. 9   P. AARON, *Trattato della natura et cognitione di tutti gli tuoni di canto figurato.* Vinegia, 1525

v. 10   P. AARON, *Toscanello de la musica.* 1529

v. 11   P. AARON, *Compendiolo di molti dubbi . . .* Milano, 1545

v. 12   P. AARON, *Lucidario in musica.* 1545

v. 13   L. FOLIANI, *Musica theorica.* Venezia, 1529

v. 14   GIOVANNI SPATARO, *Trattato di musica.* Venezia, 1531

V. 15   GIOVANNI MARIA LANFRANCO, *Scintille di musica*. Brescia, 1533

V. 16   STEPHANUS VANNEUS, *Recanetum de musica aurea*. Roma, 1533

V. 17   G. DEL LAGO, *Breve introduttione di musica misurata*. Venetia, 1540

V. 18   SYLVESTRO DI GANASSI, *Opera intitulata Fontegara*. Venezia, 1535

V. 19   S. DI GANASSI, *Regula Rubertina*. Venezia, 1542

V. 20   S. DI GANASSI, *Lettione seconda pur della pratica di sonare il violone d'arco da tasti*. 1543

V. 21   HEINRICH FINCK, *Practica musica*. Vitebergae, 1556

V. 22   VINCENZO GALILEI, *Il Fronimo, dialogo*. Venezia, 1569

V. 23   GIROLAMO DALLA CASA, *Il vero modo di diminuire. Libri I e II*. Venezia, 1584

V. 24   ADRIANO BANCHIERI, *Conclusioni del suono dell'organo*. Bologna, 1609

V. 25   PIETRO CERONE, *El Melopeo y Maestro*. Napoli, 1613

V. 26   A. BANCHIERI, *Cartella musicale nel canto figurato fermo et contrapunto*. Venezia, 1614

V. 27   ERCOLE BOTTRIGARI, *Il Patricio, overo de'tetracordi armonici*. Bologna, 1593

V. 28   E. BOTTRIGARI, *Il Desiderio*. Venezia, 1594

V. 29   E. BOTTRIGARI, *Il Melone, & il Melone secondo*. Bologna, 1602

V. 30   SCIPIONE CERRETO, *Della prattica musica vocale et strumentale*, Napoli, 1601

V. 31   A. BANCHIERI, *L'organo suonarino*. Venezia, 1605

V. 32   A. PISA, *Breve dichiarazione della battuta musicale*. Roma, 1611

V. 33   GIROLAMO DIRUTA, *Il Transilvano*. I. parte: Venezia, 1612; II. parte: Venezia, 1622

V. 34   S. ZUCCOLO DA COLOGNA, *La Pazzia del ballo*. Padova, 1549

v. 2   LEONIDA BUSI, *Il Padre Martini*. Bologna, 1891

v. 3   ANGELO SOLERTI, *Le origini del Melodramma*. Torino, 1903

v. 4   A. SOLERTI, *Musica, ballo e dramatica alla corte Medicea dal 1600 al 1637*. Firenze, 1905

v. 5   FRANCESCO VATIELLI, *Arte e vita musicale a Bologna*, Vol. I. Bologna, 1927

v. 6   STEFANO ARTEAGA, *Le rivoluzioni del teatro musicale italiano*. Bologna, 1783–88

v. 7   A. FAVARO, *L'acustica applicata alla costruzione delle sale per spettacoli*. Padova, 1882

v. 8   LUIGI TORCHI, *La musica strumentale in Italia nei secoli XVI, XVII e XVIII*. Torino, 1901

v. 9   FRANCESCO FLORIMO, *La scuola musicale di Napoli*. Napoli, 1881–83. 4 v.

v. 10   GIUSEPPE CARPANI, *Le Haydine*. Padova, 1823

v. 11   L. NERICI, *Storia della musica in Lucca*. Lucca, 1879

v. 12   A. ADEMOLLO, *I teatri di Roma nel secolo decimosettimo . . .* Roma, 1888

v. 13   R. MAROCCHI, *La musica in Siena*. Siena, 1886

v. 14   L. F. VALDRIGHI, *Musurgiana*, 1879

v. 15   F. VATIELLI, *Un musicista pesarese del secolo XVI* [*Ludovico Zacconi*], Bologna, 1912

v. 16   O. KÖRTE, *Laute und Lautenmusik bis zur Mitte des 16. Jahrhunderts*. Leipzig, 1891

v. 17   A. BERTOLOTTI, *La musica in Mantova (1400–1600). Musici alla Corte dei Gonzaga in Mantova*

v. 18   FAUSTO TORREFRANCA, *Le origini italiane del romanticismo musicale*. Torino, 1930

v. 19   F. TORREFRANCA, *Il segreto del Quattrocento*. Milano, 1939

v. 20   G. S. MAYR, *Biografie di scrittori e artisti musicali bergamaschi*. Bergamo, 1875

V. 21   Joseph von Wasielewski, *Die Violine im XVII. Jahrhundert.* Bonn, 1874

V. 22   G. de Picolellis, *Liutai antichi e moderni,* Firenze, 1885

V. 23   A. G. Ritter, *Zur Geschichte des Orgelspiels.* Leipzig, 1884

V. 24   L. Riccoboni, *Histoire du Théâtre Italien depuis la décadence de la comédie Latine.* Paris, 1728

V. 25   L. Riccoboni, *Réflexions historiques et critiques sur les différents Théâtres d'Europe.* Amsterdam, 1740

V. 26   Giovanni Battista Martini, *Serie cronologica de' Principi dell'Accademia de' Filarmonici di Bologna.* Bologna, 1776

V. 27   Oscar Chilesotti, *Studi sul liuto e la chitarra* [Collected essays from *Rivista musicale italiana* and elsewhere]

V. 28   L. Frati, *Studi e notizie riguardanti la storia della musica*

V. 29   Adrien de La Fage, *Miscellanées musicales.* Paris, 1844

V. 30   D. Muoni, *Gli Antegnati organari insigni e serie di maestri di cappella del Duomo di Milano.* Milano, 1883

V. 31   P. E. Ferrari, *Spettacoli drammatico-musicali e coreografici in Parma dal 1628 al 1883.* Parma, 1884

V. 32   L. N. Galvani, *I teatri musicali di Venezia nel secolo XVII (1637–1700).* Milano, 1879

V. 33   P. Cambiasi, *Rappresentazioni date nei reali teatri di Milano, 1778–1873*

V. 34   A. Gandini, *Cronistoria dei teatri di Modena.* Modena, 1873. 3 v.

Section IV. *Musica practica.* See **A 20**

Section V. *Miscellanea, Carteggi, ecc.*

V. 1   G. Mari, *I trattati medievali di ritmica latina.* Milano, 1899

V. 2   E. Du Meril, *Poésies populaires latines antérieures au douzième siècle.* Paris, 1843

V. 3   E. Du Meril, *Poésies populaires du moyen-âge.* Paris, 1847

V. 4   E. Du Meril, *Poésies inédites du moyen-âge.* Paris, 1854

v. 5   F. J. MONE, *Hymni latini Medii Aevi*. Freiburg, 1853–55. 3 v.

v. 6   G. CARDUCCI, *Cantilene e ballate, strambotti e madrigali nei secoli XII e XIV*

v. 7   A. CAPPELLI, *Ballate, rispetti d'amore e poesie varie . . . del secoli XIV, XV, XVI*. Modena, 1866–9

v. 8   U. SESINI, *Musicologia e filologia. Raccolta di studi sul ritmo e sulla melica del medio evo*. Bologna, 1968

v. 9   GUISEPPE VECCHI, *Studi e ricerche su testi melici del medio evo*. Bologna, 1968

v. 10–20   Not yet published?

v. 21 *ML 194 B2 16280*   ADRIANO BANCHIERI, *Lettere armoniche*. Bologna, 1628–30

v. 22   G. B. MARTINI, *Carteggio inedito*. Bologna, 1888

v. 23   *I copialettere di Giuseppe Verdi*. Milano, 1943

15
Bibliotheca organologica. Hilversum, Frits Knuf
This series consists of facsimiles of rare books on organs and organ building

v. 1 *ML 582 .K88 1962*   M. H. VAN 'T KRUYS, *Verzameling van disposities der verschillende orgels in Nederland*. 1885

v. 2 *•ML 552 .S32 1966*   JOHANN JULIUS SEIDEL, *Die Orgel und ihr Bau. Ein systematisches Handbuch*. 1843

v. 3   J. C. WOLFRAM, *Anleitung zur Kenntnisz, Beurtheilung und Erhaltung der Orgeln*. 1815

v. 4   EDWARD J. HOPKINS, EDWARD F. RIMBAULT, *The organ, its history and construction*. 3d. ed. 1877. Preface and corrections by W. L. Sumner

v. 5 *MT 190 .T9 1966*   DANIEL GOTTLOB TÜRK, *Von den wichtigsten Pflichten eines Organisten. Ein Beytrag zur Verbesserung der musikalischen Liturgie*. Halle, 1787. Ed. Bernhard Billeter

v. 6 *ML 552 .H64 1966*   ARTHUR GEORGE HILL, *The organ-cases and organs of the middle-ages and the renaissance*. London, 1883–1891. 2 v. [this reprint in 1 v.], ed. W. L. Sumner

V. 7 WINFRED ELLERHORST, *Handbuch der Orgelkunde. Der mathe-matischen und akustischen, technischen und künstlerischen Grundlagen sowie die Geschichte und Pflege der modernen Orgel.* Einseideln, 1936. Ed. P. Gregor Klaus

V. 8 GEORG CHRISTIAN FRIEDRICH SCHLIMBACH, *Über die Structur, Erhaltung, Stimmung, Prüfung . . . der Orgel.* Leipzig, 1801

V. 9   A. DE PONTECOÙLANT, *Organographie.* Paris, 1861. 2 v.

16

California. University of California. Publications in Music. Berkeley and Los Angeles, University of California Press, 1943–

V. 1, NO. 1   WALTER H. RUBSAMEN, *Literary sources of secular music in in Italy ca. 1500*

V. 1, NO. 2   ROBERT J. TUSLER, *The style of J. S. Bach's chorale preludes*

V. 2, NO. 1   SIRVART POLADIAN, *Armenian folk songs*

V. 2, NO. 2   MANFRED F. BUKOFZER, *"Sumer is icumen in": a revision*

V. 3   ROBERT U. NELSON, *The technique of variation. A study of the instrumental variation from Antonio de Cabezon to Max Reger*

V. 4   JOHN VINCENT, *The diatonic modes in modern music*

V. 5   W. THOMAS MARROCCO, *The music of Jacopo da Bologna*

V. 6   ELIZABETH MAY, *The influence of the Meiji period on Japanese children's music*

V. 7   VIOLA L. HAGOPIAN, *Italian ars nova music. A bibliographic guide to modern editions and related literature*

17

Catalogus musicus: a series of catalogues and bibliographies. International association of music libraries, International musicological society. Kassel, Bärenreiter, 1963–

V. 1   FRIEDRICH WILHELM RIEDEL, *Das Musikarchiv im Minoriten-konvent zu Wien (Katalog des älteren Bestandes vor 1789)*

V. 2   ADOLF LAYER, *Katalog des Augsburger Verlegers Lotter von 1753*

√V. 3   RICHARD SCHAAL, *Das Inventar der Kantorei St. Anna in Augsburg*

√ V. 4   MADELEINE GARROS, SIMONE WALLON, *Catalogue du fonds*
V. 5 *cop* 2 *musical de la Bibliothèque Sainte-Geneviève de Paris*
V. 6

18
Catholic University of America. Studies in music. Washington, D.C., Catholic University Press, 1954–

V. 1   DONALD WESLEY STAUFFER, *Intonation deficiencies of wind instruments in ensembles*

V. 2   CORAZON G. CANOVE, *A re-evaluation of the role played by Carl Philipp Emmanuel Bach in the development of the clavier sonata*

V. 3   GEORGE D. DURHAM, *The development of the German concert overture*

V. 4   SISTER M. J. B. CONNOR, *Gregorian chant and medieval hymn tunes in the works of J. S. Bach*

V. 5   SISTER M. J. KLEIN, *The contribution of Daniel Gregory Mason to American Music*

V. 6   L. JANETTE WELLS, *A history of the music festival at Chautauqua Institution from 1874 to 1957*

V. 7   GERALD LEFKOFF, *Five sixteenth century Venetian lute books*

V. 8   PAUL F. FOELBER, *Bach's treatment of the subject of death in his choral music*

V. 9   SISTER M. M. KEANE, *The theoretical writings of Jean-Philippe Rameau*

Cologne see **Köln**

19
Colorado College. Translations [of music theory works]. Colorado Springs, Colorado music press, 1967–

ML171   V. 1   JOHANNES DE GROCHEO, *Concerning music (De musica),*
G7413   ed. Albert Seay

JOHANNES TINCTORIS, *Concerning the nature and propriety of tones (De natura et proprietate tonorum),* ed. Albert Seay

AURELIAN OF RÉOME, *The discipline of music,* ed. Joseph Ponte

20

Columbia University studies in musicology. New York, Columbia University Press, 1935–

V. I   KARL NEF, *An outline of the history of music*

V. 2   ERNEST BRENNECKE, JR., *John Milton the elder and his music*

V. 3   WALDO SELDON PRATT, *The music of the French Psalter of 1562*

V. 4   WILLIAM TREAT UPTON, *Anthony Philip Heinrich: a nineteenth century composer in America*

V. 5   HAROLD EARLE JOHNSON, *Musical interludes in Boston, 1795–1830*

V. 6   EDWARD E. LOWINSKY, *Secret chromatic art in the Netherlands motet*

V. 7   BELA BARTOK and ALBERT B. LORD, *Serbo-Croatian folk songs*

Consejo superior . . . see **Spain**

20A

Contributi di musicologia, a cura di Lino Bianchi. Roma, Edizioni de Santis, 1967–

V. I   MASSIMO BONGIANCKINO, *The harpsichord music of Domenico Scarlatti.* Eng. trans. by John Tickner

V. 2   L. BIANCHI, *Carissimi, Stradella, Scarlatti e l'oratorio musicale*

V. 3   ALBERTO GHISLANZONI, *Giovanni Paisiello: Valutazioni critiche rettificate*

21

Corpus scriptorum de musica. Rome, American Institute of Musicology, 1950–   (cf. **A 1**)

ML170.C6 no.1 v. 1   JOHANNES AFFLIGEMENSIS (*fl. ca.* 1100), *De musica cum tonario,* ed. Joseph Smits van Waesberghe

ML170.C6 no.2 v. 2   ARIBO SCHOLASTICUS (11th c.), *De musica,* ed. J. Smits van Waesberghe

ML170.C6 no.3 v. 3   JACOB OF LIÉGE (14th c.), *Speculum musicae,* ed. Roger Bragard. 7 parts are planned; 4 have appeared so far: 1. *Liber primus*   2. *Liber secundus* (in 2 separately bound v.) 3. *Liber tertius*   4. *Liber quartus* , 5 , 6

v. 4   GUIDO OF AREZZO (*ca.* 995–1050), *Micrologus,* ed. J. Smits van Waesberghe

v. 5   Anonymus, 14th c., *Notitia del valore delle note canto misurato,* ed. Armen Carapetyan

v. 6   MARCHETTUS OF PADUA (14th c.), *Pomerium,* ed. Giuseppe Vecchi

v. 7   UGOLINO OF ORVIETO (*ca.* 1380–*ca.* 1457), *Declaratio musicae disciplinae,* ed. Albert Seay In 3 parts: 1. *Book 1*   2. *Books 2–3*   3. *Books 4–5*

v. 8   PHILIPPE DE VITRI (1291–1361), *Ars nova,* ed. Gilbert Reaney, J. Maillard, A. Gilles

v. 9   *Anonymous treatise from the Codex Vatican, Lat. 5120 (ca. 1400),* ed. Albert Seay

v. 10   JOHN HOTHBY (*d.* 1487), *Tres tractatuli,* ed. A. Seay

v. 11   GUILIELMUS MONACHUS (*fl. ca.* 1480), *De preceptis artis musicae,* ed. A. Seay

v. 12   *MS Oxford Bodley 842, Brevarium regulare musicae; MS British Museum Royal 12.C.VI, Tractatus de figuris sive de notis; Johannes Torkesey, Declaratio trianguli et scuti,* ed. G. Reaney, A. Gilles

14,

22
Detroit studies in music bibliography. General editor Bruno Nettl. Detroit, Information Service Inc., 1961–

ML128.M8N5 v. 1   BRUNO NETTL, *Reference materials in ethnomusicology*

v. 2 SIRVART POLADIAN, *Sir Arthur Sullivan: an index to his vocal works*

v. 3 DONALD W. MACARDLE, *An index to Beethoven's conversation books*

v. 4 KEITH E. MIXTER, *General bibliography for music research*

v. 5 JULIUS MATTFELD, *A handbook of American operatic premieres [1931–1962]*

v. 6 JAMES COOVER and RICHARD COLVIG, *Medieval and renaissance music on long-playing records*

v. 7 JOYCE ELLEN MANGLER, *Rhode Island music and musicians, 1733–1850*

v. 8 FRED BLUM, *Jean Sibelius, an international bibliography of books and articles on the occasion of the centennial celebrations 1965*

v. 9 KENNETH R. HARTLEY, *Bibliography of theses and dissertations in sacred music*

v. 10 CAROLINE S. FRUCHTMAN, *Checklist of vocal chamber works by Benedetto Marcello*

v. 11 THOMAS E. WARNER, *An annotated bibliography of woodwind instruction books, 1606–1830*

v. 12 SVEN H. HANSELL, *Works for solo voice of Johann Adolph Hasse (1699–1783)*

v. 13 DOROTHY STAHL, *A selective discography of solo song*

v. 14 DENA J. EPSTEIN, *Music publishing in Chicago before 1871: the firm of Root & Cady, 1858–1871*

23

Documenta musicologica. Faksimile-Reihe, herausgegeben von der Internationalen Gesellschaft für Musikwissenschaft und der Internationalen Vereinigung des Musikbibliotheken. Kassel, Bärenreiter, 1951–

Reihe I, Facsimiles of theoretical and practical works, is listed below. For Reihe II see **A 38**

v. 1 GEORG RHAU, *Enchiridion utriusque Musicae practicae I (Musica plana), Wittenberg 1538,* ed. Hans Albrecht

MT 340
. Q 1
1953

v. 2   JOHANN JOACHIM QUANTZ, *Versuch einer Anweisung die flûte traversière zu spielen. 3. Auflage, Berlin, 1789,* ed. Hans-ed. Hans-Peter Schmitz

ML100
.A2 W2 1953

v. 3   JOHANN GOTTFRIED WALTHER, *Musikalisches Lexikon oder Musikalische Bibliothek, 1732,* ed. Richard Schaal

ML100
.A23 1953

v. 4   JACOB ADLUNG, *Anleitung zu der musikalischen Gelahrtheit, 1758,* ed. Hans Joachim Moser

MT85
.M42 1954

v. 5   JOHANN MATTHESON, *Der volkommene Capellmeister,* ed. Margarete Reimann

MT 6 . A2 B6
1550a

v. 6   LOYS BOURGEOIS, *Le droict chemin de musique, 1550,* ed. P. André Gaillard

M1496
. L655 P8

v. 7   PASCHAL DE L'ESTOCART, *Les cent cinquante pseaumes de David . . . 1583,* ed. Hans Hollinger, Pierre Pidoux
5 part books. Commentary in French and German

MT 6
. A2 M33

v. 8   JOSEPH FRIEDRICH BERNHARD CASPAR MAIER, *Museum musicum, 1732,* ed. Heinz Becker

ML 171
. C675 C6

v. 9   ADRIAN PETIT COCLICO, *Compendium musices* [mid-sixteenth c.], ed. Manfred F. Bukofzer

MT 6
. A2 B96 1955

v. 10   JOACHIM BURMEISTER, *Musica poetica. Rostock, 1606,* ed. Martin Ruhnke

ML171
.B47 D4

v. 11   FRAY JUAN BERMUDO, *Declaraciòn de instrumentos musicales, 1555,* ed. Macario Santiago Kastner

MT 80
. B7 1957

v. 12   GIOVANNI BATTISTA BOVICELLI, *Regole passaggi di musica, 1594,* ed. Nanie Bridgman

ML171 . S16 1958

v. 13   FRANCISCO DE SALINAS, *De musica, 1577,* ed. M. S. Kastner

ML100 . A278 V2

v. 14   MICHAEL PRAETORIUS, *Syntagma musicum II: De organographia, 1619,* ed. Wilibald Gurlitt (cf. v. 15, 21)

ML100 . A2 P8 V3

v. 15   ——— *III: Termini musici, 1619,* ed. W. Gurlitt

MT55 . A2 P82

v. 16   PIETRO PONTIO, *Ragionamenti de musica, 1588,* ed. Suzanne Clercx

MT40
.. A2 V77

v. 17   NICOLO VICENTINO, *L'antica musica ridotta alla moderna prattica, 1555,* ed. Edward E. Lowinsky

ML 550 . A2 A2
1961

v. 18   JACOB ADLUNG, *Musica mechanica organoedi, 1768,* ed. Christhard Mahrenholz

v. 19   CHARLES BURNEY, *Tagebuch einer musikalischen Reise durch Frankreich und Italien, 1772*, ed. R. Schaal

v. 20   LOUIS SPOHR, *Violinschule* [not yet published]

v. 21   M. PRAETORIUS, *Syntagma musicum I: Musicae artis analecta, 1614/15*, ed. W. Gurlitt (cf. v. 14–15)

v. 22   JOHANN CHRISTOPH WIEGEL, *Musicalisches Theatrum*, ed. Alfred Berner

v. 23   DANIEL GOTTLOB TÜRK, *Klavierschule, 1789*, ed. Erwin R. Jacobi

v. 24–6   DOM BEDOS DE CELLES, *L'Art du facteur d'orgues, 1766, 1770, 1778*, ed. C. Mahrenholz

v. 27   PETER PRELLEUR, *The modern musick master, 1731*, ed. Alexander Hyatt King

24
Erlanger Arbeiten zur Musikwissenschaft, herausgegeben von Bruno Stäblein. München, W. Ricke, 1962–

v. 1   PETER JOSEF THANNABAUR, *Die einstimmige Sanctus der Römischen Messe in der handschriftlichen Überlieferung des 11. bis 16. Jahrhunderts*

v. 2   KARL HEINZ SCHLAGER, *Thematischer Katalog der ältesten Alleluia-Melodien aus Handschriften des 10. und 11. Jahrhunderts, ausgenommen das ambrosianische, alt-römische und alt-spanische Repertoire*

25
Erlanger Beiträge zur Musikwissenschaft, herausgegeben von Rudolf Steglich. Kassel, Bärenreiter, 1933–42

v. 1   WERNER GOSSLAU, *Die religiöse Haltung in der Reformationsmusik, nachgewiesen an den "Newen deudschen Gesengen" des Georg Rhaw, 1544*

v. 2

v. 3   WERNER MENKE, *Des Vokalwerk Georg Philipp Telemanns: Überlieferung und Zeitfolge*

26

Facsimiles of early biographies. Hilversum, Frits A. M. Knuf, 1963–

V. 1   CHARLES BURNEY, *An account of the musical performances in Westminster Abbey and the Pantheon May 26, 27, 29 and June 3, 5, 1784 in commemoration of Händel.* London, 1785

V. 2   JOHN MAINWARING, *Memoirs of the late George Frederic Handel.* London, 1760

V. 3   C. L. HILGENFELDT, *Johann Sebastian Bach's Leben, Wirken und Werke. Ein Beitrag zur Kunstgeschichte des achtzehnten Jahrhunderts.* Leipzig, 1850

V. 4   CARL PHILIPP EMANUEL BACH, *Autobiography. 1773.* Ed. William S. Newman [In preparation]

27

Facsimiles of early music dictionaries. Hilversum, Frits A. M. Knuf, 1964–

V. 1   SEBASTIEN DE BROSSARD, *Dictionnaire de musique, contenant une explication des termes grecs, latins, italiens et français . . .* Paris, 1703

V. 2   JAMES GRASSINEAU, *A musical dictionary, being a collection of terms and characters . . .* London, 1740

28

Forschungsbeiträge zur Musikwissenschaft. Regensburg, Gustav Bosse, 1954–

V. 1   MARGARETE MELNICKI, *Das einstimmige Kyrie des lateinischen Mittelalters*

V. 2   DETLEV BOSSE, *Untersuchungen einstimmiger mittelalterlichen Melodien zum "Gloria in excelsis Deo"*

V. 3   ROSWITHA TRAIMER, *Bela Bartoks Kompositionentechnik dargestellt an seinen sechs Streichquartetten*

V. 5   INGEBORG KIEKERT, *Die musikalische Form in den Werken Carl Orffs*

V. 6   HEINRICH LINDLAR, *Igor Strawinskys sakraler Gesang: Geist und Form der Christ-kultischen Kompositionen*

V. 2   HIERONYMUS DE MORAVIA, *Tractatus de musica*, ed. S. M. Cserba

V. 3   KARL GUSTAV FELLERER, *Mittelaltliches Musikleben der Stadt Freiburg im Üchtland*

V. 4   JULIUS AMANN, *Allegris Miserere und die Aufführungspraxis in der Sixtina nach Reiseberichten und Musikhandschriften*

V. 5   BÖSKEN, FRANZ, *Musikgeschichte der Stadt Osnabrück: die geistliche und weltliche Musik bis zum Beginne des 19. Jahrhunderts*

V. 6   WILHELM JERGER, *Constantin Reindl, 1738–1799: ein Beitrag zur Musikgeschichte der deutschen Schweiz im 18. Jahrhundert*

V. 7   W. JERGER, *Die Haydndrucke aus dem Archiv der Theater- und Musik-Liebhaber Gesellschaft zu Luzern, nebst Materialien zum Musikleben in Luzern um 1800*

V. 8   KIENBERGER, FRANZ JOSEF, *Studien zur Geschichte der Messenkomposition der Schweiz im XVIII. Jahrhundert*

30

Gennrich, Friedrich. Musikwissenschaftliche Studien-Bibliothek. Darmstadt, Gennrich, 1946–

V. 1/2   *Abriss der frankonischen Mensuralnotation nebst Übertragungsmaterial*

V. 3/4   *Abriss der Mensuralnotation des XIV. und der der ersten Hälfte des XV. Jahrhunderts*

V. 5/6   *Die Sankt Viktor-Clausulae und ihre Motetten*

V. 7   *Aus der Formenwelt des Mittelalters. 64 Beispiele zum Bestimmen musikalischer Formen*

V. 8   *Übertragungsmaterial zur Rhythmik der Ars Antiqua. 101 ausgewählte Beispiele aus dem Bereich der mittelalterlichen Monodie*

V. 9   *Melodien altdeutscher Lieder. 47 Melodien in handschriftlicher Fassung*

V. 10   *Mittelhochdeutsche Liedkunst. 24 Melodien zu mittelhochdeutschen Liedern*

V. 11   *Lateinische Liedkontrafaktur. Eine Auswahl lateinischer Con-
            ductus mit ihrem volkssprachigen Vorbildern*

V. 12   PEROTINUS MAGNUS (*fl. ca.* 1183), *Das Organum: Alleluia
            Nativitas floriose virginis Marie, und seine Sippe*

V. 13/14   *Musica sine Littera. Notenzeichen und Rhythmik der Gruppen-
            notation. Ein Abriss nebst Übertragungsmaterial*

V. 15/16   MAGISTRI FRANCONIS (*fl. ca.* 1250–1280), *Ars cantus mensura-
            bilis*

V. 17   *Exempla altfranzösischer Lyrik. 40 altfranzösische Lieder*

V. 18/19   *Lo gai saber. 50 ausgewählte Troubadour-Lieder*

V. 20   ADAM DE LA HALLE (*ca.* 1240–1287), *Le jeu de Robin et Marion*

V. 21   *Die autochthone Melodie. Übungsmaterial zur Musikalischen
            Textkritik*

V. 22   *Aus der Frühzeit der Motette, I. Teil: Der erste Zyklus von
            Clausulae der Hs W^1 und ihre Motetten*

V. 23   ——— *II. Teil: Der zweite Zyklus von Clausulae der Hs W^1
            und ihre Motetten*

V. 24   *Cantilenae piae. 31 altfranzösische geistliche Lieder der Hs.
            Paris, Bibl. nouv. acq. fr. 1050*

31

Gennrich, Friedrich. Summa musicae medii aevi. Langen bei Frankfurt,
1957–

Divided into five separately numbered series, but with an unmatching
set numbering as well. The following table shows the correlation of
series and set numbers.

Bibliographiae
V. 1 = V. 2
V. 2 = V. 14
V. 3 = V. 7
V. 4 = V. 8

Collectanea
V. 1 = V. 3
V. 2 = V. 4

v. 3 = v. 15
v. 4 = v. 17
v. 5 = v. 18

Facsimilia
v. 1 = v. 1
v. 2 = v. 5
v. 3 = v. 6
v. 4 = v. 11

Fundamenta
v. 1 = v. 10
v. 2 = v. 12
v. 3 = v. 16

Monumenta
v. 1 = v. 9
v. 2 = v. 13

v. 1   (Facs. 1). GUILLAUME DE MACHAUT (*ca.* 1300–*ca.* 1377), *La messe de Nostre-Dame*

v. 2   (Bibl. 1). *Bibliographie der ältesten französischen und lateinischen Motetten*

v. 3   (Coll. 1). *Der musikalische Nachlass der Troubadours, I. Teil: Kritische Ausgabe der Melodien*

v. 4   (Coll. 2). ——— *II. Teil: Kommentar*

v. 5   (Facs. 2). *Die Wimpfener Fragmente der Hessischen Landesbibliothek Darmstadt*

v. 6   (Facs. 3). *Ein altfranzösischer Motetten-Kodex. Faksimile-Ausgabe der Hs. La Clayette*

v. 7   (Bibl. 3). FRIEDRICH LUDWIG, *Repertorium organorum recentioris et motetorum vetustissimi stili: Band I/2, Handschriften in Mensuralnotation. Die Quellen der Motetten älsten Stils*

v. 8   (Bibl. 4). F. LUDWIG, *Musikalisches Anfangsverzeichnis des nach Tenores geordneten Repertorium*

v. 9   (Mon. 1). *Neidhart-Lieder. Kritische Ausgabe der Neidhart von Reuental zugeschriebenen Melodien* [*12–13 c.*]

v. 10   (Fund. 1). *Das altfranzösische Rondeau und Virelai im 12. und 13. Jahrhundert*

v. 11   (Facs. 4). *Die Jenaer Liederhandschrift. Faksimile-Ausgabe ihrer Melodien*

v. 12   (Fund. 2). *Die Kontrafaktur im Liedschaffen des Mittelalters*

v. 13   (Mon. 2). JEHANNOT DE L'ESCUREL (*d.* 1303), *Balades, Rondeaux et Diz entez sur Refroiz de Rondeaux*

v. 14   (Bibl. 2). *Bibliographisches Verzeichnis des französischen Refrains des 12. und 13. Jahrhunderts*

v. 15   (Coll. 3). *Der musikalische Nachlass der Troubadours, III. Teil: Prolegomena*

v. 16   (Fund. 3). *Studien über die Geschichte der mehrstimmigen Musik im Mittelalter*

v. 17   (Coll. 4). *Florilegium Motetorum: ein Querschnitt durch das Motettenschaffen des 13. Jahrhunderts*

v. 18   (Facs. 5). *Die Colmarer Liederhandschrift. Faksimile-Ausgabe ihrer Melodien*

32

Göttinger musikalische Arbeiten, herausgegeben von Hermann Zenck. Kasell, Bärenreiter. 1945–

v. 1   WILHELM MARTIN LUTHER, *Gallus Dressler: ein Beitrag zur Geschichte des Protestantischen Schulkantorats im 16. Jahrhundert*

33

Die grossen Darstellungen der Musikgeschichte in Barock und Aufklärung. Deutsche, französische, italienische und englische Standardwerke der Musikwissenschaft. Neuausgaben mit modernen Registern versehen von Othmar Wessely. Graz, Akademische Druck- u. Verlagsanstalt, 1964–

A facsimile series. V. which are proposed but which I do not know to have been published yet are listed in parentheses.

v. 1   WOLFGANG CASPAR PRINTZ. *Historische Beschreibung der edelen Sing- und Kling-Kunst (Dresden, 1690)*

v. 2/1   PIERRE BOURDELOT, PIERRE BONNET, *Histoire de la musique et de ses effets depuis son origine jusqu'à présent (1715)*

v. 2/2–4   JEAN-LAURENT LE CERF DE LA VIEVILLE DE FRESNEUSE, *Comparaison de la musique italienne et de la musique françoise (1704–6).* 3 v.

v. 3   GIAMBATTISTA MARTINI, *Storia della musica (1757–1781).* 3 v.

(v. 4)   MARTIN GERBERT, *De cantu et musica sacra a prima ecclesiae aetate usque ad praesens tempus (1774).* 2 v.

(v. 5)   JOHN HAWKINS, *A general history of the science and practise of music (1776).* 2 v.

(v. 6)   CHARLES BURNEY, *A general history of music from the earliest ages to the present period to which is prefixed a dissertation on the music of the ancients (1776–1789).* 4 v.

(v. 7)   JEAN-BENJAMIN DE LA BORDE, *Essai sur la musique ancienne et moderne (1780).* 4 v.

v. 8   JOHANN NIKOLAUS FORKEL, *Allgemeine Geschichte der Musik (1788–1801).* 2 v.

34
Hamburg. Schriftenreihe des Musikwissenschaftlichen Instituts der Universität Hamburg. 1956–

v. 1   HEINRICH HUSMANN, *Beiträge zur Hamburgischen Musikgeschichte*

v. 2   URSULA GÜNTHER, *Zehn datierbäre der Ars nova*

v. 3   HANS PETER REINECKE, *Experimentelle Beiträge zur Psychologie des musikalischen Hörens*

v. 4   HEINZ BECKER, *Zur Entwicklungsgeschichte der antiken und mittelalterischen Rohrblattinstrumente*

35
Harvard University. Isham Library papers. Cambridge, Mass., Harvard University press, 1958–

v. 1   *Instrumental music: a conference at Isham memorial library May 4, 1957,* ed. David G. Hughes

v. 2   *Chanson and madrigal, 1480–1530: studies in comparison and*
         contrast. A conference at Isham memorial library September
         13–14, 1961, ed. James Haar

36

Historiae musicae cultores. Biblioteca. Firenze, Casa editrice Leo S. Olschki,
1952–

v. 1   Lucca Marucci, *Mostra di strumenti musicali in disegni*
         degli Uffizi: Catalogo

v. 2   *Collectanea historiae musicae I*
         Collected essays on various subjects. II = v. 6; III = v. 17;
         IV = v. 22

v. 3   Luigi Parigi, *"Laurentiana". Lorenzo dei Medici cultore della*
         musica

v. 4   Francesco Briganti, *Giovanni Andrea Angelini-Bontempi*
         (1624–1705), musicista-litterato-architetto

v. 5   Gino Roncaglia, *La cappella musicale del duomo di Modena*

v. 6   See v. 2

v. 7   Ermengildo Paccagnella, *Palestrina, il linguaggio melodico*
         e armonico

v. 8   *Michele Carrara: la intavolatura di liuto, 1585,* ed. Benvenuto
         Disertori

v. 9   Ottavio Tiby, *Il real teatro Carolino e l'ottocento musicale*
         Palermitano

v. 10   Renato Lunelli, *L'arte organaria del Rinascimento in Roma*
         e gli organi de S. Pietro in Vaticano dalle origini a tutto il
         periodo Frescobaldiano

v. 11   Gabriella Ricci des Ferres-Cancani, *Francesco Morlacchi*
         (1784–1841). Un maestro italiano alla corte di Sassonia

v. 12   Riccardo Allorto, *Le sonate per pianoforte di Muzio Cle-*
         menti. Studio critico e catalogo tematico

v. 13   Claudio Gallico, *Un canzioniere musicale italiano del*
         cinquecento, Bologna, Con. Mus. Ms Q 21

v. 14   GEORGII ANSELMI PARMENSIS (*fl. ca.* 1424–1440), *De musica* [1424], ed. Giuseppe Massera

v. 15   LEOPOLDO GAMBERINI, *La parola e la musica nel confronto fra i documenti musicali dell'antichità e dei prima secoli del medio evo*

v. 16   MARIO FABBRI, *Alessandro Scarlatti e il Principe Fernando de' Medici*

v. 17   See v. 2   ML55. C 65

v. 18   GIUSEPPE MASSERA, *La "mano musicale perfetta" di Francesco de Brugis, dalle prefazioni ai corali di L. A. Giunta (Venezia 1499–1504)*

v. 19   *Luigi Cherubini nel il centenario della nascita. Contributo alla conoscenza della vita e dell' opera*

v. 20   GISELLA SELDON-GOTH, *Feruccio Busoni-un profilo*

v. 21   ALFREDO BONACCORSI, *Maestri di Lucca: i Guami e altri musicisti*

v. 22   See v. 2   ML55. C65

v. 23   FEDERICO MOMPELLIO, *Lodovico Viadana, musicista fra due secoli*

v. 24   A. BONACCORSI, ed. *Gioacchino Rossini*

v. 25   MARIANGELA DONA, *Espressione e significato nella musica*

v. 26   HÉLIANE DERÉGIS, *Alessandro Marcello*

v. 27   ALDO CASELLI, *Catalogo delle opere liriche publicate in Italia*

International inventory of musical sources, see Repertoire . . . , C 65

37
Internationale Musikgesellschaft [International musical society; IMG], 1899–1914 [Publications]

For *Sammelbände* (SIMG) and *Zeitschrift* (ZIMG) see section D. The following two monograph series were also issued.

1.   *Sammlung musikwissenschaftlicher Arbeiten/Abhandlungen von deutschen Hochschülen,* 1899–1900

V. 1   EDUARD BERNOULLI, *Die Choralnotenschrift bei Hymnen und Sequenzen*

V. 2   HERMANN ABERT, *Die Lehre vom Ethos in der griechischen Musik*

V. 3   HEINRICH REITSCH, *Die Tonkunst in der zweiten Hälfte des neunzehnten Jahrhunderts*

V. 4   RICHARD HOHENEMSER, *Welche Einflüsse hatte die Wiederbelebung der älteren Musik im 19. Jahrhundert auf die deutschen Komponisten?*

2.   Beihefte der IMG 1901–1914
     [First series, to 1905]

V. 1   EDGAR ISTEL, *Jean-Jacques Rousseau als Komponist seiner lyrischen Szene Pygmalion*

V. 2   JOHANNES WOLF, *Musica practica Bartolomeo Rami de Pareia*

V. 3   OSWALD KÖRTE, *Laute und Lautenmusik bis zur Mitte des 16. Jahrhunderts (unter besonderer Berücksichtigung der deutschen Lautentabulatur)*
       For a reprint of this v. see **C 14**, III, 16

V. 4   THEODOR KROYER, *Die Anfänge der Chromatik im italienischen Madrigal des XVI. Jahrhunderts*

V. 5   KARL NEF, *Zur Geschichte der deutschen Instrumentalmusik in der zweiten Hälfte des 17. Jahrhunderts*

V. 6   WALTER NIEMANN, *Über die abweichende Bedeutung der Ligaturen in der Mensuraltheorie der Zeit vor Johannes de Garlandia*

V. 7   MAX KUHN, *Die Verzierungs-Kunst in der Gesangsmusik des 16. und 17. Jahrhunderts (1535/1650)*

V. 8   HERMANN SCHRÖDER, *Die symmetrische Umkehrung in der Musik. Ein Beitrag zur Harmonie- und Kompositionslehre mit Hinweis auf die hier notwendige Wiedereinführung antiker Tonarten im Stil moderner Harmonik*

V. 9   ARNO WERNER, *Geschichte der Kantorei-Gesellschaften im Gebiete des ehemaligen Kurfürstens Sachsen*

38
Jenaer Beiträge zur Musikforschung, herausgegeben von Heinrich Besseler.
1950–

v. 2   JOHANN GOTTFRIED WALTHER, *Praecepta der musicalischen Composition,* ed. Peter Benary

v. 3   P. BENARY, *Die deutsche Kompositionslehre des 18. Jahrhunderts*

39

Kieler Schriften zur Musikwissenschaft. Herausgegeben von der Landeskundlichen Abteilung des Musikwissenschaftlichen Instituts der Universität Kiel. Kassel, Bärenreiter, 1953–

Originally called *Schriften des Landesinstituts für Musikforschung Kiel*

v. 1   WILFRIED BRENNECKE, *Die Handschrift A.R.940/41 der Proske-Bibliothek zu Regensburg*

v. 2   INGE-MARIA SCHROEDER, *Die Responsorienvertonungen des B. Resinarius*

v. 3   GERHARD HAHNE, *Die Bach-Tradition in Schleswig-Holstein und Dänemark*

v. 4   ANNEMARIE NAUSCH, *Augustin Pfleger*

v. 5   MARTIN RUHNKE, *Joachim Burmeister*

v. 6   CARLA WEIDEMANN, *Leben und Wirken des Johann Philipp Förtsch*

v. 7   PETER MOHR, *Die Handschrift B 211–215 der Proske-Bibliothek zu Regensburg*

v. 8   HANS KOELTZSCH, *Nikolaus Bruhns*

v. 9   HEINZ GOTTWALDT, G. HAHNE, *Briefwechsel zwischen J. A. P. Schulz und Johann Heinrich und Ernestine Voss*

v. 10   FRIEDRICH WILHELM RIEDEL, *Quellenkundliche Beiträge zur Geschichte der Musik für Tasteninstrumente*

v. 11   HANS PETER DETLEFSEN, *Musikgeschichte der Stadt Flensburg*

v. 12   LYDIA SCHIERNING, *Die Überlieferung der deutschen Orgel- und Klaviermusik*

v. 13   HANS HAASE, *Jobst vom Brandt*

v. 14   K. HORTSCHANSKY, *Katalog der Kieler Musiksammlung*

41
Leipzig. Die Musikstadt Leipzig. Arbeitsberichte. Leipzig, Rat der Stadt, 1966–

42
Mainz. Akademie der Wissenschaften und der Literatur: Kommission für Musikwissenschaft. Neue Studien zur Musikwissenschaft. Mainz, Schott, 1950–

V. 1   ARNOLD SCHMITZ, *Die Bildlichkeit der wortgebunden Musik Johann Sebastian Bachs*

V. 2   EWALD JAMMERS, *Der mittelalterliche Choral: Art und Herkunft*

V. 3   WILIBALD GURLITT, *Die Epochengliederung der Musikgeschichte nach musikalisch-rhythmischen Prinzipien*

43
Mainzer Studien zur Musikgeschichte. Tutzing, Hans Schneider, 1967–

V. 1   DIETER LUTZ TRIMPERT, *Die Quatuors concertants von Giuseppe Cambini*

V. 2   HUBERT UNVERRICHT, *Geschichte des Streichtrios*

44
Marburger Beiträge zur Musikforschung, ed. Heinrich Hüschen. Kassel, Bärenreiter, 1967–

V. 1   WERNER FRIEDRICH KÜMMEL, *Geschichte und Musikgeschichte. Die Musik der Neuzeit in Geschichtsschreibung und Geschichtsauffassung des deutschen Kulturbereichs von der Aufklärung bis zu J. G. Droysen und Jacob Burckhardt*

V. 2   WILFRIED KAISER, *Dietrich Tzwyvel und sein Musiktraktat "Introductorium musicae practicae", Münster 1513*

V. 3   WALTER PIEL, *Studien zum Leben und Schaffen Hubert Waelrants unter besonderer Berücksichtigung seiner Motetten*

V. 4   JOACHIM DORFMÜLLER, *Studien zur norwegischen Klaviermusik der 1. Hälfte des 20. Jahrhunderts*

45
Masterworks on singing. Champaign, Ill., Pro musica press, 1967–

V. 1   RICHARD MACKENZIE BACON (1776–1844), *Elements of vocal* science; being a philosophical enquiry into some of the principles of singing, ed. Edward Foreman

v. 2–6   Not yet published

v. 7   GIAMBATTISTA MANCINI, *Practical reflections on figured singing (the editions of 1774 and 1777)*, ed. Edward Foreman

46

Monuments of music and music literature in facsimile. Second series: Music literature. New York, Broude Brothers, 1967–

For first and third series see **A 74**. V. not yet printed are in parentheses.

v. 1   GIOSEFFO ZARLINO, *Le istitutioni harmoniche.* Venice, 1558

v. 2   GIOSEFFO ZARLINO, *Dimostrationi harmoniche.* Venice, 1571

v. 3   JEAN-PHILIPPE RAMEAU, *Traité de l'harmonie réduite à ses principes naturels; divisé en quatre livres.* Paris, 1722

v. 4   JEAN-PHILIPPE RAMEAU, *Démonstration du principe de l'harmonie.* Paris, 1750

v. 5   JEAN-PHILIPPE RAMEAU, *Code de musique pratique.* Paris, 1760

v. 6   JEAN-PHILIPPE RAMEAU, *Génération harmonique.* Paris, 1737

v. 7   JEAN-PHILIPPE RAMEAU, *Nouveau système de musique théorique.* Paris, 1726

v. 8   GIUSEPPE TARTINI, *Trattato di musica.* Padua, 1754

v. 9   FRANCISCUS BLANCHINUS, *De tribus generibus instrumentorum musicae veterum organicae dissertatio.* Rome, 1742

v. 10   VINCENZO MANFREDINI, *Regole armoniche.* Venice, 1775

v. 11   THOMAS SALMON, *An essay to the advancement of musick by casting away the perplexity of the different cliffs.* London, 1672

v. 12   ARTHUR BEDFORD, *The great abuse of musick.* In two parts. London, 1711

(v. 13)   MICHEL CORRETTE, *Le maître de clavecin.* Paris, 1753

v. 14   FRANCISCO GASPARINI, *L'armonico pratico al cimbalo.* Venice, 1708

(v. 15)   GIOSEFFO ZARLINO, *Sopplimente musicali.* Venice, 1588

(v. 16)   MATTHEW LOCKE, *The present practice of music vindicated.* London, 1673

v. 17   THOMAS MACE, *Musick's monument.* London, 1676

v. 18   ANTON BEMETZRIEDER, *Leçons de clavecin et principes d'harmonie.* Paris, 1771

v. 19   JEAN LE ROND D'ALEMBERT, *Eléments de musique.* Paris, 1752

v. 20   VINCENZO GALILEI, *Dialogo della musica antica et della moderna, contro Ioseffo Zarlino.* Florence, 1581

v. 21   FRANCHINUS GAFURIUS, *Theorica musice.* Milan, 1581

(v. 22)   THOMAS RAVENSCROFT, *A brief discourse of the true (but neglected) use of charact'ring the degrees . . .* London, 1614

(v. 23)   FRANÇOIS COUPERIN, *L'art de toucher le clavecin.* Paris, 1716

v. 24   JOHANN JOSEPH FUX, *Gradus ad Parnassum sive manuductio ad compositionem musicae regularum.* Vienna, 1725

v. 25   ORAZIO TIGRINI, *Il compendio della musica.* Venice, 1588

v. 26   JOHANNES TINCTORIS, *Terminorum musicae deffinitorium.* Venice, *ca.* 1494

v. 27   JOSEPH LACASSAGNE, *Traité général des éléments du chant.* Paris, 1766

v. 28   JOHN CHRISTOPHER PEPUSCH, *A treatise on harmony.* Second enlarged edition. London, 1731

(v. 29)   JOHN FREDERICK LAMPE, *A plain and compendious method of teaching thorough bass.* London, 1737

(v. 30)   MATTHEW LOCKE, *Melothesia, or, Certain general rules for playing upon a continued-bass.* London, 1673

(v. 31)   JEAN-JACQUES ROUSSEAU, *Traités sur la musique.* Geneva, 1781?

(v. 32)   WILLIAM HOLDER, *Treatise of the natural grounds and principles of harmony.* London, 1694

v. 33   FRIEDRICH WILHELM MARPURG, *Anfangsgruende der theoretischen Musik.* Leipzig, 1757

V. 34   MARTIN AGRICOLA, *Rudimenta musices.* Wittenberg, 1539

V. 35   JOHANN HEINRICH ALSTED, *Templum musicum, or, The musical synopsis . . . Faithfully translated out of Latin by John Birchensha.* London, 1664

V. 36   JOHANN ERNST ALTENBURG, *Versuch einer Anleitung zur heroisch-musikalischen Trompeter- und Pauker-Kunst.* Halle, 1795

(V. 37)   FILIPPO BUONANNI, *Gabinetto armonico, pieno d'istromenti sonori, indicati, e spiegati.* Rome, 1722

V. 38   FRANÇOIS DE CASTAGNÈRES CHATEAUNEUF, *Dialogue sur la musique des anciens.* Paris, 1725

V. 39   JOHANN FROSCH, *Rerum musicarum.* Strasbourg, 1535

V. 40   JAMES GRASSINEAU, *A musical dictionary.* London, 1740

V. 41   PIERRE JOSEPH ROUSSIER, *Mémoire sur la musique des anciens.* Paris, 1770

V. 42   ANTONIO SOLER, *Llave de la modulacion.* Madrid, 1762

(V. 43)   WILLIAM TANS'UR, *The elements of musick display'd.* London, 1772

V. 44   ATHANASIUS KIRCHER, *Phonurgia nova.* Kempten, 1673

V. 45   PIERRE RAMEAU, *Le maître à danser.* Paris, 1725

V. 46   MARCO FABRIZIO CAROSO, *Il ballarino, divisi in due trattati . . .* Venice, 1581

V. 47   JEAN GEORGE NOVERRE, *Lettres sur la danse et sur les Ballets.* Stuttgart, 1760

V. 48   GIOVANNI ANDREA BATTISTA GALLINI, *A treatise on the art of dancing.* London, 1772

(V. 49)   DE LA CUISSE, *Le répertoire des bals, ou Théorie pratique des contredanses . . .* Paris, 1762–5. 4 V.

(V. 50)   JEAN-BAPTISTE DE LA BORDE, *Le clavecin électrique, avec une nouvelle théorie du mécanisme et des phénomènes de l'électricité.* Paris, 1761

(V. 51)   MARCUS MEIBOM, *Antiquae musicae auctores septem. Graece et latine.* Amsterdam, 1652. 2 V.

(v. 68)   PIETRO AARON, *Lucidario in musica*. Venice, 1545

(v. 69)   PIETRO AARON, *Thoscanello de la musica*. Venice, 1523

(v. 70)   JACOB ADLUNG, *Musica mechanica organoedi, das ist: Gründlicher Unterricht von der Struktur, Gebrauch und Erhaltung, &c. der Orgeln, Clavicymbel, Clavichordien* . . . Berlin, 1768

(v. 71)   JOHANN GEORG ALBRECHTSBERGER, *Gründliche Anweisung zur Composition*. Leipzig, 1790

(v. 72)   JOHANN CHRISTIAN BACH et F. P. RICCI, *Méthode ou Recueil de connoissances élémentaires pour le fortepiano ou clavecin*. Paris, *ca.* 1790

(v. 73)   BÉNIGNE DE BACILLY, *Remarques curieuses sur l'art de bien chanter*. Paris, 1668

(v. 74)   ERNST GOTTLIEB BARON, *Historisch-theoretisch und praktische Untersuchung des Instruments der Lauten*. Nuremberg, 1727

v. 75   JEAN ANTOINE BÉRARD, *L'art du chant*. Paris, 1755

(v. 76)   ELWAY BEVIN, *A brief and short instruction of the art of musicke*. London, 1631

(v. 77)   ANTERUS MARIA DE S. BONAVENTURA, *Regula musice plane*. Brescia, 1497

(v. 78)   GIOVANNI MARIA BONONCINI, *Musico prattico*. Bologna, 1673

(v. 79)   GIOVANNI ANDREA ANGELINI BONTEMPI, *Historia musica*

(v. 80)   CHARLES BUTLER, *The Principles of Musik*. London, 1636

(v. 81)   SALOMON DE CAUS, *Institution harmonique*. Frankfurt, 1615

(v. 82)   MICHEL PAUL GUI DE CHABANON, *De la musique, considérée en elle-même et dans ses rapports avec la parole, les langues, la poésie et le théâtre*. Paris, 1785

(v. 83)   MATTEO COFERATI, *Il cantore addottrinato, ovvero Regole del canto corale* . . . Florence, 1691

(v. 84)   CHARLES COMPAN, *Dictionnaire de danse*. Paris, 1787

(v. 85)   MICHEL CORRETTE, *Méthode, théorique et pratique. Pour apprendre en peu de temps le violoncelle dans sa perfection*. Paris, 1741

(v. 86)   JACQUES GEORGES COUSINEAU, *Méthode de harpe*. Paris [1786?]

(v. 87)   RENÉ DESCARTES, *Musicae compendium*. Zyll and Amsterdam, 1650

(v. 88)   GIROLAMO DIRUTA, *Il Transilvano, dialogo sopra il vero modo di sonar organi, & istromenti di penna*. Venice, 1597

(v. 89)   *Encomium musices*. Antwerp, *ca.* 1590

(v. 90)   LEONHARD EULER, *Tentamen novae theoriae musicae*. Petropoli, 1739

(v. 91)   NIKOLAUS FABER, *Musicae rudimenta admodum brevis*. Augsburg, 1516

(v. 92)   GEORG FALCK, *Idea boni cantoris, das ist: Getreu und gründliche Anleitung wie ein Music-Scholar so wol im Singen als auch auf andern instrumentis musicalibus in kurtzer Zeit* . . . Nuremberg, 1688

(v. 93)   LODOVICO FOGLIANI, *Musica theorica*. Venice, 1529

(v. 94)   BARTHOLD FRITZ, *Anweisung, wie man Claviere, Clavecins, und Orgeln, nach einer mechanischen Art, in allen zwölf Tönen gleich rein stimmen könne* . . . Leipzig, 1756

(v. 95)   FRANCHINUS GAFURIUS, *Angelicum ac divinum opus musice materna lingua scriptum*. Milan, 1496

(v. 96)   FRANCHINUS GAFURIUS, *Apologia Franchini Gafurii musici adversus Ionannem Spatarium & complices musicos bononienses*. Turin, 1520

(v. 97)   FRANCHINUS GAFURIUS, *. . . de harmonia musicorum instrumentorum opus*. Milan, 1518

(v. 98)   FRANCHINUS GAFURIUS, *Musice utriusque cantus pratica*. Brescia, 1496

(v. 99)   FRANCHINUS GAFURIUS, *Practica musicae*. Milan, 1496

(v. 100)   FRANCHINUS GAFURIUS, *Theoricum opus musice discipline*

(v. 101)   HANS GERLE, *Musica teusch auf die Instrument der grossen und kleinen Geygen, auch Lautten* . . . Nuremberg, 1532

(v. 102)   ANDRÉ GRÉTRY, *Méthode simple pour apprendre à préluder*. Paris, 1801/2

(v. 103)   JOHANN ANDREAS HERBST, *Musica poëtica.* Nuremberg, 1643

(v. 104)   JOHANN ANDREAS HERBST, *Musica practica.* Nuremberg, 1642

(v. 105)   JOHANN ADAM HILLER, *Anweisung zum Violinspielen.* Leipzig, [1792]

(v. 106)   JOHANN NEPOMUK HUMMEL, *Ausführliche theoretische practische Anweisung zum Pianoforte-Spiel.* Vienna, 1828

(v. 107)   GEORG SIMON LÖHLEIN, *Anweisung zum Violinspielen.* Leipzig and Züllichau, 1774

(v. 108)   GEORG SIMON LÖHLEIN, *Clavierschule.* Leipzig und Züllichau, 1765

(v. 109)   ETIENNE LOULIÉ, *Eléments du principe de musique.* Paris, 1969

(v. 110)   FRIEDRICH WILHELM MARPURG, *Anleitung zum Clavierspielen.* Berlin, 1755

(v. 111)   FRIEDRICH WILHELM MARPURG, *Anleitung zur Singcomposition.* Berlin, 1758

(v. 112)   FRIEDRICH WILHELM MARPURG, *Versuch über die musicalische Temperatur.* Berlin, 1776

(v. 113)   THOMAS MORLEY, *A plaine and easie introduction to praticall musicke.* London, 1597

(v. 114)   GUILLAUME-GABRIEL NIVERS, *Traité de la composition de musique*

(v. 115)   GIOVANNI PADUANI, *Institutiones ad diversas ex plurium vocum harmonia cantilenas.* Verona, 1578

(v. 116)   JOHANN SAMUEL PETRI, *Anleitung zur practischen Musik.* Leipzig, 1782

(v. 117)   PIETRO PONZIO, *Ragionamento di musica.* Parma, 1588

(v. 118)   JEAN-PHILIPPE RAMEAU, *Dissertation sur les différentes méthodes d'accompagnement pour le clavecin ou pour l'orgue.* Paris, 1732

(v. 119)   MICHEL DE SAINT-LAMBERT, *Les principes du clavecin.* Paris, 1702

(v. 120)   MICHEL DE SAINT-LAMBERT, *Nouveau traité d'accompagnement de clavecin, de l'orgue, et des autres instruments*

(v. 121)   FRANCISCO DE SALINAS, *De musica libri septem.* Salamanca, 1577

(v. 122)   THOMAS SALMON, *A proposal to perform musick in perfect and mathematical proportions.* London, 1688

(v. 123)   JOHANN BAPTIST SAMBER, *Manuductio ad organum.* Salzburg, 1704

(v. 124)   TOMASO DE SANTA MARIA, *Libro llamado arte de tañer fantasia, assi para tecla como para vihuela, y todo instrumento* . . . Valladolid, 1565

(v. 125)   GASPAR SCHOTT, *Magia universalis naturae et artis* . . . *Pars II, Acustica.* Würzburg, 1657

(v. 126)   JOHANN GEORG TROMLITZ, *Ausführlicher und gründlicher Unterricht die Floete zu spielen.* Leipzig, 1791

(v. 127)   WILLIAM TURNER, *Sound anatomiz'd in a philosophical essay on musick.* London, 1724

(v. 128)   JOHN WEAVER, *A small treatise of time and cadence in dancing.* London, 1706

(v. 129)   DIDEROT, D'ALEMBERT, *Three excerpts from L'Encyclopédie: Musique; Chorégraphie ou l'art d'écrire la danse; Lutherie*

(v. 130)   RAOUL-AUGER FEUILLET, *Chorégraphie ou l'art d'écrire la dance* . . . *Recueil de dances* . . . Paris, 1700

(v. 131)   JOSEPH C. WALKER, *Historical memoirs of the Irish bards.* London, 1786

(v. 132)   MICHEL CORRETTE, *Méthode pour apprendre aisément à jouer de la flûte traversière.* Paris, 1710

(v. 133)   PIETRO FRANCESCO TOSI, *Opinioni de'cantori antichi e moderni...* Bologna, 1723

(v. 134)   ROBERT BREMNER, *The rudiments of music.* Edinburgh, 1756

(v. 135)   RAOUL-AUGER FEUILLET, *Recueil de Contredances.* Paris, 1706

(v. 136)   BIAGIO ROSSETTI, *Libellus de rudimentis musices.* Verona, 1529

47

München. Schriftenreihe des musikwissenschaftlichen Seminars der Universität München, herausgegeben von Prof. Rudolf von Ficker. 1935-7

v. 1   CARL WINTER, *Ruggiero Giovannelli (c. 1560–1625), Nachfolger Palestrinas zu St. Peter in Rom. Eine stilkritische Studie zur Geschichte der römischen Schule um die Wende des 16. Jahrhunderts*

v. 2   ROLAND HÄFNER, *Die Entwicklung der Spieltechnik der Schul- und Lehrwerke für Klavierinstrumente*

v. 3   THRASYBULOS GEORGIADES, *Englische Diskanttraktate aus der ersten Hälfte des 15. Jahrhunderts. Untersuchungen zur Entwicklung der Mehrstimmigkeit im Mittelalter*

48

Münchner Veröffentlichungen zur Musikgeschichte, herausgegeben von Thrasybulos Georgiades. Tützing, Schneider, 1959–

v. 1   IRMGARD HERRMANN-BENGEN, *Tempobezeichnungen. Ursprung Wandel im 17. und 18. Jahrhundert*

v. 2   FRIEDER ZÄMINER, *Der Vatikanische Organumtraktat (Ottob. lat. 3025). Organum-Praxis der frühen Notre Dame-Schule und ihre Vorstufen*
Includes facsimile of ms.

v. 3   WOLFGANG OSTHOFF, *Monteverdistudien I. Das dramatische Spätwerk Claudio Monteverdis*

v. 4   SIEGFRIED HERMELINK, *Dispositiones modorum. Die Tonarten in der Musik Palestrinas und seiner Zeitgenossen*

v. 5   RUDOLF BOCKHOLDT, *Die frühen Messenkompositionen von Guillaume Dufay*

v. 6   THEODORE GÖLLNER, *Formen früher Mehrstimmigkeit in deutschen Handschriften des späten Mittelalters*

v. 7   JÜRGEN EPPELSHEIM, *Das Orchester in den Werken Jean-Baptiste Lullys*

v. 8   STEFAN KUNZE, *Die Instrumentalmusik Giovanni Gabrielis*

Separate *Notenteil* includes previously unpublished works of Gabrieli and his circle

ML55.M6547

V. 9   MARIE LOUISE MARTINEZ, *Die Musik des frühen Trecento*

V. 10   HANS RUDOLF ZÖBELEY, *Die Musik des Buxheimer Orgelbuchs*

V. 11   KURT DORFMÜLLER, *Studien zur Lautenmusik in der ersten Hälfte des 16. Jahrhunderts*

M2.H17W4

V. 12   G. HABERKAMP, *Die weltliche Vokalmusik des 15. Jahrhunderts in Spanien*

V. 13   Not yet published

ML55.M674

V. 14   W. OSTHOFF, *Theatergesang und darstellende Musik in der italienischen Renaissance (15. und 16. Jahrhundert)*
Separate *Notenteil* includes works of Verdelot, Alfonso della Viola, Francesco Corteccia, A. Striggio, and others

v. 15 - 19   See Kardex

49

Museion: Dritte Reihe. Veröffentlichungen der Musiksammlung. Veröffentlichungen der Österreichischen Nationalbibliothek. Wien, Georg Prachner, 1962–

V. 1   JOSEF HAYDN, *Konzert für Violoncello und Orchester, D-dur, 1783. Partitur, Erstdruck nach dem Autograph mit Kadenzen von Enrico Mainardi,* ed. Leopold Nowak

V. 2   *Richard-Strauss-Bibliographie, Teil 1: 1882–1944,* ed. Oswald Ortner, Franz Grasberger

V. 3   *Katalog des Archivs für Photogramme musikalischer Meisterhandschriften. Widmung A. v. Hoboken, Teil 1,* ed. Agnes Ziffer

50

Music library association. Index series

V. 1   *An alphabetical index to Claudio Monteverdi Tutte le opere,* ed. by the bibliography committee of the New York chapter, MLA

v. 2   *An alphabetical index to Hector Berlioz Werke 1905–1907,* ed. by the bibliography committee of the New York chapter of MLA

v. 3   *A checklist of music bibliographies (in progress and unpublished)*

v. 4   Lenore Coral, *A concordance of the thematic indexes to the instrumental works of Antonio Vivaldi*

v. 5   *An alphabetical index to Tomás Luis de Victoria Opera omnia*

v. 6   *An alphabetical index to Robert Schumann Werke, part 1,* compiled by Michael Ochs

v. 7   *A Schumann index, part 2: An alphabetical index to the solo songs of Robert Schumann,* compiled by M. Ochs

v. 8   *An index to Maurice Frost's English and Scottish Psalm and Hymn tunes,* by Kirby Rogers

51

Music theorists in translation. Brooklyn, The Institute of mediaeval music, 1959–   (See **A 50**)

v. 1   Anonymous IV, *Concerning the measurement of polyphonic song,* ed. Luther Dittmer

v. 2   Robert de Handlo (*fl.* 1326), *The rules, with maxims of Master Franco,* ed. L. Dittmer

v. 3   Guillaume Gabriel Nivers, (*b.* 1617), *Treatise on the composition of music,* ed. Albert Cohen

v. 4   Constantijn Huygens (1596–1687), *Use and non-use of the organ in the churches of the United Netherlands,* ed. Ericka E. Smit-Vanrotte

v. 5   Nicholas Bernier (1664–1734), *Principles of composition,* ed. Philip Nelson

v. 6   Étienne Loulié, *Elements or principles of music,* ed. Albert Cohen

v. 7   Bénigne de Bacilly, *A commentary upon the art of proper singing,* ed. Austin B. Caswell

have 9 v. 3/73   Ac Kardey

52

Musicologica medii aevi, ed. Joseph Smits van Waesberghe. Amsterdam, Noord-Hollandsche Uitgevers Maatschappij.

v. 1   *Expositiones in micrologum Guidonis Aretini*

v. 2   *De melodieën van Hendrik van Veldekes liedern*

53

Musicological studies. Brooklyn, The Institute of mediaeval music. (See **A 50)**

v. 1   LUTHER DITTMER, *Auszug aus The Worcester Music Fragments*

v. 2   GEORGE C. SCHUETZE, *An introduction to Faugues*

v. 3   ERNEST TRUMBLE, *Fauxbourdon, an historical survey, I*
           II not yet published

v. 4   LINCOLN SPIESS, *Historical musicology*

v. 5   S. LEVARIE, *Fundamentals of harmony*

v. 6   E. SOUTHERN, *The Buxheim organ book*

v. 7   FRIEDRICH LUDWIG, *Repertorium organorum, I, 1*, ed. L. Dittmer
           for v. II see v. 17 below

v. 8   CHARLES JACOBS, *Tempo notation in renaissance Spain*

v. 9   E. THOMSON, *An introduction to Philippe (?) Caron*

v. 10   HANS TISCHLER, *A structural analysis of Mozart's piano concertos*

v. 11   V. MATTFELD, *Georg Rhaw's publications for vespers*

v. 12   EDITH BOROFF, *An introduction to Elisabeth-Claude Jacquet de la Guerre*

v. 13   F. JOSEPH SMITH, *The Speculum musicae of Jacobus Leodiensis I*
           II not yet published

v. 14   JAMES TRAVIS, *Miscellanea musica celtica*

v. 15   CLYDE W. BROCKETT, *Antiphons, responsories, and other chants of the Mozarabic rite*

v. 16   FREDERICK CRANE, *Materials for the study of the fifteenth-century basse danse*

v. 17   LUDWIG, *Repertorium II*
          See v. 7 above

54

Musicological studies and documents. Rome, American Institute of musicology. 1951–   (See **A 1**)

v. 1   JOSEPH SMITS VAN WAESBERGHE, *Cymbala (bells in the middle ages)*

v. 2   LUTHER DITTMER, *The Worcester fragments. A catalog and transcription of all the music*

v. 3   GIROLAMO MEI, *Letters on ancient and modern music to Vincenzo Galilei and Giovanni Bardi,* ed. Claude V. Palisca

v. 4   GEORG MUFFAT, *Essay on thorough bass,* ed. Hellmut Federhofer

v. 5   JOHANNES TINCTORIS, *Art of counterpoint,* ed. and translated by Albert Seay

v. 6   HEINRICH GLAREANUS, *Dodecachordon (1547),* ed. and translated by Clement A. Miller

v. 7   HANNA STABLEIN-HARDER, *Fourteenth-century Mass music in France*
          Companion v. to **A 28**, ser. 29

v. 8   RENÉ DESCARTES, *Compendium of music,* translated by Walter Robert, ed. Charles Kent

v. 9   ERCOLE BOTTRIGARI, *Il desiderio,* and VINCENZO GIUSTINIANI, *Discorso sopra la musica,* ed. and translated by Carol MacClintock

v. 10 *The codex Faenza, Bibliotheca communale, 117.*
          Facsimile of the keyboard music

v. 11 HENRY W. KAUFMANN, *Nicola Vicentino (1511–1576), life and works*

v. 12 LUDWIG FINSCHER, *Loyset Compère (c. 1450–1518), life and works*

V. 13
**M2
.B854

The MS London, British Museum Add. 29987. Facsimile, ed. Gilbert Reaney

V. 14
**ML 1729
.2
.H25

JAMES HAAR, The Tugendsterne of Harsdörfer and Staden. An exercise in musical humanism

V. 15
**M3
.E7

JEAN MAILLIARD, Lais et chansons d'Ernoul Gastinois

V. 16
** ML 410
. G11 K4

~~Not yet published~~ Kenton, Egon. Life and Works of Giovanni Gabrieli.

V. 17
**ML410
.W49 M3

CAROL MacCLINTOCK, Giaches de Wert. Life and works

V. 18

JEAN MAILLARD, Charles d'Anjou, Roi-trovère du XIIIeme siècle

V. 19
**M2
.T97

RICHARD L. HOPPIN, Cypriot plainchant of the manuscript Torino, Biblioteca nazionale, J.II.9. A facsimile edition with commentary

V. 20
**ML 171
.G12 I3

FRANCHINUS GAFFURIUS, Practica musica, ed. Clement A. Miller

V. 21
**ML3088
.C6

JUDITH COHEN, The six anonymous L'homme armé masses in Naples. Biblioteca nazionale Ms VI.E.40

V. 23 *ML 171
.C6613

V. 25 **M1520
.B38 B3
1971

55

Die Musik im alten und neuen Europa, ed. Walter Wiora. Kassel, J. P. Hinnenthal

V. I

W. WIORA, Europäische Volksmusik und abendländische Tonkunst

V. 2

WALTER SALMEN, Die Schichtung der mittelalterlichen Musikkultur in der ostdeutschen Grenzlage

V. 3

KARL M. KOMMA, Das böhmische Musikantentum

V. 4

WALTER SALMEN, Der fahrende Musiker im europäischen Mittelalter

V. 5

LOTHAR HOFFMAN-ERBRECHT, Thomas Stoltzer, Leben und Schaffen

56

ML 85
.B48 M9

Musikgeschichte in Bildern, herausgegeben von Heinrich Besseler, Max Schneider und Werner Bachmann. Leipzig, Deutscher Verlag für Musik, 1961–

The entire proposed plan of this series is given below; v. not yet published (late 1969) are given in parentheses.

v. 1   *Musikethnologie*

    Lieferung 1 PAUL COLLAER, *Ozeanien*

      Lfg. 2   P. COLLAER, *Amerika* (Eskimo und indianische Bevölkerung)

      (Lfg. 3   P. COLLAER, *Südostasien*)

      (Lfg. 4   ALAIN DANIELOU, *Südasien*)

      (Lfg. 5   SHIGEO KISHIBE, *Ostasien*)

      (Lfg. 6   ERNST EMSHEIMER, *Mittel- und Nordasien*)

      (Lfg. 7   P. COLLAER, *Vorderasien*)

      (Lfg. 8–11 *Afrika*)

      (Lfg. 12–13 *Europa*)

v. 2   *Musik des Altertums*

      Lfg. 1   HANS HICKMANN, *Ägypten*

      (Lfg. 2   WILHELM STAUDER, *Mesopotamien*)

      (Lfg. 3   LAURENCE PICKEN, FRITZ A. KUTTNER, *China*)

      Lfg. 4   MAX WEGNER, *Griechenland*

      Lfg. 5   GÜNTER FLEISCHHAUER, *Etrurien und Rom*

      (Lfg. 6   FRIEDRICH BEHN, *Alt-Europa*)

      (Lfg. 7   SAMUEL MARTI, *Alt-Amerika*)

      (Lfg. 8   *Alt-Indien*)

v. 3   *Musik des Mittelalters und der Renaissance*

      (Lfg. 1   WERNER BACHMANN, *Byzanz*)

      Lfg. 2   HENRY GEORGE FARMER, *Islam*

      (Lfg. 3   JOSEF SMITS VAN WAESBERGHE, *Musikerziehung*)

      (Lfg. 4   BRUNO STÄBLEIN, HEINRICH BESSELER, *Schriftbild der Musik*)

(Lfg. 5   *Musikinstrumente im Mittelalter*)

(Lfg. 6   EDMUND A. BOWLES, *Musikleben und Musizier-praxis im 15. Jahrhundert*)

(Lfg. 7   H. BESSELER, *Musik des 16. Jahrhunderts*)

(Lfg. 8   *Musikinstrumente der Renaissance*)

V. 4   *Musik der Neuzeit*

Lfg. 1   HELLMUTH CHRISTIAN WOLFF, *Oper*

(Lfg. 2   HEINRICH W. SCHWAB, *Konzerte und Musikfeste*)

(Lfg. 3   WALTER SALMEN, *Haus- und Kammermusik*)

(Lfg. 4–8   *Tanz, Gebrauchsmusik, Musikhandschriften und Notendruck, Musikerziehung, Musikinstrumente*)

(Supplement: *Musikerporträts*)

57

Musikwissenschaftliche Arbeiten. Herausgegeben von der Gesellschaft für Musikforschung. Kassel, Bärenreiter, 1947–

V. 1   FRIEDRICH BLUME, *J. S. Bach im Wandel des Geschichte* Translated into English and published as a separate by Oxford University Press, 1950

V. 2   WALTER LIPPHARDT, *Die Weisen der lateinischen Osterspiele des 12. und 13. Jahrhunderts*

V. 3   HANS HEINZ DRÄGER, *Prinzip einer Systematik der Musikinstrumente*

V. 4   CARL GERHARDT, *Die Torgauer Walter-Handschriften*

V. 5   D. P. WALKER, *Der musikalische Humanismus im 16. und frühen 17. Jahrhundert*

V. 6   IRMGARD BECKER-GLAUCH, *Die Bedeutung der Musik für die Dresdener Hoffeste*

V. 7   HANS JOACHIM MOSER, *Das musikalische Denkmälerwesen in Deutschland*

V. 8   HANS-PETER SCHMITZ, *Die Tontechnik des Pere Engramelle*

Musikwissenschaftliche Studien-Bibliothek, see **Gennrich**

57A
Neue Musikgeschichtliche Forschungen. Wiesbaden, Breitkopf & Härtel, 1968–

ML 1156
. R58

V. 2   GISELA SEEFRID, *Die Airs de danse in den Bühnenwerken von Jean-Philippe Rameau*

58   Bd.8· M.L 138· P63 Jaenecke

Österreichische Akademie der Wissenschaften: Kommission für Musik-forschung. Mitteilungen. 1955–

This series consists of very short studies; longer works are in the following series (**C 59**)

V. 1   OTHMAR WESSELY, *Zur Frage nach der Herkunft Arnold von Bruck*

V. 2   OTHMAR WESSELY, *Neues zur Lebensgeschichte von Erasmus Lapicida*

V. 3   O. WESSELY, *Neue Hofhaimeriana*

V. 4   CARL NEMETH, *Zur Lebensgeschichte von Carlo Agostino Badia (1672–1738)*

V. 5   O. WESSELY, *Beiträge zur Geschichte der Maximilianischen Hofkapelle*

V. 6   HELLMUT FEDERHOFER, *Die Niederländer an den Habsburger-höfen in Österreich*

V. 7   ERICH SCHENK, *Zwei unbekannte Frühwerke von Franz Schubert*

V. 8   PAUL NETTL, *Das Prager Quartierbuch des Personals der Krönungsoper 1723*

V. 9   P. ALTMANN KELLNER, *Ein Mensuraltraktat aus der Zeit um 1400*

V. 10   O. WESSELY, *Zum Leben und Werk von Matthäus Gugl*

V. 11   WOLFGANG OSTHOFF, *Zur Bologneser Aufführung von Monteverdis "Ritorno di Ulisse" im Jahre 1640*

V. 12   O. WESSELEY, *Ein unbekanntes Huldigungsgedicht auf Heinrich Schütz*

V. 13   RICHARD SCHAAL, *Quellen zu Johann Kaspar Kerll*

V. 14   ERICH SCHENK, *Ein unbekanntes Klavier-Übungstück Mozarts*

V. 15

v. 16   HERWIG KNAUS, *Wiener Hofquartierbücher als biographische Quelle für Musiker des 17. Jahrhunderts*

v. 17   H. KNAUS, *Beiträge zur Geschichte der Hofmusikkapelle des Erzherzogs Leopold Wilhelm*
ML 246
, 8   "Sonderabdruck aus dem Anzeiger der phil. hist. Klasse der
, V62A614   Österreichischen Akademie der Wissenschaften, Jg. 1966,
1966   no. 5"

v. 18   THEOPHIL ANTONICEK, *Italienische Musikerlebnisse Ferdinands II, 1598*

v. 19   RUDOLF FLOTZINGER, *Beobachtungen zur Notre-Dame-Handschrift W^1 und ihrem 11. Faszikel*

59
Österreichische Akademie der Wissenschaften: Kommission für Musikforschung. Veröffentlichungen, herausgegeben von Erich Schenk

ML410
qS313
47
v. 1   E. SCHENK, *Ein unbekannter Brief Leopold Mozarts. Mit Beiträgen zum Leben und Werk W. A. Mozarts*

v. 2   ALEXANDER WEINMANN, *Wiener Musikverläger und Musikalienhändler von Mozarts Zeit bis gegen 1860*

v. 3 ML410 HELENE WESSELY-KROPIK, *Lelio Colista, ein Romanischer*
, C745w5 *Meister vor Corelli. Leben und Umwelt*

v. 4 ML410 T. ANTONICEK, *Zur Pflege Händelischer Musik in der 2. Hälfte*
, H13A8 *des 18. Jahrhunderts*

v. 5 ML420 RICHARD SCHAAL, *Quellen und Forschungen zur Wiener*
, F88S3 *Musiksammlung von Aloys Fuchs*

v. 6 ML2933 RUDOLF FLOTZINGER, *Eine Quelle italienischer Frühmonodie*
, F6 *in Österreich*

v. 7 ML136 HERWIG KNAUS, *Die Musiker im Archivbestand des Kaiser-*
, V4262 *lichen Obersthofmeisteramtes (1637–1705), Band I*

ML410
B43
60
Orpheus. Schriftenreihe für Grundfragen der Musik. Herausgegeben von der Gesellschaft zur Förderung der systematischen Musikwissenschaft. Düsseldorf, 1961–

V. 1   MARTIN VOGEL, *Die Intonation der Blechbläser : neue Wege im Metallblas-Instrumentenbau*

V. 2   M. VOGEL, *Der Tristan-Akkord und die Krise der modernen Harmonie-Lehre*

V. 3   M. VOGEL, *Die Enharmonik der Griechen, 1. Teil: Tonsystem und Notation*

V. 4   —— *2. Teil: Der Ursprung der Enharmonik*

V. 5   ADRIAEN D. FOKKER, *Neue Musik mit 31 Tönen*

V. 6   GIUSEPPE TARTINI, *Traktat über die Musik,* ed. Alfred Rubeli

V. 7   RUDOLF HAASE, *Kaysers Harmonik in der Literatur der Jahre 1950 bis 1964*

61
Paris. Institut de Musicologie de l'Université de Paris. Centre de Documentation Universitaire.

1. [Publications] 1961 –

> V. 1   *Principes du violon de l'Abbé le Fils, 1761.* Facsimile, ed. Aristide Wirsta
>
> V. 2   ROGER COTTE, *Compositeurs français émigrés en Suède*
>
> V. 3   BARRY BROOK, *La symphonie française dans la deuxième moitié du XVIII siècle*
>
> V. 4   JEAN MAILLARD, *La lai lyrique des origines à la fin du XIV siècle*
>
> V. 5   JOHN DOWNEY, *La musique populaire dans l'oeuvre de Béla Bartók*
>
> V. 6   JACQUES CHAILLEY, *Alia musica (IX siècle), édition critique . . . avec une introduction sur l'origine de la nomenclature modale pseudo-grecque au moyen-âge*

2. *Colloques internationaux*

> 1953   *Musique et poésie au XVI siècle*
>
> 1956   *Influences étrangères dans l'oeuvre de Mozart*

1960   *La résonance dans les échelles musicales*

1962   *Debussy et l'évolution de la musique du XXe siècle*

62
Princeton studies in music. Princeton University press, 1964–

V. 1   CHARLES E. HAMM, *A chronology of the works of Guillaume Dufay*

63
Quaderni dei Padri Benedettini di San Giorgio Maggiore. Venezia, 1961–

V. 1   P. PELLEGRINO M. ERNETTI, *Parola, musica, ritmo*

V. 2   P. GIUSEPPE NOCILLI, *La messa romana, suo sviluppo nella liturgia e nel canto*

V. 3   P. PAOLO FERRETTI, *Estetica gregoriana* (V. 2)
        V. 1 was printed as a separate by La Société de Saint Jean l'Évangéliste, Paris, Desclée, 1938

64
Quaderni della Rivista Italiana di Musicologia, a cura della Società Italiana di Musicologia. Firence, Olschki, 1966–

V. 1   FRANCESCO DELGARDA, *Indici della Rivista musicale italiana, annate XXXVI–LVII [1929–1955]*

V. 2   F. DELGARDA, *Indici de La Rassegna Musicale (Annate XXIII–XXXII, 1953–1962) e dei Quaderni della Rassegna Musicale (N. 1, 2, 3, 1964–1965)*

64A
Quellenkataloge zur Musikgeschichte, herausgegeben von Richard Schaal.
Wilhelmshaven, Heinrichshofen's Verlag, 1968–

V. 1   *Die Musikhandschriften des Ansbacher Inventars von 1686,* ed. R. Schaal

v. 2   *Thematisches Verzeichnis der sämtlichen Kompositionen von Joseph Haydn zusammengestellt von Alois Fuchs 1839*, ed. R. Schaal

65

Répertoire international des sources musicales. International inventory of musical sources. Munich, G. Henle, 1960–
   Common abbreviation: RISM

Series B

v. 1/1   FRANÇOIS LESURE, *Recueils imprimés: XVIe–XVIIe siècle, I: Liste chronologique*

v. 2   FRANÇOIS LESURE, *Recueils imprimés, XVIIIe siècle*

v. 3/1   JOSEPH SMITS VAN WAESBERGHE, *The theory of music from the Carolingian era up to 1400*, I.
   Organized by country. This v. covers Austria, Belgium, Switzerland, Denmark, France, Luxembourg and the Netherlands

v. 4/1   GILBERT REANEY, *Manuscripts of polyphonic music: 11th-early 14th century, I*

v. 5/1   HEINRICH HUSMANN, *Tropen- und Sequenzenhandschriften*

66

Royal musical association. Research Chronicle. Cambridge, 1961–

v. 1   MICHAEL TILMOUTH, *A calendar of references to music in newspapers published in London and the provinces*
   The index and errata list are in v. 2

v. 2   HUGH BAILLIE, *Some biographical notes on English church musicians, chiefly working in London, 1485–1560*

v. 3   [Miscellaneous essays]

67

Saarbrücker Studien zur Musikwissenschaft. Herausgegeben vom Musikwissenschaftlichen Institut der Universität des Saarlandes. Kassel, Bärenreiter, 1966–

v. 1   *Zum 70. Geburtstag von Joseph Müller-Blattau*, ed. Christoph-Hellmut Mahling

v. 2   CARL DAHLHAUS, *Untersuchungen über die Entstehung der harmonischen Tonalität*

68
Sammlung musikwissenschaftlicher Abhandlungen (Collection d'études musicologiques), begründet von Karl Nef. Strassburg, Heitz & Co. 1930–

v. 1   ANDRÉ PIRRO, *La musique à Paris sous le règne de Charles VI (1380–1422)*
2nd ed. 1958

v. 2   P. SIEBER, *Johann Friedrich Reichardt als Musikästhetiker*

v. 3   W. LÜTHY, *Mozart und die Tonartencharakteristik*

v. 4   K. SCHUBERT, *Spontinis italienische Schule*

v. 5   K. MEYER [KATHI MEYER-BAER], *Bedeutung und Wesen der Musik*

v. 6   KARL GUSTAV FELLERER, *Choralbegleitung und Choralverarbeitung in der Orgelmusik des ausgehenden 18. und beginnenden 19. Jahrhunderts*

v. 7   E. HEGAR, *Die Anfänge der neueren Musikgeschichtsschreibung um 1770 bei Gerbert, Burney und Hawkins*

v. 8   G. PINTHUS, *Das Konzertleben in Deutschland (Ein Abriss seiner Entwicklung bis zum Beginn des 19. Jahrhunderts)*

v. 9   J. SAAM, *Zur Geschichte des Klavierquartetts bis in die Romantik*

v. 10   G. MÜLLER, *Daniel Steibelt, sein Leben und seine Klavierwerke*

v. 11   FRED HAMEL, *Die Psalmkompositionen Johann Rosenmüllers*

v. 12   L. KRÜGER, *Die Hamburgische Musikorganisation im 17. Jahrhundert*

v. 13   J. C. HOL, *Horatio Vecchi's weltliche Werke*

v. 14   EWALD JAMMERS, *Das Karlofficium: "Regnali natus". Einführung, Text und Übertragung in moderne Notenschrift*

Schweizerische Musikforschende Gesellschaft see **C 12,** ser. 2

Settimane musicali Senesi see **C 2**

69

Société Belge de Musicologie. Publications. 1947–

Series 1

      v. 1   PAUL COLLAER, *Darius Milhaud*

Series 2

      v. 1   SUZANNE CLERCX, *Le baroque et la musique*

      v. 2   J. VAN ACKERE, *Pelleas und Mélisande, ou la rencontre miraculeuse d'une poésie et d'une musique*

70

Société Française de Musicologie. Publications. Paris, 1930–

Series 1.   *Monuments de la musique ancienne see* **A 96**

Series 2.   *Documents et catalogues*

      v. 1–2 LIONEL DE LA LAURENCIE, *Inventaire du fonds Blancheton de la Bibliothèque du Conservatoire de musique de Paris (symphonies du milieu de XVIIIe siècle), publié avec l'incipit et le tableau de la composition thématique de chaque symphonie*

      v. 3–4 (in 1). *Mélanges offerts à M. L. de La Laurencie*

      v. 5–6 NORBERT DUFOURCQ, *Documents inédits relatifs à l'orgue français, extraits des archives et des bibliothéques (XIVe–XVIIIe siècles).* Cf. C77:1:1

      v. 7   L. DE LA LAURENCIE, AMÉDÉE GASTOUÉ, *Catalogue des livres de musique (manuscrits et imprimés) de la Bibliothèque de l'Arsenal, à Paris*

      v. 8   GENEVIÈVE THIBAULT, L. PERCEAU, *Bibliographie des poésies de P. de Ronsard mises en musique au XVIe siècle*

      v. 9   FRANÇOIS LESURE, G. THIBAULT, *Bibliographie des éditions d'Adrian Le Roy et Robert Ballard (1551–1598)*

      v. 10   MARIE BRIQUET, *La musique dans les congrès internationaux (1835–1939)*

V. I I   COLUMBE SAMOYAULT-VERLET, *Les facteurs de clavecins parisiens. Notices biographiques et documents (1550–1793)*

Series 3.   *Études*

V. I   JEAN ROLLIN, *Les chansons de Clément Marot, étude historique et bibliographique*

71
Spain. Consejo superior de investigaciones científicas: Instituto Español de musicologia. Barcelona

Series 1.   *Monumentos de la musica española,* see **A 72**

Series ?   *Musica hispana,* see **A 78**

Series 2.   *Anuario,* see **D 5**   ML 32 . S7 S7

Series 3.   *Publicaciones*

[Part 1] *Monografías*

ML 3921
,S 35
V. I   MARIUS SCHNEIDER, *El origen musical de los animales-simbolos en la mitologia y la escultura antigua*

✸✸ ML80
.C4 E8
V. 2   VICTOR ESPINÓS, *El Quijote en la música*

✸✸ML60.S395 D3   V. 3   M. SCHNEIDER, *La danza de espadas y la tarentela*

ML410.I79 S8✸✸
+ cop.2
V. 4   JOSÉ SUBIRÁ, *El compositor Iriarte (1750–1790) y el cultivo español del melólogo*

ML1747.8.M327 S83   V. 5   J. SUBIRÁ, *El teatro del Real Palacio (1849–51)*
+ ✸✸ cop.2

✸✸ ML55.A54   V. 6   *Miscelánea en homenaje a Mons. Higinio Anglés.* 2 v.

[Part 2] *Catalogos musicales*

ML136.M16 B5
Mus. Ref.
V. 1–3   HIGINIO ANGLÉS, JOSÉ SUBIRÁ, *Catalogo musical de la biblioteca nacional de Madrid*
✓v. 1: *Manuscritos;* v. 2: *Impresos;* v. 3: *Impresos, Música práctica*

72
Studien zur Musikgeschichte des 19. Jahrhunderts. Forschungsunternehmen der Fritz Thyssen Stiftung Arbeitskreis Musikwissenschaft. 1965–

Proposed v. (1969) are placed in parentheses.

ML196.S26

v. 1   *Beiträge zur Geschichte der Musikanschauung im 19. Jahr-
hundert,* ed. Walter Salmen
Miscellaneous essays on E. T. A. HOFFMANN, ADOLF
BERNARD MARX and other subjects

ML270.4
.E32

v. 2   URSULA ECKART-BÄCKER, *Frankreichs Musik zwischen Romantik und Moderne. Die Zeit im Spiegel der Kritik*

ML250.4
.S34

v. 3   HEINRICH W. SCHWAB, *Sangbarkeit, Popularität und Kunstlied.
Studien zu Lied und Liedästhetik der mittleren Goethezeit
(1770–1814)*

ML196.V63

v. 4   *Beiträge zur Musiktheorie des 19. Jahrhunderts,* ed. Martin
Vogel
Miscellaneous essays, including one each on the following
theorists: MORITZ HAUPTMANN (1792–1868), HUGO RIE-
MANN (1849–1919), ARTHUR VAN OETTINGEN (1836–1920),
SIEGFRIED KARG-ELERT (1877–1933), and HEINRICH SCHEN-
KER (1868–1935)

ML3915.B43

v. 5   *Beiträge der Geschichte der Musikkritik,* ed. Heinz Becker

v. 6   MARTIN VOGEL, *Apollonisch und Dionysisch: Geschichte eines
genialen Irrtums*

ML3915.K57

v. 7   HELMUT KIRCHMEYER, *Situationsgeschichte der Musikkritik
und des musikalischen Pressewesens in Deutschland, dargestellt
vom Ausgange des 18. bis zum Beginn des 20. Jahrhunderts.*
6 parts proposed:
(1. *Allgemeine musikkritische Systematik*)
(2. *System- und Methodengeschichte*)
(3. *Die romantische Idee im Spiegel ihrer Kritik*)
 4. *Das zeitgenössische Wagner-Bild*
    (1. *Die frühe Wagner-Kritik*)
    ✓2. *Dokumente 1842–1845*
    ✓3. *Dokumente 1846–1850*
(5. *Die Problematik der Neudeutschen*)
(6. *Biographisch-Bibliographisches Kritikerverzeichnis*)

ML196.D21

v. 8   *Studien zur Trivialmusik des 19. Jahrhunderts,* ed. Carl Dahlhaus

ML410.B13 G2

v. 9   MARTIN GECK, *Die Wiederentdeckung der Mattäuspassion im
19. Jahrhundert*

v. 10   IMOGEN FELLINGER, *Verzeichnis der Musikzeitschriften des 19. Jahrhunderts*

v. 11   RUDOLF HEINZ, *Geschichtsbegriff und Wissenschaftscharakter der Musikwissenschaft in der zweiten Hälfte des 19. Jahrhunderts. Philosophische Aspekte einer Wissenschaftsentwicklung*

v. 12   PETER RUMMENHÖLLER, *Musiktheoretisches Denken im 19. Jahrhundert: Versuch einer Interpretation erkenntnistheoretischer Zeugnisse in der Musiktheorie*

v. 13   HERFRID KIER, *Raphael Georg Kiesewetter (1773–1850). Wegbereiter des musikalischen Historismus*

v. 14   WALTER WIORA, *Die Ausbreitung des Historismus über die Musik*

v. 15   HEINZ BECKER, *Beiträge zur Geschichte der Oper*

v. 16   GERHARD ALLROGGEN, *Thematisch-chronologisches Verzeichnis der musikalischen Werke von E. T. A. Hoffman)*

v. 17   SUSANNE GROSSMANN-VENDREY, *Felix Mendelssohn Bartholdy und die Musik der Vergangenheit*

v. 18   KARL H. WÖRNER, *Das Zeitalter der thematischen Prozesse in der Geschichte der Musik*

Summa musicae medii aevi, see **Gennrich**

73

Studia musicologia Upsalensia, edidit Carl-Allen Moberg. Uppsala, 1952–

[First series]

v. 1   ÅKE DAVIDSSON, *Catalogue critique et descriptif des imprimés de musique des XVIᵉ et XVIIᵉ siècles conservés dans les bibliothèques suédoises (excepté la Bibliothèque de l'Université Royale d'Upsala)*

v. 2   Å. DAVIDSSON, *Catalogue critique et descriptif des ouvrages théoriques sur la musique imprimés au XVIᵉ et au XVIIᵉ siècles et conservés dans les bibliothèques suédoises*

V. 3   INGMAR BENGTSSON, RUBEN DANIELSON, *Handstilar och notpikturen i. Kungl. Musikaliska Akademie Romansamling*

V. 4   I. BENGTSSON, *J. H. Roman och hans instrumental-musik*

V. 5   Å. DAVIDSSON, *Studien rörande svenskt musiktryck före år 1750*

V. 6   BENGT HAMBRAEUS, *Codex carminorum gallicorum: une étude sur le volume Musique vocale du manuscrit 87 de la Bibliothèque de l'Université d'Upsala*

V. 7   Å. DAVIDSSON, *Dansk musiktryck intill 1700-talets mitt. 1962*

V. 8   JAN LING, *Leven Christian Wiedes vissamling. En studie i 1800-talets folkliga vissång*

Nova series. Acta Universitatis Upsaliensis: Studia musicologica Upsaliensia. 1965–

V. 1   Å. DAVIDSSON, *Bibliographie zur Geschichte des Musikdrucks*

V. 2   HANS EPPSTEIN, *Studien über J. S. Bachs Sonaten für ein Melodieinstrument und obligates Cembalo*

V. 3   JOHAN SUNDBERG, *Mensurens betydelse i öppna labialpipor . . . with an English summary: The significance of the scaling in open flue organ pipes*

74
Sweden, Publications of the library of the Royal Swedish Academy of Music.
Stockholm, 1953–

V. 1   ÅKE LELTKY, *Katalog över orkester-och körverk tillgängliga för utlåning från Kungl. Musika-Akademiens Bibliotek*

V. 2   CARI JOHANSSON, *French music publishers' catalogues of the second half of the eighteenth century*

75
Tabulae Musicae Austriaicae. Kataloge österreichischer Musiklieferung,

herausgegeben von der Komission für Musikforschung, Österreichische Akademie der Wissenschaften, unter Leitung von Erich Schenk. 1964–

v. 1   KARL SCHNÜRL, *Das alte Musikarchiv der Pfarrkirche St. Stephan in Tulln*

v. 2   *ML 93*
          . F6   RUDOLF FLOTZINGER, *Die Lautentabulaturen des Stiftes Kremsmünster. Thematischer Katalog*

v. 3   *ML 134*   HELGA MICHELITSCH, *Das Klavierwerk von Georg Christoph*
          . W 08M5 Wagenseil. Thematischer Katalog

v. 4   *ML 128*   THOEPHIL ANTONICEK, *Das Musikarchiv der Pfarrkirche St.*
          . C54 V54 Karl Borromäus in Wien

76

Utrechtse bijdragen tot de muziekwetenschap. Uitgegeven van wege het Instituut voor Muziekwetenschap onder leidung von Prof. Dr. Eduard Rieser. Bilthoven, Creyghton, 1958–

v. 1   ROBERT LEON TUSLER, *The organ music of Jan Pieterszoon Sweelinck*

v. 2   J. H. VAN DER MEER. *Johann Joseph Fux als Opernkomponist.* 3 v.

v. 3   C. VON GLEICH, *Die sinfonischen Werke von Alexander Skrjbin.* 2 v.

v. 4   WILLEM ELDERS, *Studien zur Symbolik in der Musik der alten Niederländer*

v. 5   J. VAN BIEZEN, *The middle Byzantine kanon-notation of manuscript H. A paleographic study of the melodies of 13 kanons and a triodion*

77

La vie musicale en France sous les rois Bourbons. Collection publiée par le groupe "Histoire et musique" sous la direction de Norbert Dufourcq. Paris, A. & J. Picard, 1954–

Series 1.   Études

↗ ML410
. L392 DF   v. 1   N. DUFOURCQ, *Nicholas Lebègue, organiste de la*
1954

Chapelle Royale; Nouveaux documents inédits sur l'orgue francais au XVIIe siècle. [Cf. **C 69** ser. 2, v. 5–6]

ML270.3.D8 v. 2   N. DUFOURCQ, *Dix années à la Chapelle Royale de musique, d'après une correspondance inédite Langers-Delamare (1718–1728)*

ML410.D242 D8 1957 v. 3   N. DUFOURCQ, ANDRÉ TESSIER, *Michel-Richard Delalande: Notes et références pour servir à son histoire, suivies du catalogue thématique de l'oeuvre*

xx ML410. C256 B3 v. 4   M. BARTHÉLÉMY, *André Campra, sa vie et son oeuvre*

ML410.R22 B4 v. 5   PAUL BERTHIER, *Réflexions sur la vie et l'art de Jean-Philippe Rameau*

ML424.J7 D8 v. 6   N. DUFOURCQ, *Jean de Joyeuse et la pénétration d'orgues parisiennes dans le Midi de la France au XVIIe siècle*

ML410.C855 H6 1961 v. 7   SHLOMO HOFMAN, *L'oeuvre de clavecin de François Couperin: Étude stylistique, avec catalogue thématique*

ML410.B684 D8 v. 8   N. DUFOURCQ, *Jean-Baptiste de Boesset, musicien et maître de musique des Reines Anne d'Autriche et Marie-Thérèse*

ML594.L8C6 v. 9   N. DUFOURCQ, *Le grand orgue de la chapelle Saint-Louis du Prytanée Militaire de La Flèche*

ML410.D39A75 v. 10   MICHEL ANTOINE, *Henry Desmarest, 1661–1741: biographie critique*

xx ML107.P18 B8 v. 11   YOLANDE DE BROSSARD, *Musiciens de Paris, 1535–1792: actes d'état civil d'après le Fichier Laborde de la Bibliothèque nationale*

v. 12   MARIE FRANÇOISE CHRISTOUT, *Le ballet de cour de Louis XIV, 1643–72, mises en scène*

ML410.C855 M38 v. 13   *Mélanges François Couperin, publiés à l'occasion du tricentenaire de sa naissance, 1668–1968*

ML574.D8L6 v. 14   N. DUFOURCQ, *Le livre de l'orgue français 1589–1789. Tome II: Le Buffet*

In 2 parts: 1. *Des origines à Henri IV; 2. La Buffet
d'orgue classique*

ML290.8.T887 v. 15   MARIE-THÉRÈSE BOUQUET, *Musique et musiciens
à Turin de 1648 à 1775*

*17 ML270.D79   19 ML270.8.V47 B45   21. ML574.D8L6 v.4
20 ML270. B45*

Series 2.   *Recherches sur la musique classique française,* see **D 46**

Vienna, see **Wien**

78
The Wellesley edition cantata index series. Wellesley College, 1964–

This series consists of thematic catalogues

v. 1   DAVID BURROWS, *Antonio Cesti (1623–1669)*

v. 2   IRVING EISLEY, *Mario Savioni (ca. 1608–1685)*

v. 3   ELEANOR CALUORI, *Luigi Rossi (ca. 1598–1653)*
             Part 1: Reliable attributions; Part 2: Unreliable attri-
             butions

v. 4   Not yet published

v. 5   GLORIA ROSE, *Giacomo Carissimi (1604–1675)*

79
Wien. Beiträge zur Geschichte des Alt-Wiener Musikverlags. Wien, L. Krenn,
1952–

*v. 1 ML134.L244 A Weinmann ... Joseph Lanner
v. 2 ML134.S9A58 A. Weinmann ... Johann Strauss Vater und Sohn
v. 3 ML134.S92 A4 A. Weinmann ... Josef + Eduard Strauss,*

Series 1.   None yet published?

Series 2.   *Verleger*

✳✳ML112.W443

v. 2   ALEXANDER WEINMANN, *Vollständiges Verlagsver-
             zeichnis, Artaria & Comp.*

v. 3–5   Not yet published?

v. 6   A. WEINMANN, *Verzeichnis der Musikalien aus dem
             K. K. Hoftheater-Musik-Verlag*

v. 7   A. WEINMANN, *Kataloge Anton Huberty [1727–
             1791], Wien, und Christoph Torricella*

v. 8   A. WEINMANN, *Verlagsverzeichnis F. A. Hoffmeister*

v. 9   A. WEINMANN, *Verlagsverzeichnis Tranquillo Mollo
         (mit und ohne Co.)*

v. 10   A. WEINMANN, *Verlagsverzeichnis Pietro Mechetti,
         quondam Carlo*

v. 11   A. WEINMANN, *Verlagsverzeichnis Giovanni Cappi
         bis A. O. Witzendorf*

80

Wiener Musikwissenschaftliche Beiträge, unter Leitung von Erich Schenk.
Gesellschaft zur Herausgabe von Denkmälern der Tonkunst in Österreich.
1955–

v. 1   OSKAR EBERSTALLER, *Orgeln und Orgelbauer in Österreich*

v. 2   ANTON BAUER, *Opern und Operetta in Wien*
         An index to first performances, 1629–

v. 3   JOHANN WILHELM HERTEL, *Autobiographie,* ed. Erich Schenk

v. 4   OTHMAR WESSELY, *Arnold von Bruck und die Wiener Hof-
         kapelle von 1519 bis 1545*

v. 5   HANNELORE GERICKE, *Die Wiener Musikalienhandel von 1700
         bis 1778*

v. 6   URSALA KIRKENDALE, *Antonio Caldara: sein Leben und seine
         venezianisch-römischen Oratorium*

v. 7   ERICH SCHENK, *Ausgewählte Aufsätze, Reden und Vorträge*

81

Yale University. Music theory translation series, ed. Richard L. Crocker.
New Haven, Yale school of music, 1963–

v. 1   FRANCESCO GASPARINI, *The practical harmonist at the harpsi-
         chord,* ed. Franck S. Stillings, David L. Burrows
         (*L'armonico pratico ad cimbalo,* Venezia 1708)

v. 2   GIOSEFFO ZARLINO, *The art of counterpoint,* ed. Guy A. Marco
         and Claude V. Palisca
         Part 3 of *Le istitutioni harmoniche,* 1558

82

Yale University. Yale studies in the history of music. New Haven, Yale University press

v. 1 Beekman C. Cannon, *Johann Mattheson, spectator in music*

v. 2 William G. Waite, *The rhythm of twelfth-century polyphony: its theory and practice*
Contains transcription of Wolfenbüttel Ms 677 *olim* Helmstadt 628

v. 3 Sylvia W. Kenney, *Walter Frye and the contenance angloise*

v. 4 Leon B. Plantinga, *Schumann as critic*

v. 5 Fenner Douglas, *The language of the classical French organ*

SECTION D
MUSIC PERIODICALS AND YEARBOOKS

Accademia musicale Chigiana, see **Chigiana**

1
Acta Musicologica. 1928–

The official journal of the International Musicological society. Its original title (used in v. 1–2) was: *Mitteilungen der internationalen Gesellschaft für Musikwissenschaft/Bulletin de la Société internationale de musicologie.* It includes news of society activities, announcements &.

It issues 4 numbers a year, but the numbers are often combined.

Table of contents, index: There is an annual cumulative table of contents, and from v. 27 (1952) an annual index of names in fasc. 4 of each v.

Features: Contained current book and music lists until v. 25 (1952)

V. 1–7, 25 have been reprinted by Johnson Reprint Corporation, New York

2
American Musicological Society

A. **Bulletin,** June, 1936–Sept. 1948
    Contains abstracts of papers read at chapter meetings

B. **Papers** read by members at the annual meeting, 1936–41

C. **Journal of the American Musicological Society,** 1948–

    Common abbreviation: JAMS
    Issued 3 times yearly
    Annual index, cumulative table of contents
    Features: Reviews of books and scholarly music editions, Society news, communications &.
    Special issue: v. 13 (1960), nos. 1–3 combined in 1, *A musicological offering to Otto Kinkeldey upon occasion of his 80th anniversary*

D. **Studies and Documents,** see C 3

3

Analecta Musicologica. Veröffentlichungen der Musikabteilung des Deutschen Historischen Instituts in Rom, herausgegeben von Friedrich Lippmann. Köln, Böhlau, 1963–

Published irregularly
Feature: Bibliographies of articles on music in non-musical Italian
periodicals
Special issues: v. 1–5 have the title *Studien zur italienisch-deutschen
Musikgeschichte.* v. 6: *Vincenzo Bellini und die italienische Opera seria
seiner Zeit*

4

Annales Musicologiques: Moyen-Âge et Renaissance. Publication de la
Société de musique d'Autrefois, direction de Geneviève Thibault. 1953–
1963?

v. 1–5 (1953–7);   v. 6 (1963)
Table of contents in back of each v.
Articles of *ca.* 100 pp. or longer:

v. 1   FRANÇOIS LESURE, G. THIBAULT, "Bibliographie des éditions
            musicales publiées par Nicolas du Chemin (1549–1576),
            pp. 269–374. Additions and corrections v. 4 p. 251; v. 6,
            p. 403

v. 3   NANIE BRIDGMAN, "Christian Egenolff, imprimeur de mu-
            sique" pp. 77–177
            F. LESURE, "Le traité des instruments de musique de Pierre
            Trichet", pp. 283–387 and v. 4 pp. 175–248

v. 5   EDWARD E. LOWINSKY, "The Medici Codex. A document of
            music, art, and politics in the Renaissance", pp. 61–178
            WALTER H. RUBSAMEN, "The international "Catholic" reper-
            toire of a Lutheran church in Nürnberg (1574–1597)" [Nürn-
            berg, Germanisches Museum Ms 8820], pp. 229–327

5

Anuario musical. Consejo superior de investigaciones científicas: Institute
Español de musicologia. Barcelona, 1946–

Published annually
Table of contents; no index

Special issues:

v. 18   (1963). *En homenaje al Exc. Sr. D. José Subirá en su 80 aniver-
             sario*

v. 21   (1966). "Dedicado a A. de Cabezon (1510–1566) en el IV
             centenario de su muerte"

Anticle of *ca.* 100 pp.: Marius Schneider, "A propósito del influjo árabe:
Essayo de etnografie de la España medieval", v. 1, pp. 31–152

6

L'Approdo musicale. Revista trimestrale di musica, ed. Alberto Mantelli.
Edizioni Radio Italiana, 1958–

Issued in separately paged numbers, about four each year until 1962:
1958: nos. 1–4
1959: nos. 5–8 (7–8 in 1)
1960: nos. 9–12
1961: nos. 13–17 (14–15 in 1; 16–17 in 1)

These nos. included book reviews and an annual index in the last no. of
each year. However, with no. 18, the set changed to undated numbers,
each entirely devoted to a specific subject. The latest no. was 21; nos. 19–20
were combined in 1.

Most nos., even before 18, single out a specific subject for several articles:
1.   *Omaggio ad Alfredo Casella,* pp. 1–29
5.   Richard Strauss, pp. 5–120
7–8.   Claude Debussy, pp. 1–160
9.   Gian Francesco Malipiero, pp. 1–149
10.   Leos Janacek, pp. 1–108
11.   Joseph Haydn, 1–164
12.   Sergei Prokofiev, pp. 1–160
14–15.   Alberto Basco "Il corale organistico di J. S. Bach", pp. 1–264
16–17.   Gustav Mahler, pp. 1–196
18.   *La cultura musicale nella scuola italiana*
19–20.   *Il grupo dei sei*
21.   Ildebrando Pizzetti

7

Archiv für Musikforschung, ed. Rudolf Steglich, H. J. Therstappen. Leipzig, 1936–1943

Superseded *Zeitschrift für Musikwissenschaft* **(D 61)** as the publication of the Deutsche Musikgesellschaft from 1936 to 1943.

8

Archiv für Musikwissenschaft. Leipzig, Breitkopf & Härtel, 1918–1926 [v. 1–8]

Reprinted by Georg Olms, Hildesheim, 1964
——— Trossingen, Gohner-Stiftung, 1951–   [v. 9–]
———, *Beihefte,* see **8a** below
Common abbreviations: AfM, AfMw
Published quarterly
Features: short book reviews, v. 1–8; current book and music edition lists v. 9–
Articles of *ca.* 100 pp. or longer:
HANS MERSMANN, "Grundlagen einer musicalischen Volksliedforschung", v. 4 (1922) pp. 141–154, 284–321; v. 5 (1923) pp. 81–135; v. 6 (1924) pp. 127–164.

HEINRICH BESSELER, "Studien zur Musik des Mittelalters"
   I.   "Neue Quellen des 14. und beginnenden 15. Jahrhundert" v. 7 (1925) pp. 167–252
   II.   "Die Motette von Franko von Köln bis Philipp von Vitry", v. 8 (1926), 137–258

8a

Archiv für Musikwissenschaft: Beihefte, herausgegeben von Hans Heinrich Eggebrecht. Wiesbaden, Franz Steiner, 1966–

√ v. 1   WILIBALD GURLITT, *Musikgeschichte und Gegenwart: eine Aufsatzfolge. Teil I: Von Musikgeschichtlichen Epochen*

√ v. 2   ———. *Teil II: Orgel und Orgelmusik. Zur Geschichte der Musikgeschichtsschreibung*

√ v. 3   WERNER BREIG, *Die Orgelwerke von Heinrich Scheidemann*

√ v. 4   FRITZ RECKLOW, *Der Musiktraktat des Anonymus 4. Teil I: [Edition]*

√ v. 5   ———. *Teil II: Interpretation der Organum purum-Lehre*

√ v. 6   CHRISTOPH WOLFF, *Der stile antico in der Musik Johann Sebastian Bachs. Studien zu Bachs Spätwerk*

✓ v. 7   Brinkmann. Schoenberg Op. 11

✓ v. 8   Michels. Johannes de Muris

9

Beiträge zur Musikwissenschaft. Herausgegeben vom Verband deutscher Komponisten und Musikwissenschaftler. Berlin, Neue Musik, 1959–

> Published quarterly
> Annual table of contents; no index
> Features: Book reviews; selective list of current Russian, East German musicological publications; news of East German scholarly music societies; from v. 5 lists musicology courses in East German universities. Special issues:
> v. 6 (1964), *Beilage: Fünf neu aufgefundene Briefe von Richard Wagner* [facsimiles]
>   v. 9:3–4 (1967; pp. 178–336). *Sonderheft. 1917–1967. Sowjetische Musikwissenschaft, I. Teil*

Bouwsteenen . . . see *Vereeniging . . .*, **D 59**

Caecilien-Calendar see *Kirchenmusikalisches Jahrbuch*, **D 27**

10

Chigiana. Rassegna annuale de studi musicologici. Accademia Chigiana, Siena. Firenze, Olschki, 1964–

> Supersedes *Settimane musicali Senesi* of the *Accademia* (**C 2**); v. 1 of *Chigiana* being v. 21, or *nuova serie* v. 1 of *Settimane*

> Published annually? 3 v. to date.

Collectanea historiae musicae see *Historiae musicae cultores*, **C 36,** v. 2

11

Les Colloques de Wégimont. Cercle international d'études ethno-musicologiques, rédacteur-en-chef Paul Collaer. Bruxelles, 1956–

Published irregularly; may have ended. v. 1–4 (1954–7), v. 5 (1960) have appeared.

V. 1, 3, 5 are concerned with ethnomusicology; v. 2 is entitled *L'ars nova;* v. 4 is entitled *Le "baroque" musical*

12

Il Convegno musicale. Rassegna trimestrale, Giacomo Alessandro Caula, direttore. Torino, Bottega d'Erasmo, 1964–

"Quarterly" issues often combined.

13

Current musicology. Published under the aegis of the music department, Columbia University. New York, 1965–

Published twice a year

Features: reviews of dissertations, summaries of the musicological programs of American universities, lists of foreign dissertations.

14

Dansk Aarbog for Musik Forskning. Udgivet af Dansk Selskab for Musikforskning. København, 1961–

Published annually, but 1964/5 combined in 1.

Articles in several languages

15

Darmstadt. Institut für neue Musik und Musikerziehung. Darmstädter Beiträge zur neuen Musik. Mainz, B. Schotts Söhne, 1958–

Published irregularly. From v. 5 each v. is devoted to a single subject. V. 6–7 not yet published? Special issues:

v. 5   Pierre Boulez, *Musikdenken heute, I*

v. 8   *Informationstheorie und Computermusik,* ed. Lejaren A. Hiller, Jr.

v. 9   *Notation neuer Musik,* ed. Ernst Thomas

v. 10   *Form in der neuen Musik,* ed. E. Thomas

16

Darmstadt. Institut für neue Musik und Musikerziehung. Veröffentlichungen.
Berlin, Merseburger, 1961–

Published irregularly, 8 v. to date. Each v. consists of collected essays
about a rather broad topic of modern music

ML3845.S75 1965   v. 1   *Stilkriterien der neuen Musik*

ML390.S76 1961   v. 2   *Stilporträts der neuen Musik*

ML3830.W24 1965   v. 3   *Der Wandel des musikalischen Hörens*

MT75.V55 1963   v. 4   *Vergleichende Interpretationskunde*

ML197.T36   v. 5   *Terminologie der neuen Musik*

MT6.N268 1967   v. 6   *Neue Wege der musikalischen Analyse*

MT1.P767   v. 7   *Probleme des musiktheoretischen Unterrichts*

MT90.V47   v. 8   *Versuche musikalischer Analysen*
ML55.43,1968 v.9   ML3915.433 v.11
ML3795.S84 v.10

17

Deutsches Jahrbuch der Musikwissenschaft. Leipzig, Peters, 1957–
M.372.30   [Jg. 1 = 1956]
A continuation of *Jahrbuch der Musikbibliothek Peters* (**D 24**)
Published annually.
Features: Current publication lists; German dissertations from v. 2 on;
necrology (usually).

18

Ethnomusicology. Journal of the society for ethnomusicology. 1953–

Originally called *Ethnomusicology News letter,* nos. 1–5 (1953–5), and
mimeographed. Now printed, 3 times yearly.

Annual index; separate index for v. 1–10
Features: book and record reviews, current bibliography

19

Études grégoriennes. Publiées par les moines de Solesmes sous la direction
ML3082.E8   de Dom Joseph Gajard. Solesmes, 1954–

Published irregularly: v. 1 (1954), v. 2 (1957), v. 3 (1959), v. 4 (1961),
v. 5 (1962), v. 6 (1963), v. 7–8 (1967)
Table of contents in each v; no index.
Includes book reviews.
Article over 100 pp.:

v. 4   Dom A. Le Roux, "Aux origines de l'Office Festif: Les an-
            tiennes et les pseaumes de Matines et de Laudes pour Noël
            et le 1er Janvier", pp. 65–172

20

Fontes artis musicae. Review of the international association of music
libraries. Publié sous les auspices du Conseil international de la musique,
avec l'aide de l'UNESCO. Kassel, Bärenreiter, 1954–

Published twice yearly.
Multilingual
Index in each v.
Features: Selective lists of new music and music literature publications;
general emphasis on bibliography.
Special issue:

v. 13/1 (1966): *Mélanges offerts à Vladimir Fedorov à l'occasion de son
soixante-cinquième anniversaire*

21

Galpin Society Journal. An occasional publication. London, 1948–

V. 1–19 (1958–65) have been reprinted by Swets & Zeitlinger, Amsterdam,
1967.
Despite its sub-title has so far appeared regularly once a year.
There is a collective index for v. 1–5 in v. 5.
Features: Articles on musical instruments; book reviews; music reviews
from v. 19 on

22

Internationale Musikgesellschaft. Sammelbände. Leipzig, Breitkopf &
Härtel, 1899–1914. 15 v.

Common abbreviation: SIMG

A reprint has been announced by Olms, Hildesheim, for 1968.
Table of contents in each v.; no index.
Articles of *ca.* 100 pp. or longer:

Ludwig Schiedermair, "Die Oper an den badischen Höfen des 17.
u. 18. Jahrhunderts", v. 14, pp. 191–207, 369–449, 510–550

Otto Riess, "Johann Abraham Peter Schulz' Leben", v. 15, pp. 169–270

23

Internationale Musikgesellschaft. Zeitschrift. Leipzig, Breitkopf & Härtel,
1899–1914. 15 v.

Common abbreviation: ZIMG
Reprints have been proposed by Johnson Corporation and by Broude
Bros. (both New York) for some time now, but have not yet appeared.
Originally issued monthly
There is a collective table of contents in each v.
Features: book reviews, reports on musicological courses in universities,
alphabetical lists of periodical contents, society news.

24

Jahrbuch der Musikbibliothek Peters. Leipzig, C. F. Peters, 1895–1940. 47 v.

Common abbreviations: JMP, JMbP
Reprinted by Kraus Reprint Corp., N.Y., 1965
Continued by *Deutsches Jahrbuch der Musikwissenschaft* **(D 17)**
Index of v. 1–20 in v. 20; index of v. 1–40 in v. 40.
Features: annual list of books, occasional necrology
Special issue: v. 28 (1922) *Festgabe zum siebzigsten Geburtstage Max
Friedlanders,* ed. Rudolf Schwartz

25

Jahrbuch für Liturgik und Hymnologie. Kassel, Johannes Standa-Verlag,
1955–

Issued yearly.
Detailed index in each v.

Features: General emphasis on German Protestant church music; book reviews in that field.
Multilingual
Special issues: v. 2. *Beilage:* Facsimile reprint of *Achtliederbuch* of Jobst Gutknecht, Nürnberg, 1523/4
v. 10   Beilage: *"Maria zart" Liederblatt, gedruckt bei Jakob Köbel, Oppenheim (um 1515)*

26

Jahrbücher für Musikalische Wissenschaft, herausgegeben von Friedrich Chrysander. Leipzig, 1863, 1867. 2 v.

Reprint by Olms, Hildesheim, in 1 v.
Articles of over 100 pp.:

F. CHRYSANDER, "Geschichte der Braunschweig-Wolfenbüttelschen Capelle und Oper vom 16. bis zum 18. Jahrhundert", v. 1 pp. 147–286
F. CHRYSANDER, "Henry Carey und der Ursprung des Königsgesangs *God save the king"*, pp. 287–407
Das Locheimer Liederbuch nebst der Ars Organisandi von Conrad Paumann, ed. Friedrich Wilhelm Arnold. v. 2, pp. 1–234

26a

Journal of Music Theory. A publication of the Yale school of music. New Haven, 1957–

Issued twice yearly
Index in v. 5, 6; no others.
Features: Book reviews; bibliography of current periodical articles in the field; general emphasis since v. 5 on contemporary music.

27

Kirchenmusikalisches Jahrbuch, 1876–

Publishing history: Originally named *Caecilien-Calendar* and published under that name 1876–1885 (10 nos.). In 1886 it received its present name, but continued a double numbering of each v. for many years (1886 = v. 1 and v. 11); however eventually omitted the numbering which started in 1876 in favor of that started in 1886. In 1911 the publication ceased with v. 24, starting again in 1925 and ceasing in 1935 with v. 33. It again resumed publication in 1950 and has issued a v. yearly since.

Indices: Index of the 10 nos. of *Caecilien-Calendar* in no. 10 (1885); index of those and of the first 20 v. of *Kirchenmusikalisches Jahrbuch* (1876–1907) in v. 20.

Features: Editions of sacred compositions of the renaissance in v. 1–20 (1886–1907), listed below. These were collected and printed separately as *Repertorium musicae sacrae,* ed. F. X. Haberl.

A series of articles by P. Otto Kornmüller, "Die alten Musiktheoretiker" appeared at the beginning of v. 1–4 (1886–1889), v. 6–8 (1891–1893), and v. 18 (1903)

Music editions:

v. 1 (1886)   G. F. ANERIO, *Missa brevis*

v. 2 (1887)   CLAUDIO CASCIOLINI, *Missa pro defunctis*

v. 3 (1888)   JOANNE CRUCE [GIOVANNI CROCE], *Missa prima sexti toni*

v. 4 (1889)   LUDOVICO GROSSI DA VIADANA, *Missa Cantabo Domino*

v. 5 (1890)   O. DI LASSO, *Missa Puisque j'ay perdu*

v. 6 (1891)   G. M. NANINI, *Quinque Lamentations*

v. 7 (1892)   G. CROCE, *Missa tertia, octavi toni*

v. 8 (1893)   Anon. (16th c.), *Falsibordoni super octo tonos cantici Magnificat*

v. 9 (1894)   PALESTRINA, *Missa O admirabile commercium*
v. 10 (1895)   FRANCESCO SORIANO, *Passio Domini nostri*

v. 11 (1896)   VICTORIA, *Officium hebdomade sanctae,* I

v. 12 (1897)   ———, II

v. 13 (1898)   ———, III, with index

v. 14 (1899)   G. CROCE, *Missa secunda, tertii toni*

v. 15 (1900)   L. MARENZIO, *Motets 1–7*

v. 16 (1901)   ———, *8–14*

v. 17 (1902)   ———, *15–21*

v. 18 (1903)   ———, *22–27*

v. 19 (1905)   F. SORIANO, *VIII Magnificat*

28

Miscellana musicologica. Adelaide studies in musicology. University of Adelaide, 1968–

Features: Some coverage of Australian ethnomusicology; *Research synopsis*, listing with brief comments articles in recent music periodicals.

29

Monatshefte für Musikgeschichte, herausgegeben von der Gesellschaft für Musikforschung, redigiert von Robert Eitner. Leipzig, 1869–1905. 37 v.

Common abbreviations: MfM, MfMg
Reprint by Annemarie Schnase Reprints, New York (*ca.* 1963)
Cumulative index 1869–1878 only; table of contents for each v.
Organization: Originally issued monthly, usually including one or more annual *Beilagen.* Both articles and *Beilagen* were frequently issued in installments, and it may require patience and persistence to locate all of any given one. *Beilagen* are usually paged separately, but some parts, especially music sections, may not be paged at all. In the original set the location of *Beilagen* will undoubtedly vary according to the decisions of past librarians or book binders. In the reprint edition they have been assembled, each one usually in the location of its last part. It is the latter which is followed below.
Some of the more extensive and important articles and editions are listed below in categories. Eitner is the author or editor unless otherwise stated.

1. Library catalogs of *ca.* 30 pp. or longer
   Augsberg. *Katalog der in der Kreis- und Stadt-Bibliothek, dem Städtischen Archive und der Bibliothek des historischen Vereins . . . befindliche Musikwerke,* by H. M. Schletterer. *Beil.* 10–11
   Basel. *Katalog des Musik-Sammlung auf der Universitäts-Bibliothek . . .* by Julius Richter. *Beil.* 23–4
   Berlin. Joachimsthalschen Gymnasium. *Katalog der musikalien-Sammlung . . . Beil.* 16–17, 30
   Brieg. *Beschreibendes Verzeichnis der alter Musikalien: Handschriften und Druckwerke, des Kgl. Gymnasiums . . . Beil.* 27
   Dresden. *Katalog der Musik-Sammlung der Kgl. öffentlichen Bibliothek . . . Beil.* 22
   Göttingen. *Die Musikwerke der Kgl. Universitäts-Bibliothek . . .* by A. Quantz. *Beil.* 15
   Liegnitz. *Katalog der in der Kgl. Ritteracademie . . . befindlichen Gedruckten und Handschriftlichen Musikalien . . .* v. 1, v. 21

London, Westminster Abbey. *Musik-Katalog* . . . by William Barclay
Squire. *Beil.* 35

Stuttgart. *Katalog über die Musik-Codices des 16. und 17. Jahrhunderts
auf der Kgl. Landes-Bibliothek* . . . by August Halm. *Beil.* 34–5

Vatican. *Bibliographischer und thematischer Musikkatalog des Päpstlichen Kapellarchives* . . . by F. X. Haberl. *Beil.* 19

Zwickau. *Bibliographie der Musikwerke in der Ratsschulbibliothek* . . .
by Reinhard Vollhardt. *Beil.* 26

2.   Miscellaneous indices

EITNER. *Verzeichnis der im Druck erschienenen musikhistorischen
Arbeiten von Robert Eitner. Beil.* 25

HASSLER, HANS LEO. *Chronologisches Verzeichnis seiner gedruckten
Werke. Beil.* 6

VINCENTI, ALESSANDRO. *Indice di tutte le opere de musica* . . . by
F. X. Haberl. *Beil.* 14–15

*Verzeichnis neuer Ausgaben alter Musikwerke aus der frühsten Zeit
bis zum Jahre 1800. Beil.* 2–3. *Nachtrag* v. 9, *passim*

3.   Editions and extensive studies of music and theory

Das alte deutsche mehrstimmige Lied und seine Meister. v. 25, 26

BUCHNER, JOHANN, *Fundamentum* . . . ed. W. Nagel. v. 23

Das Buxheimer Orgelbuch. Beil. 20

Cantaten des 17. und 18. Jahrhunderts. Beil. 18
Editions of works by Heinrich Albert, Buxtehude, K. H. Graun,
J. A. Hasse, R. Keiser, G. C. Schurmann, G. H. Stölzel

Das deutsche Lied des XV. und XVI. Jahrhunderts. Beil. 8–9, 12–15
Includes edition of *Schedelsches Liederbuch* (called *Münchener
Liederbuch*)

GUIDO D'AREZZO, *Micrologus* (German translation by Raymond
Schlecht). v. 5

KRIEGER, JOHANN PHILIPP, [*Works*]. v. 29–30

Musica enchiriadis (German translation by R. Schlecht). v. 6

PHILIPPE DE VITRY, *Ars nova* (German translation by Peter Bohn). v. 22

SCHLICK, ARNOLT, *Spiegel des Orgelmacher (1509); Tabulaturen
etlicher Lobgesang . . . (1512).* v. 1

STADEN, SIGMUND GOTTLIEB, *Seelewig (Singspiel,* 1644*). Beil.* 13

Tänze des 15.–17. Jahrhunderts. Beil. 6–7

4.   Other

NAGEL, WILIBALD, *Annalen der englischen Hofmusik von der Zeit*

Heinrichs VIII bis zum Tode Karls I (1509–1646). Beil. 26–7
WALDNER, FRANZ, *Nachrichten über der Musikpflege am Hofe zu Innsbruck nach archivalischen Aufzeichnungen. I. Unter Kaiser Maximilian. I. Beil.* 29–30

30

Music and Letters. A quarterly publication. London, 1920–

Reprinted by Swets & Zeitlinger, Amsterdam, 1965
Indices: Cumulative index in separate v. for v. 1–40; annual index, annual table of contents
Features: Book reviews, music reviews, record reviews until 1940, current book and record lists, occasional short musical supplements.
Special issues:

> v. 8 nos. 2–3 (1927). BEETHOVEN
> v. 9 no. 4 (1928). SCHUBERT
> v. 16 nos. 3–4 (1935). BACH and HÄNDEL

31

The Music Forum. New York, Columbia University press, 1967–
To be issued annually
Indexed

32

Music Library Association. Notes. Series 1, 1934–43 (15 nos.), Series 2, 1943–

All of series 1, and series 2 v. 1–21 (1943–64) have been reprinted by AMS Press, New York.
Series 1 was mimeographed; series 2 is printed and appears quarterly.
Features: Emphasis on music bibliography. Book reviews, music reviews, current book and music lists, lists of current dealers' catalogs, index to current record reviews, Association news, necrology.

33

Music Review. Cambridge, 1940–

Reprint of v. 1–25 (1940–1964) by Kraus, New York, 1967.
Issued quarterly.
Features: reviews of books, records, and concerts

34

Musica Disciplina. Rome, American Institute of Musicology, 1946–

Title of v. 1: *Journal of Renaissance and Baroque music*
Originally issued quarterly, now issued annually.

Features: General emphasis on medieval and renaissance music; bibliography, list of European and American dissertations. Often includes facsimile pages of Mss; specializes in inventories of the contents of medieval and renaissance manuscripts, the most extensive of which are listed below, together with articles of *ca.* 100 pp. or longer.

1. Manuscripts

Aosta. *A recently discovered source of early fifteenth century music* . . . by Guillaume de Van. v. 2, p. 5
Bologna [Museo civico] Ms Q 15. *An inventory* . . . by G. de Van. v. 2, p. 231
Bologna, Museo civico Ms Q 16. *A report* . . . by Edward Pease. v. 19, p. 57; v. 21, p. 231
Bologna, Bibl. univ. Ms 2216. . . . by Heinrich Besseler. v. 6, p. 39
Chantilly, Musée Condé Ms 1047 . . . by Gilbert Reaney. v. 8, p. 59; v. 10, p. 55
Edinburgh, Nat'l lib. Ms Adv.5.1.15 . . . by Denis Stevens. v. 13, p. 155
Edinburgh, Univ. lib. Ms Dc 1.69. Seventeenth-century songs and lyrics . . . by John P. Cutts. v. 13, p. 170
Faenza, Bibl. Comm. Ms 117. [Facsimile], by Armen Carapetyan. v. 13, p. 79; v. 14, p. 65; v. 15, p. 63; v. 17, p. 57
Lucca . . . . by Frederico Ghisi, Nino Pirrotta, and Ettore Li Gotti. v. 1 suppl., v. 3, p. 119; v. 4, p. 111; v. 5, p. 115
Old Hall. . . . *A re-appraisal and an inventory,* by Andrew Hughes and Margaret Bent. v. 20, p. 97.
Paris, Bibl. Nat. f. it. 568. . . . by G. Reaney. v. 14, p. 33
Paris, Bibl. Nat. nouv. acq. fr. 6771 (Codex Reina). . . . by Kurt von Fischer. v. 11, p. 38

2. Other

Jacques Handschin, "The summer canon and its background". v. 3, p. 55; v. 5, p. 65

35

The Musical Antiquary. London, 1909–1913. 4 v.

Reprinted by Gregg Press, New York, 1967
Index in each v.
Special emphasis on English music

36
The Musical Quarterly. New York, G. Schirmer. 1915–

V. 1–50 (1915–1964) reprinted by AMS Press, New York.
Common abbreviation: MQ
Indices: Annual index from v. 28. Cumulative indices by Herbert K.
Goodkind for v. 1–43 (1915–1959) and v. 44–46 (1960–62). Special index
by Hazel Gertrude Kinsella: "Americana index to the *Musical Quarterly*"
[1915–1957] in *Journal of research in music education,* 6:2 (1958)
Features: Book reviews from v. 31 (1945) on; *Current chronicle* (concert
reviews and reports) from v. 34 (1948) on; record reviews from v. 38 (1952)
on; quarterly book lists.

Special issues:

v. 13 no. 2 (1927). BEETHOVEN
v. 14 no. 1 (1928). SCHUBERT
v. 18 no. 1 (1932). American music
v. 18 no. 2 (1932). HAYDN
v. 21 no. 2 (1935). BACH and HANDEL
v. 22 no. 3 (1936). LISZT
v. 42 no. 2 (1956). MOZART (also printed separately)
v. 45 no. 2 (1959). HÄNDEL
v. 46 no. 2 (1960). The Princeton seminar in advanced musical
studies [on contemporary music]
v. 48 no. 3 (1962). STRAVINSKY
v. 51 no. 1 (1965). Contemporary music in Europe: a comprehensive survey (also printed separately)

37
Musik und Kirche. Kassel, Bärenreiter, 1939–

6 issues a year
Features book reviews, performance reviews, music supplements.
General emphasis on Protestant German church music

38

Die Musikforschung. Herausgegeben im Auftrag der Gesellschaft für Musikforschung und in Verbindung mit dem Institut für Musikforschung Berlin, dem Landesinstitut für Musikforschung in Kiel und dem Institut für Musikforschung in Regensburg. Kassel, Bärenreiter, 1948–

Originally quarterly, now semi-annual.
Annual index, table of contents
Features: Book reviews; annual list of dissertations and music seminars in Germany and Switzerland in 2nd issue each year.

39

Note d'Archivio per la storia musicale. Periodica trimestrale diretto da Rafaelle Casimiri. Roma, 1924–42. 19 v.

Annual index, table of contents
Features: Book and music reviews, book lists.
Articles of 100 pp. or longer:
R. CASIMIRI, "I diarii Sistini [Sistine chapel archives 1535–*ca*. 1560].
v. 1 p. 85, p. 140, p. 267; v. 3 p. 1, p. 169, p. 257; v. 4 p. 256; v. 9 p. 53, p. 150, p. 260; v. 10 p. 45, p. 149, p. 261, p. 326; v. 11 p. 76, p. 300; v. 12 p. 56, p. 126, p. 249; v. 13 p. 59, p. 147, p. 201; v. 14 p. 19, p. 73, p. 128, p. 297; v. 15 p. 42, p. 129, p. 200, p. 281; v. 16 p. 74; v. 17 p. 65.

BRAMANTE LIGI, *La cappella musicale del duomo d'Urbino,* v. 2, pp. 1–369
RICCARDO PAOLUCCI, "La cappella del Duomo di Fano". v. 3 pp. 79–168; v. 4 pp. 100–115
GIUSEPPE VALE, "Contributo alla storia dell'Organo in Friuli", v. 4 pp. 1–99
G. VALE, "La cappella musicale del Duomo di Udine". v. 7 pp. 87–201

40

Nuova Rivista Musicale Italiana. Bimestrale di cultura e informazione musicale. Roma, Edizioni Radiotelevisione Italiana. 1967–

Features: Book, music, and record reviews.

41

Organo. Rivista di cultura organaria e organistica. Brescia, Gruppo musicale "Girolamo Frescobaldi", 1960–

Published with 2 numbers to each v. Appears irregularly; 3 v. so far.
Features: Reviews of books, music, new organs.

42
Perspectives of New Music. Princeton, Princeton University Press, 1964–

Published semi-annually.
Features: Book reviews, book lists.

43
Quaderni della Rassegna musicale. Torino, Guilio Einaudi, 1964–

Issued annually; supersedes Rassegna musicale **(D 45)**
Features: Book reviews, book lists. Index of v. 1–3 in **C 64** v. 2
Each v. consists of essays on a single topic:

> v. 1   *L'opera di Goffredo Petrassi*
>
> v. 2   *L'opera di Luigi Dallapiccola*
>
> v. 3   *La nuova musicologia italiana*
>
> v. 4   *Musica e le arti figurative*

44
Quadrivium. Studi di filologia e musicologia. Antiquae musicae italicae studiosi, Istituto di Filologia Latina e Medievale, Universita degli Studi di Bologna. Bologna, Arnaldo Forni, 1956–

V. 1 contains 2 separate issues; 1 annual issue since.
A related series is *Biblioteca di "Quadrivium", Serie musicologica* and *serie liturgica* (also an unnumbered *serie estratti*), all of which consist of separate reprints of articles from *Quadrivium*.

45
Rassegna musicale. Turin, 1928–43, 1947–52. 22 v.

Superseded *Il Pianoforte* (1920–27; is superseded by *Quaderni di Rassegna musicale* **(D 43)**

Indices. Separate complete index for v. 1–22; annual index in each v.
Features: Book and record reviews, lists of contents of some scholarly music periodicals.

46

Recherches sur la musique classique francaise. Publiées par la groupe "Histoire et musique". Paris, A. & J. Picard, 1960–

Série 2 of *La vie musicale en France sous les rois Bourbons* **(C 77).**
Issued annually.
Index of v. 1–5 in v. 5 (1965).
Features: book, music, and record reviews

47

Die Reihe. A periodical devoted to developments in contemporary music. Bryn Mawr, Theodore Presser, in association with Universal Edition. 1958–

This is the English translation of the German *Die Reihe,* which began in 1955.
Published annually? 7 v. so far.
Each v. contains essays on a special topic:

v. 1	Electronic music
v. 2	ANTON WEBERN (1883–1945)
v. 3	Musical craftsmanship
v. 4	Young composers
v. 5	Reports, analyses
v. 6	Speech and music
v. 7	Form-Space

48

Revue Belge de Musicologie. Schotin, P. Lombaerts, 1946–

Originally issued in 4 numbers (2 or 3 of which were often combined) each year; since 1958 (v. 12). has been annual.
Table of contents in back of each v.

Features: Book reviews, periodical reviews, news of *Société Belge de Musicologie* activities.

Special issues and lengthy articles:

v. 8 nos. 2–4 (1954). *Hommage à Charles Van den Borren à l'occasion de son quatre-vingtième anniversaire*

v. 13 nos. 1–4 (1959). *Musique expérimentale*

v. 14 (1960). ALBERT VAN DER LINDEN, "Lettres de Vincent D'Indy à Octave Maus". pp. 87–125; v. 15 pp. 55–160.

v. 16 (1962). Special Debussy section pp. 43–149

v. 18 (1964). *Hommage à Charles Van den Borren à l'occasion de son quatre-vingt dixième anniversaire*

v. 20 (1966). *Hommage à André Souris*

49

Revue de Musicologie. Publiée par la Société Française de Musicologie. Paris

Publishing history:

Phase 1: Title: *Bulletin de la Société Française de Musicologie.* Published twice yearly 1917–1921. Each issue numbered separately (nos. 1–10) and combined in numbered v.: v. 1 = nos. 1–5 (1917–19); v. 2 = nos. 6–10 (1919–21).

Phase 2: Title: *Revue de musicologie, Nouvelle série.* Each of these issues was also numbered individually, 4 each year composing a v. which carried both a v. no. and a year of publication no., as follows:

v.	année	nos.	date
3	6	1–4	1922
4	7	5–8	1923
5	8	9–12	1924
and so on, through:			
20	23	69–72	1939

Phase 3: Title: *Société Française de Musicologie: Rapports et communications.* Issued as follows:

v.	année	no.	date
21	—	Serie special 1–2	1942
22	—	" " 3–4	1943
23	—	" " 5	1944

Phase 4: Title: *Revue de musicologie*. Appeared twice each year, but with each issue numbered as double:

v.	année	nos.	date
24	27	73–4, 75–6	1945
25	28	77–8, 79–80	1946

and so on, through:

v.	année	nos.	date
29	32	93–4, 95–6	1950

after which the v. nos. were dropped:

	33	97–8, 99–100	1951
	34	101–2, 103–4	1952
	35	105–6, 107–8	1953

Phase 5: Title the same, but numbering of individual issues ceased. The format changed, and two issues have appeared regularly each year since 1954. However, the issues of 1954 carried the *volume number 36,* and the set has been so numbered since then.

There is no index, but there is a cumulative annual table of contents in all v. except 1942–4.

Features of present magazine: Book and music reviews; tables of contents of current periodicals in second issue each year.

Special issue: v. 47 (1962) *Claude Debussy (1862–1962). Textes et documents inédits*

50
Revue Grégorienne. Études de chant sacré et de liturgie. Directeur M. le

Chanoine Norbert Rousseau avec le concours des Bénédictins de Solesmes. Paris, Tournai, 1911–1939, 1946–?
    Issued 6 times a year.
    Annual index, table of contents
    Features extensive annotated current bibliography.

51

La Revue Musicale. Directeur, Henry Prunières. Paris, 1920–

Publishing history: Started publication in November, 1920 and issued 11 numbers yearly (monthly except September), until 1940. It resumed publication in 1946 with 4 numbers a year until 1948. Nothing then appeared until 1952, when publication was resumed actively but somewhat irregularly. In 1954 the issues ceased to be dated, and since that time publication has become increasingly irregular.

Numbering: No. 1 having appeared in Nov., 1920, the third no. (Jan. 1921) carried the description "Deuxième année". This year of publication numbering continued, with the year changing in November, until the end of 1929, at which point, by omitting two issues, the eleventh appeared in December. In January, 1930, a new numbering was started, this issue being no. 100, and each issue since then has been consecutively numbered. The year of publication numbering was continued until 1948 (21st year = 1940, 22nd–24th years = 1946–8), but abandoned thereafter.

A reprint of nos. 1–259 (1920–1964) has been issued by Swets & Zeitlinger, Amsterdam.

There is an index of v. 1–11 in v. 11.

Features: 1. From the beginning, 2 monthly issues each year were devoted to special topics. Sometimes these were called "Numéro spécial". Since 1952 all numbers have been devoted to special topics. These are all listed below.

2. Almost every issue of the first ten years, and several later issues, included a separate musical composition. These are generally short pieces, and most, though not all, are by 20th century French composers.

Date	Year	No.	Title
12/1920	1		Debussy
7/1921	2		La musique Russe contemporaine

Date	Year	No.	Title
12/1921	3		Le ballet au XIX^c siècle
10/1922	3		Gabriel Fauré
12/1922	4		César Franck
8/1923	4		Eduard Lalo
12/1923	5		Igor Stravinsky
5/1924	5		Ronsard et la musique
1/1925	6		Lully et l'opéra français
4/1925	6		Maurice Ravel
12/1925	7		Ernest Chausson
5/1926	7		La jeunesse de Claude Debussy
4/1927	8		Beethoven
12/1928	10		Schubert
4/1929	10		Albert Roussel
1930	11	106	Julien Krein
1930	11	108	Hindemith
1931	12	113	La musique autrichienne [20th c.]
1931	12	117–18 [in 1]	Géographie musicale 1931 : ou Essai sur la situation de la musique en tous pays
1931	12	121	Chopin
1932	13	122	Vincent d'Indy
1932	13	125	Goethe et la musique
1932	13	129	Les instruments de musique
1932	13	130	Bach
1933	14	140	L'opéra-comique au XIX^c siècle
1933	14	141	Mozart
1934	15	151	Le Film sonore
1935	16	156	Bellini
1935	16	161	Schumann
1936	17	166	Paul Dukas
1937	18	172	Musique d'orgue et musique religieuse
1937	18	173	Le rythme et la danse
1937	18	174	Autour de Beethoven et Wagner
1937	18	175	La musique dans l'exposition de 1937
1937	18	176	Autour de Vincent d'Indy
1937	18	178	A la mémoire d'Albert Roussel

Date	Year	No.	Title
1938	19	182	Le ballet contemporain
1938	19	183	Autour de Debussy et Satie
1938	19	184	Questions d'esthétique et d'histoire
1938	19	185	Sur quelques musiciens français
1938	19	187	Hommage à Maurice Ravel
1939	20	191	Igor Stravinsky
1940	21	196	La musique dans les Pays Latins
1947	23	206	Maurice Emmanuel
1952		210	La littérature française et la musique (1900 à nos jours)
1952		211	L'œuvre du XXe siècle
1952		213	Les carnets critiques: Arguments de "Wozzeck" d'Alban Berg et de "Billy Budd" de Benjamin Britten
1952		214	Erik Satie: son temps et ses amis
1952		215	Carnets critiques [miscellany]
1952		216	La musique 1900–1950 . . . Tableau chronologique des principales œuvres musicales . . .
1952		217–18	Carnets critiques
1953		219	La musique et le ballet
1953		220	La musique polonaise d'aujourd'hui
1953		221	Carnets critiques
1953–4		222	La musique religieuse française de ses origines à nos jours
1953–4		223	Carnets critiques

no. title
224. BELA BARTOK
225. *Une valse inédite de Frédéric Chopin,* ed. S. Chainaye
226. *Aspects inédits de l'art instrumental en France des origines à nos jours,* ed. Norbert Dufourcq
227. ARMAND MACHABEY, *La cantillation manichéenne*
228. MADELEINE O'NEILL, *Les deux passions de J. S. Bach dans la lumière des évangiles*
229. *Autour de Frédéric Chopin: sa correspondance—ses portraits*
230. *Sampiero Corsi et Henri Tomasi*

231. *Mozart*
232. *Hommage à Mozart et Schumann* [program for concert]
233. *Hector Berlioz*
234. *Le martyre de Saint-Sébastien*
235. O. D'ESTRADE-GUERRA, *Les manuscrits de Pelleas et Mélisande*
236. PAUL SCHAEFFER, *Vers une musique expérimentale*
237. *La vérité de Jeanne. Oratorio . . . musique d'André Jolivet*
238. GENEVIÈVE CALAME-GREAULE, BLAISE CALAME, *Introduction à l'é-tude de la musique Africaine*
239–40. *La musique sacrée: III congrès international de musique sacrée*
241. FRANÇOISE GERVAIS, *La notion d'arabesque chez Debussy*
242. *La musique dans le monde: Les semaines musicales de Bus*
243. ARMAND MACHABEY, *Messe de Tournai*
244. *Expériences musicales: musiques concrète, électronique, exotique,* ed. Pierre Schaeffer, François Mache
245. *Le concours Marguerite Long-Jacques Thibaud*
246. *Henrik Neugeborn, dit Henri Nouveau, 1901–1959*
247. *Carnets critiques*
248. ROBERT TANNER, *La musique antique Grecque*
249. *Carnets critiques*
250. *Traveaux de médecins à propos de musique*
251. *Carnet critique*
252. *Alexandre Tcherepnine*
253–4. IANNIS XENAKIS, *Musiques formelles*
255. Université radiophonique et télévisuelle internationale. *La musique légère et la musique à danser du moyen âge au XXᶜ siècle. Premier cycle: Du moyen âge à la fin du XVIIᶜ siècle*
    Part 2, *Du XVIIIᶜ siècle au XXᶜ siècle* = no. 262
256. JACQUES DURON, *Mozart et le mythe de Don Juan*
257. *Iannis Xenakis et la musique stochastique*
258. *Claude Debussy 1862–1962*
259. ———— supplement: programs of D. performances in 1962
260. *Jean-Philippe Rameau (1764–1964)*
261. ———— supplement
262. See no. 255
263. *Claude Ballif: Essais, études et documents*
    Includes piano piece: *Passe-temps*
264. ———— supplement: Ballif program 3/7/68
265–6 (in 1). *Varese, Xenakis, Berio, Pierre Henry*
267. ———— supplement: program of *Journées de musique contemporains de Paris* 25–31 Octobre 1968

52

Rivista Musicale Italiana. Torino, Fratelli Bocca. 1894–1955. 57 v.

Continued by Nuova Rivista Musicale Italiana **(D 40)**
Annual table of contents and index; cumulative index for v. 1–20,
21–35. Separate index for v. 35–57 in **C 64**, v. 1
Features: Book and music lists and reviews, lists of periodical contents.
Section "Arte contemporanea" on current performances of new works

Articles of *ca.* 100 pp. or longer:

v. 2   N. D'ARIENZO, "Origini dell'Opera comica", v. 2 pp. 597–
         628; v. 4 pp. 421–59; v. 6 pp. 473–95; v. 7 pp. 1–33

v. 3   A. POUGIN, "Essai historique sur la musique en Russie",
         pp. 37–77, 452–6; v. 4 pp. 44–94

v. 4   LUIGI TORCHI, "La musica istrumentale in Italia nei secoli
         XVI, XVII, e XVIII", pp. 581–630; v. 5 pp. 64–84, 281–320,
         455–89; v. 6 pp. 253–88, 693–726; v. 7 pp. 233–51; v. 8 pp. 1–
         42
         Also printed as a separate book in 1901. Reprint **C 14** ser. 3,
         v. 8

v. 5   JOHN GRAND-CARTERET, "Les titres illustrés et l'image au
         service de la musique", pp. 2–63, 225–80; v. 6 pp. 289–329;
         v. 9 pp. 559–635; v. 11 pp. 1–23, 191–227

v. 8   [1901; several articles on Verdi pp. 277–412]
         ROMUALDO GIANI, "Il "Nerone" de Arrigo Boito", pp. 861–
         1006

v. 9   MICHEL BRENET, "La jeunesse de Rameau", pp. 658–93,
         860–97; v. 10 pp. 62–85, 185–206

v. 10   ALBERTO CAMETTI, "Donizetti a Roma", pp. 761–88; v. 12
         pp. 1–39, 515–54, 689–713; v. 13 pp. 50–90, 522–45; v. 14
         pp. 301–32, 616–55

v. 12   CICILIO DE RODA, "Un quaderno di autografi di Beethoven del
         1825", pp. 64–108, 592–622, 734–67

v. 13   FRANCESCO PIOVANO, "Baldassare Galuppi", pp. 676–726;
         v. 14 pp. 333–65; v. 15 pp. 233–74

v. 16   F. PIOVANO, "Notizie storico-bibliografiche sulle opere di
         Pietro Carlo Guglielmi (Guglielmini) con appendice su Pietro

Guglielmi", pp. 243–70, 475–505, 785–820; v. 17 pp. 59–90, 376–414, 554–89, 822–77

v. 17   JULIEN TIERSOT, "Lettres de musiciens, écrites en français, du XVᵉ au XXᵉ siècle", pp. 1–58, 359–75, 505–53, 878–915; v. 18 pp. 233–75, 549–600; v. 19 pp. 315–61, 882–97; v. 20 pp. 89–128; v. 21 pp. 52–85, 451–91; v. 23 pp. 413–52; v. 29 pp. 541–71; v. 30 pp. 14–46; v. 33 pp. 558–89; v. 34 pp. 34–62, 190–209, 325–75, 512–54; v. 36 pp. 1–25, 408–29; v. 37 pp. 1–20, 185–203, 329–49, 529–50; v. 38 pp. 1–20, 207–24, 369–88; v. 39 pp. 237–62, 441–66
ANDRE POUGIN, "Gounod écrivain", pp. 590–627; v. 18 pp. 747–68; v. 19 pp. 239–85, 637–95; v. 20 pp. 453–86, 792–820

v. 18   ENRICO CELANI, "Musica e musicisti in Roma 1750–1850", pp. 1–63; v. 20 pp. 33–88; v. 22 pp. 1–56, 257–300

v. 19   SESTO FASSINI, "Il melodramma italiano a Londra ai tempi del Rolli", pp. 35–75, 575–636
CARLO SONIGLI, "L'attuale situazion e la nuova produzione operatoria teatrale negli Stati Uniti dell'America del Nord", pp. 898–915; v. 20 pp. 353–76; v. 21 pp. 514–77; v. 22 pp. 651–89

v. 20   FAUSTO TORREFRANCA, "Le origini della sinfonia" [about Sammartini], pp. 291–346; v. 21 pp. 97–121, 278–312; v. 22 pp. 431–46

v. 24   GAETANO CESARI, "Giorgio Giulini, musicista", pp. 1–34, 210–71 (including symphony score)

v. 28   F. TORREFRANCA, "Le origini dello stile mozartiano", pp. 263–308; v. 33 pp. 321–42, 505–29; v. 34 pp. 1–33, 167–89, 493–511; v. 36 pp. 373–407

v. 31   [Articles on Boito pp. 161–444]

v. 32   MARIA M. BRONDI, "Il liuto e la chitarra", pp. 1–39, 161–95, 317–62; v. 33 pp. 1–20, 181–209

v. 43   [Articles on Gabriele d'Annunzio pp. 161–301]

53

Royal Musical Association. Proceedings . . . for the investigation and discussion of subjects connected with the science and art of music. London, 1874–

Originally *Proceedings of the Musical Association* (commonly abbreviated PMA), the word *Royal* was added in 1945.
Issued annually
Reprint of v. 1–74 (1874–1944) by Kraus Reprints, New York
Features: includes floor discussion of papers read at meetings

54

Schweizerisches Jahrbuch für Musikwissenschaft. Basel, Helbing & Lichtenhahn, 1924–1938.

Each v. was edited by a different local chapter of the Swiss musicological society. Some are monographs.

v. 1   *Festschrift zum musikwissenschaftlichen Kongress in Basel 26. bis 29. September 1924*

v. 6   ARNOLD GEERING, *Die Vokalmusik in der Schweiz zur Zeit der Reformation: Leben und Werke von Bartholomäus Franck, Johannes Wannenmacher, Cosmas Alder*

v. 7   WALTER ROBERT NEF, *Der St. Galler Organist Fridolin Sicher und seine Orgeltabulaturen*

55

Score. A music magazine. London, 1949–61. 28 nos.

Later title: *The Score and IMA [International music society] magazine*
Published irregularly from 2 to 4 issues annually.
Some emphasis on contemporary music
Special issues:
no.   8 (Sept. 1953). English music [current scene]
no. 12 (Sept. 1955). American music [current scene]
no. 17 (Sept. 1956). A tribute to Roberto Gerhard on his sixtieth birthday

Settimane musicale Senese see **C 2**

Société Belge de Musicologie see **D 48**

Société de musique d'Autrefois see **D 4**

Société Française de Musicologie see **D 49**

56

Studia musicologica. Academiae Scientarum Hungaricae. Budapest, Akadémiai Kiadó, 1961–

> Published in 4 fascicles yearly, but fascicles often combined
> Multilingual
> Includes book reviews

> Special issues:

v. 3   *Zoltano Kodály octogenario sacrum*

v. 5   *Report of the second international musicological conference, Budapest, 1961*
             On Liszt (pp. 27–338), and Bartok (pp. 339–596)

v. 7   *. . . Papers read at the International Folk Music Council held in Budapest in August 1964*
             Forms the second part of the *Journal of the* I. F. M. C., vol. 22

Studien zur italienisch-deutschen Musikgeschichte see **D 3**

57

Studien zur Musikwissenscuaft. Beihefte der Denkmäler der Tonkunst in Österreich, unter Leitung von Guido Adler, 1931–34, 1955–

> The old set published 1 v. annually (except in 1917); the new set is less frequent, 6 v. having appeared since 1955.

> Annual table of contents, no index.
> Articles of *ca.* 100 pp. or longer:

v. 1   EGON WELLESZ, "Cavalli und der Stil der venezianischen Oper von 1640–1660", pp. 1–103
             MAX NEUHAUS, "Antonio Draghi" p. 104–192
             ERNST KURTH, "Die Jugendopern Glucks bis Orfeo", pp. 193–277

v.   2   GUSTAV DONATH, "Florian Leopold Gassmann als Opernkomponist", pp. 34–211
LOTHAR RUDINGER, "Carl von Dittersdorf als Opernkomponist", pp. 212–349

v.   6   E. WELLESZ, "Die Opern und Oratorien in Wien von 1660–
1708", pp. 5–138
ALBERT SMIJERS, "Die kaiserliche Hofmusik-Kapelle von
1543–1619", pp. 139–86; v. 7 pp. 102–42; v. 8 pp. 176–206;
v. 9 pp. 43–81

v. 25   *Festschrift für Erich Schenk*

58

Vereeniging vor Nederlandsche Muziekgeschiedenis. Bouwsteenen. Amster-
dam, 1869–81, and **Bouwsteenen voor een geschiedenis der toonkunst in de
Nederlanden** (Documenta et archivalia ad historiam musicae neerlandicae),
Amsterdam, 1965–

The old set published 3 v. (v. 1, 1869–72; v. 2, 1872–74, v. 3, 1874–81)
consisting of extensive lists of Dutch musicians, publishers, instrument
makers &, all unindexed. It served as the yearbook of the *Vereeniging,*
but was superseded by the *Tijdschrift* **(D 59)**. The contents of the new series
are similar.

59

**Vereeniging voor Nederlands Muziekgeschiedenis. Tijdschrift voor Noord-
Nederlands Muziekgeschienenis.** Amsterdam, 1882–

See **D 58**. In 1948 the title was changed to *Tijdschrift voor Muziekweten-
shap.*
Publishing history: Published 1, or sometimes 2 nos. annually, and grouped 4 nos. to each v. The dates of each v. are:

v.   1 = 1882–5
v.   2 = 1885–7
v.   3 = 1888–91
v.   4 = 1892–4
v.   5 = 1895–7
v.   6 = 1898–1900
v.   7 = 1901–4

v.   8 = 1907–8
v.   9 = 1909–14
v. 10 = 1915–22
v. 11 = 1923–5
v. 12 = 1926–8
v. 13 = 1929–32
v. 14 = 1932–5
v. 15 = 1936–9
v. 16 = 1940–46

From here on individual nos. are undated. Completion date given:

v. 17 = 1955
v. 18 = 1959
v. 19 = 1963

The recent volumes are multilingual

A complete cumulative table of contents appears in v. 19, nos. 1–2 (1960–61)

Features: Long articles which were divided among different numbers are broken at the end of a page, perhaps in the middle of a sentence. Also there are several unpaged sections, or sections which are independently paged.

Articles of *ca.* 100 pp. or longer:

v.   1   J. P. N. LAND, "Het Luitboek van Thysius beschreven und togelicht", pp. 129–95, 205–64; v. 2 pp. 1–56, 109–74, 178–94; 278–349; v. 3 pp. 1–60
         Also printed as a separate book by the society

v.   2   J. C. M. VAN RIEMSDIJK, "Jean Adam Reinken" pp. 61–195

v.   7   J. W. ENSCHEDÉ, "Cornelis de Leeuw", pp. 88–148, 157–232 (including music)
         Starting in v. 7, separately paged sections of a book appear: D. F. SCHEURLEER, *Bijdragen tot een repertorium der Nederlandsche Muziekliteratur.* v. 7/1: pp. 1–16; v. 7/3: pp. 17–32; v. 7/4: pp. 33–48; v. 8/1: pp. 49–64; v. 8/2: pp. 65–96; v. 9/1: pp. 97–112; v. 9/2 pp. 129–54.

v. 11   A. SMIJERS, "De Illustre Lieve Vrouwe broedershap te 's-Hertogenbosch" [1399–1535], pp. 187–210; v. 12 pp. 40–62, 115–67; v. 13 pp. 46–100, 181–237; v. 14 pp. 48–105; v. 16 pp. 63–106, 216 (see also v. 16 pp. 1–32, v. 19 pp. 32–43, 163–72)

60

Vierteljahrsschrift für Musikwissenschaft, herausgegeben von Friedrich Chrysander, Phillip Spitta, Guido Adler. Leipzig, Breitkopf & Härtel, 1885–1894. 10 v.

Index, annual table of contents in each v.; cumulative index for all 10 v. ed. Rudolf Schwartz.

Features: Bibliography, reviews.

Articles of *ca.* 100 pp. or longer

v. 1   Philipp Spitta, "Sperontes 'Singende Muse an der Pleisse'", pp. 35–127, 350–55
Fr. X. Haberl, "Wilhelm du Fay. Monographische Studie über dessen Leben und Werke", pp. 397–530

v. 2   Oskar Fleischer, "Denis Gaultier", pp. 1–181

v. 3   F. X. Haberl, "Die römische 'Schola cantorum' und die päpstlichen Kapellsänger bis zur Mitte des 16. Jahrhunderts", pp. 189–297
Emil Vogel, "Claudio Monteverdi", pp. 315–459

v. 4   Wilhelm Bäumker, "Niederländische geistliche Lieder nebst ihren Singweisen aus Handschriften des XV. Jahrhunderts", pp. 153–254

v 5   Carl Paesler, "Fundamentbuch von Hans von Constanz", pp. 1–193

v. 7   Max Seiffert, "J. P. Sweelinck und seine direkten deutschen Schüler", pp. 145–260
Hermann Gehrmann, "Gohann Gottfried Walther als Theoretiker", pp. 468–578
Friedrich Chrysander, "Lodovico Zacconi als Lehrer des Kunstgesanges", pp. 337–396; v. 9 pp. 250–310; v. 10 pp. 531–67

v. 10   Karl Held, "Das Kreuzkantorat zu Dresden. Nach archivalischen Quellen bearbeitet", pp. 239–410

61

Zeitschrift für Musikwissenschaft. Herausgegeben von der Deutschen Musikgesellschaft. Schriftleitung Dr. Alfred Einstein. Leipzig, Breitkopf & Härtel, 1918–1935. 17 v.

Published monthly; year started in October.

Detailed annual index

Features: Book reviews, music reviews, reports on musicology courses.
Current periodical index as follows:

v.   1: Jan., Feb.

v.   2: May

v.   3: June

v.   4: June

v.   5: Sept.

v.   6–13: Sept. each year

v.   14: June, Sept.

v.   15: Sept.

v.   16–17: lacking

INDEX

Bruck, Arnold von, *ca.* 1470–*ca.* 1554   A 4; 32:99; 33:34; C 58:1; 80:4

Bruckner, Anton, 1824–1896   **B 15**

Brudieu, Joan, *fl. from* 1538, *d.* 1591   A 14:1

Bruers, Antonio   C 1:15; 2:6

Brugis, Francesco de, *fl. ca.* 1500   C 36:18

Bruhns, Nicholas, *ca.* 1665–1697   A 43:c9:1–2; C 39:8

Brumel, Antoine, *ca.* 1475–*ca.* 1520   A 22:68; 60:8; 100; **B16**

Bruna, Pablo, 17th c. Spanish   A 14:20

Brunetti, Geatano, 1753–1808   A 23:3

Bruning, E.   A 64:7

Brunold, Paul   B 28:1:1, 6, 11–12

Bruollis (Brolo), Bartholomaeus de, *fl. ca.* 1430–1440   A 32:61

Buchner, Johann (Hans of Constance), 1483–*before* 1544   D 29:3; 60:5

Buck, Percy C.   A 99

Budapest. Academiae Scientarum Hungaricae   D 56

Bugge, Arne   A 66:a6

Buhle, Edward   A 33:35–6

Bukofzer, Manfred F.   A 76:8; C 16:2:2; 23:9; 68:21

Bull, John, *ca.* 1562–1628   A 76:9, 14, 19

Bulletin de la Société Internationale de Musicologie   D 1

Bulletin of the American Musicological Society   D 2A

Buonanni, Filippo, *fl.* 1722   C 46:37

Buonauguria da Tivoli, Guiliano, ca. 1500–1567   A 55:1–2

Buranello, Il, = Galuppi

Burbach, *P.* Josef Hermann   C 40:34

Burck, Joachim von, *ca.* 1541–*ca.* 1610   A 4; 88:22

Burgh, Cornelius, *fl.* 1618–1635   A 34:6, 9

Burghauser, Jarmil   B 32:1 *passim*; 32:2

Burgundian composers   A 28:11:2; C 68:23 (before Dufay)

Burmeister, Joachim, *fl.* 1606   C 23:10; 39:5

Burney, Charles, 1726–1814   C 23:19; 26:1; 33:6; 68:7

Burrows, David   A 101:5; C 78:1

Burtius (Burzio, Burci), Nicolaus, *ca.* 1450–*after* 1518   A 6:mon 2:1; C 14:II 4

Busch, Gudrun   C 40:12

Busi, Leonida   C14:III 2

Busnois, Antoine, *fl. from* 1467, *d.* 1492   A 69:I:1:2; 100

Busoni, Feruccio, 1866–1924   C 1:22; 36:20; 40:41

Bussi, F.   C 13:5

Buszin, Walter   A 92:7

Butler, Charles, *d.* 1647   C 46:80

Buttstedt, Johann Heinrich, 1668–1728   A 43:a9; C 9:3

Buxheimer Orgelbuch (Munich, Bay. Staatsbibl. Ms cim 352 ᵇ *olim* Mus. 3725):
— facsimile   A 38:1
— complete transcription   A 43:a 37–9
— excerpts   A 16; D 29:3
— studies   C 48:10; 53:6; D 29:3

Buxtehude, Dietrich, 1637–1707   A4; 33:11; 56:6; **B 17**; C 39:15; 40:31; D 29:3

Buys, Hans Brants   A 64:1

Byrd, William, 1542/3–1623   A 41; 56:10; 76:27–8; 99:2; **B 18**

Byzantine music   A 3:13; 66; C 56:3:1; 76:5

Cabanilles, Johannis, 1644–1712   A 14:4; 20

Cabezòn, Antonio de, 1510–1566   A 56:3; 72:27–9; 74:I 32; **B 19**; D 5:21

Caccini, Francesca, *b.* 1581   A 94:7

Caccini, Giulio, *ca.* 1546–1618:
— *Euridice*   A 15:3; 88:10
— theory   A 74:I 29

Caecilien-Calendar   D 27

Caffagni, M.   A 6:mon 11; 7:mon c2

Caffarelli, Filippo   B 68

Calame, Blaise   D 51:238

Calame-Greaule, Geneviève   D 51:238

Caldara, Antonio, 1670–1736   A 17; 22:25 C 80:6

Caldwell, John   A 40:6

California. University of California. *Publications in music*   C 16

Calmus, Gregory   C 37:2:2:6

Calouste Gulbenkian Foundation, Lisbon   A 86; B 10:2

Caluori, Eleanor   C 78:3

Cambert, Robert, *ca.* 1628–1677   A 19: 2–3

Cambiasi, P.   C 14:III 33

Cambini, Giovanni Giuseppe, 1746–1825   C 43:1

Cambio, Perissone, *before* 1520–*after* 1551   A 22:106

Camerata, Florentine   A 54:a4   *See also individual names*

Gabrieli, Andrea (*cont.*)
22:96; 24:5; 54:a1–2; 87:10; 98:2–3
Gabrieli, Giovanni, 1557–1612   A 16;
22:10,67;   48:70;   53:a1–2;   98:2;
B 38; C 2:19; 48:8
— pupils of   A 22:35
Gabussi (Gabucci, Gabutius), Giulio Cesare,
ca. 1555–1611   A 7:exc 1
Gafurio (Gaffuri, Gafori &), Franchino,
1451–1522   A 12:1–5; **B 39**; Theory:
A 47:7; C 4:4; 15:II 5–7; 37:2:2:2;
46:21; 46:96–100; 54:20
Gagliano, Marco da, *ca.* 1575–1642   A 15:4,
7; 88:10; 98:4
Gagnebin, Henri   B 46:1
Gaillard, Paul-André   A 93:3; C 23:6
Gajard, *Dom* Joseph   A 83; D 19
Gál, Hans   A 32:63, 68; B 13
Galeno, Giovanni Battista, *ca.* 1550–*after*
1626   A 32:90
Galilei, Vincenzo, *ca.* 1520–1591   A 54:a4;
94:8; C 14:II 22; 46:20,62; 54:3
Gallican chant   A 83:a 13
Gallico, Claudio   A 71; C 36:13
Galliculus, *see* Hähnel, Johannes
Gallino, Giovanni Andrea Battista, *fl.* 1772
C 46:48
Gallo, F. Alberto   A 8:mon a1; 62:III:1,
3; C 4:1:1; 4:3:1; 7:2
Gallus, Jacobus (Jakob Handl), 1550–1591
A 4; A 32:12, 24, 30, 40, 48, 51–2, 78,
95, 117
Galpin, Francis W.   C 68:33
Galpin Society Journal   D 21
Galuppi, Baldassare, *called* Il Buranello,
1706–1785   A 25:6;   C 1:18;   2:5;
D 52:16
Galvani, L. N.   C 14:III 32
Gamberini, Leopoldo   C 36:15
Ganassi,   Sylvestro   di,   *fl.*   1535–1542
C 14:II 18–20
Gandini, A.   C 14:III 34
Gardano, Antonio, *fl.* 1538–1569   A 44:8
Gardano, Johannes, 16th c.   A 82:6
Gardano (16th c. Venetian publishers)
A 15:42,50; 25:1; 53:1
Garros, Madeleine   C 17:4
Gascogne, Matthieu, *fl.* 1521–1554   A 65:
9
Gaspari, G   C 14:III 1
Gasparini, Francesco, 1668–1727   C 46:14;
81:1

Gasparini, Querino, *fl. from* 1760, *d.* 1778
B 64:1:3:2
Gassmann,   Florian   Leopold,   1729–1774
A 32:42–4, 83; D 57:2
Gastinois, d'Ernoul   C 54:15
Gastoldi, Giovanni Giacomo, *ca.* 1550–1622?
A 48:23–4; A 89:10
Gastoué, Amédéé   A 96:10; B 28:1:9–10;
C 70:2:7
Gatto, Simone, *ca.* 1545–1594/5   A 32:90
Gaultier, Denis, *ca.* 1600–1672   A 96:6–7;
D 60:2
Gautier de Coinci, 1177/8–1236   A 96:15
Gebhardt, Armin   C 28:20
Geck, Martin   C 39:15; 72:9
Geering,   Arnold   A   43:a10,15;   93:5;
B 86:2,4–7; C 12:II 1; D 54:2
Gehrmann, Hermann   A 33:2; B 87:10;
D 60:7
Geiringer,   Karl   A   22:25;   32:70;
B 52:2:32:1
Geist, Christian, *ca.* 1640–1711   A 43:a 48
Gemblaco, J. Franchois de, *fl. ca.* 1425–30
A 32:76; 39:71; 39:I:a 11
Geminiani,   Francesco,   1687–1762
A 48:173–4, 178; 94:1
Genée, Rudolph   B 64:5
Gennrich, Friedrich   A 3:2; C 30–31
Georg-Friedrich-Händel-Gesellschaft
A 50:2
Georgiades, Thrasybulos   C 47:3; 48
Georgii, Walter   A 3:1
Georgius a Brugis (Trent codices composer)
A 32:61
Georgius, Joannes de (Giorgi, Giovanni), *fl.
ca.* 1723   A 35:12–13;   36:6–8;
61:I:c 2; 61:III,IV
Gerardello (Gherardello) da Firenze, 14th c.
A 28:8:1
Gerber, Rudolf   A 22:9, 16, 26, 32, 35, 46,
49,60; 43:a 21,25,27–9,32; B 5:2:VI 1;
44;   44:I:1:4,7,10;   70:1–2,10–12;
84:13–14; C 57:21
Gerbert, Martin, 1720–1793   C 33:4; 68:7
Gerdes, Gisela   A 82:3
Gerhard, Roberto, 1896–   A 14:9, 14 (editor), D 55:17 (composer)
Gerhardt, Carl   C 57:4
Gerhartz, Leo Karl   C 11:15
Gericke, Hannelore   C 80:5
Gerle, Hans, 1500–1570   C 46:101
Gerlin, Ruggiero   A 24:12–13

Index